Pearl Harbor
we must never forget
the sacrifices made for
our freedom.

Semper Fidelis

Jerome T. Hagen
B.Gen. USMC (Ret)

WAR IN THE PACIFIC

Volume II

Al Bodenlos
804th ENGRS - 7th AiR Corps
Dec 7, 1941

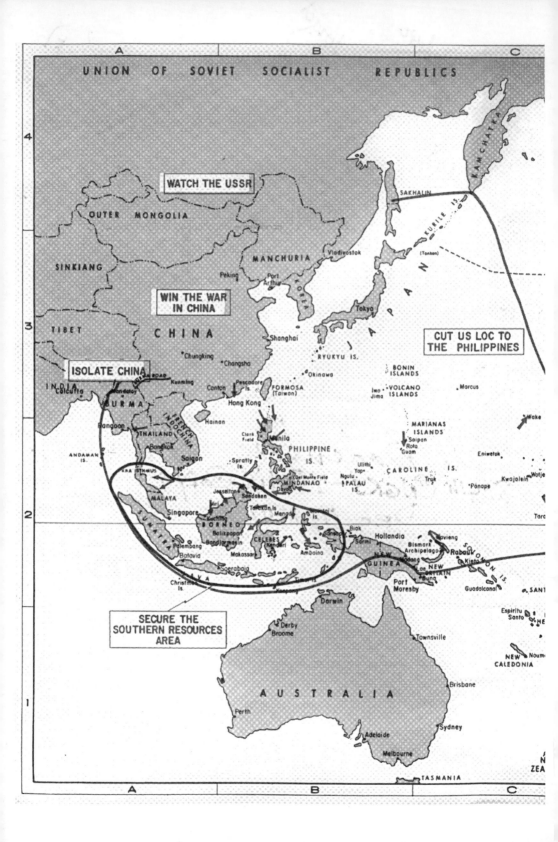

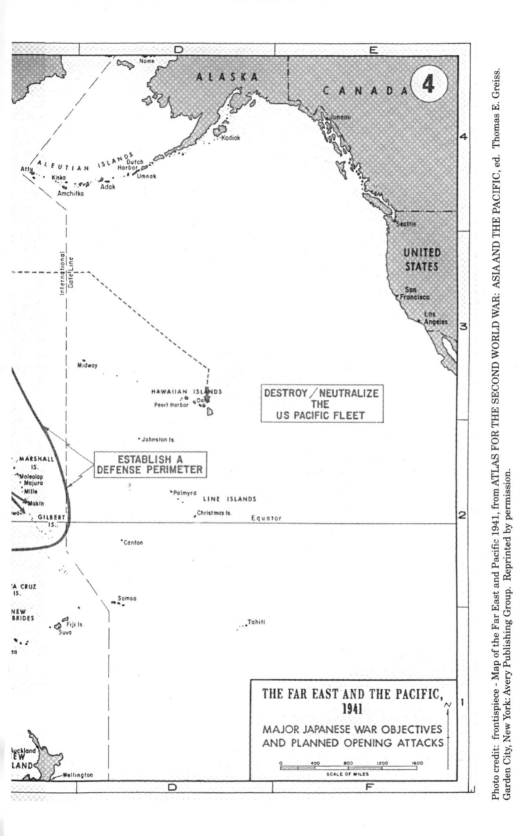

Photo credit: frontispiece - Map of the Far East and Pacific 1941, from ATLAS FOR THE SECOND WORLD WAR: ASIA AND THE PACIFIC, ed. Thomas E. Greiss. Garden City, New York: Avery Publishing Group. Reprinted by permission.

太平洋戦争

WAR IN THE PACIFIC

Jerome T. Hagen
Brigadier General, United States Marine Corps (Retired)

Volume II

HAWAII PACIFIC UNIVERSITY
Honolulu

Published by Hawaii Pacific University

Copies of the book are available from the author at 47-446 Lulani St., Kaneohe, HI, 96744 (Fax: 808-239-1053)

Printed in the United States of America by Malloy, Inc.
Ann Arbor, MI 48106-1124

Library of Congress Cataloging in Publication Data

Hagen, Jerome T.
    War in the Pacific / Jerome T. Hagen.—1st ed.
        p. cm.
    Bibliography:
    Includes index
    ISBN: 0-9762669-1-1
    1. World War, 1939-1945-Campaigns-Pacific Ocean.
    2. Islands of the Pacific. 1. Title.

    D767.H34 1996   96-77738
    940.54'26-dc   CIP

Photo credit: cover- Task Group 38.3 entering Ulithi anchorage near
    Palau after conducting air strikes against Japanese positions in the
    Philippines. Leading are carriers *Langley,* and *Ticonderoga.*
    Following are battleships *Washington, North Carolina, South Dakota,*
    and cruisers *Santa Fe, Biloxi, Mobile,* and *Oakland.* The photograph
    was taken in December 1944, and is reprinted with permission of
    the National Archives.

Frontispiece- Map of the Far East and Pacific 1941, from
*ATLAS FOR THE SECOND WORLD WAR: ASIA AND
THE PACIFIC,* ed. Thomas E. Greiss. Garden City, New York:
Avery Publishing Group. Reprinted by permission.

PREFACE

My purpose in writing Volume II remains the same as the earlier volume, to ensure that our youth understand how this war really was. Since publishing Volume I, it has become obvious that a single volume cannot adequately describe all of the important events and personalities of the war.

Since World War II in the Pacific began in China, not Pearl Harbor, several additional chapters on China and Chiang Kai-shek are included. From the Japanese perspective emerge such major personalities as Admiral Nagumo, leader of the raid on Pearl Harbor; Saburo Sakai, Japan's leading air ace; and Generals Masaharu Homma and Tomoyuki Yamashita, proven and capable leaders who were tried, convicted, and executed by a "rump" court convened by General Douglas MacArthur in the Philippines.

American personalities include Navy Captain Jimmy Daniels and Marine Corps PFC Richard Fiske, heroes of December 7, 1941; Gregory Boyington (Baa Baa Black Sheep); Claire Chennault (The Flying Tigers); Admiral Chester Nimitz; General Curtis LeMay (Firebombing of Japan); Jonathan Wainwright (Hero of Corregidor), and senior American Prisoner of War.

Also included are chapters describing the Coastwatchers of the Solomon Islands and Navajo Code-Talkers, units that played pivotal roles in the Allied victory at Guadalcanal. The chapters on Comfort Women, Horrors of Sandakan, Nagano (There's More Than Snow), and Shiro Ishii, describe the atrocities that were commonplace during this war.

The contents of this book appeared in the Walla Walla, WA Union-Bulletin as specials to their Sunday papers from November 2001 through November 2002. The chapters have been modified to reflect comments from the paper's readership.

As in Volume I, Japanese names appear in the Western style: i.e., personal name followed by family or surname.

ACKNOWLEDGEMENTS

I owe tremendous thanks to my friend, Rick Stepien. After his long work week, Rick edited all chapters of this volume. It is appropriate to say that without his editing, Volume II would still be in the draft stage.

I am indebted to the thousands of readers of Volume I that continue to encourage me to complete and publish Volume II. Especially helpful were the comments from the readers of the Walla Walla, Wa. *Union-Bulletin.* They were able to read most of the Volume II chapters in the Sunday edition of the *Union-Bulletin,* and provided valuable comments that I have incorporated into this book. Rick Doyle, editor of the *Union-Bulletin* proposed the arrangement to print the draft chapters to supplement his already significant effort to keep alive the importance of this war. I am most grateful for his initiative.

Special thanks to George Moyer, John Connor, and Don Boyer for reading and commenting upon many of the draft chapters. They made significant changes to the drafts. Robert Carlson of Dynamic Data Designs did the typesetting, layout, composition and graphics for Volume II. He made significant improvements to the design process, and worked closely with the printers. Much of the credit for the final product goes to Robert.

CONTENTS
VOLUME II

ILLUSTRATIONS

Photographs

Maps and drawings

1

THE 1927 TANAKA MEMORIAL

Many of today's youth might be surprised to learn that World War II in the Pacific did not begin on the morning of December 7, 1941, at Pearl Harbor. Most historians agree the war started on July 7, 1937, at the Lukouchiao (Marco Polo) Bridge near Peking (now Beijing), China.

One could also argue that Japan's aggression in China had been in full bloom since the Kwantung Army assassinated Manchurian Marshall Chang Tso-lien in 1928, and created the "Manchurian Incident," at Mukden on September 18, 1931. The clash at Mukden is still referred to as the start of the 10-year war between China and Japan.

In reality, Japan's dream of empire goes back to 1873 when they seized Formosa and the Ryukyus (Okinawa), and 1894 when they invaded Korea and forced China to cede them the Pescadores and the Liaotung Peninsula. Japan's aggression was simply following the master plan (The 1927 Tanaka Memorial) for world conquest.

Baron Giichi Tanaka was born in Yamaguchi, Japan, in 1863, the son of a samurai. He entered adult life as a soldier and was commissioned in the army at the age of 24. While a soldier, he married a blood relative of Prince Yamagata, "father of the Japanese army." He was military attaché in the Japanese embassy in St. Petersburg, Russia, served as minister of war under two premiers of Japan, and headed the aggressive military faction of Japan. He retired from the army in 1925, and became premier in 1927.

Tanaka served as premier for almost two years. Emperor Hirohito rebuked him in 1928 for his tactless handling of the assassination of Marshall Chang Tso-lien, the warlord of Manchuria. Tanaka took his own life by taking poison in the apartment of a favorite geisha. He was not considered a great statesman and his political party was ripe with corruption when he died. Diplomatically, his death in 1929 was timely as it was clearly time for reorganization and new leadership.

Baron Giichi Tanaka was Japan's 26th premier, and served in that capacity from April 20, 1927, to July 2, 1929.

Japan's Office of the Cabinet Archives

2

Tanaka's legacy to the world is contained in a document purported to be a memorial to the divine ruler of Japan, the Mikado. The document first surfaced in China in 1927, and was published by newspapers in Tiensin. Researchers and publishers worldwide debate the authenticity of the document. Mr. Upton Close, a newspaper correspondent in China from 1917-1922, and chief of foreign affairs for China under Wu Pei-fu, argues that, " The thing that matters about the Tanaka Memorial is that since September 18, 1931, Japan has been consistently and relentlessly carrying out the program outlined therein."[1]

Leon Trotsky writing for "Liberty" on November 18, 1933, stated that, "General Tanaka's famous memorial of 1927 sets forth a program of Japanese expansion, involving the defeat of America and Russia, in which Japanese imperialism is raised to the height of insane megalomania. It is an astounding document. Official Japanese claims that the Tanaka Memorial is a forgery do not weaken its persuasive force by one iota. THERE IS NO FORGING SUCH A TEXT! IN ANY CASE, JAPAN'S POLICIES DURING THE PAST TWO YEARS SUPPLY IRREFUTABLE PROOFS OF THE AUTHENTICITY OF THIS DOCUMENT!"[2]

Tanaka's dream of world conquest, as presented to the Emperor of Japan on July 25, 1927, begins by reminding the emperor of Japan's interest in Manchuria and Mongolia since the reign of emperor Meiji. Tanaka's right to memorialize the direct descendant of the Sun God is explained thusly by Tanaka. "I was returning to Japan from Manchuria by way of Shanghai. At the wharf a Chinese attempted to take my life. An American woman was hurt but I escaped by the divine protection of my emperors of the past. It seems that it was by divine will that I should assist your Majesty to open a new era in the Far East and to develop the new continental empire."[3]

Tanaka begins his memorial by blaming the Nine-Power Treaty, initiated by the United States, as the basis for Japan's problems.

He perceives the treaty as a way of national suicide, and a way for Great Britain and the United States to crush Japan's influence in China. Tanaka recommends that Japan void her participation in the treaty agreement and take immediate steps to consolidate her hold on both Manchuria and Mongolia. Tanaka warns that in carrying out its policy of "Blood and Iron in China," Japan will have to crush the United States. Tanaka also reminds the emperor, "in order to conquer the world, we must first conquer China. In order to conquer China, we must first conquer Manchuria and Mongolia."[4]

Once Japan controls the 74,000 square miles and 28 million people of Manchuria and Mongolia, it will be an easy matter to penetrate and gain control of the rest of China. Once China's entire resources are at Japan's disposal, reasons Tanaka, "Japan shall proceed to conquer Asia Minor, Central Asia, and even Europe."[5] If Japan wants to secure the permanent prosperity of its empire, the conquest of Manchuria and Mongolia is the only way.

Tanaka goes on to argue that Manchuria and Mongolia are not now, and have never been, part of China. He does admit that this issue is a problem since Japan recognized China's sovereignty over these regions when Japan declared war on Russia, and when Japan signed the Nine-Power Treaty. Tanaka recommends ignoring such recognition and negotiating directly with local governments for Japan's access.

Already there are 19 Japanese retired officers in important positions in the government of Mongolia. Hereafter we shall send secretly more retired officers to live among them. They should wear Chinese clothes in order to escape the attention of the local government, and then seek to dominate the affairs of government.[6]

Tanaka proposed to use one million yen from the secret funds of the Army Department's budget to send 400 retired officers into inner and outer Mongolia to, "lay the foundation for Japan's takeover and our national interests for the next hundred years."[7]

The memorial contains 55 pages wherein Tanaka provides specific recommendations for the development of railways in Manchuria and Mongolia, the establishment of a Colonial Department, and the need for schools in the occupied regions to build goodwill among the people toward Japan. The railways are needed to move the resources of China to Japan, and Japanese military forces throughout China. Tanaka gives detailed cost expenditures for the exploitation of raw materials from China, and compares the development cost to the fortune flowing to Japan from such things as coal, iron and steel, petroleum, ammonia sulfate, soda and soda ash, magnesium and aluminum. Tanaka estimates that there is sufficient coal in Manchuria to keep Japan self-sufficient for 70 years. Iron and steel exports will be worth 35 billion, 120 million yen.[8]

Tanaka explains that a Colonial Department is needed to ensure secrecy of operations and provide unity of control in the occupied regions. Tanaka also warns against Chinese migration into the occupied areas. He sees these immigrants as a threat to Japanese immigration since the Chinese work for less wages. Tanaka recommends the use of police to put a stop to Chinese migration into the occupied areas.

The theme of Tanaka's Memorial is closely linked with the philosophy of Dr. Shumei Okawa, one of Japan's militarists in the 1920s. Okawa wrote that, ". . . since Japan was the first state in existence, it was Japan's divine mission to rule the world."[9] Tanaka simply takes the next step by providing a strategy to accomplish Japan's divine mission.

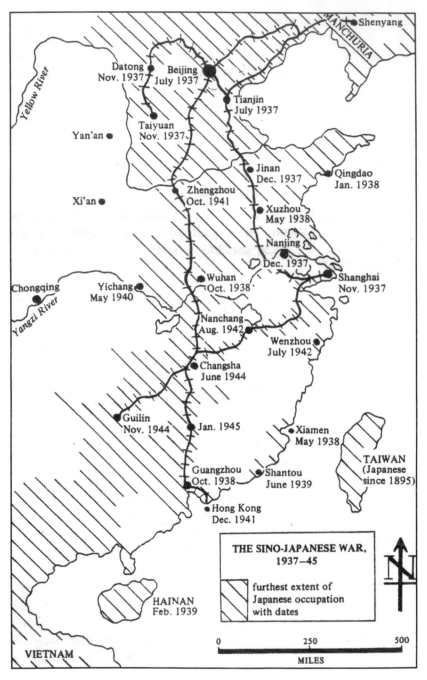

THE SINO-JAPANESE WAR, 1937–45

furthest extent of
Japanese occupation
with dates

US Navy

6

2

CHINESE MILITARY VICTORIES

Although the Chinese enjoyed few military victories against the Japanese, such was not the fault of the Chinese soldier. In many ways, it was amazing that the Chinese soldiers fought at all against the superbly trained and far better equipped Japanese army. The fact that they did so is a testament to their courage and fighting spirit.

The Imperial Army, and even the Kwantung Army (Japan's army in China) were well-trained, had a strong loyalty to their emperor and nation, and ranked among the best armies in the world in terms of supporting arms (artillery, tanks, naval gunfire, and close-air-support.)[1] They were well-supplied with weapons, ammunition, clothing, and medical care.

The average Chinese soldier was taught to fire a weapon, any weapon that was available, and that was about the extent of his training. He was forced into service at an early age, dragged from his village, and sent to some distant place to serve officers who were similarly illiterate, untrained, and incapable of commanding military units of any size.

Chinese conscripts were paid U.S. $1.50 per day, but much of that was withheld by various commanders. The food ration was 22 ounces of rice per day, and one ounce of salt. He was constantly hungry, undernourished, and exhausted. He had no uniform, just rags as he could find. His footwear was usually straw sandals that he made himself. If he became sick or wounded, he was either left to fend for himself, or be shot by his fellow soldiers as an act of mercy, since "he would only die anyway."[2] Being left alive to fend for himself was not an easy task, since he was alone among the very farmers who resented the foraging he was forced to do to stay alive.

But, the Chinese soldier did fight, and he was not afraid to die. All too often the battles were lost due to faulty leadership, and commanders who had no stomach for dying. Major David D. Barnett, assistant U.S. military attaché to Peking, observed that, "The Chinese soldier is excellent material, wasted and betrayed by stupid leadership."[3] Colonel "Vinegar Joe" Stilwell, never one to mince words, when speaking of Chinese leadership said, "The offensive spirit is not in them." Our ambassador to China, Nelson T. Johnson, summarized the attitude of the Chinese upper and middle class as being, "let us fight to the last drop of coolie blood." Perhaps the finest compliment to the Chinese soldier was paid by Japanese Count General Hisaichi Terauchi, when he told a group of visiting newsmen that, "The Chinese junior officers and enlisted were courageous and tenacious fighters, but their superior officers lacked training and offensive spirit."[4]

Prior to 1937, Japanese aggression in China had been restricted to Manchuria and Mongolia, territories that officials such as Baron General Giichi Tanaka insisted were not Chinese territory and never had been.[5] The intent of the Kwantung Army at this time was to establish an autonomous regime of the five northern Chinese provinces: Hopei, Shansi, Chohar, Suiyuan, and Shantung. This area comprised some 400,000 square miles (more than Texas and California combined), and 90 million people.

Chiang Kai-shek was fully committed to unifying China, and did not have sufficient military strength or political support to oppose the Kwantung Army in the north. Consequently, Chiang did not react to the Japanese assassination of Manchuria's Marshall Chang Tso-lien in 1928, the Mukden incident in 1931, or the Japanese establishment of Manchukuo as a separate nation in 1932. Indeed, the opposition to the Japanese on July 7, 1937, at Lukouchiao, was a decision of the local commander on the scene, and not Chiang Kai-shek.

For most Chinese, the Sino-Japanese war began on July 7, 1937, at Lukouchiao. Battles were fought throughout much of China on a near daily basis from that time until the end of the war, but Chinese victories were few.

Lukouchiao (Lugau) Bridge

About a dozen miles west of Peking (Beijing), near the village of Lukouchiao, on the Yongding River, stands a monumental stone bridge, named after the Venetian explorer, Marco Polo. More than seven centuries ago, Polo marveled at the width of the bridge, and its arches and piers topped with elephants, lions, and turtles that had been chiseled from marble. The bridge has changed very little since Polo discovered and described it to the West. The giant marble tortoises, elephants, and lions still form the initial side supports for the bridge at both ends, and guard it from intruders. Both sides of the entire 500-yard length of the bridge are decorated with more than 500 stone lions. Only a few of the original lions have been damaged and replaced.

The tracks of millions of carts, wagons and other wheeled vehicles have worn deep depressions into the stone roadway of the bridge, and the bridge is now closed to vehicular traffic except for bicycles. A series of temporary metal fences has been erected to prevent tourists and pedestrians from rubbing or damaging the carved stone figures. With minor exceptions, the bridge remains as it did on July 7, 1937, when the Japanese Kwantung Army chose Lukouchiao as the site for the next contrived incident that would propel them to seize Peking and other large sections of north China. Besides the bridge over the Yongding River, Lukouchiao was located at the junction of the railway from Tientsin and the Peking-Hankow line. This made the area especially valuable to the Kwantung Army.

On the night of July 7, the Japanese army was conducting field exercises near Lukouchiao. During the maneuvers, the Japanese commander accused the Chinese of kidnapping one of his troops, and demanded access to the nearby Chinese fort at Wanping. The Chinese commander, Colonel Hsing-wen Chi, refused the Japanese request and fighting broke out. By morning, the Japanese had three infantry regiments, a tank company, and a field artillery regiment in place, and attack aircraft overhead.

The Lukouchiao (Lugau or Marco Polo) bridge near Beijing, China.

J. T. Hagen

One of the marble tortoises that guard and support the entrance to the Lugau bridge. There are also marble lions and elephants.

J. T. Hagen

Some of the more than 500 marble lions that line both sides of the Lukouchiao (Lugau) bridge.

J.T. Hagen

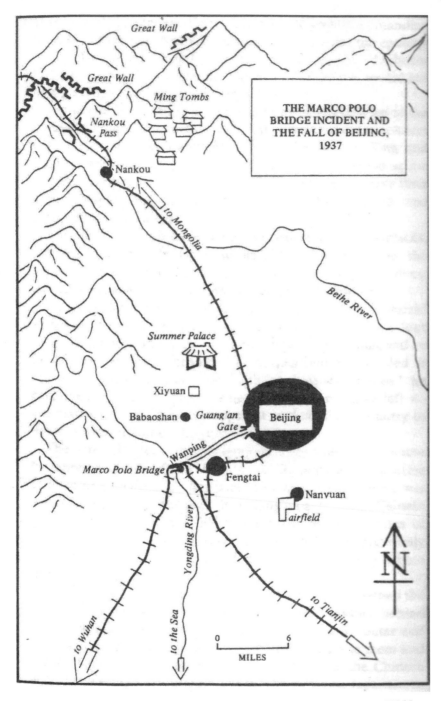

THE MARCO POLO
BRIDGE INCIDENT AND
THE FALL OF BEIJING,
1937

US Navy

The following day, Colonel Joseph W. Stilwell, the American military attaché in Peking, drove to Wanping to talk to Colonel Chi in an effort to defuse the situation. Stilwell never reached Wanping, the fighting from both sides was much too heavy. Additional Japanese reinforcements arrived on July 11, and Wanping fell. Simultaneously, some 150,000 Japanese poured into Peking, Tientsin, and the surrounding areas. Chinese resistance was generally futile and short-lived. Following a four-hour bombing raid on the 29th, General Seichhiro Itagaki's troops took Tientsin on the following day, as the Chinese 38th Division retreated south.

The Chinese 132nd Division choose not to defend Peking, and while withdrawing from the Nan Tai airfield, some of its elements were ambushed and massacred by a Japanese patrol. Unlike Japanese conduct at Shanghai and Nanking, there was no looting or burning of Peking.

A very brief Chinese victory occurred on July 29, when the Chinese garrison at Tungchow ran amok and massacred some 300 Japanese civilian officials and their families. The Chinese chopped off the heads of the Japanese and hung them in baskets, while the decapitated bodies were left in the streets for the dogs and flies. The victory and celebration was very short-lived. The next day, the Japanese bombed, strafed, mortared, and pounded the village with artillery fire. They broke down the gates and beheaded every Chinese male they could find. The women were raped, mutilated and killed. The village was then sacked and set afire. Not a single Chinese survived in the blackened ruins. The first substantive Chinese victory over the Japanese military came two months later at Pinghsingkuan.

The Battle of Pinghsingkuan Pass: September 23, 1937

Early on the morning of September 23, 1937, the lead brigade of the Japanese 5th "Samurai" Division, commanded by General Seishiro Itagaki, left Weishan, China to destroy the Chinese communist guerrilla units that had been harassing his lines of communications, in Suiyuan province. The division proceeded in a single column of infantry, followed by its motorized units and supply convoy. The advance element, the 21st Brigade, was stopped some eight miles northeast of Pinghsingkuan Pass, (also spelled Pingxing) by Chinese troops firing from the hills. After all-day fighting on the 24th, the Chinese forces withdrew, and the division continued its march.

The Chinese troops that had attacked the Japanese brigade belonged to the Communist Eighth Route Army under General Chu Teh. Chu sent his 115th Division under General Lin Piao to march 300 miles from Shensi province to arrive in the mountains near Pinghsingkuan on the 29th. They were delaying the Japanese advance just long enough for Lin to place his troops on the sides of the road through the Inner-Great-Wall that the Japanese would have to follow.

The road was through deep, yellow, loamy soil. For generations, the road had been cut deeper and deeper by the wooden and iron-wheeled carts used by the traders that plied the route. Now, the roadbed lay some 15 feet deeper than the walls that rose steeply on both sides. Once in the pass, it was virtually impossible to exit during its seven-mile length.

At 7:00 A.M., the Japanese entered the pass. Some troops rode on horseback, many were carried in trucks, and some walked, periodically whipping the Chinese coolies that had been pressed into service as pack animals. The Japanese were dressed in leather boots, steel helmets, and woolen overcoats. They carried their rifles loosely, talked, laughed, and seemed very much at ease as they worked their way through the ankle-deep, yellow-muck churned up by trucks and horses in front of them. Next came more than 100 motorized vehicles carrying troops and supplies. Following the trucks came some 200 horse-and mule-drawn carts of supplies, ammunition, and large caliber artillery pieces.

As the Japanese progressed through the pass, the trail became clogged with men, horses, and trucks to such an extent that some trucks tried to turn around and go back. This maneuver created confusion and provided the ideal moment for General Lin' Piao's attack. The first warning available to the Japanese commander was heavy firing and shouting coming from the front of the column. He was not able to move to the front to determine the cause of the shooting because of the steep sidewalls. Soon, there was a confused tangle of troops and equipment trying to move forward, and a mass stampede to the rear for those that survived the initial ambush. Now that Lin had the column stopped, the ridges on both sides of the pass roared with the explosion of hand grenades, mortars, and machine guns. Hundreds of Japanese were killed in the initial ambush. Trucks burst into flames and collided with other vehicles and horses.

About 1:00 P.M., the 687th Chinese Regiment, commanded by General Sun Chu-shous, arrived at the entrance to the pass and eliminated any hope of escape for the Japanese. General Lin ordered a charge and completely annihilated the Japanese in the pass. For miles, all that could be seen were thousands of Japanese bodies, dead horses, and burned-out trucks. In similar manner, the Second Brigade of the Fifth Division was torn apart. By 3:00 P.M., what little remained of the Japanese Fifth Division was in full retreat.

Lin's 115th Division of 9,000 men, captured 100 trucks loaded with supplies; all the codes, maps and records of the 21st Brigade; field guns; and huge amounts of equipment, ammunition, clothing, and other supplies. The Japanese lost all of their headquarters staff personnel and more than 3,000 men. Lin suffered 400 killed or wounded.

General Chu explained three reasons for the Chinese victory. "The fighting was done in a narrow mountain pass where the Japanese could not use their tanks, airplanes, or artillery effectively.

The Chinese enjoyed the principle of surprise. The Japanese had little, if any, opportunity to organize defensive positions. This was also one of the first times that Chinese Nationalists and Communist forces coordinated an attack against the Japanese." General Zhu was most kind to include the 687th Regiment in his praise. The Nationalist regiment was supposed to have sealed the exit from the pass, but arrived far too late to do so, and barely got involved in the action. Zhu could have also mentioned that General Itagaki, the Japanese division commander, made a major tactical error in not conducting long-range aerial reconnaissance and providing air cover.

The Japanese advance into Suiyuan province yielded another advantage to China. The Soviet Union, concerned about Japan's intentions in northern China signed a treaty of friendship with China on August 29. The treaty opened the way for much needed military aid for China, including loans and air support.

The Battle for Tierhchuang: March 1938

Tierhchuang was a walled village of narrow streets and alleys within a one-mile-long and one-half-mile-wide area, 200 miles southwest of Tsingtao, China. Tierhchuang contained nothing of value to the Japanese, but it lay across their route to Hsuchow, a major junction of important rail lines.

Since early January, 1938, the Japanese had advanced in three columns from the north towards Hsuchow. Fighting on both sides was marked by many acts of heroism and sacrifice. The Japanese advance was made predominately along the railroad, and the few roads capable of supporting heavy equipment. As a result, the Chinese forces were able to strike the Japanese on their flanks and rear, while cutting their lines of communications and supply.

On March 14, the Japanese Fifth Division, with a strength of about 10,000 men, struck P'ang Ping-hsun's 40th Chinese Corps at Linyi, 25 miles north of Tierhchuang. P'ang was reinforced by two divisions of Chang Tse-chung's 59th Corps on the following day, and the Chinese held their positions until March 18, when the Japanese retreated to the northeast. Both sides suffered heavy casualties.

By March 23, the Japanese had refitted and the 10th division sent a battalion reinforced by tanks and armored cars to a hilly area near Tierhchuang to rout a Chinese brigade under General Ch'ih. The Chinese refused to give ground. The Japanese sent a second battalion which slipped behind Ch'ih to attack his forces from the rear.

Fortunately, he previously detached one of his battalions to wait in concealment in his rear. When the Japanese attacked, they were surprised and mauled by Ch'ih's detached battalion. The Japanese force withdrew to the northwest and were reinforced to a strength of 5,000 during the night.

At first light on the 24th, the Japanese attacked Ch'ih's right flank which Ch'ih again let fall back to let the Japanese pass. By 7:00 A.M., momentum carried the Japanese force past Ch'ih's position and he turned to attack the Japanese flank. About 4:00 P.M., the Japanese were further reinforced, and Ch'ih was forced to withdraw into the town of Tierhchuang where he drove the Japanese back after long hand-to-hand fighting. The Japanese attacked again at 6:00 A.M., the next morning, but were again repulsed. The Japanese retreated, as they so often did, and brought up their artillery and close-air-support to hammer the Chinese positions throughout the remainder of the day.

That evening, Ch'ih's forces counterattacked and by midday on the 26th, the Japanese were again forced to withdraw. Later in the day, the Chinese 27th Division arrived at Tierhchuang and were positioned on the line with one brigade in reserve.

Early on the 27th, the Japanese made a mass attack but the Chinese held, and then counterattacked. The hard-fought battle left thousands of casualties from both sides on the bloody battlefield. Fierce fighting continued over the next several days, with the Japanese attacking, falling back, and then blasting the Chinese positions with supporting arms. Fighting within the town was vicious, and done with rifles, pistols, hand grenades, bayonets, and knives.

On March 31, General Sun Lien-chung arrived to take command of his Second Army Group. The Japanese welcomed him with a tank and armored vehicle attack, but the Chinese held, destroying 19 tanks and armored vehicles with their 37-mm anti-tank guns. Heavy fighting continued until April 2, when General T'ang En-pos arrived with the remainder of the Second Army. Now the Japanese 19th Division was in danger of being surrounded and having its supply lines cut. The Japanese responded by sending another brigade to Tierhchuang, but General T'ang blocked their route of advance and sent a division to attack their flank. The Japanese brigade was forced into the same encirclement situation.

On April 3, the Japanese, in a desperate attempt to break out of the entrapment, used tear gas and 90 tanks and armored vehicles to attack the Chinese positions. The fight continued through April 5, by which time both sides were physically exhausted. This time however, it was the Japanese that were severely short of food and water. The Chinese attacked and attacked. Slowly, the Japanese defensive perimeter collapsed. Japanese tanks became useless without fuel. Artillery could not fire without ammunition, and the Japanese infantry was reduced to fighting with machine guns, mortars, and finally, bayonets. The Chinese showed no mercy, as they decimated the trapped Japanese.

Early on the morning of April 7, the 2,000 exhausted remnants of General Isogai's 10th and General Itagaki's Fifth Division fought their way through a narrow space in the Chinese encirclement and fled north. The following morning revealed an unusual sight for the Chinese defenders. More than 16,000 Japanese soldiers lay in the wheat fields surrounding Tierhchuang and in the town itself. Forty tanks, 70 armored vehicles, 100 trucks, all of the Japanese artillery, and thousands of machineguns and rifles were confiscated by the Chinese. Led by some bold, resourceful commanders, the Chinese soldiers had won a great victory over the superior Japanese forces. Victory was sweet, but it cost 5,000 Chinese lives.

The First Battle for Changsha: October 1938

Changsha, with a population of more than 500,000, was the largest city in Hunan. It occupied a strategic position in the lake region, south of the Yangtze River, and was only 250 miles from Chunking, the new capital of China. Changsha was a prize that could not be ignored by the Japanese invaders. General Nasakichi Okamura, commanding the 11th Japanese Corps, was assigned five divisions with 120,000 men, plus more than 100 gunboats and watercraft to capture Changsha. The Chinese Ninth War Area, under General Ch'en Ch'eng, had 47 divisions with an approximate strength of 365,000 men for the defense.

The Japanese effort to capture Changsha involved three separate, coordinated operations. The first phase started on September 13, when the Japanese 106th Division attacked the Chinese at Huifu on the Chin River. The Chinese withdrew on the 17th and were reinforced by the 183rd Division on the 22nd. After several days of severe fighting, the Chinese fell back to Kanfang, where they were reinforced with two more divisions. The Japanese took Kanfang, but were forced back by a Chinese counterattack on October 1. The Japanese fell back to the north with the intent of consolidating their forces in the area, but Chinese 32nd and 60th Corps attacked their flanks and caused numerous casualties.

Four additional Chinese divisions arrived on October 3, and the Japanese began a retreat to Shawoli to the east. By now, the

Chinese were anticipating victory and continued to attack the retreating Japanese 106th Division with vengeance. The Chinese pushed the Japanese division back to Wuning, where their advance had started. The Japanese advance had been a complete failure. They suffered many casualties and gained a greater respect for the fighting qualities of the Chinese soldier.

The second phase began 100 miles north of Changsha in early September when the Japanese 33rd Division began its push south. Although the Japanese division was constantly engaged and suffered heavy casualties, it did succeed in capturing Nanlouling and Taoshukang on the 26th. By October 3, the Japanese had overextended their advance, and began to pull back to the north under constant attack on its flanks. The Chinese 98th and 82nd Divisions kept pressure on the Japanese during their withdrawal, which by now was becoming a rout. On October 8th, the Chinese 197th Division ambushed the Japanese 33rd Division as it retreated through the lower ridges of the Chiuking Mountains. Unable to use their artillery in the narrow mountain pass, the Japanese were massacred. Once again, the landscape was strewn with dead and wounded Japanese, discarded weapons, and equipment. Chinese leadership and determination to drive the Japanese back had won a significant victory.

The third phase of the Changsha offensive began at Yochow, 75 miles north of Changsha on September 18. The Japanese Corps under General Neiji Okamura was supported by gunboats on Tung Ting Lake, and heavy air and artillery barrages. By September 23, the Chinese had been forced back to the Milo River, 40 miles north of Changsha. On September 26, the Japanese forced a crossing of the river against strong Chinese resistance and suffered heavy casualties.

General Ch'en Ch'eng then prepared a plan to trap the Japanese just north of Changsha. He sent his 52nd Corps 20 miles south to prepare ambush positions while holding the Japanese advance with two divisions. On September 27th, the Chinese delaying force began to fall back from the Milo River positions, pressed hard by the Japanese 3rd and 5th Divisions. On September 30, the Japanese reached a position 15 miles north of Changsha, and General Ch'en sprang his trap. That night, Chinese struck from every direction. Some 60,000 screaming Chinese threatened the very existence of the Japanese army. In retreat, the Japanese suffered thousands of casualties and lost large amounts of arms and equipment. Changsha was saved.

The Second Battle of Changsha: September-October 1941

The last battle of the Sino-Japanese war in 1941 was a major Chinese victory. Changsha was defended by General Hsueh Yuch, perhaps Chiang's most able general. General Tadaki Anan was the Japanese commander with the mission to destroy Hsueh, his Ninth War Area Command, and to sack Changsha, which had become a symbol of success for the Chinese. Anan had the Japanese 11th Corps, with 125,000 ground troops, more than 100 bomber and fighter aircraft, and numerous gunboats. Hsueh had 300,000 men, but lacked the artillery and other supporting arms available to Anan. Hsueh established his defensive positions near Tung Ting Lake, and made no effort to interfere with the Japanese troop dispositions, which took 10 days to complete. On September 12, the Japanese crossed the river in four separate columns and moved south toward Changsha against minimal Chinese resistance. On September 20, Anan's forces reached the Milo River, and on September 26, were only 7 miles east of Changsha. Chinese resistance had been minimal.

Suddenly, General Hsueh changed his tactics. He ordered his forces to give no further ground. All night on the 26th, the Chinese held against furious Japanese attacks. Morning revealed hundreds of dead and dying soldiers, as many Japanese as Chinese. In an effort to create panic in the Chinese rear areas, Japanese paratroopers were dropped behind the Chinese lines, and plain-clothes troops infiltrated into the city. Within a day, both the paratroopers and infiltrators were caught and executed. Next, General Hsueh sent 29 divisions against the flanks of the Japanese, and 11 divisions against the Japanese rear. All four Japanese columns were now cutoff. Nine more Chinese divisions attacked from the east, pinning the Japanese Corps of 100,000 men between three Chinese forces, in an area of approximately 10-by-15 miles. The Japanese had no hope of reinforcement and could only try to fight their way through the Chinese lines and retreat back to Yochow.

The Japanese fought their way across the Laotao River and fled north, badly demoralized and defeated. Repeated ambushes took a heavy toll in dead, wounded, and lost weapons. Japanese stragglers and wounded were gathered into groups and shot. Neither side took prisoners.

For the remainder of the war, Chiang Kai-shek paid far more attention to the Chinese communist army in China than he did to the Japanese Kwantung Army. Chiang understood very well that the United States would eventually defeat Japan, and that the long-term threat to his government would come from the communist forces of Mao Tse-tung.

3

CHUNGKING: 1937-1941

The western city of Chungking in Szechuan province slumbered along for hundreds of years away from the turmoil found in cities such as Peking, Shanghai, Hong Kong, and Nanking. In the spring of 1937, Chungking was a trading outpost for the agricultural produce of Szechwan. The city was located at the intersection of the Yangtze and Chialing rivers, and connected China to the high plateaus of the Himalayan mountains. All that changed abruptly in the summer, following Japan's "Rape of Nanking," China's nationalist capital.

Chiang Kai-shek, China's president, believed that the rugged terrain surrounding Chungking, its precipitous gorges, rapid river currents, and distance from east coast ports would provide a location safe from Japanese attack. Chiang, as commander-in-chief of all Chinese military forces, moved his military headquarters from Nanking, prior to the Japanese attack on the city, to the strategic city of Wuhan, 500 miles down the Yangtze river from Chungking, but directed that the nationalist capital be established at Chungking.

The exodus from China's interior started immediately. To Chungking trekked the wealthy, the educated, the politically influential, students, professors, skilled laborers, and a few patriots. They came to Chungking not because they respected Chiang Kai-shek or believed in his government, but because they feared life under the Japanese. They came to Chungking by boat, cart, and on foot, carrying as much of their worldly possessions as they could. Regardless of their social status, they all shared the chill, damp climate of Chunking's winters, the humid heat of summer, and the stench of the open sewers for more than six years, until Chiang and his government were forced to flee to Formosa.

From December 13, 1937, when Nanking fell, until August 1938, when the Japanese captured Wuhan, Chungking became saturated with more than a million people, equipment, small factories, rolling stock, and anything that could be dismantled and moved.

When the entire industrial base of central China had been moved to Chungking, the Chinese tore up the railroad tracks as they went, and carried them to their new capital.

Several thousand of the poorest refugees sought shelter within the confines of the old city walls. The rest — the rich or wealthy— built impressive villas on the surrounding hills. Perhaps the most splendid home was that of Generalissimo and Mme. Chiang Kai-shek. Chiang also had a more modest home in his headquarters compound, and a group of villas on the other side of the city that were used to entertain state guests, such as Colonel Joseph W. Stilwell, the American military attaché, who called on Chiang on December 28, 1938.

Other impressive buildings were the Russian Embassy, atop the highest hill in Chungking, a huge house in the late Victorian style, where Soviet Ambassador Paniushkin received official guests, and the home of the British ambassador.[1]

The Communist Eighth Route Army, in disarray and unpaid since January 1941, kept a representative named Chou En-lai at Chungking. Although the communist organization was illegal and detested by Chiang, Chou was tolerated and even permitted to publish a newspaper, subject to heavy censorship. It is impossible for a westerner to understand why Chiang would tolerate the presence of his foremost enemy in his capital. To the Chinese, it was a matter of official courtesy and political tradition.[2]

During the winter of 1938, Chungking enjoyed the safety of rain and fog that shrouded the city and prevented Japanese air raids. The Japanese began to bomb Chungking during May 1939. The first raid occurred on May 3, and caused 5,000 casualties. Chiang's defenders had insufficient antiaircraft guns and bomb shelters to disrupt the bombing raids that continued through the summer and resumed again in the spring of 1940. By this time, shelters had been dug into the hillsides and under the city itself. During 1941, the longest interval between the raids was five hours, the shortest interval was an hour-and-a-half.

Despite the bombings, the city had a pulse that throbbed constantly. Like Shanghai or New York City today, Chungking never slept. The Yangtze was immense, fast flowing and dirty, with hundreds of battered junks and boatmen toiling along the channels. The cries of the boatmen and coolies echoed throughout the area. Every drop of water, every object used by the people in the city, and in the majestic villas, had to be carried on the shoulders of coolies, from the life-giving river up hundreds of steps carved into the cliffs. The beating heart of China was probably best understood by listening to the chants of the coolies on the river and those climbing the steps to Chungking.

A short 2,000-foot concrete runway built on an island in the Yangtze River, and a tenuous link to Burma called the Burma Road, provided the only link to more distant places than the river traffic could provide.

Half a million Chinese lived in bamboo shacks built one upon another on crowded slopes leading down to the Yangtze River. There was no fire-fighting equipment, but even had there been, such equipment would have been unable to traverse the crowded, steep slopes where the poorer Chinese lived. The highly combustible wood and bamboo buildings quickly ignited and burnt fiercely in the firestorm following a Japanese bombing attack. Chinese were burned alive in alleys, streets, and the business district. A third of all homes were destroyed and another third severely damaged. About 5,000 Chinese were killed and many thousands more injured by this first bombing attack on Chungking, a city with a land area smaller than Manhattan Island, New York. Photographer Carl Mydans of *Life* magazine described the attack as, ". . . the worst bombing a city has ever received." [3]

From 1939 to 1942, the Japanese dropped more than 3,000 tons of bombs on Chungking. The resourceful Chinese moved their industry into the sides of the sandstone cliffs that surrounded Chungking. A system of visual-warning outposts was established to give some degree of warning of impending air attacks. Red paper lanterns were run up poles, and sirens were sounded when air attacks were expected. People would hurry to one of the thousands of shelters dug into the cliffs and under the city itself.

The shelters were not always safe. Following a heavy air raid on June 5, 1941, residents were leaving Chungking's largest shelter, a mile-and-a-half long tunnel under the center of the city, when suddenly the signal for a second raid was sounded. Guards slammed the gates to the shelter closed, and, in the panic that followed, 4,000 Chinese were suffocated or trampled to death. This tragedy led to residents being assigned to specific shelters and having to show a pass to gain entrance.

Over time, the Chinese learned to cope with the constant air attacks. Casualties declined to about 50 per air raid, and the population began to increase. Two births were being recorded for every casualty suffered during the three years of bombings. Each winter when the rain and fog prevented Japanese air attacks, workers would clear and widen streets, and start new construction amid the rubble and devastation.

On March 6, 1942, when Lieutenant Gen. Joseph W. Stilwell arrived in Chungking to become Chiang's chief of staff, Stilwell wrote to his wife that, "Chungking isn't half bad when the sun shines. The city lies on a rock promitory and we live on the Kialing [river] side. Views up and down the stream which is busy with

26

boat traffic. Clear water. Prices are fantastic. $80 for a pair of garters; $200 for a charcoal iron. Coolies go around with $50 bills. Clothes are nowhere to be had."[4]

Bodies of Chunking residents fill the entrance to a shelter that they never reached during a Japanese air attack.

Carl Mydans

Anor Adet and Meimei Lin, two Chinese teenagers who accompanied Adet's parents to Chungking in 1941, described Chungking as a bustling, highly patriotic city, where everyone worked hard for the glory and gain of the Chiang government. [5] Their description of Chungking is quite different than that of Edgar Snow who described the population of the city as having a philosophy of, "Let Sam do it." [6] Sam being Uncle Sam. Snow wrote that, " . . . inflation, hoarding, speculation, corruption and bribery were essentially unchecked by the Chiang government. Money became the foremost priority, the war was secondary." [7]

Regardless of one's source of information, it seems clear that Chungking was an exciting place to be in 1941. Passengers arriving at the Chungking airport were amazed to find that the airport was in the middle of the Yangtze River, the only flat area that was long enough to accommodate the runway. A temporary shed that later became permanent served as the baggage terminal. After collecting their baggage, visitors were faced with the task of climbing more than 300 stone steps carved into the hillside that led to the homes and businesses of Chungking. While climbing the stairs, people had to be quick to duck the poles of the water carriers and sedan-chair porters. The water carriers were men who made a living carrying water from the river to the city. Water was carried in two clay pots tied one on each end of a long pole that fit across a man's back. If one could not climb the steps, chair porters would carry the person to the top in a palanquin type seat for a fee. The steps were so steep that chair passengers were carried to the city in a near vertical position.

According to Adet and Lin, the first thing they saw upon reaching the city were hundreds of shelters dug into the hillsides for protection against the Japanese air raids. The shelters also provided homes for many Chungking residents who lost their homes in the bombings. If one arrived in Chungking in winter or spring, there is a good chance that it would be raining and the streets would be a muddy mess, filled with puddles, potholes, and barefoot children playing in the dirty water next to coffin shops.

The second thing the teenagers noticed were the crowds of people from Shanghai, Canton, Nanking, Peking, Hankow, Yunnan, Kweichow, and Hong Kong who were all moving about the streets, all fleeing the Japanese. It seemed that everyone in Chungking comes out to the street, even in the rain. There were many army uniforms in the crowd, students with their books, and people from all walks of life, working, and talking. Blacksmiths plied their trade as did shoemakers, bakers, tailors, and butchers. Close to the businessmen, the wife worked over a stove, and the daughter or daughter-in-law washed clothes. Grandpa sat on the curb reading a paper and sucking on a long pipe, already smoked out. Everyone seemed busy, but with enough time to engage in gossip and news with one's neighbor. All this activity went on while the crowd surged up and down the street.

Most of the residents of Chungking wore cheap cotton clothing, usually with the shirt outside the trousers. Everyone had a straw hat and a shirt. Some residents wore cloth shoes or sneakers, but there are few leather shoes since they cost $75 a pair. Many feet were bare. Anyone found wearing bright clothing like red or white, which were especially visible from the air, could be tried as a traitor. Most people wore army green-colored clothing so that if they were caught outside the city during an air raid, they could lie down and blend in with the background.

Adat and Lin found that the air raid shelters that were carved into the hillside had winding corridors and that the caves were wet and dark, since none of them had ventilation or electricity. There was also a constant chinking sound that seemed to emanate from everywhere, and yet nowhere in particular. The sounds were found to come from hundreds of laborers using hammers and chisels to create more room in the sandstone shelters.

There were no hotels in Chungking in 1941: earlier bombings destroyed them all. In order to stay in Chungking, one must have made arrangements to stay with family or a friend. Once in Chungking, the visitor discovered that the cost of living was expensive. Sedan-chair carriers earned as much as $200 per month, and ricksha pullers earned $300 per month. A can of coffee cost $22, while a small can of condensed milk cost $6. Large oranges cost 70 cents to $1, small melons were 60 cents, and an iron to press clothes cost $25.

Slogans were everywhere, but especially prominent on the hillsides. The two most popular slogans seemed to be, *"Those who have money give money; those who have strength give strength"* and, *"Victory in resistance; success in reconstruction."* [8]

The teenagers recounted that there was a large wasteland where 500 Chinese burned to death during an air raid in May 1941. As the Chungking residents were fleeing the Japanese firebombs, they became trapped against the stone wall of the German Legation. The wall was too high to climb, and there was no turning back. The people suffocated and burned to death. The bare lot, without even a blade of grass, was a wordless memorial to those who perished.

Residents of Chungking crowd into one of the thousands of air raid shelters prior to a Japanese air attack.

Carl Mydans

Breakfast in Chunking in 1941 consisted of a bowl of congee, bean curd, peanuts, and pickles. Lunch might be green-pea soup and an orange. Food taken to the air raid shelters was usually boiled eggs and bakery buns, washed down with tea. Biscuits, bread, and cookies were always in demand and were not available for days at a time following a bombing.

The daily Chungking newspaper was difficult to read because it was printed in color. One day it was printed in pink, and another day in green, purple, or yellow. The reason for the color was to hide the impurities in the paper. Good quality paper was too expensive to use for newspapers. Of course, the government strictly controlled the news that appeared in the paper.

Those who stayed in Chungking for more than two days during the summer, could expect a Japanese air-attack. Often two or three attacks would be conducted a few hours apart, forcing Chungking residents to spend nine or ten hours in the shelters. The Japanese bombers flew in perfect formation. Sometimes there were as few as 27 bombers with their fighter escorts. Other times, there were as many as 81 bombers in each of two or three formations.

The first signal for an air raid was the raising of flags or lighted red lanterns on poles that could be seen by most of the residents. This signal meant that Japanese planes had taken off at Hankow and could attack Chunking. The next signal was the sound of sirens which meant that the Chungking area is the projected target and all residents should go to the shelters. The shelters were always dark and wet. People would trip over one another as they forced their way deep into the caves. When they fell, they usually landed on their hands and knees in the mud. Since there was no place to clean up, they had to spend the next three to four hours in the same filthy condition.

People would cry out and scold the interloper when their foot or hand was stepped on, but there was little that could be done. Most people accepted the many hours spent in the tunnels as the

31

best of a bad and terrifying situation. Some would talk quietly to family members; some would sleep, or try to sleep; and others would share the small amounts of food and water they brought with them with their less fortunate neighbors.

The third siren meant that an attack would occur shortly. People outside the shelters would panic and government workers not yet in the tunnels would quickly store their equipment in blast-proof storage bins and run for safety. The aircraft would walk their bombs toward the center of the city. The explosions became louder until they were like hammer blows to the heads of the people in the shelters. Air was sucked out of the tunnels and then rushed back in. The changing air pressures terrified the children and old people. People would cry and scream, believing that the next 800-pound bomb would penetrate the tunnel and kill everyone inside. People were knocked to their hands and knees, again and again. Constant day and night bombings left all the survivors in an exhausted and stressful condition.

When the bombing ended, and if there was not a follow-on attack, people would exit the tunnels with pounding heads and sore bodies. The first thing they would see was the destruction next to the shelter. Wooden buildings would have disappeared into the black smoke that was visible for many miles. Only a few baked bricks lying among small pieces of glass and metal remained. Now and then one might see a child digging in the rubbish for a doll or keepsake. The ruin of one's home or business would impart a feeling of futility. One could not help but recall the many years and hardships involved in developing the home or business, and the fears that it would be impossible to start over again. A common sight would be the crews loading the dead onto carts to be taken outside the city for burial. Finally, residents would begin the trek home to find if they still had a place to live. Many did not.

On June 24, 1942, the Japanese dropped firebombs on Chungking. The smell of sulfur permeated the entire city. This was the first bombing of Chunking in four days. Previously the

Japanese bombed Chungking for ten consecutive days and then announced by radio that they would not bomb again for a week. On the fifth day they came with the firebombs. Fires were too large to extinguish with the antiquated fire-fighting equipment available. Yellowish-green sulfur covered everything. The body and coffin details had to cover their faces with handkerchiefs to remove the burnt corpses. The whole riverfront district burned to the ground; businesses, homes, poles, everything.

The August 1942 bombings have been described as the most violent that Chungking experienced. The bombs were directed against many of the tunnels sheltering the residents. The sandstone tunnels shook from one direct hit after another. All the air was sucked out of many of the tunnels, and the lamps extinguished.

Everyone was knocked down and few tried to rise. Most lay in the mud, eyes closed, breathing with great difficulty, and feeling the cave shaking constantly from the high-explosive bombs. The silence that followed the bombing was so quiet that it would startle the residents. Many were afraid to leave the shelters. When they did, they found blocks and blocks of Chungking destroyed, and the rest of it in flames, dust, and smoke.

Within minutes, men began clearing rubble and filling in bomb holes. Others dug holes, erected new poles, and started stringing new electric and telephone wires. When families could afford it, the dead relatives were put in coffins for burial. Families whose homes were destroyed moved in with neighbors or found shelter in one of the caves. Within 24 hours, life was back to normal, awaiting the next bombing attack that was sure to follow.

Adet and Lin spent much of their time in China in a small village 50 miles distant from Chungking. This was the only place that the family could find a home to rent. Like Chungking, the village was subjected to air attack on a near-daily basis. Villagers were warned of an impending attack by signals similar to the ones used in Chungking.

When warning of an attack was received, the youngsters would accompany their parents and other villagers to one of the caves dug in the nearby hills. It was not uncommon to spend the entire day in the cave. Their home was destroyed in one such air-raid, as were the homes of many of their neighbors. The loss of their home and the constant danger from Japanese bombs and bullets forced Adet's parents to make the decision to leave China in late 1941. Their flight to Hong Kong and Los Angeles was uneventful, but the sights, sounds, and smells of war, death, and dying, remained with them for the rest of their lives.

Chiang Kai-shek was not forgotten in his war against Japan. Starting in the spring of 1942, the United States began to fly supplies to China over the Himalayan Mountains from northeastern India to Kunming, China. From Kunming, the supplies were moved by road to Chungking. The 500-mile air route from India was nicknamed "the Hump" by the pilots who flew three or four missions per day. The Hump passed over some of the most inhospitable terrain in the world.

The 10,000-foot Naga Hills were home to the Naga head-hunting tribe, and thick jungle covered most of the areas between the Irrawady, Salween, and Mekong rivers. The 15,000-foot Santsung range had to be overflown by the heavily loaded C-46, two-engine workhorses. Monsoon rains from May to October, winds with gusts up to 248 miles-per-hour, and Japanese fighters made flying "the Hump" a dramatic change of pace from the dreary and dismal air bases in India. The Hump took a heavy toll of planes and aircrews. More than 1,000 pilots and crewmen were killed, and 600 planes lost while transporting 650,000 tons of supplies to China.

While supplies were being delivered to China via the Hump, U.S. Army engineers began a 500-mile road from Ledo in Assam, India, to Mong Yu in Burma. The plan was to link the new road (the Ledo Road) with the old Burma Road that ran from Mong Yu to Kunming, China. The road would provide a crucial supply line and a fuel pipeline to China. In addition to the problems of jungle, weather, and lack of equipment, the engineers were working in regions under Japanese control. Engineers were frequent targets of Japanese snipers, with 130 being killed and hundreds more, including laborers, lost due to drowning, accidents, disease, and supply-plane crashes. More than 28,000 engineers and 35,000 native workers labored for two years to complete the Ledo Road. The $150-million highway stands as one of the great engineering feats of World War II. It was completed seven months before the end of the war.

In addition to airlift and highway construction, the American Volunteer Group (AVG) Flying Tigers, under command of newly promoted Brigadier Gen. Claire Chennault, provided offensive air support against the Japanese attackers. Chennault based one of his squadrons at Kunming to protect the terminus of the Burma Road. Another was based at the RAF airfield at Mingaladon, near Rangoon, to protect the harbor and capital city of Burma. A third squadron was rotated to various airfields in China and Burma to protect the Burma Road. Although the AVG compiled an impressive record in the China-Burma-India Theater, there were never enough planes, fuel, ordnance, or maintenance to push back the Japanese.

By August 1945, when Japan surrendered to the Allies, much of China was overwhelmed by anarchy. Chiang Kai-shek's Nationalist government in Chungking was drained by eight years of war with Japan and 18 years of conflict with China's communists. The Japanese and Russians had ravaged large areas of China. Cities were in ruins, and river vessels, the core of China's transportation system, were destroyed or beached. China's railroads were torn up; bridges, tunnels, and rolling stock destroyed. Highways were impassable and there were few vehicles to use them. Huge areas of farmland had been torched, and starvation and disease were rampant.

Chiang re-established his capital at Nanking on May 1, 1946, after an absence of nine years. Two-and-a-half years later, the last battle of China's civil war began just north of Nanking. Within two months, a half-million soldiers were committed on each side. The last soldiers loyal to Chiang Kai-shek departed Nanking on April 23. At 7:00 A.M., the next morning, the Peoples Liberation Army (PLA) under the command of General Ch'en Yi, marched into Nanking. The inhabitants watched in silence as the communist forces set an example of discipline that the nationalist armies should have envied. There was no looting or rape, and foreigners were left alone.[9]

What remained of Chiang's government fled south to Canton, then back to Chungking, and finally to Chengtu, even deeper into Szechwan province. On December 10, Chiang departed China and joined two million Chinese in their migration to Formosa, where he re-established his government and proclaimed Formosa as the Republic of China.

4

CHIANG KAI-SHEK

As one followed the events leading up to World War II, Chiang Kai-shek seemed to epitomize Abraham Lincoln, John Wayne, and a knight on a white horse combined. He became a hero figure to some, and stood for justice and equality. He stood up to the Japanese who were attempting to conquer his country, and he did so against overwhelming odds. Then something happened that many of us knew little about. The communist menace in China grew in power and claimed more and more of Chiang's attention, energy, manpower, and finances. We began to read of his brutal government that no longer fought against the Japanese invaders, but seemed intent upon alienating the masses. By reading Edgar Snow's books, *People on our Side, Journey to The Beginning,* and *Red Star Over China,* one can begin to understand why the people of China preferred Mao Tse-tung and Chou En-lai's communism to Chiang's brand of democracy.

Americans were enraptured by the 1943 visit of Madame Chiang Kai-shek to the U.S. She made speeches in Chicago, New York City, Washington, DC, the Senate and House of Representatives, and at the Hollywood Bowl in California. Americans worshipped her. She could do no wrong. President Roosevelt said that America would send aid to China, "as fast as the Lord will let us." Madame Chiang added that, "the Lord helps those who help themselves."[1]

What happened in China from 1925 until 1945 that caused the Chiang Kai-shek government to fall from being such a powerful force to one that was forced to flee to Formosa? More importantly, from our viewpoint, what happened to Chiang Kai-shek that turned his vision from The Three Principles of government (of, by, and for the people), as set forth by Sun Yat-sen, to Chiang's total grasp of authority, separation of government and the people, and repression of civil liberties? The following pages will attempt to describe what occurred.

Chiang Kai-shek was born on October 31, 1887 at Ningpo, China. He attended local schools until 1906, when he entered the Paoting Military Academy. A year later, he went to Japan to study military science, and while there, met the revolutionary leaders, Sun Yat-sen and Chen Chi-mei. In 1909, he returned to China and played a minor role in the 1911 revolution that overthrew the Manchu dynasty. Chiang became a disciple of Sun Yat-sen, the "Father of the Revolution." Sun recognized Chiang's military and political talents and his devotion to a unified China.

From 1912 to 1920, Chiang was a penniless jobber at the Shanghai stock exchange. He was an unknown, living in a cubicle without windows. His greatest achievement being that he was able to establish lasting relationships with leading bankers and merchants. Later, these businessmen would finance Chiang's revolution in return for his keeping the leftists out of the government.

Chiang was attracted to Miss Mayling Soong, the younger sister of Dr. Sun's wife, Chingling. Mayling was the daughter of a Chinese Christian minister and a powerful family in China. Mayling recently completed her education in America, returned to China, and entered into the best circles of Chinese society. Because her older sister was married to Sun Yat-sen, the president of China, she soon met the young soldier Chiang Kai-shek.

Each time Chiang would approach Dr. Sun for advice on how to proceed with the romance, Sun would advise Chiang to wait. Sun was well aware of the Soong family determination that non-Christians would not marry into the family. His own marriage with Chingling occurred only because Chingling left home, moved in with Sun, and announced her engagement. Madame Soong was crushed. Dr. Sun was twice as old as Chingling, was already married with three children, and did not divorce his first wife. At least Sun was a Christian, Madame Soong rationalized. Even Chingling sided with the family on the issue of Christianity and announced that she, "would rather see her little sister dead" than as the wife of Chiang.[2]

Generalissimo Chiang Kai-shek

In 1920, Chiang was appointed head of the Whampoa Military Academy, founded by Dr. Sun. Russian military personnel staffed the academy and its purpose was to produce trained officers for the nationalist (Kuomintang) army in order to defeat the various warlords and unite China. Chiang visited Moscow in 1923 as Sun Yat-sen's emissary. He returned with a distrust of the Russians and a hatred of communism. Sun did not share Chiang's feelings for the Russians and relied upon them to organize the Chinese government.

The Whampoa cadets were trained in six years, and following Dr. Sun's death in March 1925, Chiang became commander-in-chief of the army and began to conquer the independent provinces. Chiang's forces conquered Kwangtung and Kwangsi provinces, and in 1926, turned north to Peking and the northern provinces. These provinces surrendered individually allowing Chiang's forces to occupy Hankow, Hangchow, Shanghai and Nanking. Chiang established his capital at Hankow and prepared to move on Shantung province and Peking.

During the Kuomintang's conquest of the provinces, indiscriminate looting, especially at Nanking, greatly diminished the prestige of Chiang. Chiang blamed the Russian elements of the army for the looting, and had them expelled, much to the displeasure of certain nationalist elements in the Russian organized government. This created a division within the Kuomintang, whereby Madame Sun Yat-sen and the Russians established a government at Hankow while the more conservative elements established a rival government at Nanking. Despite the split, Chiang pressed ahead with his goal of unifying China.

Chiang established an alliance with the "Christian General" Feng Yu-hsiang for a two-pronged attack on Peking. As Chiang and his army moved through Shantung, they were strongly resisted by provincial commanders loyal to the warlord Chang Tso-lin. General Feng saw this as an opportunity to gain power and threw his support to the opposition. In disgust, Chiang announced his

40

resignation as commander-in-chief of the army, and from all government positions. In August 1927 he returned to Chekiang, his native province. During his conquest of the provinces, Chiang had not forgotten Mayling Soong.

Mayling was born September 5, 1898. When she was five years old, she was enrolled at the McTyeire School in Shanghai, a Methodist and English-speaking elementary school, intended for the daughters of upper-class Chinese families. She was admitted to Wellesley College when she was ten years old, and graduated in 1917. She had been away from China for nine years, traveled the United States extensively, and had essentially forgotten her native Shanghai dialect. When she returned to China, she had to learn to read and write Chinese. "The only thing Chinese about me is my face," she said.[3] Many thought she didn't even look Chinese. In America, she developed a culture and self-assuredness quite unusual for a Chinese woman, especially for someone still in her teens.

After a lengthy attempt to meet with Madame Soong, Chiang was finally successful and promised her that he would study Christianity, read the bible, and pray for divine guidance. Chiang's response secured Madame's approval for the marriage with her youngest daughter, but a wedding was not so simple. The pastor refused to marry the couple in the church because Chiang was not divorced from a previous wife, and refused to marry them in a private ceremony at home for the same reason. Finally, the pastor agreed to come to the home and pray with the couple. At the session, the blessing of God was asked upon the couple and that satisfied the Soong's. The December 1927 wedding was a magnificent affair in Shanghai, uniting as it did the powerful house of Soong with the leader of China's armies.

After a week-long honeymoon, Chiang was persuaded to come back as the head of the government, and when General Fung promised to support him, he agreed to do so. The Chiang's went to Nanking, where Mayling began to learn about the real China.

Nanking was a mixture of old ruins and new construction, with far more dirt, crowding, and squalor than she had ever imagined. Most of the government wives refused to live there and stayed in Shanghai or other more luxurious locations. To Mayling's credit, she stayed with Chiang and went with him in his battles to unify China.

In July 1928, Chiang's army entered Peking. In December, the "Young Marshall" Chang Hsueh-liang, the son of Chang Tso-lin, announced his support for Chiang's government, and Mukden, the capital of Manchuria, was brought under the central government. In theory, at least, China was unified.

On October 10, Chiang became, in effect, if not in name, President of the Republic of China. As chairman of the state council, and Generalissimo, he had sole authority to receive diplomats from foreign countries. Chiang was 41 years of age, headed an army of two million men, and his power seemed absolute.

Chiang was successful in defeating the communists in Shanghai in 1927, and later in Canton. Extermination of the remaining communist threat remained Chiang's number one priority and he kept pressure on the remaining communist fighters. When Japan invaded Manchuria in 1931, Mao proclaimed China the Chinese Soviet Republic. Mao was elected president, and Chou En-lai vice president. Chiang immediately launched three attacks against the communist base at Kiangsi. Chiang himself led the third attack in July 1931 with 300,000 men. All three "Campaigns of Extermination," as Chiang called them, ended as communist victories.

It is now obvious that Chiang made the wrong decision when he decided not to fight the Japanese invaders in Manchuria. On September 11, 1931, Chiang directed the Manchurian warlord, Chang Hsueh-liang "to avoid any enlargement of the Mukden incident and to resolutely maintain the principle of nonresistance."[4] Chiang intended to drive the Japanese out of China, but only after he had truly united China. The Chinese people expected Chiang to resist the Japanese invaders now. Had he done so, he could have united the warlords against the Japanese in a common cause. By failing to do so and fighting Chinese when there was a national emergency, Chiang weakened his authority and gave fuel to the communists who claimed they were the true defenders of China

Indeed, China was still disunited and weak in 1931, and was not capable of defeating the well-trained and well-equipped Japanese Kwantung Army. Chiang's responsibility should have been to unite the country under a common cause of fighting an aggressor nation. Instead, he continued to pursue the communists and leave the Japanese alone. Chiang's "communists first, Japan later" philosophy was the basis for his subsequent kidnapping in 1936 by Chang Hsueh-liang. Chang and others wanted Chiang to forget the communists and fight the Japanese.

Before Chiang's kidnapping, spontaneous gatherings of students took place at Nanking. In November 1931, 12,000 students marched on the government of Nanking demanding a declaration of war against Japan. On December 15, 70,000 students invaded Nanking and demanded that Japan be thrown out of China. Chiang let them wait for twenty-four hours in the bitter cold, and then appeared on a balcony to tell the students that the government would deal with the Japanese as it saw fit. The students attacked the Kuomintang headquarters building, foreign ministry, and destroyed the plant and offices of the *Central Daily News*. In frustration, Chiang resigned all his posts and flew to his native village in the Chekiang hills.

Within a few days, the government and students implored Chiang to return, but to adopt a new policy toward Japan. Chiang did return but his policy towards the Japanese did not change. On January 28, 1932, when the Japanese Army struck at Shanghai, only the Communist 19th Route Army defended Shanghai. They received no material support from Chiang, but fought bravely for 33 days before falling back in the face of Japanese reinforcements. The 19th Army commanders became heroes throughout China. Their names were equated with Washington and Nelson as the greatest heroes in history. As the final tribute, their names were stamped on brands of cigarettes and other articles for sale. Money in the amount of Chinese $40 million poured in from overseas Chinese for the 19th Army.

While Chinese were being killed by the thousands by the Japanese, the Yangtze River flooded near the junction with the Han River and drowned an estimated two million Chinese.[5] Where was Chiang Kai-shek? Where were the Principles of Sun Yat-sen (of, by, and for the people)? The intellectuals and peasants alike began to turn against Chiang and toward the man who seemed to be a leader, Mao Tse-tung.

On February 18, 1932, Japan declared the three eastern provinces of Manchuria plus Jehol to be the independent nation of Manchukuo, and they installed Henry Pu-yi as emperor. Chiang still had the communists as his priority and attacked the popular 19th Route Army located at Fukien. In two weeks, Chiang defeated and scattered the remains of the 19th Army.

By 1934, Chiang had been fighting the communists for seven years. He was able to defeat the communists in many of the battles, but he was never able to exterminate them. In complete frustration, he assembled an army of 900,000 men with 400 aircraft, heavy guns and German strategists to plan and help conduct the campaign. After seven months and one million communist casualties, Mao, Chou En-lai, Chu The, and P'eng The-huai made the decision to abandon Kiangsi and march 6,000 miles north to Shensi. They departed on March 16, 1934.

About 100,000 people took part in the march, including men, women, children, and old people. They carried their printing press, bullet-making equipment, and weapons. They received the assistance of the peasants throughout their travel, and one year later joined about 10,000 communists already in Shensi. Author Edgar Snow did much to glamorize the sacrifice, suffering and courage of the communists during the march. Westerners read Snow's books and articles and began to turn against Chiang for his persecution of the only Chinese who were fighting the Japanese.

On December 9, 1935, 10,000 students demonstrated in Peking against the Japanese. Students also protested in Hangchow, Shanghai, Wuhan, Changsha, and Wuchow. It was a major embarrassment for Chiang and a major gain for the communists. When Chiang's oldest son wrote to his mother and hailed the Chinese communists for their fight against the Japanese and for their support for the working people, it was another blow to Chiang. Yet, he did nothing to change his priorities from the communists to the Japanese.

Chiang was always aware of his precarious power base. It depended on the warlords and their willingness to support him. If he used his military against the Japanese and was defeated, he believed the warlords would divide whatever remained and the unification of China would come to a standstill. So, he waited, fought the communists, and looked for more support from the warlords.

On November 21, 1936, a communist army in Kansu province defeated Chiang's famous first army commanded by General Hu Tsung-nan. Two infantry brigades and a regiment of cavalry were decimated and destroyed, losing all their weapons in the process. Another Kuomintang regiment defected to the communists. On December 7, Chiang flew to Sian to meet with Chang Hsueh-liang to discuss another "suppression campaign" against the communists.

At Sian, Chiang was captured and held under house arrest until December 25, when he and his wife were flown back to Nanking. The *coup d' e'tat* was poorly conceived and executed. Chiang was injured during his attempt to escape, 40 of his bodyguards were murdered, and many of his government officials were arrested. Chiang was kept under house arrest and lectured daily by Chang Hsueh-liang and others as to why he must cease the war against the communists, resist Japan, and implement Dr. Sun's principles. Chiang refused to listen to his captors and demanded that he be allowed to return to Nanking.

By December 12, it became apparent to the coup plotters that they lacked support from the people and from other warlords to force Chiang to do much of anything. Chou En-lai was brought in to talk to Chiang about a truce and a joint effort against the Japanese. An Australian, W. H. Arnold, was brought in to serve as a mediator, and Mme. Chiang and her brother T.V. Soong arrived to plead Chiang's case. He was released on December 25, and emerged much stronger from the ordeal. He had not agreed to the terms presented to him by the plotters, and had not signed anything. There was an understood agreement however that Chiang would cooperate with the communist army to fight the Japanese.

Chang Hsueh-liang and Yang Hu-ch'eng, the two major coup plotters lost everything. Chang was sentenced to ten years in prison, but Chiang kept him under house arrest and took him to Formosa in exile. Yang was imprisoned and murdered in Chungking in 1949. The communists were the big winners. For the near term at least, they gained respectability and were no longer attacked by the nationalist forces. Mao was able to foresee the nationalists being defeated and humiliated by the Japanese Kwantung Army. While Chiang fought the Japanese, Mao would consolidate his base of power, claim credit for guerrilla warfare success in the rear areas, regain their strength, and be ready to conquer China once the Allies defeated Japan.

By 1937, China's nationalist army totaled 1.7 million men, with a navy of 59 assorted ships, and 200 aircraft commanded by Claire Chennault, a medically retired U.S. Army Air Corps captain, hired by Chiang to develop and train his air force. Japan's response to Chiang's buildup of force came on July 7, at the Marco Polo

Bridge, 15 miles from Peking. The Kwantung Army had prepared for the incident well in advance, and using the incident as a pretense, went on to seize Peking, Tientsin, large parts of North China and Inner Mongolia.

Rather than fight in the north, Chiang decided to challenge the Japanese at Shanghai. The battle started on August 8, 1937, and ended with the Rape of Nanking in December. The exact figure is still unknown. Japan suffered more than 60,000 casualties. Once Shanghai fell, the Kwantung Army pushed rapidly towards Chiang's capital of Nanking. Nanking fell on December 12. Between 200,000 and 300,000 soldiers and innocent civilians perished during the Japanese rape at Nanking.

Chiang evacuated the capital on December 7, leaving it defenseless, and flew to Hankow where he established his military headquarters. The civilian government was relocated to Chungking. Following the loss of Nanking, Chiang relinquished all of his political titles and concentrated on military missions. He had some success: at Taierhchwang, he defeated the Japanese Army and caused 42,000 casualties. At Chengchow, his forces dynamited the breakwaters of the Yellow River, drowning thousands of Japanese and sinking large quantities of equipment. Seldom mentioned is the fact that two million Chinese in eleven cities lost their homes in the man-made flood. Incidents such as these further alienated the people from Chiang and caused them to welcome Mao's brand of communism.

Hankow fell to the Japanese on October 25, 1938. By the end of the year, Japan claimed control of 1.5 million square kilometers of Chinese territory with a population of 170 million people. Casualties to date, according to Japanese reports, were 800,000 Chinese and 50,000 Japanese killed.[6] For the next six years, Japan undertook no major military operations. Chiang had traded space for time, and settled in Chungking as his capital. During the lull in fighting, the communist Eighth Route Army grew from 45,000 in 1937 to 400,000 in 1940. The communist's new Fourth Army grew from 15,000 to 100,000 during the same period. The two communist armies surrounded and disarmed several nationalist forces, either killing them or causing them to join the communist army.

In May 1939, the Japanese began to bomb Chungking. The first air raid caused 5,000 casualties, and the raids continued throughout the summer and into 1941, the worst year of the capital's aerial bombardment. Through it all, Chiang showed little initiative to take the offensive against the Japanese. He was content to outwait the Japanese, believing that the Americans and perhaps the Russians would be drawn into the war against Japan, and he would be rewarded for tying up one million Japanese in China.

A problem with Chiang's strategy was that the communists were engaging the Japanese and cutting ever deeper behind their lines. The battles were not necessarily large, but on each occasion, the communists gained greater support from the Chinese people. By staying in Chungking, Chiang was losing touch with the populace and with the warlords that still retained the forces in their areas. The warlords fought well enough to defend their own towns, but would not go on the offensive outside of their own areas. In 1940, Japan pressured the French to close the Hanoi-China railroad, and forced Great Britain to close Hong Kong and the Burma Road for three months. China stood alone without logistic support from any country. Finally, on December 8, 1941, the United States and Great Britain declared war on Japan. For Chiang, China seemed saved.

On December 8, 1941, (China time), Chiang proposed a joint conference with representatives from, China, Russia, and the United States to plan for the war against Japan. Stalin was not ready for the Russians to participate in such a war, but Great Britain and the U.S. sent representatives to Chungking on December 23. The defense of Burma and the Burma Road were declared the top priorities.

General Joseph Stilwell arrived in Chungking on March 6, 1942, to be Chiang's chief of staff, command all American forces in the China - Burma - India theater (CBI), to control lend lease, and to represent the U.S. on all joint committees. Stilwell's titles and his way of carrying out his duties were irksome and humiliating for Chiang. The British and Russians could utilize their lend lease aid as they saw fit, only Chiang had to submit his request for lend lease through Stilwell, and obtain his permission to use such aid. Major differences between the two were inevitable.

Stilwell also alienated Claire Chennault by limiting the amount of support Chennault's Chinese Air Force could receive. While Chiang slowly emerged as a great leader, Mao Tse-tung gained complete control over the Chinese Communist Party and issued demands upon Chiang for recognition of those areas controlled by the communists and greatly increased manpower for the communist armies. Chiang rejected the demands and the communist began to "lobby" the members of the American consulate in Chungking. Chiang was slow to expel the communists from Chungking and they made major inroads in converting American opinion in favor of the communists.

By 1943, Chiang's regime and power were on the decline. He became authoritarian to the extreme. His government officials had to wait weeks to see him. He had his own system, which allowed only three men to assist him. They were Ch'en Li-fu for Kuomintang affairs, Ho Ying-ch'in, for military affairs, and H.H. K'ung for actual government business. The real secret of Chiang's power was his manipulation of these groups. For the remainder of the war, male peasants were kidnapped, roped together, and dragged off for duty in the military. Small wonder that many deserted to the communists at the first chance.

For many of the peasants, service in the military meant death from starvation, sickness, or wounds. Thousands of conscripts died before ever reaching their assigned units. Training was minimal and many did not have a weapon. Tuberculosis, typhus, dysentery, malaria, scabies, beriberi, influenza, and worms took a heavy toll. Wounded troops were usually left to fend for themselves. There was an average of only one doctor per division and little in the way of medicine.

Because their own treatment was so brutal, the soldiers often treated the farmers in the same way. They took whatever the farmer had in the way of food, clothing and shoes without recompense. Mao's forces did just the opposite. They treated the farmers with respect, paid them for what they took, helped with the harvest, and refrained from raping and looting. Chiang seemed ignorant of the sufferings of his people. Perhaps he was too far away in Chungking. Perhaps he was not about to risk another kidnapping by going to the front line areas where his troops were suffering. Perhaps he was too busy writing his book, *China's Destiny,* which was published on March 10, 1943. The book was in response to Mao's book, *On the New Democracy,* and was made mandatory reading for students in all Chinese schools and colleges, for all army officers, all civil servants, and all members of the Kuomintang Youth Corps. The tone of the book is anti-western and antiliberal. It was never published in English.

During 1943, Chiang was given a great boost in popularity by Mme. Chiang's visit to America. Through her speaking engagements, she captivated the American public and besides goodwill, obtained money, planes, and promises of support. Her speaking engagements were reported in detail in Chungking. In October 1943, Vice Adm. Lord Louis Mountbatten arrived in Chungking to become supreme allied commander, South-East Asia command. Stilwell, because of his differences with Chiang was near a point where he was going to be recalled by President Roosevelt. Mountbatten advised Stilwell to apologize to Chiang, which Stilwell did, and for a short time Chiang and Stilwell reconciled.

In November, Chiang attended the Cairo Conference as one of the "Big Three," with Roosevelt and Prime Minister Winston

Churchill. Chiang obtained agreement that all territories seized by Japan (Manchuria, Formosa, and the Pescadores) would be returned to China. Roosevelt also pledged to blockade Burma, train and equip 90 Chinese divisions, and take the offensive in 1944 to drive the Japanese out of Burma. In return, Chiang was to resolve his differences with the communists.

"For me," said Chiang Kai-shek, "the big problem is not Japan, but the unification of my country. If I let Mao Tse-tung push his propaganda across all of free China, we run the risk — and so do you Americans — of winning for nothing. I say this because behind Mao there is a religion of communism — and in consequence, Russia."[7]

The American war leaders could not understand Chiang's desire to kill Chinese communists rather than Japanese. Since 1938, Chiang had essentially left the Japanese armies alone. His best forces were engaging the communists in the northwest of China. President Roosevelt, General George Marshall, military chief of staff, and the U.S. State Department were bombarded by misinformation and anti-Chiang reports from Stilwell; Clarence Gauss, our ambassador in Chungking; and Owen Lattimore, a political advisor to Chiang. Most of the reports inferred that the Kuomintang was evil, and, therefore, the communists must be good. Roosevelt was seriously considering shifting our China aid to the communists who were described as "communists" in name only.

The situation changed in October 1942 when defeated presidential candidate Wendell Wilkie came to Chungking. Wilkie came, saw, and was conquered by Mme. Chiang. Wilkie was so impressed with her charm that he insisted she come to America and tell China's story to the American people. Madame Chaing did come to America as the guest of President and Mrs. Roosevelt, and she won the hearts and respect of the American people. She had an appealing dignity, spoke English perfectly, and blended Chinese and American prose and stories to illustrate her points. At times, her voice would choke, and she would stop her story as if overcome by emotion. She urged Chinese Americans to have pride in their culture and to support their native land. Her visit made a marked change in our government's support of the Chiang government.

Chiang was forced to fight the Japanese in late 1943 and 1944, because the Kwantung Army went on the offensive. In November 1943, Japan seized Changteh in northern Hunan (a province south of the Yangtze) after a 15-day battle. Only 30 of the city's 10,000 buildings were left standing and the populace that was not killed by bombing or poison gas fled the area. A week later, nationalist forces recaptured the city. In March and April 1944, another Japanese offensive involving 1.8 million well-fed, well-equipped, and well-disciplined troops took place against Honan province (to the north of the Yangtze). The province had not yet recovered from a disastrous famine caused at least in part by the nationalist army's seizure of the province crops. Estimates of 200,000 deaths due to starvation and similar numbers of farmers forced to flee the province seemed accurate.

By November 1944, Japan controlled Kiangsi province and destroyed the U.S. air bases at Hengyang, Lingling, Paoching, Tanchuk, Kweilin, and Liuchow. Chungking lay only 200 miles away. Chiang began gathering forces to defend Chungking, but once again seemed oblivious to the real perils of China. He had surrounded himself with "yes men," and brokered no opposition. Prices were skyrocketing, there were food shortages, the educated class began seeking other allegiances, and all signs pointed to chaos and dissension.

During July, President Roosevelt, at the request of General Marshall, tried to have Stilwell appointed supreme commander of all American and Chinese forces in China. Messages flew between Washington and Chungking with the result that on September 25, Chiang demanded that Roosevelt relieve and replace Stilwell.

Roosevelt replaced Stilwell in two weeks with General Albert Wedemeyer, and replaced Ambassador Gauss the following month with General Patrick Hurley. Both men were anti-communist and determined to support Chiang. Chiang was delighted with both appointments.

The Yalta conference with Stalin, Churchill, and an exhausted Roosevelt met in the Crimea on February 4, 1945. Roosevelt seemed incapable of standing up to Stalin's demands and Churchill listened impotently. As a result, Roosevelt signed away China's territorial rights. For the Soviet Union to enter the war against Japan, Russia got the Kurile Islands, Outer Mongolia, South Sakalin Island, and control over the port and rail facilities in Manchuria. The conference adjourned, and Chiang was not informed of the results. By February 12, however, rumors of "a deal" at Chiang's expense began circulating, and Chiang immediately requested a meeting with President Roosevelt. The U.S. replied that there was no time for such a meeting due to the forthcoming San Francisco conference. Chiang then requested to be included in the San Francisco conference. He did not receive a reply.

Roosevelt died on April 12, 1945, and the rationale for his "China" decision died with him. Chiang looked desperately for a way to salvage something from the end of the war. On May 15, General Hurley advised Chiang that the Russians would enter the war against Japan on August 8, and gave him the official results of the Yalta conference. Outwardly, Chiang remained calm, but inwardly he seethed. He suggested that America and Great Britain should be included with Russia for use of the Port Arthur Naval Base, and that all four countries should discuss the Sakhalin Islands. Hurley had no authority to agree to anything. The U.S. stood behind the Yalta agreement.

China sent a delegation to Russia on August 7 to discuss the implications of the Yalta agreement. On August 6, the first atomic bomb was dropped on Hiroshima. Two days later, the port city of

Nagasaki absorbed the effects of the second bomb, and the Soviet Union Army poured across the Manchurian border into China.

For Chiang and China, one war was over and another was about to begin. The collapse of Japan was too swift for Chiang. His government was totally unprepared.

Generalissimo Chiang Kai-shek and General Stilwell linked by Madame Chiang.

National Archives

5

CAPTAIN CLAIRE CHENNAULT: THE FLYING TIGERS

It is safe to say that if there had been no Claire Lee Chennault, there would have been no "Flying Tigers." The need for an aviation organization to fight the Japanese would probably have been realized, but the organization would have lacked the character and flamboyance of the "American Volunteer Group" (AVG) recruited and trained by Claire Chennault.

Founder of the Flying Tigers, Major Gen. Claire L. Chennault, "Old Leatherface," in front of one of his P-40s.

US Air Force

Chennault was one of those confident, gregarious, egocentric characters that seemed to be in abundance in China, Burma, and India during the 1930s. Chennault, a native of Louisiana, had been a country schoolteacher and had an obsession for hunting and fishing. This passion for the two hobbies gave him a weathered appearance that provided instant recognition. His pilots in the AVG, after seeing his leathery facial skin, furrows, and wrinkles, nicknamed him "Old Leatherface."

As a fighter pilot in the army air corps, Chennault was ahead of his time. The leaders of Army aviation were promoting unescorted and invulnerable bombers as the super weapon of the next war. Chennault, like Baron Manfred Von Richtofen, believed that fighter aircraft, operating as a team, had an important role in future wars.

Chennault may have been a prophet, but not to his own service. The tactical fighter school at Maxwell Field, Alabama, stopped teaching fighter tactics in 1936. Chennault retired from active duty the following year as a 47-year-old captain. His discharge was for medical reasons, partial deafness and chronic bronchitis. Due to Chennault's advocacy for fighter aircraft, his short temper, and periodic insubordination, there were more than a few in the army air corps that were happy to see him leave.

Some of the Chinese fighter pilots were trained in the United States and knew of Chennault's fighter-pilot advocacy. By May 1937, he was in China as a $15,000-per-year consultant, with the rank of colonel in the Chinese air force. He was tasked with training and transforming the ragtag Chinese air force into an effective fighting organization. Chiang Kai-shek, president of unified China, was fully occupied with fighting both the Japanese and the Chinese communists, so he turned over management of the air force to his wife, Madame Chiang (the former Mei-ling Soong). Chennault was captivated by Madame

56

Chiang, and she, in turn, became Chennault's greatest supporter.

The Chinese air force was pathetic in the late 1930s. Men were assigned as pilots more due to their social standing than flight ability. Chennault recalls seeing them destroy six of their 13 aircraft during takeoffs and landings in just one day.[1] Simply stated, they were no match for the well-trained and better-equipped Japanese pilots.

By the summer of 1940, one-hundred Japanese planes per day were bombing Chungking, capital of China, and Kunming, terminus of the Burma Road. The Japanese bombers required no fighter escort because the Chinese had no fighters to oppose them. The bombers would fly a level-bombing approach at 6,000 feet that permitted excellent accuracy. Chiang authorized Chennault to fly to Washington to lobby for U.S. aircraft, pilots, and support crews to fight the Japanese.

Chennault's initial request for U.S. support was for 500 B-17 bombers to bomb the mainland cities of Japan. With the support of Mr. Tse-ven Soong, one of the richest men in the world, and brother of Madame Chiang, Chennault was able to brief Secretary of the Treasury Henry Morganthau. Morganthau became a supporter and briefed President Roosevelt and his cabinet on December 19, 1940. Roosevelt and most of his cabinet supported the plan, but Secretary of War Henry Stimson was less certain. Stimson chaired a meeting of Morganthau, Secretary of the Navy, Frank Knox, and Chief of Staff of the Army, George C. Marshall, to further study the plan.

General Marshall and army air corps Chief of Staff, Henry "Hap" Arnold had no use for the renegade Chennault or his AVG plan. Marshall opposed any operation outside of the army chain of command and not subject to army control. He went on to say that the U.S. did not have the bombers or trained crews to spare. In Marshall's opinion, the bombing of Japan by American bombers with American crews would provoke a

Japanese attack against the U.S. when we were still unprepared for war. Chennault's plan was too dangerous, too costly, and too unorthodox.

When the President learned of Marshall's objections, he withdrew his support for the bombers, but did authorize the sale of 100 P-40 fighters. The President also approved a secret plan that permitted Chennault to recruit pilots from the other services through an existing aircraft maintenance company based in China.

In this manner, Chennault was able to purchase 100 P-40 Tomahawk fighter airplanes that Great Britain rejected as being obsolete, and to recruit 112 pilots and 128 ground-support personnel from the navy, marine corps, and army air corps for duty in the China-Burma-India theater (CBI). The pilots were allowed to resign from their current service with the verbal understanding that they would be allowed to rejoin their service when their volunteer duty was complete. The pilots and maintenance personnel were well paid for their adventure. Pilots received $600 to $750 per month at a time when a new car cost about that amount. Maintenance personnel received $250 per month. Pilots also received a bonus of $500 for every Japanese plane they destroyed.

The pilots, known as the American Volunteer Group (AVG), arrived at Loiwing, China, on the Burma border in late summer 1941, for training in the tactics developed by Chennault. The flamboyant group painted the noses of their aircraft with the eyes and teeth of a shark and promptly christened themselves as the Flying Tigers.

The P-40 was no match for the nimble Japanese Zero or Kate fighter in aerial dogfighting, but it was heavy and durable. It also had thick armor plate to protect the pilot. Chennault's tactics could best be described as "hit-and-run." AVG pilots were trained to use the diving speed of the heavy Tomahawk to make diving, firing passes on the more maneuverable Japanese fighters and then dive away. When possible, the pilots, who were always to fight in pairs for mutual protection, could return for another high-speed pass. Pilots were ordered never to try to outmaneuver or dogfight the Japanese pilots. Such tactics, Chennault cautioned, "were nonhabit-forming."[2]

Flying Tiger pilots at Chengkung base in China scramble for their P-40 aircraft.

US Air Force

The AVG was a group of free spirits. Pilots dressed pretty much as they pleased. Some pilots flew in cowboy boots, and salutes and military discipline were not practiced. Many pilots and maintenance men socialized with local girls and partied into the wee hours of the morning. A story is told of how a group of AVG pilots in Rangoon convinced a C-47 cargo plane pilot to fly a bombing mission over Hanoi, French Indo-China. The well-liquored pilots loaded an ample store of spirits into the aircraft, and then filled the fuselage of the C-47 with old Chinese, French, and Russian bombs. Over Hanoi, they pushed the bombs out the door.[3]

There were many characters in the AVG, but, other than

Chennault, only one other living legend. Gregory "Pappy" Boyington outfought, outdrank, and outbrawled all of his compatriots. Following his exploits with the AVG, where he was credited with shooting down six Japanese planes, Boyington rejoined the U.S. Marine Corps and commanded Marine Fighter Squadron 214 on Guadalcanal. He was shot down in January 1944, after personally shooting down 28 Japanese planes. He was carried as missing during the remainder of the war. Following the American occupation of Japan, Boyington was freed from a Japanese POW camp in Yokohama.

The Flying Tigers flew their first combat mission on December 20, 1941. Four "Tigers" intercepted ten Betty bombers as they neared Kunming at 6,000 feet. The Japanese bombers jettisoned their bomb loads and fled for Hanoi, their airfield in French Indo-China. Soon, ten more shark-painted "Tigers" joined the fray, blasting the unescorted bombers from the sky. Only one Betty survived to limp back to Hanoi.

Chennault's Flying Tigers were Chiang Kai-shek's first line of defense.

US Air Force

On February 25, 1942, nine P-40s met 166 Japanese aircraft on the way to bomb and strafe Rangoon. The AVG shot down 24 Japanese aircraft and lost only three. The following day, more than 200 Japanese aircraft raided Rangoon. The Japanese were met by six AVG P-40s. Eighteen Japanese planes were shot down without any losses to the AVG.

By changing the numbers on the fuselage and frequently repainting the noses of the P-40s, the AVG caused the Japanese to believe they had far more aircraft than they actually had. During the fall of 1942, Tokyo radio promised to destroy all 200 of the Flying Tiger aircraft. There were only 29 aircraft operational at the time.

Chennault split the AVG between Burma, where they assisted the British in the defense of Rangoon, and Kunming, China, as a protective screen for western China. When Rangoon fell to the Japanese on March 7, 1942, Chennault moved his entire force to China and continued the attack on the Japanese that were moving north on the Burma Road.

Although the AVG imposed impressive losses on Japan's air forces, their own existence was precarious. Chennault's airfields were about as far from their supply source as they could get. Supplies had to survive the 12,000-mile trip from the United States to Bombay, then 1,500 miles by rail and barge to Ledo in Assam, India. From Ledo, the supplies were flown 500 miles over "The Hump" to Kunming, China. It would often take eight weeks for ox carts and trucks to deliver fuel and supplies the 400 to 700 miles from Kunming to the airfields. Airlift from Kunming was hardly the answer. Cargo planes delivering fuel from Kunming used three gallons of the precious liquid for every two gallons they delivered. Chennault estimated that for every ton of ordnance he was able to drop on Japanese targets, 18 tons had to be delivered to the ports at Rangoon or India.[4] The entire AVG was once grounded for 33 days due to lack of fuel.

Shortages of fuel and spare parts were not the only problem faced by Chennault. The AVG contract with William Pawley's company, Central Aircraft Manufacturing Company, CAMCO, called for CAMCO to provide mechanics, tools, and equipment to repair battle-damaged planes at CAMCO's facility at Loiwing. On January 1, 1943, Pawley notified Chennault that he would no longer repair AVG planes. Chennault lashed out at Pawley in letters to Soong and many others. Chennault accused Pawley of selling AVG supplies and keeping the money. Pawley responded by charging that the AVG's lack of spare parts and maintenance personnel was due to Chennault's negligence and refusal to accept Pawley's advice. Charges and countercharges continued throughout the war and even after the war as both men tried to claim success for the AVG operation.[5]

Chennault and Lieutenant Gen. Joseph W. Stilwell, chief of staff to Chiang Kai-shek, and commanding general U.S. Army Forces in CBI, developed serious differences of opinion as to how the war should be conducted. Chennault argued that his AVG could drive the Japanese out of China, and, if given long-range bombers, could bomb mainland Japan on a daily basis. Stilwell was strongly biased against airpower, and insisted that the war in China and Burma would be won with the bayonet and rifle.

During March 1942, Colonel Clayton Bissell, army air corps, arrived in Chungking to serve as Stilwell's air officer. Bissell and Chennault were old adversaries, having disagreed about fighter tactics long ago at Maxwell Field, Alabama. Chennault considered Bissell to be a parade-ground, spit-and-polish officer who knew nothing of the situation in Burma and China. Bissell, according to Chennault, "represented everything negative about the military."[6] Bissell was sent to China by General Hap Arnold, chief of staff, U.S. Army Air Corps, with the task of dissolving the AVG and introducing an army air corps fighter group. These plans did not include Chennault.[7]

Chennault was aware of Arnold's plans to eliminate the AVG

and had been busy lobbying Madame Chiang and influential friends in Washington in an effort to keep the AVG intact. On March 29, Generalissimo and Madame Chiang, Lieutenant Gen. Stilwell, Colonel Bissell, and Chennault met in Chungking to decide the fate of the AVG. Chiang reluctantly agreed to give up the AVG for a complete U.S. Army Air Corps fighter group if Chennault would command the group and be promoted to brigadier general. Stilwell and Bissell agreed to those conditions, but insisted that the AVG be dissolved by April 30. Chennault argued that army air corps personnel could not possibly relieve the AVG in such a short time and that Chiang needed air support while the new personnel were trained. Madame Chiang was able to obtain agreement to disband the AVG on July 4, the day that most of the AVG contracts expired.[8]

Chennault was returned to active duty in the army air corps on April 15, 1942, as a colonel. Nine days later, he was promoted to brigadier general, as was Bissell, whose date of rank was one day senior to Chennault.[9] The fact that Chennault was now an active duty officer commanding the civilian AVG organization had a negative morale factor on the pilots and support personnel. In late May, one entire AVG squadron refused to fly especially hazardous missions because of broken-down, worn-out airplanes. The men were also physically exhausted and believed that Chennault was simply trying to get the last ounce of blood out of them before their contracts expired. Chennault was furious, but there was little he could do. An army air corps general had no authority over civilian pilots in a volunteer organization in China.

In late April 1942, President Franklin Roosevelt called Chennault back to Washington to learn more about his "six-month-to-drive-the-Japanese-out-of-China-plan." General Marshall was infuriated by Chennault's bypassing the proper chain of command, and ordered Stilwell to return to Washington at the same time. The president had separate meetings with the two protagonists, but was most persuaded by Chennault's presentation. He invited Chennault to communicate directly with him in the future.

63

Both Stilwell and Chennault were invited to speak to the American and British leaders who had assembled in Washington for the Trident conference. Both gave their strategy for future operations in the CBI theater. Chennault's plan to use aviation to slow down the Japanese offensive was strongly resisted by Stilwell and the American chiefs of staff. The British supported Chennault's plan, as did Roosevelt. The result was that Chennault was given the go-ahead for his air offensive and was given priority for supplies flown over the Hump. Stilwell, Arnold, and Marshall were frustrated and angry with Chennault for his intervention.[10]

During May and June, Chennault argued, implored and threatened his pilots to stay on and join the army air corps. He was even successful in obtaining an appeal from President Roosevelt asking the AVG pilots to stay on until properly relieved by the reinforcements. The pilots were having none of it. They had been in China too long. They also wanted no part of the forthcoming military organization. Flying as a civilian and being paid well was one thing. Flying for less pay and having to put up with "chicken" regulations was something else.

Some army air corps personnel started to straggle into China by mid-June, but it was clear to Chennault that he would not have an air capability on July 4, unless the AVG pilots extended their contracts. Chennault called a mass meeting and begged his pilots and ground crews to extend their contracts for two weeks to allow the new men to prepare. If the army air corps is wiped out, it will be your responsibility, Chennault told the AVG.[11] More to the crews' credit than Chennault's, 19 pilots and 36 ground crewmen extended their contracts. Three of the pilots were shot down in the next two weeks.

Burma fell to the Japanese in May 1942. Chinese resistance collapsed, and by May 5, a Japanese armored column on the Burma Road penetrated 75 miles into China. There was no organized Chinese army to stop the Japanese advance into Kunming, the only distribution center for Allied aid to China. Only the AVG and the Salween River gorge stood between the Japanese and Kunming. On May 5, the Japanese reached the mile-deep gorge with thousands of Chinese soldiers and civilians fleeing just ahead of them. Terrified drivers trying to flee the Japanese advance went off the sides of the narrow road, causing hundreds of passengers to fall to their death at the bottom of the gorge.

Some of the first Chinese to cross the suspension bridge across the Salween cut the bridge, trapping thousands of refugees that were killed when the Japanese directed their artillery on them. Chennault was certain that the AVG could stop the Japanese at the gorge, but he knew that the Chinese refugees would also die. He sent a message to Madame Chiang advising her of the situation and asking for orders. Her response came back the same day, "destroy the enemy."[12]

An AVG reconnaissance flight on May 6 reported a solid mass of people, trucks and animals jammed on the narrow road cut through the rock in the gorge. Behind the mass of humanity, Japanese vehicles and troops were stalled bumper-to-bumper waiting for the engineers to construct a pontoon bridge to cross the Salween.

Chennault had recently received seven new P-40 E-model aircraft with external bomb racks. He sent these aircraft, flown by some former navy dive-bombing pilots, to attack the 20-mile column of trucks and people. The bombers were escorted by older model P-40 B-models, that were armed with six .50-caliber machine guns. The P-40 bombers dropped old, Russian-made, 570-pound bombs that destroyed vehicles and broke off sections of the cliff, closing the road and trapping the Japanese.

Next, the AVG used smaller fragmentation bombs and strafed the enemy columns, destroying nearly everything on the road. When the P-40Es left to rearm and refuel, more P-40Bs continued the deadly strafing runs. There was no escape for the Japanese. They died by the hundreds, amid the smoke and fire of burning vehicles, gasoline, and exploding ammunition. Chennault continued the attack for four days and was able to report that the only movement on the Burma Road was a few stragglers heading back to Burma. Besides the Japanese trucks, tanks, and troops, the AVG burned every village along the Burma Road that the Japanese could have used for points of supply. The Japanese never did cross the Salween. This victory by the AVG, in itself, was more than enough to justify their existence.

The "Tigers" existed as the AVG for seven months, December 1941 to July 1942. During that period they compiled a record of success that included the destruction of 300 Japanese planes, strafing and bombing of Japanese forces on the ground, and, perhaps equally important, provided a much-needed morale boost for both America and China.

The relationship between Stilwell and Chennault continued to worsen at the same time that Stilwell's relationship with Chiang Kai-shek and Vice Adm. Lord Louis Mountbatten, supreme commander Southeast Asia, soured.

During the spring of 1944, the Japanese launched a massive strike against Chennault's airfields in retaliation for the punishment that they had been receiving from Chennault's 14th Air Force. For two years, Stilwell had warned Chennault that the Japanese would conduct such an operation and that there were insufficient Chinese ground forces to protect the airfields. Chennault responded that he could protect the airfields with air power alone. He was wrong.

The Japanese advanced on the airfields in east China with 15 divisions commanded by General Shenruki Hata. The meager Chinese resistance fell apart. The airfields were destroyed and plowed into land suitable for planting. The Japanese were especially vicious. Civilians were brutally terrorized and murdered. Businesses, homes, and entire cities were burned to the ground. The civilians of such cities as Kwelin, Hengyong, and Liuchow panicked, overwhelming the transportation system, and making an orderly retreat impossible. China's man-made disasters were compounded by a series of droughts, floods, illness, and deaths that left many Chinese eating soil, tree bark, peanut husks, and even some of the three million dead.[13]

With the situation becoming desperate, Chennault, hat in hand, was forced to ask Stilwell to divert supplies from a new base being developed at Chengtu in west-central China for his use in east-China. Stilwell predictably refused. Animosity between the two men reached a flash point. Chennault went directly to Chiang with his request despite being ordered by Stilwell not to do so. He placed the blame for the loss of airfields and Japanese terrorism on Stilwell for not providing the necessary aviation supplies. Stilwell termed Chennault's action an intolerable act of insubordination and tried to relieve him. Chennault was very popular with the American public, however, and had a friend in the President. Back in Washington, his relief was deemed not possible.

Stilwell had played his last card. On September 24, 1944, Chiang sent Roosevelt a message demanding that Stilwell be recalled. "General Stilwell is unfitted for the vast, complex, and delicate duties which the new command will entail," he said.[14] Roosevelt tried compromises, but Chiang would have none of it. On October 18, President Roosevelt ordered the withdrawal of General Stilwell. Chennault would follow some nine months later.

President Roosevelt died in office on April 12, 1945. His death left Chennault without a friend in high places. General Marshall and General Arnold moved quickly to dismiss Chennault. Knowing that Chennault would not retire willingly, plans were developed to force Chennault's retirement. General Albert C. Wedemeyer, Silwell's successor as Chiang's chief of staff, was notified that Chennault's 14th Air Force in China was to be replaced by the 10th Air Force currently in India. Most of Chennault's squadrons would join the 10th Air Force, and Chennault's depleted unit would be sent north of the Yangtze river, where there were few targets and fewer supplies. This was the final insult to the old warrior.

On July 8, 1945, Chennault submitted his retirement letter which was promptly accepted by General Wedemeyer. He left China on August 8, a bitter and angry man. For eight years he had fought the Japanese, and now with final victory so close, he was prevented from sharing in the glory of the victory celebration.[15]

Claire Chennault died from cancer on July 27, 1958. President Eisenhower called him at his hospital bed on July 25, and promoted him to lieutenant general. Chennault was survived by his two sons, both career Air Force officers, and his widow, Anna Chan, a charming woman, 35 years younger than the general. Claire and Anna were married in China in December 1946, while Chennault was founding the highly successful airline, Civil Air Transport (CAT).

Chennault was buried at Arlington cemetery. Attendees at his funeral included Madame Chiang, T. V. Soong, many of the pilots who served with him in China, and such senior generals as Nathan Twining, Curtis LeMay, Albert Wedemeyer, Carl Spaatz, and George Kinney. Chennault traveled the hard road from the dirt airfield in Louisiana, where he saw his first airplane, to the jungles of Burma, the suffering of China, and, finally, Arlington National Cemetery. Certainly no one could question the respect and love he earned from those who served with him, nor the thanks expressed by Madame Chiang from a grateful nation.

6

DID ROOSEVELT KNOW?

President Franklin D. Roosevelt began his speech to a joint session of Congress on December 8 with these words. "Yesterday, December 7, 1941: a date which will live in infamy: the United States was suddenly and deliberately attacked by the naval and air forces of the Empire of Japan."[1]

Thirty-three minutes later, Congress passed a war resolution against Japan with only one dissenting vote. It has been 60 years since Roosevelt made the speech to Congress and many of those living at the time are no longer alive. Those who remain, and generations since, believe that the lessons learned from the Pearl Harbor attack resulted in our government developing sophisticated systems to warn against surprise attacks in the future. But warnings are not always enough. What if there is warning, but the human element fails to respond properly?

Historians have documented evidence that our government and military services had ample warning of a possible attack on Pearl Harbor, but for a number of reasons failed to respond. Some historians such as Robert Stinnet, in his book, *Day of Deceit*, have gone even further to suggest that the responsibility for the Pearl Harbor disaster falls upon President Roosevelt, and that the president took deliberate measures to destroy records that could have proven his guilt.

Why would the President or his staff not have alerted the Pearl Harbor commanders if they had foreknowledge of the Japanese intention? The story goes that Roosevelt made secret promises of assistance to British Prime Minister Winston Churchill, and that he did not believe he had the necessary public support to provide such assistance without an event that would galvanize our country and Congress to go to war. Pearl Harbor provided such an event.

The story continues that in order to get America into the war, Roosevelt engineered events that led Japan to attack Pearl Harbor and then convened investigative bodies to ensure Admiral Husband E. Kimmel, commander-in-chief U.S. Fleet at Pearl Harbor, and Lieutenant Gen. Walter E. Short, army commander at Pearl Harbor, were found responsible for the debacle that occurred.

The most commonly asked question history students and visitors at the USS Arizona Memorial ask is: "Do you think Roosevelt knew Pearl Harbor would be attacked on the morning of December 7, 1941?" The question implies that Roosevelt knew more than his military commanders at Pearl Harbor, and, therefore, is guilty of negligence for not providing such information to those area commanders.

The President may have had substantially more intelligence available concerning the attack on Pearl Harbor than the two Hawaii area commanders. It's not the job of the president, however, to provide intelligence directly to force commanders. The military has departments, service chiefs, and intelligence networks to analyze and disseminate such information. The 39 volumes and 15,000 pages of evidence from the Joint Committee of Investigation revealed that human error played a major role in the tragedy of Pearl Harbor, but pointed to a collective responsibility for the disaster rather than singling out an individual. The single greatest cause was a shared disbelief that Japan would dare to attack the Pacific Fleet. Perhaps one could better argue that the President failed to provide intelligence to his staff, department heads, and service chiefs, or that service chiefs failed to provide such information to Admiral Kimmel and Major Gen. Short, the area commanders. Rear Adm. Edwin T. Layton, fleet intelligence officer for Admiral Kimmel, places the fault and, therefore, the responsibility for not providing such information on the office of the Chief of Naval Operations (CNO) in Washington, D.C.

70

Layton in his book, *And I Was There,* cites information from seven of the nine separate official investigations into the attack on Pearl Harbor to pinpoint responsibility on the plans division, office of CNO, and specifically on Rear Adm. Richmond Kelly Turner, chief (director) of war plans within the plans division.[2]

Layton might be expected to display a favorable bias toward his former boss, Admiral Kimmel, but his denunciation of Admiral Turner stems from his professional relationship with Turner and knowledge obtained subsequent to the attack on Pearl Harbor. Layton testified at all but one of the secret inquiries into the Pearl Harbor attack and referred to Turner as an "opinionated, stubborn fool," who failed to provide Admiral Kimmel with the vital intelligence information that might have saved Pearl Harbor.[3]

Troubles in the CNO office reached a peak in April 1941, when Turner took control of all intelligence estimates within his plans division and made decisions on distribution of estimates without coordination with the Office of Naval Intelligence (ONI). Heretofore, ONI had collected, interpreted, and disseminated estimates known as Enemy Intentions and had assured both Kimmel and Layton that they would be sent every piece of pertinent information.

The Director of ONI, Captain Alan C. Kirk, resisted Turner's takeover and was forced to take the issue to the CNO, Admiral Harold R. Stark. Stark was described by Secretary of War Stimson as, "a timid and ineffective man to the post he holds."[4] Stark's own CNO staff manual gave ONI the responsibility for securing "all classes of pertinent information pertaining to naval and maritime matters." Stark, lacking the necessary fiber to referee a service roles-and-missions dispute, refused to concern himself with the real issue.[5] Since he was impressed with Turner's demonstrated abilities, and censorship was becoming a national concern, he approved Turner's position. From that date forward, the commanders at Pearl Harbor received only edited intelligence information personally approved by Turner. Kimmel learned of the paucity of the information provided to him during the testimony given during the Pearl Harbor Attack investigations. The fact that Stark's staff manual was never changed to reflect the change in responsibility confused the various investigative groups and made ONI, rather than the plans division, the eventual scapegoat for Kimmel's lack of information.

Purple was the name of the most secret U.S. code used to decrypt Japanese messages to their ambassador in Washington. The decryption process of the Japanese Purple code was termed Magic. There was an understandable concern at the highest levels of our government that dissemination of Magic material might lead to a compromise of our capability. General Marshall assumed authority for approval for all army Magic dissemination. This concern for security was one of the reasons for Turner's takeover in the navy plans department and his personal involvement in the dissemination of all Magic information, not just to Kimmel and Short, but other operational commanders and services as well.

Other reasons listed for Turner's failure to provide adequate intelligence information to Admiral Kimmel included Turner's desire to dictate strategic intelligence regardless of whether he had sufficient information to do so. As early as April 1941, and until December 6, 1941, Turner insisted that the Soviet Union, not the Philippines, Malaya, Thailand, Hawaii, or anywhere else was the target of Japan's forthcoming offensive. On December 6, he revised his opinion to make the British possessions potential targets of Japan's attack. If one believes his own intelligence summaries, small wonder that Turner bothered Kimmel with any such information. Gradually, Turner created a system whereby he would bring his ideas directly to Stark who would rubber-stamp them, often keeping the other staff officers ignorant of his actions.

Turner's dominating influence within the CNO office created much resentment and bad blood, especially among the professionals within the intelligence field. In addition, army intelligence found him to be a difficult person with whom to work. As a result, they seldom did. This inter- and intra-service squabbling worked to the detriment of the operational commanders, especially those far removed from Washington.

In addition to information collected by each service and allied intelligence agency, President Roosevelt received information from the Federal Bureau of Investigation (FBI); his secretary of war, Henry L. Stimson; State Department dispatches; a small and secretive fact-finding body headed by columnist John Franklin Carter;[6] a neophyte Central Intelligence Agency headed by William J. "Wild Bill" Donovan;[7] and personal phone calls from Winston Churchill, the British prime minister. Despite these sources of information, Layton states that even the president was denied reports of vital intelligence for several month-long periods. The army had become so security conscious that they refused to deliver actual Magic intercepts to the President and provided summarized briefings instead. This situation occurred in the fall of 1941, causing Layton to speculate that if the " . . . commander in chief could be denied details of vital intelligence for a whole month, a situation that recurred in the fall (of 1941) . . . must once and for all cast doubt that an omniscient Roosevelt had advance warning of the Japanese attack."[8] To Layton's credit, he states unequivocally that " . . . there is no evidence that any presidential directive was issued restricting the flow of intelligence to Pearl Harbor — or anywhere else."[9]

Author James Rusbridger and Eric Nave, the "father of British code-breaking in the Far East," state unequivocally that Churchill deliberately withheld vital intelligence derived from British intercepts of the Japanese naval code, JN-25. This information, if provided to Roosevelt, would have alerted the president to the Japanese attack on Pearl Harbor.[10] Churchill, according to Rusbridger, feared that if he alerted Roosevelt to the Japanese plan to attack Pearl Harbor, Roosevelt would set a trap that would either destroy Admiral Yamamoto's attack force, leaving the U.S. with no immediate need to join Britain in its war against Germany, or purposefully alert Japan to the trap, causing them to cancel the attack on Pearl Harbor and abandon its use of the JN-25 code.

Either way, according to Rusbridger and Nave, Churchill saw Great Britain as the loser. Churchill's gamble not to alert Roosevelt brought America into the war and temporarily, at least, saved the British empire.

Much of the highly classified information that was not provided to Admiral Kimmel would not have caused a significant change to fleet readiness on the morning of December 7. Some information, however, may well have made a difference. For example, on October 7, a message was decrypted in Washington and provided to the CNO. The message was from Tokyo and was addressed to the Japanese consulate in Honolulu. The message asked for continuous reports on the fleet anchorage at Pearl Harbor. The request was for information on the Pacific Fleet training schedule, the days and times the fleet returned from training, and where each ship anchored. In addition, the harbor was to be divided into a grid of five parts.

One might assume the grid was to plan bombing attacks against the ships located inside each grid. One might also assume that if the CNO had provided such information to Kimmel, it would have caused Kimmel to ask what other information CNO had about Japan's interest in Pearl Harbor.

The following day, another message was decrypted that revealed Japan would send a special courier to return the information to Tokyo. Both messages were routed to the military departments in Washington on October 9 and 10, but nothing was sent to Kimmel. On November 25, Secretary Hull warned the president's inner cabinet that "relations were extremely critical and . . . we should be on the lookout for a military attack anywhere by Japan at any time."[11] This information was not sent to Kimmel nor was Japan's deadline of November 25 for an end to negotiations.

Japan's ambassador had been meeting with Cordell Hull frequently in an effort to prevent Japan's militarists from going to war. Japan's negotiating position promised to remove troops from China and Indochina in 1966 (25 years in the future), and to make no aggressive moves to the south. For that, the U.S. must provide Japan's oil needs. Secretary Hull held firm that, in order to negotiate at all, Japan must agree to three points:

1. Japan to cease movement of military forces everywhere in the Pacific.
2. Japan agree not to invoke the tripartite pact (Germany, Japan, and Italy) even if the U.S. becomes involved in the war in Europe.
3. Japan to guarantee China's autonomy.

In response, the U.S. would resume economic relations, provide some oil and rice now, with more to be provided later.

On November 19, Ambassador Nomura was directed by Tokyo to present Japan's final offer to the U.S. with no further concessions possible. If the U.S. could not agree to the proposals and sign an agreement by November 25, "negotiations will have to be broken off."[12] Nomura and special envoy Kusuru visited Secretary Hull on November 21 and made Japan's final proposal. The proposal included Japan's willingness to evacuate southern French Indochina in return for the U.S. supplying some of Japan's oil needs. Hull had known Japan's final offer for more than a week, courtesy of Magic intercepts, but gave Nomura no such indication. Hull was primarily concerned with extending negotiations well into December, or, hopefully, for three months so the U.S. military could further reinforce the Philippines. The two sides agreed to meet the afternoon of November 26.

During the morning of November 26, President Roosevelt received intelligence information confirming that a Japanese expedition force was approaching Indochina. This act of treachery so inflamed the president that he directed Hull to give the Japanese a new proposal with ten conditions including: Japan must withdraw all military forces from China and Indochina; support the government of Chiang Kai-shek in China; and abrogate the Tripartite Pact.[13]

Secretary of State Cordell Hull arrives at the White House with Japanese Ambassador Kichisaburo Nomura (left) and Special Envoy Saburo Kurusu (right) on November 17, 1941 for a 70-minute conference with President Franklin D. Roosevelt in a "final attempt at peace."

The Awani Press

As Nomura read the conditions, he realized that negotiations had come to an end. Too stunned to speak, he turned to special envoy Kurusu, who asked Hull about the abrupt change in the U.S. position and asked if they could discuss the proposal before sending it to Tokyo. A tight-lipped Hull refused to discuss the conditions. The meeting was over and, in retrospect, the attack on Pearl Harbor was assured. Much speculation exists as to other reasons for Roosevelt's abrupt reversal, including a visit from Ambassador Dr. Hsu Shih on the evening of November 25. Naturally, Chiang Kai-shek was against any appeasement of the Japanese. Still other historians speculate that Roosevelt received information from Churchill that Japan was about to wage war against Great Britain and the United States. British intelligence sources will not yield any information in the near term since Great Britain placed a 75-year "closure" on Japanese intelligence reports following the war.

When informed of the Japanese response, President Roosevelt had concerns that Japan might go to war within a few days, ". . . for the Japanese are notorious for attacking without warning."[14] The more difficult proposition confronting the U.S., according to the president, was how to maneuver Japan into being the aggressor without suffering too much from the Japanese attack.

Ample evidence existed that the Japanese attack would be against Malaya, Singapore, Thailand, or the Philippines. On the morning of November 26, General Marshall convened an emergency meeting with the war and navy departments in his office. He informed the attendees that he expected the Japanese to terminate discussions and to "assault the Philippines."[15] General Douglas MacArthur was directed to carry out orders to attack threatening convoys and begin reconnaissance flights over Formosa, even at the risk of provoking hostilities. Stark was told to ferry fighter aircraft from Hawaii to Wake Island and Midway Island.

The army convened a joint board an hour later with General Hap Arnold, deputy chief of staff, army air corps, agreeing to use two B-24 bombers to photograph Jailut and Truk islands to determine Japanese naval buildups. Stark radioed Kimmel and gave him this information plus the need to move aircraft to Wake and Midway. Neither Marshall, Stark, nor Kimmel raised any objection to the depletion of Hawaii's fighter aircraft. Later, Kimmel testified that he took the movement of aircraft from Hawaii to mean that there was no threat to the fleet. A war warning predicting an aggressive move by Japan within the next few days was drafted and sent to General MacArthur and Admiral Thomas C. Hart, Asiatic fleet commander, in Manila.[16] The message repeated that Japan had to commit the first overt act before offensive action was taken.

Kimmel received the war warning on November 27. Layton noticed that Guam was not listed as a potential target, but the Philippines, Thailand, and possibly Borneo were. He was then directed to forward the warning to General Short in Hawaii and did so. Task Force 8 with USS *Enterprise* left Pearl Harbor on November 28 to ferry a marine attack squadron to Wake Island. Task Force 12 with USS *Lexington* departed on December 5 with support for Midway Island, and Task Force 5, several cruisers traveling without a carrier, went south to conduct landing exercises at Johnston Island.

On November 30, *The Honolulu Advertiser* announced that "Japan May Strike over the Weekend." The story had been printed in the *New York Times* a few days earlier. For the next several days, the other Hawaii daily paper, *The Star Bulletin,* notified its readers that, "Japan Envoys Resume Talks amid Tension," and "Japan Gives Two More Weeks to Negotiations." Apparently, no one paid attention to any of the information.

In Washington, on December 6, during Secretary Knox's morning meeting with Admiral Stark, there was a long discussion regarding Japanese intentions. Finally, Knox asked, "Gentlemen, are they going to hit us?" "No, Mr. Secretary," responded Turner, generally regarded as the spokesman for Stark. "They are going to attack the British. They are not ready for us yet."[17] During the evening President Roosevelt sent a personal message to the Japanese emperor seeking to diminish the likelihood of war. When informed of the message, special envoy Kurusu termed it "a clever move," since the emperor could neither approve or disapprove Roosevelt's request, and it was certain to cause more thinking in Tokyo.

By 9:30 P.M., the first 13 parts of a 14-part Purple message from Tokyo to Ambassador Nomura had been intercepted, decoded, and delivered to the President. Secretary Knox read the message at the same time as the president and both determined that the message meant war. A meeting with Stimson and Hull was scheduled for 10:00 the next morning.

Early on December 7, the 14th part of the message arrived and was decoded. The message specified that the Japanese ambassador was to deliver the entire message to Secretary Hull at 1:00 P.M. (7:00 A.M. Hawaii time). Admiral Stark, three blocks away at the navy department, received the message at 2:30 P.M. "Why don't you pick up the telephone and call Kimmel?" one of Stark's staff members asked. Stark lifted the receiver as if to comply but then changed his mind and called the president. When told that the president was not available, Stark put down the phone and did not follow up. President Roosevelt was with Dr. Hu Shih, the Chinese ambassador, and informed him about his message to the emperor. "This is my last effort for peace," Roosevelt said. "I am afraid it may fail."

Much of the intelligence information received by Kimmel's command concerned Japanese submarines. During the evening of December 6, five two-man midget submarines were released from their mother subs just outside the entrance to Pearl Harbor. Their mission was to enter the harbor and torpedo the American ships. Five large Japanese submarines that carried seaplanes to reconnoiter ahead of the Japanese carrier force joined a force of 20 additional submarines to blockade Oahu. At 7:00 A.M. on December 7, the Japanese submarine *I-26* attacked the American freighter *Cynthia Olson* and the *Lahaina*, one thousand miles north of Hawaii. It took the *I-26* more than three hours to sink the small freighters. There were no survivors. That was the extent of the damage inflicted by Japanese submarines. By then, the American fleet at Pearl Harbor was in ruins.

At the White House, Roosevelt was having lunch and chatting with his aide, Harry Hopkins, when the phone rang. The operator explained that it was an urgent call from the secretary of the navy. Hopkins glanced at his watch. It was 1:40 P.M. Roosevelt initially seemed stunned. He turned "white as a sheet, and was visibly shaken." He questioned Knox out of sheer disbelief, but Knox insisted that it was true. Japan had just attacked the U.S. Fleet at Pearl Harbor. Hopkins interrupted Roosevelt's pronouncement by insisting, "This can't be true, this must mean the Philippines."[18] Roosevelt's pride in his navy was so great that he had difficulty acknowledging that the navy had been caught unaware.

Following the numerous investigations into the attack and the relief of Admiral Kimmel and General Short, one thing seems obvious. Neither officer should have been relieved in disgrace for the debacle at Pearl Harbor. It is clear that they lacked the necessary information to have acted differently. Relief may have been appropriate under the circumstances, but both officers should have been reassigned to other positions within their service. Perhaps Congress, in time, will direct the Department of the Navy to rectify the disgrace of Admiral Husband Kimmel and Lieutenant Gen. Walter Short, scapegoats for the navy's mistakes at Pearl Harbor.

Major characters in this chapter

Franklin D. Roosevelt, President
Cordell Hull, Secretary of State
Henry L. Stimson, Secretary of War
Frank Knox, Secretary of the Navy
James V. Forrestal, relieved Frank Knox

Japanese Dignitaries
Saburu Kurusu, special Japanese envoy
Nomura, Kichisaburo, Japanese ambassador

Joint Chiefs of Staff, Washington
General George C. Marshall, Chief of Staff, U.S. Army and Chairman
Admiral Harold R. Stark, Chief of Naval Operations
Admiral Ernest J. King, relieved Stark and became CINC U.S. Fleets
Major Gen. H. "Hap" Arnold, Deputy Chief of Staff, army air corps

Navy Department, Washington
Admiral Richmond Kelly Turner, Chief (Director) of War Plans
Division, CNO

Commander in Chief, Navy, Honolulu
Admiral James O. Richardson, CINCUSFLT, relieved by
Admiral Husband E. Kimmel as CINCUSFLT (Feb 1, 1941), relieved
by Admiral Chester W. Nimitz, CINCPACFLT (Dec 31, 1941)

Hawaii Commanders
Lieutenant Gen. Walter C. Short, Commander, Hawaii Army
Major Gen. F. L. Martin, Commander Hawaiian Army Air Corps

CINC US Fleet Staff
Capt. Edwin C. Layton, Fleet Intelligence Officer
Lieutenant Cmdr. Joseph J. Rochefort, Communications Security Unit

On December 8, 1941, President Roosevelt asked congress to declare war on Japan.

Associated Press

7

GREGORY "PAPPY" BOYINGTON

It would be difficult, if not impossible, to write about personalities of the Pacific war and not include "Pappy" Boyington. Without question, Boyington is one of most colorful characters to emerge from that war.

Major Gregory "Pappy" Boyington, commanding officer VMF-214.

US Marine Corps

Gregory Boyington was born in Cour d'Alene, Idaho, on December 4, 1912. It was 1935, before Greg realized his last name was Boyington, not Hallenbeck. His mother married a man named Hallenbeck shortly after Greg was born, but his biological father was Boyington. Greg Hallenbeck graduated from the University of Washington, where he was on the wrestling team. He married under the name Hallenbeck, and was a draftsman for the Boeing Aircraft Corporation in Seattle. He wanted to fly for the Marine Corps, but the corps would not accept married men at the time. When he learned that his father was not Hallenbeck, he joined the Marine Corps as Gregory Boyington, the name on his birth certificate, as a bachelor second lieutenant. By 1941, Boyington was deeply in debt, his marriage was failing, and his future in the corps was dim.

In mid-1941, Brigadier Gen. Claire Chennault, United States Army Air Force (USAAF retired), started organizing the All Volunteer Group (AVG), which would later become known as The Flying Tigers. President Franklin Roosevelt approved a secret plan that authorized Chennault to recruit 112 pilots and 128 ground support personnel from the army air corps, navy, and marine corps to fight the Japanese in China. Chennault was also able to purchase 100 P-40 "Tomahawk" aircraft that the British rejected as being obsolete. The pay was impressive at the time: $600 to $750 per month for the pilots, plus $500 for each Japanese plane shot down. Maintenance personnel received $250 per month. The arrangement was for the pilots to be released from their service, serve their term in the AVG, and then return to their service without any loss of rank or time in service.

Boyington was well aware that he would not be selected for promotion to the grade of captain, the result of being too far in debt, and being too much of a "party animal." He was a flight instructor at the Naval Air Station, Pensacola, Florida, at the time Chennault's agents visited the command. With scant future in the corps, Boyington seized the opportunity to join the AVG. It seemed to him to be the solution to most of his problems.

84

His resignation from the marine corps took four hours to process. When finished, Boyington had a passport with his picture and the statement, "A member of the clergy," stamped on the passport.[1]

Boyington arrived in Rangoon in mid-November 1941, and proceeded to Toungoo, where he met some AVG pilots, groundcrews, and Claire Chennault.[2] Boyington was credited with downing six Japanese planes during the six months that he was with the AVG. He continued his heavy drinking and brawling, and had serious differences of opinion with Brigadier Gen. Claire Chennault.

Once, when restricted by Chennault to two drinks per day, the result of a raucous party involving a live leopard, Anglo-Burmese girls, target practice with personal weapons, and drums of scotch whiskey, Boyington insisted that he could be trusted to stick to his punishment. He located the two largest water glasses in Burma, and had them filled with scotch each evening before the party began. In this manner he stuck to the two drinks per day routine.[3] There were many "characters" in the AVG, but only two living legends, Boyington and Chennault. Boyington outfought, outdrank, outcursed, and outbrawled all of his fellow pilots. It was inevitable that differences would occur.

Boyington returned to the United States in June 1942, and found that the secret arrangement that sent him to the AVG was so secret that the Marine Corps knew nothing about it. He had to seek the help of the secretary of the navy to be reinstated into the Marine Corps. He was sent to the Pacific Theater in January 1943, and served as the executive officer of Marine Fighter Squadron-122 on Guadalcanal. He broke his leg in a barroom brawl, was shipped to New Zealand to recuperate, and was back at Espiritu Santo, in the New Hebrides, waiting for orders when the marines needed a commanding officer for a new squadron that was being formed. Boyington, then a major, was an experienced combat pilot; he was available; he got the job. The rest is history.

Boyington's fighter squadron, VMF-214, was nicknamed the Black Sheep Squadron and flew the new F4U Corsair aircraft. The Corsair was a clean, gull-wing airplane with a 2,000-horsepower engine. It had a speed of 415-miles-per-hour, substantially faster than the Japanese Zero, and mounted six 50-caliber machine guns, three in each wing. Boyington, then age 30, was nicknamed "Pappy" by his pilots.

During the next 84 days, the Black Sheep led the attacks that destroyed Japanese aerial opposition in the Solomon Islands, and "Pappy" Boyington led the Black Sheep. He earned the nation's highest decoration, the Medal of Honor, for shooting down 26 enemy planes during the period September 12, 1943 to January 3, 1944.

Boyington's Black Sheep pilots were credited with destroying 94 aircraft during the same period, and one additional *Zero* on January 6, 1944.

An F4U-Corsair aircraft and the Black Sheep pilots in the Solomon Islands. The baseball caps were provided by the Saint Louis Cardinals baseball team, one cap for each Japanese plane shot down.

US Marine Corps

His medal citations included his actions on October 17, when he led a flight of 24 fighters over Kahili airfield in the Solomons.

When the Japanese would not launch their aircraft to fight, Boyington challenged the Japanese over the radio to "come up and fight," and continued to circle the airfield until the Japanese finally launched 60 fighters to give battle. The Black Sheep shot down 20 Japanese fighters without a single loss.

Boyington was shot down on January 3, 1944, after shooting down his 27th and 28th Japanese aircraft.[4] He was carried as missing for the remaining 20 months of the war. He was captured by a Japanese submarine and transported to Rabaul, the Japanese base on New Britain that he had just attacked. He was blindfolded, tied, and prodded along the coral streets of Rabaul until jerked to a sudden stop. "How would you like to be with your friends?"[5] a voice asked in perfect English. Boyington, startled, replied, "I don't believe I know what you mean." "Oh, you'll find out soon enough," the voice replied.[6] Boyington was loaded on a truck and taken to a building in town where he underwent his first interrogation.

The English speaker turned out to be Edward Honda, a graduate of McKinley High school in Honolulu in 1929. "Eddy's" parents were Buddhist and sent Eddy to Japan to receive a formal religious education. Eddy was an assistant coach for the Nagoya Dragons baseball team, was married, and renounced his American citizenship in 1941. He joined the Japanese navy as an interpreter in 1942, and arrived in Rabaul in August 1943. Pappy's interrogation did not go well. A petty officer was called to beat Boyington and the interrogators extinguished their cigarettes by pushing them into the neck and shoulders of the marine.

When the officers left the interrogation room for a break, Eddy suggested that Boyington should make it easy on himself or he would be treated very badly. "These Japs are going to question you again and again on the same subjects. If you are going to tell them a line, stick to the same story and be consistent; otherwise, they will think you are lying and it will get very rough for you."[7] For the next month, Boyington followed Honda's advice. His treatment may also have been better because of the stench associated with his wounds. Denied medical attention, his putrid wounds and lack of hygiene made his presence so offensive that his interrogators tended to keep their distance. Boyington's lack of military secrets also helped him. He was told many times that he was the stupidest major the interrogators had ever met. Boyington felt like replying that there were many marines back on Guadalcanal that would agree.

Another American, Lieutenant John Arbuckle, USN, was shot down, captured, and taken to Rabaul in December 1943. He recalled his interrogations by Eddy Honda as being quite reasonable. Honda would ask him such questions as, "Why was MacArthur called Dugout Doug?" and "Is President Roosevelt really a Jew?" Some of the questions were ridiculous and Arbuckle would respond, "Aw come on." Honda would just shrug his shoulders and continue. Arbuckle said Honda acted tough when the officers were around, but he never hit the POWs. He never gave his real name but he did say that he grew up in Hawaii and played professional baseball in Japan. He also said, "I'm going to get out of Rabaul, you just wait and see."[8]

The Allied prisoners on Rabaul did not have long to live. Tokyo had informed the headquarters at Rabaul to stop sending POWs to Japan, and Imperial Navy policy was to execute prisoners once all information had been obtained. Prior to February 1944, the Japanese Army's Sixth Field *Kempei Tai* (secret police) executed prisoners by decapitation with samurai swords and cremated the remains. After February, remains were not cremated for fear of attracting Allied bombing and strafing attacks. A mass execution of more than 30 Truk POWs was carried out by the *Kempei Tai* in retaliation for the March 3, 1944, bombing attack that destroyed downtown Rabaul.[9] Following the war, it was learned that 60 Australian civilians from Kavieng, New Ireland, were murdered aboard the Japanese ship *Akikaze* enroute to Rabaul.[10]

Honda knew that it was only a matter of time before the Allies would overrun Rabaul. His plan was to use several prisoners as a way to get himself back to Japan before the Allied attack came. In early February, civilian interpreter Edward Honda convinced his military superiors that the prisoners had valuable military information and should be taken to Japan for further questioning. His superiors agreed, and Honda was ordered to escort six prisoners back to Tokyo as soon as possible. Honda gathered the six on February 15, 1944. They included Boyington; John Arbuckle; Captain Charles Taylor, an army air corps P-38 pilot; Major Don Boyle, USMC, an F4U pilot; an Australian RAAF pilot; possibly Harry Dawkins; and a New Zealand RAAF pilot, possibly Brian Stacy.[11]

The POWs were blindfolded, handcuffed, and had their legs tied. Besides the two pilots of the *"Betty"* bomber, there were only three Japanese on the plane; Honda, a guard, and the rear gunner. Boyington seriously considered taking over the plane but was begged not to try it by his fellow prisoners. The plane would fly to Truk, a four-hour flight, refuel, and then fly to Saipan and Tokyo. Shortly before the plane landed at Truk, the Hellcat fighters, dive bombers, and torpedo planes of Vice Adm. Marc Mitscher's Fast Carrier Task Force 58 also arrived and subjected Truk Lagoon to two days and one night of constant bombardment. Honda untied the legs of the POWs, and they rolled in a ditch alongside the runway as the bombs rained down. The Japanese plane that carried the POWs to Truk exploded in flames and smoke, as did most other aircraft on the ground. Boyington called it, "The best Navy Day program I ever expect to see."[12]

Boyington later recalled that he was able to peek from under one corner of the blindfold, and observed a Jap Zero land near the ditch. The pilot crawled out and announced, "I'm a Japanese pilot."[13] Boyington told him to get his butt in the ditch because our planes are coming back. And they did come back, with machine guns blazing. The attack went on for hours. Honda told the POWs to stay there while he ran for cover to a real foxhole nearby. Honda's place was taken by four Zero pilots that had no idea the Allied POWs were in the ditch. "They cursed us and threw dirt on us," recalled Arbuckle. When Mitscher's nine carriers finished their raid, at least 31 Japanese ships (137,000 tons) were sunk, including 10 warships, and 270 planes destroyed.[14] Truk was never again a threat to Allied forces. Following the attack, the POWs were loaded on an captured American DC-3 aircraft, flown to Saipan and then to Tokyo.

Nothing more was heard from Boyington until August 30, 1945, when the Fourth Marine Regiment landed near the Omori POW camp on the Tokyo waterfront. Commander Harold Stassen, USN, later a senator from Minnesota, directed the release of the POWs in the camp, including "Pappy " Boyington.

Boyington returned to the United States as a war ace and international hero. He was met at Oakland on September 12, 1945, by 21 remaining Black Sheep pilots and told his story to numerous reporters. He was sent on a tour of the country promoting the sale of war bonds, met the remainder of the Black Sheep, and was presented his Medal of Honor by President Harry Truman.

The possibility of a wonderful future lay within Boyington's grasp. He could have become a congressman, governor, corporation head, or been appointed to various positions in government agencies. Unlike Joe Foss, another marine corps Pacific war ace and Medal of Honor winner, who went on to become governor of his home state and commissioner of the American Football Conference, Boyington had nothing but trouble. He remained the drinking, pugnacious character that he personified as a marine. He went through several well-publicized marriages and divorces, and went from jobs as beer salesman, stock salesman, and jewelry salesman, to a job as a wrestling referee. In 1958, he published *Baa, Baa, Black Sheep*, a best-selling book based on his wartime experiences. In 1976-77, he was technical director for the television series of the same name. Neither the book nor the television series was true-to-life and embarrassed many of the remaining Black Sheep.[12] When criticized for his connection with the show, Boyington would reply, "I only did it for the money."[15]

Toward the end, Boyington became an entertainer (guest speaker), sometimes unable to entertain because he was drunk. The one constant in his life was alcohol. Perhaps F. Scott Fitzgerald was closest to the truth when he said, "Show me a hero and I'll write you a tragedy."[16]

The Army Counter Intelligence Corps (CIC) in Japan arrested Edward C. Honda after the war. He was transported to Guam to be tried by the War Crimes Tribunal. While being interrogated, it was noticed that he was wearing a watch that belonged to Boyington. He was charged with treason, for being in charge of the Nisei intelligence corps, and with theft of the watch. When contacted, Boyington replied that he had given Honda the watch. "It was broken, so I had no use for it, and told him he could fix it up and keep it. He (Honda) is a good gent, treat him right, and please wish him the season's greetings. . . ."[17] The theft charges were dismissed. When it was proven that Honda had renounced his American citizenship, the treason charge was also dropped. Eddy spent six months on Guam, playing baseball, enjoying the post exchange, and having the time of his life. He became a public relations consultant and was active in postwar baseball.

Don Boyle and John Arbuckle were both alive in 1996. Gregory Boyington died on January 11, 1988, at age 75. His remains are interred in Arlington National Cemetery. [18]

Colonel Gregory Boyington (at left) after receiving the Medal of Honor from President Harry Truman. Lieutenant Col. Frank Walton is at the right of the picture.

US Marine Corps

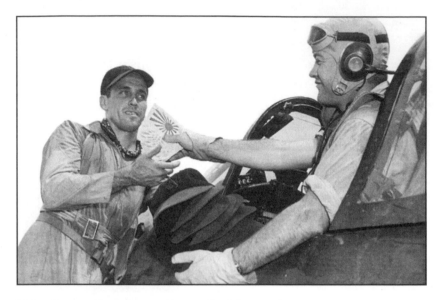

Major Gregory Boyington exchanges 48 stickers, each one representing a Japanese plane shot down, for 20 St. Louis Cardinal baseball caps.

U.S. Marine Corps

8

HECTOR C. BYWATER

Most historians credit the genius of Admiral Isoroku Yamamoto, commander of Japan's combined fleet, for the strategy that gained Japan a huge advantage at the start of WW II. This chapter argues that the architect of Japan's strategy was not Yamamoto, but rather Mr. Hector C. Bywater.

Hector Bywater was born in London on October 21, 1884, the youngest of four children. He died in Richmond, near London on August 16, 1940. Bywater did not live to see his strategy implemented by Yamamoto, but had he lived, he would have been pleased to see his predictions fulfilled.

October 21, Bywater's birthday, is also Trafalgar Day in England which celebrates Admiral Horatio Nelson's victory over the combined French and Spanish fleets in 1805. Each year on Hector's birthday, the Royal Dockyards are opened to the public in honor of Nelson's stunning victory, and in memory to Nelson who lost his life in the battle. Bywater recalled that these annual visits to the dockyards were the closest thing to heaven that he could imagine. To be able to see and touch the mighty warships that made history around the world was more important than toys, bicycles, or pellet guns to young Bywater. Bywater's lifelong preoccupation with ships, armament, and naval strategy began with these visits.

At age 10, Bywater wrote, and had accepted for publication, an essay about the Battle of the Yalu River, the decisive sea battle of the Sino-Japanese war. Bywater examined the tactical and technical reasons for the Japanese success against the more powerful German-built Soviet ships. For his 14th birthday, Bywater received a copy of *Ironclads in Action,* the most penetrating study of naval warfare to that time. The book detailed the battle between *Monitor* and *Merrimack* as well as other ironclad vessels and battles. Bywater had already memorized the ship statistics in Brassey's *Naval Annual,* and Jane's *All the World's Navies,* much like other boys would memorize baseball or soccer statistics.

The Bywater family in 1892. Hector is standing at the right rear of picture. Hector considered the Royal Dockyards as the closest thing to "Heaven" at this time.

Jeffrey Holman

Much of Bywater's youth was spent at sea with his family crossing and recrossing the Atlantic Ocean while his father sought suitable employment. The Bywaters spent four years in Cambridge, Massachusetts, which gave Hector the opportunity to visit the Charleston Navy Yard and explore *Old Ironsides.*

The Bywater family returned to England, but shortly after Hector's 13th birthday put to sea again. The family lived briefly in Canada, the United States, West Africa, and, for a longer time, in Germany. At age 17, Hector was in New York working as a streetcar conductor, and as a clerk for the Union Railway Company in Brooklyn. Bywater spent much of his free time at the Brooklyn Navy Yard. His continuing interest in naval strategy prompted him to write an article for the *New York Herald* newspaper. As a result, he was hired, at age 19, as a reporter for the *Herald.*

Shortly after Bywater started work for the *Herald,* Japanese torpedo boats surprised the Russian fleet at Port Arthur, China. Admiral Heihachiro Togo sent eleven small torpedo boats, without warning or a declaration of war, to attack the great Soviet Fleet. The attack destroyed a cruiser, two battleships, and confined the remainder of the Soviet Fleet to the Port Arthur harbor. Bywater's knowledge of ship capabilities, translation of the message traffic, and detailed analysis of the Japanese sneak attack earned him great respect and praise throughout naval and journalism circles.

Bywater sailed for England on February 12, 1905, as the *Herald's* European naval correspondent. The war between Russia and Japan had lasted 15 months. After his sneak attack, Admiral Togo bottled up the Soviet Fleet in Port Arthur and destroyed any Russian ships that tried to put to sea. The ancient Russian Baltic Fleet was sent on an 18,000-mile mission to break the Japanese blockade, but Togo was waiting in the Straits of Tsushima. The battle took place on May 27 and 28 and resulted in another stunning Japanese victory. The Russians, under Admiral Zinovi Rojestevsky, lost all 14 ships and 4,380 men. Togo did not lose a single ship and suffered only 17 casualties.[1]

Bywater's account of the battle was carried on the front pages of the *Herald* and established Bywater as the premier writer of naval strategy and tactics. Bywater also developed the concept whereby a country (Japan) with inferior naval forces and a much inferior economic and production capability could defeat a country (Russia) with a much stronger navy and a superior economic and production capability. Bywater understood that superior forces and national capability were worth little if the stronger country (Russia) could not bring all its potential to bear against the enemy. This concept would sustain Bywater in future years when his strategy for Japan's dominance of the Pacific Ocean would be challenged.

James Gordon Bennett, publisher of the *New York Herald,* and Bywater's boss, shared Bywater's infatuation with the sea. Since 1897, when Japan protested the United States annexation of Hawaii and sent her cruiser *Naniwa* to Hawaii to enforce her protest, Bennett believed that Japan and the United States would fight a war in the Pacific, and that the war would begin with Japan striking the first unannounced blow. Bennett's beliefs dominated much of Bywater's subsequent thinking about naval strategy.

From 1909 to 1910, Bywater remained in Germany, where he wrote articles for the *Herald,* spied for Great Britain, with the pay and allowances of a lieutenant commander, passed himself off as a United States citizen in order to obtain a job in the U.S. Consular Service, and worked full time as copy editor for the *Daily Record*, an English-language newspaper published in Dresden. Bywater's positions gave him entry to many German navy yards and naval air stations where he obtained important information for Great Britain.

Bywater returned to England in 1910. He worked for the *Herald* until 1927, but following the death of publisher Bennett, he became the naval correspondent for *The Daily Telegraph*. When Germany surrendered her fleet on November 21, 1918, Bywater stated that naval power had shifted from West to East. The center of maritime affairs now resided in Tokyo he claimed. In 1920, Bywater's interest in the Pacific was rekindled following the announcement by Josephus Daniels, U.S. secretary of the navy, that the U.S. Pacific Fleet would remain in the Pacific, and that he wanted to build a $75 million facility in San Francisco to house the fleet. Daniel's announcement caused Bywater to write, *"Sea Power in the Pacific,"* an essay postulating that Japan could seize Guam and the Philippines and, quite possibly, avoid a war with the United States due to the problems of distance and the lack of naval support facilities for the U.S. fleet. Although not stated at the time, Bywater's concept of placing superior resources at the point of battle was much in evidence.

Three weeks later, Bywater wrote, *"Pacific Armaments,"* in which he declared a naval arms race underway between Japan and the United States. When Washington announced that all future battleships would be armed with 18-inch guns, Tokyo responded that the battle cruiser *Hatuse* would receive 18-inch guns. Each power, Bywater wrote, was trying to outdo the other in both surface ships and submersibles.

Other writers called attention to Japan's desire to dominate the Pacific. What separated Bywater from such writers was his precise statements as to how Japan would accomplish such dominance and how far they could go before the United States would go to war to combat Japan's drive for dominance. In *Sea Power in the Pacific: A Study of the American-Japanese Naval Problem,* Bywater saw Guam as being critical for Japan's expansion. If the United States fortified and defended Guam, then support facilities for the U.S. fleet would make it impossible for Japan to threaten and conquer the Philippines. If Guam were left undeveloped with only its primitive anchorage, Japan, with much shorter lines of supply and communications, would surely seize both Guam and the Philippines.

A significant chapter of Bywater's study was entitled, *"Possible Features of a War in the Pacific."* In this chapter, Bywater projected Japan's surprise attack against the U.S. Pacific Fleet. After all, Japan attacked China's Fleet in 1804, and the Russian Fleet at Port Arthur without warning. Why would they not do so again? Bywater considered such an attack inevitable. The Japanese would not attack with a few torpedo boats as they did at Port Arthur, Bywater warned. The Japanese attack would be a major naval force capable of destroying the Pacific Fleet. With the U.S. Pacific Fleet impotent, Japan could seize Guam, the Philippines, the Caroline, Marshall, and Gilbert islands, thus confronting the United States with a huge problem and a paucity of answers. Bywater further explained that once Japan established such a defensive perimeter, she could pull her fleet back to the home islands, concentrate her forces, and destroy any enemy forces that may be sent to attack her.

Sea Power in the Pacific was published in 1921. Within two months, the Office of the Imperial General Staff in Tokyo had the book translated, mimeographed, and distributed to its senior officers for study. So heavy was the demand for Bywater's book that the navy General Staff authorized the book to be published and widely distributed within the Japanese navy. Much of the Japanese excitement over Bywater's book was due to the offensive nature of his strategy. The Japanese contingency plan for war with the United States was adopted in 1907 and was purely defensive in nature. Few Japanese officers liked the current war plan. Bywater's strategy was like a breath of fresh air. It may be that few Japanese military officers read the entire book. If they did so, they seemed not to realize that Bywater projected the United States as the ultimate winner of such a war. Even Bywater acknowledged that, given time, the United States would be able to project superior national power to the area where the confrontation would occur. Yamamoto read the entire book and was quick to agree that Japan could not win a protracted war against the United States.

The Washington Conference System, a series of treaties dealing with stability in China, naval shipbuilding limitations, and arms embargoes in 1920 and 1921, was widely hailed as stabilizing shipbuilding and precluding a war in the Pacific. Bywater did not agree. He praised the naval shipbuilding ratio agreed to by Great Britain, France, Italy, Japan, and the United States, but criticized the United States for agreeing not to develop naval stations west of Hawaii. "The United States may regret," Bywater wrote, "that she has made Japan strategically supreme in that corner of the globe."[2]

A 1915 U.S. State Department photo of Hector C. Bywater.

National Archives

Shortly after the Washington Conference was completed, Bywater began a much-publicized debate with former Secretary of the Navy Franklin D. Roosevelt. The issue was whether or not a Japanese-American war in the Pacific was possible due to the distance of the ocean that separated the two powers. Roosevelt believed that war would not occur, stating that Japanese-American relations had never been better. Bywater warned that war between the United States and Japan was not only possible, but "was a deadly possibility."[3]

Bywater was so certain that Japan would expand its outer defensive perimeter in the manner he prophesied that he next developed the strategy by which the United States would have to fight the war. He also realized that the United States would not risk invading the Japanese home islands without adequate fleet-support facilities. Bywater established three possible naval routes to Japan. The northern route went through Dutch Harbor, Alaska, enroute to the Japanese northern island of Hokkaido. A fleet operating from Dutch Harbor in the Aleutians would have serious weather and logistic-support problems compared to the Japanese Fleet operating from Hokkaido and fighting a sea battle in their home waters.

The second approach to Japan was a central route from Hawaii through Midway Island and Guam. The third possible approach would be a southern route from Hawaii through Samoa, Truk, and the Philippines. The fact that Japan would have captured and fortified all these potential bases except Dutch Harbor, Hawaii, and, perhaps, Samoa, made the invasion of Japan much more difficult.

One question that continued to bother Bywater was how the United States might force a fleet confrontation if Japan chose to hide behind her defensive perimeter and attack the U.S. Fleet as it approached the home islands. Bywater found the answer by playing Jane's naval war-games. Bywater called on a number of his friends and, with the use of ship models, conducted miniature naval engagements on Keston Pond, five miles from his home. During one war game, the last puzzle of the Pacific naval confrontation between Japan and the United States was solved. Bywater found that anytime the U.S. Navy approached an island in the Pacific that constituted part of Japan's defensive perimeter, the Japanese Fleet was forced to challenge the advance. This proved true regardless of whether the island was Wake, Midway, Truk, or Guadalcanal. Forcing the Japanese to fight at distances from her home islands mitigated somewhat the logistic advantage enjoyed by Japan's navy in a confrontation with the U.S. Navy.

Bywater also debated *The Great Pacific War* with several other writers and columnists. One of these, Sir Frederic Maurice, had been director of military operations of the Imperial General Staff during WW I. Maurice argued that it was impossible for Japan, with few raw materials and a poorly developed economy, to compete against the United States, a country with a highly developed industry and the greatest supply of raw materials in the world. Bywater reminded critics of how Japan courted disaster when she attacked Russia in 1904. At that time, Japan's treasury was depleted. Japan had no reserves of coal, iron, petroleum, and other necessary war materials, and all her major warships had been constructed abroad, as had her heavy artillery. Critics like Maurice, Bywater stated, were quick to forecast a short war, perhaps only a few weeks, because Japan would exhaust her meager resources. Instead, the war lasted for two years with Japan winning the war. Bywater concluded that Japan's present condition was not as bad as in 1904.

The error of Maurice and others, said Bywater, was in confusing potential resources with actual resources. Japan was able to employ every resource she had at the opportune time. Russia was able to deploy only a small part of her strength in the war zone. A war between Japan and the United States would be very similar, Bywater concluded.

Isoroku Yamamoto returned to Japan in 1928 following a two-year tour of duty as naval attaché at the Japanese Embassy in Washington, D.C. While in the United States, Yamamoto traveled extensively, paying particular attention to the production capacity and petroleum reserves of the United States. He also read Bywater's book and reported extensively back to Japan on the debates that followed the book's publication. Shortly after his return to Japan, Yamamoto lectured to a large military audience at the Yokosuka naval base. The topic was the Pacific war, and Yamamoto used Bywater's strategy as his own.[4]

Yamamoto predicted that Japan would lose an extended war with the United States if Japan adopted a defensive strategy. Japan's only hope of victory lay with destruction of the U.S. Pacific Fleet, the seizure of the necessary raw materials, and establishment of a defensive perimeter. Yamamoto then predicted that the aircraft carrier would replace the battleship as the supreme weapon of war, and that carrier aircraft should accomplish the attack on the U.S. Pacific Fleet at Pearl Harbor.

Yamamoto's selection of Pearl Harbor as the location of the Pacific Fleet was not in the same visionary league of Bywater. In 1928, Pearl Harbor was only a navy yard and supply depot with no commissioned warships based there. However, in 1926, while he was in Washington, Yamamoto reported on the U.S. Navy's plans to remove nine million cubic feet of coral from Pearl Harbor in order for the base to accommodate the Pacific Fleet. The development was being done at a cost of 50 million dollars. Yamamoto realized that the warships at this new base would have to be eliminated if his offensive strategy to seize Guam and the Philippines was to be successful.

In 1924, the Joint army and navy Planning Board developed a contingency plan, code-named *Orange*, to combat Japanese expansion in the Pacific. The plan directed a 4,800-mile race across the Pacific Ocean by the navy to respond to a Japanese attack on the Philippines. Bywater, though not privy to top secret war plans, made the point on numerous occasions that the Japanese could land, occupy, and fortify the Philippines long before the American fleet could arrive.

Finally, in 1938, with war with Japan likely, the United States Joint Planning Committee dropped their idea of reinforcing the Philippines after a Japanese attack. They conceded that it would be impossible to recapture the Philippines without advanced naval bases such as Guam. The committee further acknowledged the accuracy of Bywater's Pacific strategy by adopting his approach routes through the Marshalls, Carolines, Marianas, Yap, the Palaus, and Guam in order to attack the Japanese homeland.

Yamamoto and Bywater were not total strangers. Yamamoto respected Bywater's knowledge and strategic analysis of the Pacific theater, and met with Bywater at least twice to exchange views. The first occasion was near the end of the Preliminary Naval Limitation Conference in London in 1930 when they spent an evening together discussing international relations in the Pacific. The second meeting was on December 3, 1934, when Bywater visited Yamamoto at his suite in the Grosvenor House in London. These meetings were extremely cordial, but did nothing to change Japan's position on naval shipbuilding limitations. As early as 1935, at the London Disarmament Conference, Yamamoto made it clear that Japan would refuse to accept any naval limitaions that could make her fleet inferior to Great Britain or the United States.

During January 1941, Yamamoto wrote the strategy that was to decide the fate of the Pacific war on the first day. There were several differences between Bywater's strategy and Yamamoto's. Bywater saw the attack on the U.S. Pacific Fleet being accomplished by battleships and conventional naval forces. Yamamoto prescribed the daring sneak attack to be led by massed aircraft carriers defended by fast capital ships. Yamamoto's plan also prescribed in detail the attack on all of Japan's planned acquisitions in the Pacific. The plan was so ambitious that when it was briefed to the navy general staff in November, the plan was approved without a serious review because the general staff believed it was far too ambitious to ever be implemented.

Yamamoto proceeded with his grand strategy despite the lack of support from most of the senior naval leadership. In October, following table maneuvers simulating the attack on Pearl Harbor, there was so much opposition to the strategy that Yamamoto was forced to announce, "So long as I am Commander in Chief of the Combined Fleet, Pearl Harbor will be attacked. I ask for your fullest support."[5]

Admiral Nagumo's lack of success against the American carriers at Pearl Harbor made it clear to Yamamoto that the war was not settled by the surprise attack. He conceived the Battle of Midway in order to destroy the U.S. Fleet and then pursue political negotiations for peace terms.

During the Battle of Midway, Yamamoto followed Bywater's strategy of forcible entry from the ocean perfectly. What should have been a decisive Japanese victory was foiled by American codebreakers at Pearl Harbor. Thanks to the cryptoanalysis breakthrough, Admiral Chester Nimitz, commander of the Pacific fleet, was aware of the trap being set by Yamamoto, and set a trap of his own. The resulting naval battle, perhaps the greatest sea battle ever fought, resulted in the loss of four Japanese carriers, and turned the war forever in favor of the Allies.

Bywater died in August 1940. Yamamoto's aircraft was ambushed and he was killed on Aril 18, 1943. Had these gentlemen survived the war, it would have been most interesting to hear their versions of why Bywater's Pacific strategy was adopted by Yamamoto, and to speculate on what might have occurred in the Pacific if Yamamoto had not attacked the fleet at Pearl Harbor.

Many of Yamamoto's fellow officers who survived the war agree that Yamamoto was strongly influenced by the writing of

Bywater. Mitsuo Fuchida, a confidante of Yamamoto, and the leader of the air attack on Pearl Harbor, agreed that both of Bywater's books, *Sea Power in the Pacific* and *The Great Pacific War*, greatly influenced Yamamoto's strategy.[6]

Perhaps the most important lesson to be learned from Bywater's books and early strategy is that the "treacherous and deceitful" Japanese attack on Pearl Harbor, as announced by President Franklin Roosevelt, was not so treacherous and deceitful. The strategy was conceived by an Englishman in 1920, published in newspapers, magazines, and books by an American in 1921, widely read and debated for the next 20 years, and finally executed by a Japanese in 1941.

Isoroku Yamamoto in 1934, at the time he met with Bywater.

AP/Wide World

9

ENSIGN JIMMY DANIELS, U.S. NAVY

When the Japanese naval task force attacked Pearl Harbor on December 7, 1941, the U.S. Pacific Fleet had three aircraft carriers. USS *Saratoga* was on the West Coast undergoing scheduled repairs. USS *Lexington* departed Pearl Harbor as Task Force 12 on December 5, accompanied by heavy cruisers *Chicago, Portland, Astoria,* and five destroyers. The task force was commanded by Rear Adm. John H. Newton, and was proceeding to a point near Midway Island, where on December 7 they would launch replacement aircraft for the defense of Midway.

USS *Enterprise* departed Ford Island on November 28, as Task Force Eight. The task force was commanded by Vice Adm. William F. Halsey, Jr. The cruisers *Northampton, Chester, Salt Lake City,* and nine destroyers of the task force were commanded by Rear Adm. Raymond Spruance. The task force expected to be at sea for two weeks of training with plans to be back in port by mid-December for a Christmas holiday standdown. The story that actually unfolds is best told by Jimmy Daniels, an ensign assigned to Fighting Squadron Six aboard *Enterprise.*[1]

Following a normal briefing in the pilot's ready room at Ford Island, pilots of Fighting Six flew their aircraft aboard *Enterprise,* which was already at sea. Initially, the 18 TBD Devastator torpedo bombers, 36 Dauntless dive bombers, and 18 F4F Wildcat fighters were lowered to the hangar deck as events proceeded normally.

What wasn't normal, according to Daniels, was that instead of resuming flight operations, the navy pilots were ordered to their ready rooms while a flight of 11 marine F4F Wildcat fighters from Marine Fighter Squadron 211 followed them aboard *Enterprise.* In the ready rooms, the pilots were informed that *Enterprise* was now operating under war conditions, and that the task force was headed west to Wake Island to deliver replacement aircraft for the marines on Wake.

Ensign James G. "Jimmy" Daniels, leader of the second section of F4Fs of Navy Fighter Squadron Six. Daniels was the only pilot in a flight of six aircraft to land safely at NAS Ford Island on the evening of December 7, 1941.

US Navy

Just to make sure everyone understood he was serious about going to war, Admiral "Bull" Halsey had warheads fixed to the torpedoes, live 500-pound bombs hung on the dive bombers, and thousands of rounds of machine gun ammunition loaded into the aircraft guns. Scout aircraft from *Enterprise* flew ahead of the task force, searching for enemy planes, ships, submarines, or torpedo wakes. Halsey also had Captain Murray, commanding officer of

Enterprise, issue the following Battle Order.

At Sea, November 28, 1941

BATTLE ORDER NUMBER ONE

1. *Enterprise* is now operating under war conditions.

2. At any time, day or night, we must be ready for instant action.

3. Hostile submarines may be encountered.

4. The importance of every man being specially alert and vigilant while on watch at his battle station must be fully realized by all hands.

5. The failure of one man to carry out his assigned task promptly, particularly the lookouts, those managing the batteries, and all those on watch on deck might result in great loss of life or even the loss of the ship.

6. The Captain is confident all hands will prove equal to any emergency that may develop.

7. It is part of the tradition of the navy that, when put to the test, all hands keep cool, keep their heads, and FIGHT.

8. Steady nerves and stout hearts are needed now.

> G.D. Murray
> Captain, U.S. Navy
> Commanding

Approved: November 28, 1941
W. F. Halsey
Vice Admiral, U.S. Navy
Commander Aircraft, Battle Group

Major Paul Putnam's marine pilots had only 15 to 20 hours of flight time in the F4F fighters. Their carrier landings aboard *Enterprise* were their first arrested landings in the Wildcat. Enroute to Wake, navy pilots of Fighting Squadron Six gave Putnam's pilots training in tactics, bombing techniques, and aircraft recognition features.

While the pilots were being schooled, Marine Fighter Squadron 211's aircraft were repaired or replaced, and the marines were provided with a 12th Wildcat, courtesy of "Fighting Six."

On the morning of December 4th, the marines launched their fighters for Wake Island. Daniels recalls that a seaplane from Wake flew out to lead the marine squadron into Wake, and that he gave a pint of whiskey to a marine pilot named John Kinney with the comment that, "you will probably need this more than I will." Daniel's words proved to be most prophetic, although Kinney did survive Japanese captivity. (Refer to the chapter on Wake Island in this book to fully understand the hardships of the Wake Island POWs.)

The task force was scheduled to refuel on December 5 (there were two December 5s, since the task force crossed the international date line heading west.) However, a tropical storm some 200 miles south of Midway prevented the scheduled refueling and Halsey slowed the task force in consideration for the destroyers that were rolling badly in the heavy seas. The delay in the forward advance of the task force meant that instead of returning to Pearl Harbor on the morning of December 6, they would now arrive on the 7th.

At 6:15 A.M. on December 7, two Dauntless SBD dive-bombers were launched from *Enterprise* enroute to Ford Island to report on the Wake Island aircraft delivery. The first plane was piloted by the air group commander, Howard L. "Brigham" Young. Lieutenant Cmdr. Young was the godparent to Jimmy Daniels daughter, a fact that would soon become an important matter. Shortly after the launch of the first two aircraft, *Enterprise* launched 16 more SBDs which would scout ahead of the carrier, and then land at Ford Island.

By 8:20 A.M., Lieutenant Cmdr. Young and his wingman, Ensign Perry L. Teaff, were close enough to Pearl Harbor that they could see smoke, antiaircraft fire, and planes attacking the marine corps air station at Ewa. As Young tried to analyze the situation, a Japanese Zero attacked him and his wingman, putting holes in both aircraft. Young quickly terminated his analysis of the situation, and dove for the runway at Ford Island. Both pilots managed to avoid both Japanese and friendly fire, and, after landing, scrambled for the safety of a nearby building.

Ten minutes after Commander Young's flight landed at Ford Island, the 16 aircraft of Scouting Squadron Six approached Pearl Harbor. Lieutenant Cmdr. Hallstead Hopping, the squadron commander, was able to send a warning message to *Enterprise*, and after flying through "friendly antiaircraft fire," landed safely at Ford Island. Ensign John Vogt got into a dogfight with several Zeros and appeared to be holding his own until he collided with one of the Zeros. Both aircraft crashed and burned near Ewa. Lieutenant (jg) Clarence E. Dickinson and Ensign John McCarthy fought with Zeros near Ewa and were shot down. Both pilots parachuted safely although McCarthy suffered a broken leg.

About the same time that Lieutenant Cmdr. Hopping landed at Ford Island, Lieutenant (jg) Frank (Pat) Patriarca landed at the army air corps' Burns Field, an auxiliary field on the Island of Kauai.[2] Patriarca and his wingman, Ensign Walt Willis, came under Japanese Zero attack near Ewa. Patriarca broke away from the Zero attack but was unable to find *Enterprise,* and with hardly any gas remaining, made it to Kauai. No trace of Willis or his crewman were ever found.

Patriarca was taken off flight status by an army doctor on Kauai, probably due to the stress of flying five-and-a-half grueling hours. His gunner, Joe DeLuca, along with his 30-caliber machine gun and ammunition, was "drafted" into the Kauai ground-defense force. It would be a full week before Patriarca and DeLuca were able to rejoin their squadron.[2]

Ensign Weber and Ensign Gonzalez were surprised by Zeros some 25 miles out to sea. Gonzalez was shot down and never heard from. Ensign Edward Deacon and his wingman Ensign Bill Roberts were shot up by friendly fire. Roberts was able to land at Hickam field, but Deacon was forced to ditch in the ocean, just short of the runway at Hickam. Only six of the 18 aircraft of Scouting Six made unopposed landings at Ford Island. These aircraft flew the southernmost search sectors and arrived at Pearl Harbor after the Japanese attack.

Late in the afternoon, Ensign "Bucky" Walters reported a Japanese task force to the south of Oahu. This was the news for which Halsey had hoped. *Enterprise* launched 19 torpedo bombers, six dive bombers, and six fighters. An extensive search revealed only a small force of U.S. cruisers and destroyers that had escaped the attack on Pearl Harbor and were trying to join Halsey's task force. The bearing reported by Ensign Walters was the reciprocal bearing of the Japanese fleet. The enemy was well to the north and moving away from Hawaii.

Admiral Halsey relayed the news that Pearl Harbor was under attack to all ships in the task force and immediately launched planes to search for the Japanese carriers. Four fighters searched the area around *Enterprise* and later three more aircraft were launched to extend the search area and protect the task force. These combat-air-patrols (CAP) were relieved about every three hours during the remainder of the day. Some of the search aircraft went as far as 175 miles to the northwest and northeast but failed to find the enemy carriers.

Ensign Daniels, one of the six fighter pilots escorting the torpedo planes, recalls that "It was about as black a night as I have ever seen. There was no moon and no lights of any kind. We flew formation by lining up the faint red interior lights from the cockpits and the white exhaust light from the exhaust manifold." Finally, after a long and unsuccessful search, Lieutenant Cmdr. Gene Lindsey, commander of the torpedo group, flipped his exterior lights on briefly, the signal to return to the carrier.

Finding the carrier without navigational aids, communications, or lights had been an adventure. Daniels recalls that, "When Lieutenant (jg) Hebel briefly turned on his exterior lights and blinked them as a signal that they were over the carrier, I was amazed." With nothing but a simple plotting chart and some dead-reckoning knowledge, Hebel had put the flight directly over *Enterprise*, as evidenced by the four long phosphorescent wakes trailing the screws of the blacked out carrier. The escorting fighters, first aircraft to return to the carrier, reached a low fuel state while waiting for the Devastators to be recovered and were ordered to land at Ford Island. Hebel, with his flight of five ensigns, began the 100-mile-trip to Pearl Harbor.

The heavily loaded Devastators with their three-man crews and 2,000-pound torpedoes were the first aircraft to be recovered. The first Devastator to "catch a wire," became the first aircraft to land aboard a carrier with a live torpedo. There was some excitement associated with the recovery, but all aircraft were safely recovered. One torpedo broke loose from its aircraft and went sliding down the deck, spewing smoke with its arming wires windmilling. Individual acts of heroism contained these moments of horror.

Hebel led his flight of six fighters past what is now NAS Barbers Point and then down the coastline to the entrance to Pearl Harbor. The only lights on Oahu visible to the pilots was the lighthouse at Diamond Head. Somehow, the lighthouse beacon was never turned off, although every other light on Oahu was out. As the planes neared the entrance to Pearl Harbor, they noticed what appeared to be burning sugar cane fields. The flames were actually from the burning battleships in Pearl Harbor. As the aircraft approached Pearl Harbor at 1,000 feet, Hebel signaled for the aircraft to move into right echelon formation, and called the tower for permission to land. Ensign Daniels was flying in the number five position.

After a short delay which indicated that the tower had no knowledge that the aircraft were expected, the flight was told to make a normal approach for landing. Hebel and his flight made a normal break over the field for a normal approach and landing. As the aircraft turned on their lights and broke formation,". . . . every antiaircraft gun, machine gun, rifle, pistol, rock, wrench, and piece of metal pipe that was available, was fired or thrown at the aircraft." In an instant, according to Daniels, "The sky was filled with so much metal, you could have walked on it."

Lieutenant (jg) Hebel broke away from the antiaircraft fire and proceeded to Wheeler Army Air Field near Schofield Barracks. The army personnel at Wheeler, after hearing all the shooting at Pearl Harbor, reacted the same way, and shot Hebel down on his final approach to the runway. Hebel suffered a fractured skull and died shortly thereafter.

Ensign Herb Menges, pilot of the number two plane in the flight was hit by ground fire from Pearl Harbor and crashed into the Palms Hotel near the Pearl City Tavern. The hotel burned to the ground without any civilian casualties, but Menges was killed.

Ensign Gayle Hermann, pilot of the number three plane, took a five-inch shell through the forward part of his fuselage which tore off the engine. Hermann spun to the ground near the golf course on Ford Island, climbed out of the wreckage, and, carrying his parachute, walked to the squadron hangar.

Ensign Davy Flynn, flying the number four aircraft, broke away from the carnage at Pearl Harbor and flew toward the Barbers Point area. He bailed out of his damaged plane, wrenched his back, and had to concern himself with a group of army security personnel who were trying their best to kill him as a suspected Japanese paratrooper. Flynn's loud and earthy cussing won the day and saved his life.[3]

Jimmy Daniels, flying in the number five position, was directly above Davy Flynn when the shooting started. Daniels turned off his exterior lights, dove for the approach end of the runway, and then sped toward the channel entrance at low altitude. Ensign Eric "Ethan" Allen, pilot of the number six aircraft, was killed by a 50-caliber bullet as he tried to bail out of his damaged aircraft.

Of the six men who tried to land at Ford Island, only one was still airborne. Daniels was in the vicinity of Fort Weaver, near the channel entrance, when a voice from the Ford Island Tower came over the radio and demanded, "Who is there?"

Daniels, now extremely low on fuel answered, "Six Fox Five," his squadron call sign. The voice from the tower then asked, "What is your name?" Daniels recognized the voice as that of Lieutenant Cmdr. Young, the air-group commander. Tired after a long day in the air, weary from being shot at by friendly fire, and low on fuel, Daniels was in no mood for word games. Yet, there was little he could do but to comply if he expected to land his aircraft at Ford Island.

"What is my nickname?" Young continued. "Brigham," responded Daniels. "What is your middle name?" asked Young. "You tell me what my middle name is," the exasperated Daniels retorted. "Ganson," said Young, and then added, "I know you are low on fuel. Put your wheels down and come in low and fast."

Daniels manually cranked the 26 turns of the landing gear lever to fully extend the gear, and flew up the channel low and fast. The next thing to startle him was USS *Nevada,* aground near Hospital Point. Nevada was directly in front of Daniels flight path and its superstructure towered over him. "I dropped my left wing, missed *Nevada,* corrected to the right, and touched down on the runway at Ford Island. I was going so fast that my flaps did not come down until I was halfway down the runway." The flaps on the F4F would start to come down when airspeed dropped below 130 knots.

According to Daniels, "I was going too fast to stop at the end of the runway, so I ground looped around and managed to accomplish the maneuver without damaging the plane." As he taxied to the hangar area, a heavy machine gun, manned by a marine in a revetment, began firing at Daniels' plane. The marine was stitching a row of 50-caliber bullets directly over Daniels' head. Only the unexpected intervention of Ensign Gayle Hermann saved Daniels. Hermann had walked to the hangar from his crashed aircraft, saw the marine shooting at Daniels, and got the marine's attention by smashing a borrowed rifle over his head and convincing the marine that Daniels was one of ours.

As Daniels stopped the plane near the hangar, Hermann bolted to the aircraft, and climbed up to the cockpit, where both pilots babbled incoherently for a few moments before climbing down and heading for the tower to report to Lieutenant Cmdr. Young. It was now 9:30 P.M. on December 7, 1941.

Enterprise cruised with her supporting ships off Kauai. A few hundred miles north, *Akagi, Kaga, Hiryu, Shokaku, Soryu,* and *Zuikaku,* steamed on a course away from Hawaii. Battleships protected both flanks of the six carriers while heavy cruisers protected the front and rear of the task force. Destroyers sped ahead of the column to protect it against enemy submarines. Daniels, in retrospect, recalls "How futile it would have been if the tiny *Enterprise* task force had located the 500-plane Japanese fleet."

Following the Japanese attack on Pearl Harbor, Admiral Nimitz remarked several times that, ". . . . the outcome of the attack was the best that could have been hoped for. Had advance notice of the attack been received, the Fleet would have sortied to meet the threat, and underpowered, undergunned, and understrength, would have been sunk in the depths of the Pacific, never to be recovered and never to fight again."

10

OPERATION WATCHTOWER
THE BATTLE FOR GUADALCANAL

The Battle for Guadalcanal began on Friday, August 7, 1942. It ended on February 1, 1943, after six months of the most brutal and exhausting combat experienced by both the Americans and the Japanese.

Strategically, Japan wanted Guadalcanal for two reasons. First, to provide an airfield and logistics base for their attack and planned occupation of Port Moresby, Papua New Guinea. Once Japan controlled Port Moresby they could sever the sealines of communications between Australia and both mainland United States and Hawaii. Northern Australia would then be defenseless. Second, occupation of Guadalcanal would support the expansion of Japan's outer defensive perimeter that included Palau, Truk, and the Marshall and Gilbert Islands.

Opposing Japan's continued expansion in the Pacific was Admiral Ernest J. King, commander-in-chief, United States Navy. Admiral King concurred in the "Europe First" strategy adopted by the United States and Britain, but he was unwilling to accept a strictly defensive posture in the Pacific. King's "limited offensive" strategy was strongly opposed by General George C. Marshall, army chief of staff, and chairman of the Joint Chiefs of Staff, and General H. H. "Hap" Arnold, commander army air corps, on the grounds that such a strategy would take forces away from the European theater.

Admiral King was able to send small marine corps units to strengthen Samoa, and 3,500 army troops to occupy Canton and Christmas Islands on the route to Samoa. He succeeded in establishing a refueling base at Bora Bora (near Tahiti) with army forces, and having the 17,000 men of the Americal Division (Americans in New Caldonia) stationed in New Caldonia to protect the valuable nickel and chrome deposits there.[1] These deployments of army forces to the Pacific severely strained service relationships resulting in both the army and army air corps refusing to consider additional force deployments to the Pacific.

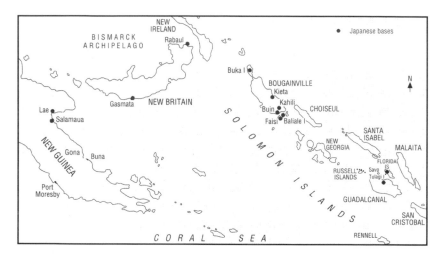

The Solomon Islands with Japanese-held bases marked.

Time/Life

Japan captured Rabaul on January 23, 1942, and Singapore fell on February 15. These losses caused British Prime Minister Churchill and Australian Prime Minister Curtin to request the United States to assume responsibility for the defense of Australia and New Zealand. President Roosevelt responded four days later by ordering the 41st Infantry Division to Australia, sending the USS *Lexington* carrier group to the South Pacific, and made plans to send the 32nd Infantry Division to Australia and the 37th Infantry Division to New Zealand.

During a March 5 meeting with the Joint Chiefs of Staff, President Roosevelt made clear his intention to hold Australia and seemed to favor Admiral King's plan for a small offensive in the South Pacific. General Marshall and Lieutenant Gen. Arnold held their ground, however, and outvoted Admiral King. There would be no additional army forces sent to the Pacific.

Japan seized the anchorage of Tulagi, across the channel from Guadalcanal on May 3 and started construction of a new airfield on Rabaul to support their invasion of Port Moresby. Thanks to this Japanese initiative, Admiral King was able to gain reluctant support from the Joint Chiefs of Staff to conduct "Operation Watchtower," the seizure of Tulagi and Guadalcanal, so long as no army forces were involved.

On July 5, Allied reconnaissance planes discovered that the Japanese had started work on an airfield at Guadalcanal. Admiral King ordered immediate preparations for the execution of "Watchtower." King created a new South Pacific Force and Area, under Vice AdmiralRobert L. Ghormley. Ghormley expressed grave misgivings about the operation. He argued that he had insufficient and untrained forces, insufficient shipping, and not enough time to prepare for the operation. Subsequent events would prove him right on all counts. Due to the paucity of forces and hasty planning, the operation was nicknamed "Operation Shoestring" by the planners. Admiral King told Ghormley to stop griping and to execute "Watchtower" on August 1, 1942.

In support of Watchtower, Naval Construction Battalion "Seebees" made their first appearance in the Pacific in April. They constructed an airfield on Vila, and began work on a bomber strip on Espiritu Santo. By June, more than 50 percent of their force was immobilized by malaria.

Major Gen. Alexander A. Vandegrift, commanding the First Marine Division, landed at Wellington, New Zealand, on June 14. The marines had scarcely unloaded their equipment when Vandegrift was designated as the commander of the Guadalcanal landing force. Vandegrift's subsequent planning and intelligence collection for the operation met more roadblocks than it gained support. Ghormley opposed the operation and provided little in the way of maps, charts, or information on weather and tides. Vandegrift's request to send a small reconnaissance party to Guadalcanal was disapproved by Ghormley as being too dangerous.

Even the New Zealand longshoremen seemed to be against Operation Watchtower. While marines worked in heavy rain to load their ships for the amphibious operation, the dockworkers refused to work during inclement weather. Relations between the longshoremen and marines became so bad that the dockworkers had to be removed by Wellington police. Marines continued to work around the clock in pouring rain in order to meet their embarkation schedule. Cardboard cartons of clothing, food, medicine, cigarettes, and candy bars became soaked and fell apart on the docks. A soggy mess of cornflakes, chocolate bars, shoes, socks, and cigarettes littered the dock area. Vandegrift embarked his 19,000 marines in 19 transports on July 22, and sailed for Guadalcanal.

Four days later, at a meeting of all the operation commanders except Ghormley, who remained at his headquarters in Noumea, Vice Adm. Frank Jack Fletcher, overall commander of the expedition force and commander of the task force, stated that he was opposed to the operation and predicted that it would be a failure. Fletcher blamed Rear Adm. Kelly Turner, commander of the amphibious force, as being the proponent of the operation.

Fletcher then announced that he intended to depart the objective area with his carriers after two days of off-loading. Vandegrift and Turner argued at length with Fletcher that it would take at least five days to put the forces, equipment, and supplies ashore. Fletcher seemed uninterested and abruptly terminated the meeting.[2] This would be the last meeting between Fletcher, Turner, and Vandegrift before the amphibious assault, now scheduled for August 7, 1942.

Former British commissioner for Guadalcanal turned coastwatcher, Martin Clemens, probably enjoyed the finest view of an amphibious operation seen in the entire Pacific war. Clemens had been forced higher and higher into the jungle since the Japanese arrived on Guadalcanal and started construction of the airfield. On the morning of August 7, he was startled by the gunfire of USS *Astoria,* the first ship to begin the bombardment. From his view at the 2,000-foot level, he could see the Allied cruisers and destroyers neatly aligned between Florida, Savo, and Guadalcanal islands, and the gray amphibious ships transporting marines to the beaches. A hundred miles south, and out of Clemen's sight, were the carriers *Saratoga, Wasp,* and *Enterprise,* screened by the battleship *North Carolina,* six cruisers, and 16 destroyers.

Rear Adm. Richmond Kelly Turner, left, explains to Major Gen. Alexander Vandergrift, commander of the marines on Guadalcanal, that the transport vessels would be pulled out of the landing area before enough supplies were offloaded.

National Archives

Clemens and the other two coastwatchers, "Snowy" Rhoades and Lieutenant D. S. MacFarlane, were not the only ones surprised by the Allied invasion. So, too, were the Japanese on Guadalcanal. The 3,500 men of two construction units beat a hasty retreat into the jungle, leaving their airfield-construction equipment, food, munitions, and many other items the marines would need in the weeks to come.[3]

Guadalcanal, 90 miles long and 30 miles wide, is huge compared to Florida Island with its two anchorages of Tulagi and Gavutu. Gavutu is 500 yards long and 300 yards wide. Yet, it was on Tulagi, and especially Gavutu, where the marines encountered their greatest opposition. It was noon, Saturday, August 8, before Tulagi was secured at a cost of 99 marine casualties, and Gavutu fell a short time later with 84 marine casualties, a loss rate of more than 20 percent of the landing force.

Japanese reaction to the landing was both predictable and punctual. At 11:15 A.M., the first Japanese air raid from Rabaul arrived. Due to advance warning from the coastwatchers on Bouganville, U.S. Navy carrier-based aircraft were in position to meet this raid and another in mid-afternoon. Of the 51 Japanese aircraft that attacked the beachhead, 30 did not return to Rabaul. One of the pilots who did make it back was Saburo Sakai, Japan's all-time leading ace, with 64 confirmed kills. Sakai landed at Rabaul with two 50-caliber bullets in his skull, blind in one eye, and an empty fuel tank. Although he survived the war and wrote about his experiences, Sakai did not fly any more missions against Guadalcanal.[4]

Early Saturday morning, the greatest problem facing the landing force was not the Japanese, but rather the huge backlog of crated equipment, supplies, and fuel drums that were piling up on the landing beaches. Landing craft would dump their load of supplies wherever they could and the supplies were becoming targets for Japanese aircraft. Fuel drums were being dumped in areas marked for ammunition, and medical supplies were in the areas marked for rations and water. The stacks of supplies were choking access to the beach and no one seemed interested in moving them into supply dumps in the jungle.

Admiral Turner learned of the beach problem about noon on

Saturday, but, by then, he had an even greater problem. Turner invited newly promoted Major Gen. Vandegrift and British Rear Adm. V.A.C. Crutchley, commander of the escort group of cruisers and destroyers, to his flagship, USS *McCawley*, for a conference. When they arrived, Turner showed them an operational priority message that he just received from Vice Adm. Fletcher. The message notified Turner that Fletcher was withdrawing his fast carriers, battleship, and other escort ships from Guadalcanal. The message did not ask for comments.

Fletcher's decision to abandon the landing force meant that Turner, without Fletcher's air support, would also have to stop offloading and withdraw the amphibious force. Hardly any of the heavy equipment for airfield construction had come ashore. Still in the transports were the marines' food, water, ammunition, barbed wire, sandbags, tools, anti-tank weapons, mines, grenades, and a host of other items needed for sustained operations ashore. Vandegrift's marines immediately went on reduced rations of two meals per day, much of the food being what the Japanese left. Fletcher's withdrawal of navy support created a rift between the two services that has never completely healed. Even today, in Geiger Hall at the Marine Corps Amphibious Warfare School at Quantico, Virginia, marines are warned not to become dependent upon their sister services.

Vandegrift had the supplies on the beach moved inland to secure dump sites, relocated his artillery and front lines to provide protection for his newly exposed rear, and then began to examine the equipment left by the Japanese. Found serviceable were four heavy-duty tractors, six road rollers, and a dozen trucks. This equipment plus the one bulldozer unloaded before Turner's departure, provided enough equipment to begin work on the runway. Other items left by the Japanese were bicycles, picks and shovels, stoves, radios, rice, cigarettes, tinned meat and crab, saki and beer, sliced beef, candy, and medical equipment. The amount of this bonanza would not supply a marine division for any length of time, but it was a welcome treat while it lasted.

Guadalcanal was the first three-dimensional campaign in the Pacific. Land, air, and sea forces were combined and coordinated by the adversaries to a degree never before seen. For six months, the Japanese coordinated their resources in an effort to retake Guadalcanal. The marines fought back with their own air and land forces. In time, the navy managed to resupply the marines during the day when marine aviation could protect them, and leave before nightfall, when the Japanese still owned the waters around Guadalcanal.

Two carrier battles, six major naval surface battles, and some 30 smaller naval battles were fought in support of a dozen land battles and almost daily air engagements. The air, naval, and ground battles for Guadalcanal are described in following chapters, as are the coastwatchers.

Vice Adm. Frank Fletcher.

National Archives

11

MARTIN CLEMENS: COASTWATCHER

"The Coastwatchers saved Guadalcanal, and Guadalcanal saved the Pacific."

Admiral William F. Halsey, Jr., USN[1]

The six-month battle for Guadalcanal produced a record number of heroes and heroic events. Now, 60 years later, the names of "Pappy" Boyington, "Red" Mike Edson, Joe Foss, Kiyano Ichiki, Saburo Sakai, Chesty Puller, Raizo Tanaka, and Archer A. Vandegrift come quickly to mind. Similarly, the night battle of Savo Island, the fight for Edson's Ridge, the battles of the Tenaru and Matanikau Rivers are all events that should never be forgotten.

There is another group of heroes and heroic actions associated with Guadalcanal that are seldom given the recognition they deserve. These are the coastwatchers, technically civilians and their native scouts, pressed into service in the Bismarck Archipelago and Solomon Islands to report on Japanese activities as Japan began to run amok in the southwest Pacific. Men such as Martin Clemens, Eric Feldt, Donald MacFarlan, F. Ashton "Snowy" Rhoades, E.D. "Wobbie" Robinson, Sergeant Yauwika, and Jacob Vouza typify these brave men. This chapter focuses on the activities of only two such men, Martin Clemens and Jacob Vouza.

About 3,500 Europeans and 95,000 Melanesian natives occupied the British Solomon Islands Protectorate in 1941. British rule was administered by the civilian Colonial Service. If force was necessary, it came from a native police force and a small European militia, since there were no British forces available to defend the Solomon Islands. The bulk of British and Australian troops were committed to the war in Europe, and the few troops remaining had been posted to Rabaul, Timor, and Ambon to defend the airfields and port facilities.[2]

Recognizing their inability to defend the Solomons, the Royal Australian Navy created a network of 1,000 civilian observers, called coastwatchers, to report on Japanese activities in the southwest Pacific. By fall 1941, the organization was commanded by Lieutenant Cmdr. Eric A. Feldt, and by the fall of 1941, consisted of 800 men and 64 teleradios. Coastwatcher stations extended 2,500 miles from Rabaul in New Britain Island, to the straits of New Ireland Island, Northern New Guinea, the Hebrides, and the Solomons.[3]

Coastwatcher teams were equipped with "teleradios," large battery-powered portable radios that had to be disassembled into ten separate sections for transport by native porters. Teleradios worked best from higher elevations and could transmit and receive to a distance of about 500 miles. The short range meant that many relay stations had to be established to retransmit the messages to Port Moresby, Papua New Guinea, thence to Townsville, Australia, and finally to naval headquarters at Pearl Harbor.

It is no exaggeration to claim, as Admiral Halsey does in the introduction to this chapter, that the coastwatchers saved Guadalcanal. By early July, 1942, a month before the Allied landings on Guadalcanal and Tulagi, Clemen's scouts were bypassing Japanese guard dogs and gaining information about the location of antiaircraft guns, and the type of equipment being used to prepare the runway on Guadalcanal. A few hours after the First Marine Division waded ashore on Guadalcanal on August 7, 1942, Coastwatcher Mason, from his jungle hideout on Malabita Hill, 400 miles from Guadalcanal, heard the noise of aircraft headed south. He was able to visually sight the aircraft and radioed, "From STO. Twenty-four torpedo bombers headed yours." Twenty-five minutes later Pearl Harbor had the information and radioed the warning throughout the Pacific.[4]

When HMAS Canberra, an Australian cruiser supporting the Guadalcanal invasion received the warning, the Allied fleet had two hours and fifteen minutes to prepare for their arrival. The boson's mate piped over the loudspeakers, "The ship will be attacked at noon by twenty-four torpedo bombers. All hands will pipe to dinner at eleven o'clock."[5]

The Japanese aircraft arrived on schedule and were met by fighters from U.S. carriers and anti-air gunfire from the fleet. Only one Japanese bomber survived and no damage was done to Allied ships. Similar warnings were repeated many more times during the invasion and throughout the six-month battle for Guadalcanal.

Clemens joined the British Colonial Service in 1937, and was sent to the Solomons to supervise development projects. He became the district officer in November 1941, and volunteered for military service following Japan's attack on Pearl Harbor. He was tasked to remain in the Solomons as district officer and to form a coastwatcher team. His first challenge was to assist in the evacuation of the Europeans and Chinese laborers from Tulagi. He accomplished the task despite a breakdown in the civil government, minimal shipping, and daily attacks by Japanese bombers.

Clemens' formed his coastwatcher detachment from his own native police force and administrative personnel from his district office. The detachment was forced to move from Tulagi to the hills of Guadalcanal by the Japanese bombing attacks and their landing of troops and engineers at Tulagi and Guadalcanal.

The detachment established radio contact with "Snowy" Rhoades, whose team was located on Vila, New Hebrides, and with Donald MacFarlan, also located on Guadalcanal. Clemens began reporting on the Japanese airfield construction immediately. Through communications with MacFarlan, he learned that he had been promoted to the grade of captain in the Australian army. He had no uniform, rank insignia, or identification papers, and his appointment as an officer would have been of little help had the Japanese captured him.

Clemens' existence on Guadalcanal was always threatened. Besides disloyal natives informing the Japanese of the location of the caucasians for a bit of food, Japanese search parties, guided by shipboard signal intercepts, constantly searched for coastwatchers and made them move further into the jungle and higher into the mountains. Food supplies were always scarce. Even loyal natives would slip away to find some sweet potatoes and fail to return.

Martin Clemens, top center, poses with six of his native scouts. Clemens was a planter on Guadalcanal before the Japanese occupation. He became a coastwatcher for the Australian government after the occupation, and joined the 1st Marine Division as an intelligence officer when the Marines captured Guadalcanal.

National Archives

Once the tinned food, clothes, supplies, and medicines that had been cached before the Japanese invasion ran out, the coastwatchers and native scouts were largely on their own. Without some means of pay or foodstuffs it became increasingly difficult to retain the natives' loyalty. Some went to work for the Japanese, either through force or as volunteers.

By July 6, Japanese patrols forced Clemens to move his camp to a mountain ridge called Vungana. The several-mile climb up slippery animal trails took several days to negotiate and took a toll on the coastwatcher party as they tried to absorb the weight of the teleradio and heavy batteries each time they fell or slipped on the steep slope.

The position on Vungana was cold, wet, and often enveloped in clouds. It was not an ideal observation post, having no water supply nearby, excessive condensation that caused the teleradio to malfunction, and no tall trees from which the radio antenna could be draped.

Clemens' spirit was dashed the first day of operation at Vungana. He spotted a convoy of five Japanese cruisers, but when he tried to send the message, the teleradio would not work. Two days later he was able to repair the teleradio and alone, surrounded by Japanese, and depressed, he sent the following message to the commissioner in Australia. "Coastal natives no longer amenable-Japs intend infiltrating weather coast-looks like search for us will be on both coasts-can trust very few natives-administration almost impossible-cannot do very much for much longer-STOP. Have you got any instructions?" The commissioner had no instructions.[6]

Following the landing of the First Marine Division on Guadalcanal and Tulagi on August 7, 1942, the marines learned of Clemens and his team from Jacob Vouza, one of Clemens native scouts who rescued a downed navy pilot and returned him to the marines. Vouza was sent to bring Clemens back to the marine division headquarters to provide vitally needed intelligence information. Despite not having any boots to traverse the jungle trails, Clemens' and Vouza's patrol evaded the Japanese and arrived at the marine front lines on August 15.[7]

Clemens had much to offer Major Gen. Alexander Vandegrift, the division commander. He was able to correct the faulty maps being used by the marines and provide information on the likely routes of advance of the Japanese forces being landed to recapture Guadalcanal. His scouts reported each morning on the night landings of Japanese troops and equipment at Taivu Point. As a result of such information and planning, marines were able to slaughter the "crack" Ichiki detachment at the battle of the Tenaru on August 20, 1942.

General Vandegrift took an immediate liking to Clemens and had him assigned as the British liaison officer to division headquarters. Clemens was allowed to retain his civil post as district officer of Guadalcanal. This dual mission suited Clemens well. He would be able to assist the marines in the defeat of the Japanese and integrate his coastwatcher team into the marine operations. He could also maintain communications with the native population and warn them to stay away from projected naval gunfire, artillery, and air-dropped ordnance.

Dealing with the native population remained risky for all concerned since a native with any American-made product was executed on the spot as a spy.

During mid-August, marines on listening posts continued to report ship traffic at night to the west of their positions. To find out what was happening, Vandegrift sent out patrols and asked Clemens to investigate. Jacob Vouza, a retired constable of Island Police, volunteered to lead the patrol to search west of the marine positions and departed on August 19.

Just before sunrise on the 21st, a seriously wounded and tortured native dragged himself into the marine defensive lines. Vouza had returned. Martin Clemens was summoned and found his native scout barely alive. Vouza had a huge hole in his throat, several bayonet wounds to his chest, and was battered and bleeding over his entire body. Vouza, in great pain, gasping and chocking on his own blood, reported to Clemens that he had been captured by the Japanese. When he refused to provide information about the Americans, he was tied to a tree, beaten with rifle butts, and used for bayonet practice.

Jacob Vouza, one of Clemens' native scouts, weilds a Japanese Sword.

National Archives

When he passed out, the Japanese thinking him dead, left him tied to the tree. He later regained consciousness, chewed through his ropes, and after crawling 20 miles, found the marine's defensive lines. Vouza survived to lead many more patrols on Guadalcanal.[8] He was awarded the Silver Star for bravery and made an honorary sergeant major in the United States Marine Corps.

Clemens was able to report on the arrival of Japan's 35th Brigade at Tasimboko in early September. He led a detachment of his scouts and two companies of Mike Edson's Raider battalion on a raid that destroyed General Kiyotake Kawaguchi's 35th Brigade's base camp and captured a large quantity of valuable intelligence material. When the material was analyzed back at marine headquarters, Clemens was able to help plan the deployment of Edson's Raider Battalion along "Bloody Ridge," resulting in the total defeat of Kawaguchi's famed brigade over a three-day period.

Perhaps Clemens' greatest contribution to the Guadalcanal campaign came in the latter stages of the six-month-long battle when army and marine forces were keeping offensive pressure on the Japanese. Clemens knew the Koli Point and Aola areas well and was able to support Vandegrift's plan to hunt down and destroy all Japanese stragglers in the area before they could be reinforced and take the offensive. Reinforced with Clemens' scouts, the allied force was able to kill 450 Japanese with a loss of 17 marines. Impressed by these actions, the Melanese natives turned against the Japanese and killed hundreds more.

Clemens was promoted to major in December 1942, and became the commanding officer of the Special Service Battalion, an organization of Solomon Islanders, Fijians, and Tongans, The battalion was used to train Americans in guerrilla warfare and also served with distinction in the central Solomons campaign. Once again, Martin Clemens led many of the missions.

Following the battle, the United States awarded Clemens the Legion of Merit and Great Britain presented him the Military Cross. Regardless of his military decorations, Martin Clemens and the coastwatchers made a difference in the battle for Guadalcanal, a battle that was always in doubt. Without his contribution, the result may have been far different.

Perhaps historian and author Allan Millet pays the best tribute to Clemens in his preface to Clemens' book, *Alone on Guadalcanal.* Millet says that when Martin Clemens enters a room, the command should be given, "Stand gentlemen, he served on Guadalcanal."[9]

12

THE GROUND BATTLE FOR GUADALCANAL
AUGUST-SEPTEMBER 1942

Admiral Ernest King, commander-in-chief, United States Fleet, had long been frustrated in his desire for an offensive action in the Pacific. The army and army air corps opposed his plan because it would take assets away from Europe, which had been allocated first priority for forces and equipment. King was finally able to gain approval for a naval assault on Guadalcanal, and set in motion the plans and forces that landed the First Marine Division on Guadalcanal and Tulagi on August 7, 1942.

Admiral King's offensive could well have ended at noon the next day. At that time, Rear Adm. Kelly Turner, commander of the Guadalcanal amphibious force, received notice that Vice Adm. Frank Fletcher was withdrawing his fast carriers, battleships, and other escort ships from Guadalcanal. Fletcher's message did not ask for comments, saying simply that there were large numbers of Japanese torpedo and bomber aircraft in the vicinity, and that his ships were critically short of fuel. In actuality, Fletcher was making good an earlier statement when he expressed his opposition to the assault of Guadalcanal, and said he would depart with his carrier task force after two days of off-loading.

Fletcher's departure left Turner and marine Major Gen. Archer Vandegrift, commander of the landing force, in a terrible position. Turner's amphibious ships were not even half-unloaded. They needed at least another three days, but could not remain at anchorage without Fletcher's air support. Vandegrift had only one bulldozer ashore with which to build an airfield, and little in the way of food, water, ammunition, and medical supplies. America's first amphibious operation in the Pacific seemed doomed to failure.

As Fletcher's carrier forces departed the objective area, Vice Adm. Gunichi Mikawa entered the "slot" north of New Georgia Island with a force of seven cruisers and a destroyer. Mikawa was moving towards the Guadalcanal beachhead at 30 knots with the single-mindedness of a salmon moving upstream to spawn. His instructions were simply to destroy the main enemy force and the landing force with torpedoes and gunfire.

Mikawa had no reason to be so bold. Rear Adm. V.A.C. Crutchley's screening force outnumbered Mikawa's with eight cruisers and eight destroyers. One of the cruisers, *San Juan*, had a new surface-search radar and two of the allied destroyers with radar were positioned to detect and warn of the approach of enemy ships. The allies also received four separate sighting reports of Mikawa's advance, plus visual observation of the float planes that Mikawa subsequently launched to reconnoiter the Allied task force.

The Japanese had a few advantages of their own. One was the long-lance torpedo, the finest weapon in any navy at the time. The torpedo was oxygen-fueled, 24 inches in diameter, traveled at 50 knots, and had a range in excess of four miles. The warhead contained 1,210 pounds of high explosives, and the weapon performed perfectly, time after time. Another advantage enjoyed by the Japanese; one which offset the American radar sets, were the specially trained night observers who could distinguish ship targets at more than four miles on a dark night.[1] Armed with powerful night-vision glasses, these human observers proved superior to technology on many occasions. Regardless of numerical and technical advantages, this battle would favor the bold.

Mikawa, in his flagship *Chokai*, drove his force past the sleeping picket destroyer *Blue*, sighted the cruisers *Canberra* and *Chicago* on his starboard side, and launched torpedoes. *Canberra* went down in flames, and *Chicago* staggered toward Cape Esperance with her bow blown off. HMAS *Australia* was spared because Crutchley had taken the cruiser 20 miles south to visit Admiral Turner. Next, Mikawa's force turned northeast, where they sighted and illuminated

Astoria, Quincy, and *Vincennes*. Within six minutes, *Astoria* was hit by torpedoes and hundreds of 8-inch naval-gunfire rounds. A few minutes later, *Quincy* was stopped by torpedoes and shells. Ablaze from bow to stern, she slid under the black waters, the first of 50 ships that would give the waters the name "Ironbottom Sound." Now the fury of Mikawa turned on *Vincennes*. Four torpedoes and hundreds of shells ripped her apart and she sank.

Mikawa, satisfied that he had destroyed the allied fleet and not knowing the whereabouts of Fletcher's fast carrier force, ordered his ships to withdraw to the north of Savo Island. On their way up "The Slot," the Japanese force encountered destroyer *Ralph Talbot*. Three of Mikawa's cruisers worked the destroyer over and left her dead in the water. The U.S. Navy, in its first ever night engagement, suffered its worst defeat. (The loss at Pearl Harbor was not a fleet engagement.)

Sunday morning revealed more than 1,000 oil-soaked, burned, and wounded sailors clinging to anything that floated in Ironbottom Sound. During the night, their bleeding had attracted sharks that circled the weary sailors. Now and then, one of the men would disappear beneath the surface of the ocean with only a thrashing of arms to momentarily mark the spot where he had been. During the morning, rescue operations saved 709 of the men, but 1,270 sailors died. Lost were four cruisers, *Astoria, Canberra, Quincy*, and *Vincennes*. Two destroyers, *Ralph Talbot* and *Jarvis*, plus cruiser *Chicago* were badly damaged.

The most serious damage to Mikawa's fleet was suffered by *Chokai*, which took three shells from *Quincy's* battery. *Chokai* had 34 killed and 48 wounded but had no serious structural damage.[2] The Battle of Savo Island was a major defeat for the U.S Navy. Japanese newspapers declared the Solomon Islands victory one of the greatest in the history of Japan. On Sunday morning, following Mikawa's departure, Admiral Turner and the amphibious transports disappeared through Lengo channel. The marines were on their own.

On Guadalcanal, thanks to the hurried departure of the Japanese construction units from the beachhead, the marines found some abandoned engineer equipment and food supplies that they put to good use.

On August 11, Japanese reconnaissance aircraft confirmed the departure of the U.S. Navy from the Guadalcanal beachhead. Efforts to recapture Guadalcanal began immediately by aerial bombing of the marine positions on Tulagi and Guadalcanal by day, and naval bombardment at night. On August 16, a Japanese destroyer landed supplies and a 200-man detachment to support the Japanese forces west of the Matanikau River.

The marines were spoiling for a fight. They had been ashore for nine days and had been subjected to daily air raids and nightly ship bombardment. Many had developed acute dysentery and were losing weight by the hour. They had fungus infection and the first signs of malaria. One in five were not combat effective, but the other four could not wait to fight the Japanese. The first confrontation took place on August 17. Vandegrift sent three companies to clean out the Japanese from the West Bank of the Matanikau River. As the marines surrounded a small Japanese force near the beach, they were startled by the first *banzai* charge of the war. The charge lasted ten minutes and ended with 65 dead Japanese. Four marines were killed and 11 wounded.

Reports of ship traffic at night, to the west of the marine positions, continued to bother Vandegrift. He correctly assumed that the traffic meant Japanese reinforcements were being landed. He maintained an aggressive patrol using both marines and native scouts to learn the Japanese intentions.

On August 18, one of the marine patrols near Koli Point ambushed Japanese troops moving towards the airfield and killed 34 of the 37 Japanese in the group. Examination of the bodies and map cases revealed that the Japanese were reinforcing with combat veterans of earlier victories. The Japanese casualties wore pressed uniforms complete with colored ribbons and polished boots. Casualties from a regiment of the Imperial Army on Guam were identified. Other soldiers fought in China, Singapore, and the Philippines. The Japanese were also in far greater numbers than Vandegrift anticipated.

During the intensive patrol action, Marine Air Group-23 arrived at Guadalcanal with 31 fighters and dive-bombers. They were the first aircraft to land on the 4,000-foot runway built almost entirely with Japanese equipment. Army air corps P-400 fighters arrived on August 21, and all aircraft were put to immediate use as close air support, combat air patrol, reconnaissance, and interdiction against Japanese shipping and facilities on nearby islands.[3]

Vandegrift christened the Guadalcanal airfield as "Henderson Field," in memory of Major Lofton Henderson, a squadron commander who lost his life leading torpedo planes against the Japanese invasion force at Midway.

All of the naval battles in and around Guadalcanal were conducted to support the Japanese army mission of recapturing the island. While Colonel Kiyano Ichiki was moving his battalion from Taivu to destroy the Americans, General Headquarters (GHQ) transferred control of operations on Guadalcanal from the navy to the army. Lieutenant Gen. Harukichi Hyakutake, commander of the 17th Army, ordered Major Gen. Kiyotaki Kawaguchi to move the 35th Brigade at Truk to Guadalcanal, assume command of all Japanese forces there, and destroy any enemy forces that might elude Ichiki.

Just after midnight on the 21st, men of the Ichiki detachment massed on the east bank of the Tenaru River. Colonel Kiyano Ichiki's 28th infantry regiment had been on Guam, but one battalion of 915 men were moved by six destroyers and arrived on Guadalcanal on August 18. The remaining 1,500 men of the regiment were scheduled to arrive by destroyer within a few days.

Colonel Ichiki was a respected officer with a distinguished record. He had been directed to delay his attack until his entire regiment was in place, but his ego got the best of him. Ichiki was so certain that he could defeat the abandoned and demoralized marines with his single battalion that he attacked immediately. Supported by machine guns and automatic weapons fire, they charged the marine positions.

Screams of *banzai* changed to moans of pain as artillery fire met the attackers at point blank range. When the first wave failed to reach the marine defensive positions, Ichiki launched a second charge. The attackers became entangled in the few strands of barbed wire that the marines were able to bring ashore, and were cut down with machine gun and artillery fire.

The marines, under command of Lieutenant Col. Edwin Pollock, threw back Ichiki's fanatical attacks, but there were still plenty of Japanese on the far bank of the Tenaru. Vandegrift approved a plan for the marines to cross the river and surround the Japanese before they could conduct another attack or retreat into the jungle. The Japanese, with no way to escape, fought valiantly but were compressed into smaller and smaller pockets until they were annihilated. Colonel Ichiki burned the regimental colors and committed suicide. Marines counted 800 Japanese bodies and took 15 prisoners, only one of which was not wounded. Perhaps 30 wounded Japanese escaped into the jungle. marine casualties were 53 wounded and 43 men killed.

This brief action gave a tremendous boost to American morale. By eliminating one of Japan's elite storm detachments, the marines destroyed the myth of invincibility that had been attached to the Japanese army. Ichiki and his men died following the code of the samurai, "death before dishonor," or *bushido*. The Japanese asked for no quarter and gave none. So it would be for the rest of the Pacific war.

At the time, Rear Adm. Raizo Tanaka was transporting the

Yokosuka Fifth Special Naval Landing Force and the rest of Ichiki's regiment in transport *Kinryu Maru* and four destroyers. Tanaka's night-running destroyer transports were becoming a major problem for the Americans because the marines could not locate the ships at night with their fighter aircraft from Henderson field. The marines named Tanaka's night runs "The Tokyo Express." While Tanaka was enroute to Guadalcanal, Admiral Isoroku Yamamoto, commander-in-chief Combined Fleet, received reports that Admiral Fletcher's carrier group was back in the Solomon sea area. Yamamoto ordered Nobutake Kondo's Second Fleet battleships and Vice Adm. Chuichi Nagumo's Third Fleet carriers to leave Truk, locate and destroy the American carriers, smash the airfield at Guadalcanal, bombard the marine positions, and provide support to the Japanese troop landings there.

Vandegrift received warning of the Japanese fleet's departure and launched all of Guadalcanal's aircraft to meet the threat, but a solid weather front with zero visibility forced the aircraft to return without sighting the enemy. On the morning of August 24, aircraft from Fletcher's carriers found the Japanese decoy carrier *Ryujo* and left it burning. Admiral Kondo had detached *Ryujo* and cruiser *Tone* to cruise south as decoys to help locate Fletcher's carriers. Nagumo's aircraft located and attacked *Enterprise* just before 5:00 P.M. The "Big *E*" suffered three bomb hits, and, although severely damaged, survived and returned for repairs. The 11 SBDs and 12 TBFs that were airborne while *Enterprise* was being attacked, landed at Guadalcanal and were donated to Vandegrift's "Cactus Air Force."

Japanese General Headquarters (GHQ) in Tokyo reacted to the Ichiki catastrophe by transferring control of operations on Guadalcanal from the navy back to the imperial army. Major Gen. Kiyotaki Kawaguchi, commander of the 35th Infantry Brigade at Truk, was designated commander of all forces on Guadalcanal, and moved his veteran forces from Borneo to Truk on August 31.

Once ashore on Guadalcanal, Kawaguchi established a supply base at Taivu and directed his engineers to cut a path through the jungle to Henderson Field. Kawaguchi had no appreciation for the terrain and lacked maps of the area. Disregarding his orders to conduct a reconnaissance of the marine positions to determine if he had sufficient forces to attack, Kawaguchi followed Ichiki's example and sent his four battalions along the jungle trail as fast as they came ashore. Kawaguchi was in no mood to "view" the enemy, he meant to destroy the marines as quickly as possible. September 13 was set as the day he would capture the airfield. Kawaguchi was so certain of success that he invited senior army officers from Rabaul to fly into Guadalcanal on the 13th to participate in the surrender ceremony of the marines.

Like many Japanese offensive actions, Kawaguchi's plan was overly complicated and difficult to coordinate. He planned a three-pronged attack in which he would lead the main element consisting of one of his battalions and two battalions of the former Ichiki regiment, which had come ashore on August 23. They would attack the marines at the south end of the runway. A second battalion would cross the Tenaru and attack the marines from the east. A third battalion would cross the Matanikau River and strike the marines from the northwest.

On September 1, a cadre of 392 very welcome Seabee officers and men arrived on Guadalcanal to relieve the marine engineers in the maintenance and improvement of Henderson Field. The Seabees brought two bulldozers and other equipment with them and were able to start work on such other projects as roads, wharf, and bridge construction, as well as fuel farms, shelters, and other projects that the marines had not been able to work on.

Seabees learned to judge which bombs or shells were likely to impact in their immediate area, and while the projectiles were falling, would run and take cover in the closest foxhole. As soon as the "crump" of the exploding projectile was heard, they dashed from their foxhole back to the job. Needless to say, Seabees and marines became fast friends.

While Kawaguchi's forces slogged through the jungle, Lieutenant Col. Merritt Edson's First Raider Battalion landed by small boat at Taivu and destroyed Kawaguchi's supply base. The Raiders destroyed antitank guns, ammunition; captured canned food and rice, and killed 21 Japanese. The Raiders departed with Japanese notebooks, papers, maps, and charts, which later proved to be valuable in planning for Kawaguchi's attack. As the Raiders departed in their small boats, they staggered under heavy loads of tinned crabmeat, sliced beef in soy sauce, 21 cases of beer, and 17 half-gallon flasks of sake.[4]

Marine Brigadier Gen. Roy Geiger arrived at Henderson Field on the evening of September 2, to take command of all aviation assets. Geiger arrived without advanced notice, and the Marines had to improvise runway lighting with the headlights of half-a-dozen jeeps. Geiger and Vandegrift took an immediate liking to one another. Geiger was short on conversation, cold, and, to some, he seemed ruthless. Like Vandegrift, Geiger was not content to let the Japanese enjoy the initiative. The following day, the Marine Wildcat fighters began bombing Kawaguchi's suspected trails through the jungle.

Geiger found that he had but 11 fighters in flyable condition. He had critical shortages of starter cartridges, bombs, oxygen, ammunition, tires, oil, and gasoline. His pilots were near exhaustion and many had developed malaria. Geiger's aviation assets improved somewhat on September 10, when 24 Wildcat aircraft from USS *Saratoga* landed at Henderson Field. *Saratoga* was torpedoed by the submarine *I-8* on August 31, and her aircraft had been parked in New Caledonia and New Hebrides. The following day, "Fighting Five" pilots from *Saratoga* joined marines in downing 16 of the Zero fighter escorts that supported the daily Japanese bombing raid against Henderson Field. A total of 60 replacement aircraft were flown into Henderson Field during the next three days, but despite their success against the Japanese Zero, the Japanese were able to reinforce their area air units by twice that number.

On September 11, right on Kawaguchi's schedule, the target for the Japanese bombing attacks switched from Henderson Field to a ridge above it. The ridge, later to be called "Edson's Ridge," was being softened up for Kawaguchi's attack on the 13th.

Later in the afternoon, between air raids, Rear Adm. Kelly Turner flew into Henderson Field with a message from the commander of Southwest Pacific Forces and Area (ComSoPac). Vice Adm. Ghormley, as ComSoPac, had been opposed to the Guadalcanal operation from the start. He now advised that the marines were once again "on their own." Ghormley said that overwhelming Japanese forces were being concentrated on Rabaul and Truk for use against Guadalcanal. He said that Japanese air strength had doubled, and that several dozen enemy transports were loading troops and equipment for action against Guadalcanal. Ghormley went on to say that he could no longer support the marines on Guadalcanal.[5]

Admiral Turner asked if he should begin evacuating the marines. Vandegrift handed the message to Colonel Gerald Thomas, his operations officer, and to General Geiger. Thomas and Geiger reasoned that there was much more at stake than just the marines or an airfield on Guadalcanal. The United States could ill afford another Bataan Death March. It was time for the nation to make a commitment in the Pacific, and, if necessary, the marines would lead the way. Colonel Thomas replied to Admiral Turner that, "We (the marines) will go into the hills, to the headwaters of the Lunga. We will take our food and our bullets." But, the marines would not leave.[6]

Admiral Ghormley's message was no surprise to the marines. By September 1942, it had become obvious to everyone that the navy-marine corps team had greatly extended itself in the Solomon Islands. Perhaps Admiral King had expected another Midway Island victory with the Japanese slinking away in defeat. That would not be the case on Guadalcanal. Not only was the U.S. Navy overextended, it had failed to develop supply and support facilities for an extended campaign. The first amphibious operation of the Pacific had truly become "Operation Shoestring."

The marines lacked everything from food to fuel, bayonets to barbed wire, shovels to shoes, and Band-Aids to bullets. They had insufficient air cover for themselves and could not assist in the escort of vital resupply convoys. When Assistant Secretary of the Navy James Forrestal visited Guadalcanal in September, he told Admiral Ghormley that if the American people knew of the actual conditions, [on Guadalcanal] there would be a revolution.

It must have come as a surprise to Admiral Turner that after his offer to evacuate them "alive," the marines decided to stay. History has failed to properly recognize the senior marine commanders for their decision. Guadalcanal was not to be another Wake Island, Bataan, or Singapore. Instead, three marines, Vandegrift, Geiger, and Thomas, made the decision that it was time for the United States to make a stand. The marines would not evacuate Guadalcanal and they would not surrender. They would stay and fight.

Henderson Field on Guadalcanal.

National Archives

Left — Lieutenant Gen. Harukichi Hyakutake, commander of the Japanese 17th Army, at his headquarters in Rabaul. Above — Major Gen. Kiyotaki Kawaguchi, ordered by Hyakutake to move the 35th Brigade at Truk to Guadalcanal, assumed command of all Japanese forces there.

National Archives

13

THE GROUND BATTLE FOR GUADALCANAL
SEPTEMBER-OCTOBER 1942

While Admiral Kelly Turner and the senior marine officers discussed the subject of evacuating the First Marine Division from Guadalcanal, Japanese bombers attacked Edson's (Bloody) Ridge, working 500-pound explosive bombs from the ridge to the edge of the jungle. A second wave of bombers dropped 250-pound bombs with extended fuses (daisy cutters) which exploded 18 inches above the ground, stripping the vegetation and clearing the six foot high kunai grass. This was the final warning call for Edson's Raiders who made certain that they were dug in and ready to receive the Japanese attack.

At 10:00 P.M. on the evening of September 11, a heavy rain started and three Japanese destroyers began shelling the ridge above Henderson Field. As soon as the naval gunfire ended, Major Gen. Kiyotaki Kawaguchi's 35th Infantry Brigade and two battalions of the Ichiki Regiment began their probing attacks. Marines answered with rifle, machinegun, mortar, and artillery fire. One of Edson's platoons was forced to fall back to a stronger position. When they were established in their new position, seven marines were missing. Their bodies were never found. In the morning, Edson's men dug deeper holes, doubled their communications wire, and ate a hot meal. Guidance to the troops was, "dig, wireup, and get some sleep."[1]

Kawaguchi was frustrated and losing patience. He had lost communications with two of his three attacking forces, and even worse, he could not contact Rabaul. He knew that senior officials were planning to fly to Henderson Field to receive the marines' surrender. His problem was that the marines still owned the airfield.

Japanese reconnaissance planes were unable to determine who controlled the airfield. A decision was made in Rabaul not to bomb the airfield or the ridge in case Kawaguchi's forces were there. Instead, 26 Betty bombers, escorted by a dozen Zeros, bombed and strafed Kawaguchi's former supply base at Taivu. Army officials at Rabaul believed the marines had occupied the base after their raid. Personnel from Kawaguchi's recently landed signal and supply detachment were slaughtered as they signaled in vain to the attacking aircraft to stop their attack.

On the afternoon of September 13th, Kawaguchi established communications with Rabaul and coordinated his night attack. At 9:00 P.M., seven destroyers illuminated Henderson Field and began their bombardment. One hour later, two of Kawaguchi's battalions attacked along the ridge in two waves. The marines fired mortar and artillery fire at point blank range, tearing huge gaps in the attacking force, but still they came. Personal insults were exchanged as the fighting became hand-to-hand with bayonet, knives, and fists. The marines held and Kawaguchi withdrew to organize his next attack.

The second attack came at midnight and was supported by Japanese mortar and artillery fire, which kept the marines in their holes. Once again, artillery took a terrible toll of the attackers. The Japanese kept coming and the artillery fire was adjusted closer and closer to the marine positions. It became impossible to distinguish friend from foe. Japanese soldiers were jumping into marine foxholes to escape the whistling death of the artillery shells. Both sides suffered many casualties from the artillery fire, but it stopped the Japanese attack.

At 2:00 A.M., on the 14th, Kawaguchi launched his first *banzai* attack. Screaming and shouting, the Japanese poured from the jungle and fought to within yards of the marine defensive positions before they were stopped. More halfhearted *banzai* attacks continued until just before sunrise when Kawaguchi led his tattered remnants back along the same trail they had worked so hard to cut through the jungle. Kawaguchi left more than 700 corpses on "Edson's Ridge,"and some 500 wounded were doomed to die as they struggled through the jungle towards Taivu. Marine losses were 49 killed and 250 wounded.

Kawaguchi's retreat toward the west bank of the Matinikau was necessarily slow. His men were carrying 400 litter patients and the carriers had a most difficult time maintaining footing on the wet, slippery surfaces. Vines would catch and trip the carriers, and the heat and humidity sapped their strength. Lack of food became an even greater enemy than the marines. Men were forced to eat bark from trees, roots from plants, grass, palm tree buds, and leaves. Some of the soldiers chewed their leather rifle slings in an effort to obtain nourishment. Water was only available from puddles and streams, with the result that dysentery became epidemic.

Mortars, machineguns, and most ammunition were discarded the first day of the retreat. Rifles, helmets, packs, binoculars, and even officer's pistols were thrown away or buried during the following days, as the men became weaker.

After eight days of agony, the advanced units of Kawaguchi's forces crawled into the rear area at Point Cruz. Stragglers would continue to arrive until the end of the month. A Japanese naval officer observing the pitiful soldiers remarked that they must have been used to fighting the Chinese.[2] There was more than an element of truth to the observation.

Henderson Field aircraft located Tanaka's "Tokyo Express" landing force 100 miles off Guadalcanal on the morning of August 24. SBDs sank Tanaka's flagship Jintsu and put a 1,000-pound bomb into the center of the 9000-ton transport *Kinryu Maru*. As the SBDs departed, a flight of B-17s arrived from New Hebrides. They sank *Mitsuki* and damaged *Yayoi*. Tanaka shifted his flag to destroyer *Kagero* and withdrew to the Shortlands. The first major attempt to retake Guadalcanal from the sea had failed.

Admiral Tanaka was back at dusk on the 28th with four modified destroyers, but his attempt to land troops was also foiled as Henderson Field aircraft sank *Asagiri*, left *Shirakumo* dead in the water, and badly damaged *Yugiri*. Tanaka's landing attempts on the 30th and 31st were successful however, and General Kawaguchi and most of his brigade were landed at Taivu. Another attempt to land Kawaguchi's forces on September 5 was spotted and attacked by allied aircraft 21 miles north of Taivu. Of the 1,000-man force, at least 400 perished at sea.

Rear Adm. John S. McCain, commander, Aircraft, South Pacific, reported to Admiral Nimitz on August 30 that immediate reinforcement by two squadrons of aircraft and crews must be provided, and, "If reinforcement requested is not made available, Guadalcanal can not be supplied and hence can not be held."[3] The U.S. Navy may have been about ready to write Guadalcanal off, but Japanese Imperial General Headquarters GHQ) was not.

As soon as GHQ learned of Kawaguchi's defeat, the 38th Division, which fought at Hong Kong, Timor, Java, and Sumatra was ordered to proceed from the Dutch East Indies immediately for Guadalcanal. Assisting them would be the Third Battalion, Fourth Infantry Regiment, which arrived on Guadalcanal on September 11, with the rest of the regiment due three days later.

While the Japanese were reinforcing Kawaguchi, Admiral Turner convinced Ghormley to release the Seventh Marine Regiment stationed at Samoa. Turner's request was approved, and he embarked the regiment on the 14th for Guadalcanal, with five transports and two supply ships. The amphibious ships were escorted by battleship *North Carolina*, seven cruisers, 13 destroyers, and two carriers, *Wasp* and *Hornet*.

At 2:00 P.M., Commander Takaichi Kinashi located the convoy

and patiently worked his submarine *I-19* around the *Wasp* escort group until he had *Wasp* between him and the *Hornet* group. That way, if he missed *Wasp* with his torpedoes, there was a fair chance that they would continue and strike a ship in the *Hornet* group.

Kinashi worked as close as he could and fired a spread of six torpedoes from his forward tubes. Three torpedoes struck *Wasp*, causing the ship to burn fiercely. Within an hour, orders were given to abandon ship. Three-hundred-seventy-five wounded sailors were rescued from the ocean, but 200 died in the fires. *Wasp* was a wreck and was torpedoed by U.S. destroyer *Landsdowne* the following day. The loss of *Wasp* left *Hornet* as the only operational U.S. carrier in the South Pacific.[4]

Three torpedoes from I-19 entered the *Hornet* group, where one of them struck *North Carolina* and penetrated below the ship's armor belt. The missile blew out 400 square feet of the battleship's port side and created a hole 32-feet-long and 18-feet-high.[5] *North Carolina* survived and returned to the mainland for repair, but destroyer *O'Brien*, which dodged the fifth *I-19* torpedo, could not evade the sixth, and suffered a mortal blow which would cause her to sink.

Commander Kinashi, with six torpedoes, was responsible for sinking a carrier, crippling a battleship, and sinking a destroyer. Although the American destroyers darted across the ocean searching for the Japanese submarine, the *I-19* escaped unharmed. The loss of *North Carolina*, left *Washington* as the only battleship in the Pacific. The Japanese had nine, including the monsters, *Musashi* and *Yamato*.

Back on Guadalcanal, Vandegrift now had nine battalions plus a depleted raider battalion, artillery, and two companies of light tanks. In an effort to keep the pressure on the Japanese, he sent Lieutenant Col. Lewis Puller with one of his battalions to rout the Japanese from the west bank of the Matinikau. Puller's men could

149

not force a crossing, so Vandegrift sent Edson and his Raiders plus another battalion to coordinate a flanking attack with Puller's battalion. The attack failed miserably. Once again, the jungle dictated the speed of movement of forces, not the commander. Communications broke down in the jungle and units were forced to operate independently without air or artillery support.

By the time the marines withdrew, they had 192 casualties, including 67 dead. It was a tragic lesson learned. Twice the Japanese had tried complicated tactics in the jungle and failed. Perhaps the marines would not make the mistake a second time.

While the future of Guadalcanal was precarious, help arrived from a most unexpected source. "Hap" Arnold, commanding general U.S. Army Air Corps, arrived in Noumea for a staff visit. Arnold later reported that the navy headquarters at Noumea (Ghormley's command) seemed to be "office bound," and had little idea of what was happening on Guadalcanal. He reported that the navy and marines were taking "one hell of a beating," and were hanging on by a shoestring. He said the navy supply system was inadequate to ensure success and that the navy had paid virtually no attention to the needs of the marines. He went on to question the competence of both Vandegrift and Geiger.[6]

Major Gen. Alexander Patch, commander of the army's Americal division on New Caldonia, was quick to second Arnold's evaluation. The marines would be barefoot, he said, if he had not sent them 20,000 pairs of boots from his own supplies.[7]

Following Arnold's visit, Admiral Chester Nimitz, commander Pacific Fleet paid the marines a visit. As his B-17 taxied between holes in the runway, dirty marines in stinking utility uniforms made wagers whether the plane contained nurses, Red Cross girls, or candy bars. Instead they received the slim, graying figure of Admiral Nimitz.

Vandegrift and Geiger had plenty to show Nimitz. Between Japanese air raids, they took him to the operations office at Henderson Field for a quick briefing, then to Edson Ridge, and the hospital where Nimitz visited the wounded. Before he left, Nimitz promised Vandegrift support to the maximum of his resources. Subsequently, the 164th regimental combat team from North Dakota was detached from General Patch's Americal division and sent to Guadalcanal. More importantly, Nimitz saw enough to convince him to relieve Admiral Ghormley as Commander South Pacific.

While the U.S. services were castigating one another for the situation on Guadalcanal, Lieutenant Gen. Harukichi Hyakutake, commanding the 17th Army on Rabaul made the decision to direct the capture of Guadalcanal himself. Hyakutake ordered the 38th division, the remainder of the Second (Sendai) Division, and his own headquarters to make the move to Guadalcanal. Hyakutake was assisted in his decision by General Headquarters in Tokyo, who reminded him that the fate of the "Greater Far East Asia War" depended upon his recapture of Guadalcanal.

Vandegrift, thanks to marine and native patrols, was aware of the Japanese reinforcements. He directed five battalions to cross the Matanikau, envelop the Japanese forces there, and drive them into the sea. The attack would be coordinated with artillery and air support. The plan was rather simple but ran into complications when it was discovered that the Sendai Division was ashore and preparing to attack the marines on the east bank of the river. Japanese air attacks increased in number and ferocity, a sure sign of an impending attack. At this time, Hyakutake had more than 200 aircraft for use against Guadalcanal.

Shortly after dawn on October 7, Edson's five battalions reached the east bank of the Matanikau and dug in to wait to attack the next morning. Before they could launch their attack, a torrential rain began and flooded the river, making it impassable.

The riverbanks were under water and river approaches became swamps. Henderson Field aircraft were grounded by the weather. Vandegrift postponed the attack for 24 hours.

A few minutes after midnight, in heavy rain, the Japanese rose from their flooded holes and rushed the marine positions on the east bank. The battle raged in the rain and darkness for 45 minutes and then abruptly stopped. So did the rain. Corpsmen worked by flashlight to save as many of the wounded as possible. When morning arrived, 59 Japanese were found dead. marine losses were 12 killed and 22 wounded.

Vandegrift's attack then developed according to plan. The Japanese were forced towards the sea and marine corps artillery kept them from organizing a counterattack. Puller's battalion counted more than 700 Japanese dead. Marine casualties totaled 200, most of which were wounded.

Hyakutake and his staff arrived on Guadalcanal on October 9, only to learn of the demise of one of his regiments. What was left of the regiment had been withdrawn two miles west of the river. Hyakutake's staff quickly gathered information and made their report to the general. There was a severe shortage of food and medicine. Roads and trails had not been properly developed. Artillery ammunition was in short supply, and the prepared offensive positions for the attack of Henderson Field had been captured by the marines. Hyakutake's chief of staff recommended that the general postpone his attack plans and wait for additional reinforcements. Hyakutake listened to his staff, and then like others before him, announced that the attack must go on as planned.

Just after sunrise on Tuesday, October 13, Admiral Turner's transport group dropped anchor off Lunga point and off-loaded 3,000 soldiers from the 164th Division with their jeeps, trucks, antitank guns, ammunition, and supplies for 70 days. Under the category of supplies were hundreds of cases of candy bars. By

9:30 A.M., a brisk trading was taking place on the beach. Marines traded Japanese rifles, sabers, pistols, helmets, and flags for the candy. Rumor has it that a samurai sword was worth three dozen large Hershey bars, and a rising sun (meatball) flag was worth a dozen. Samurai swords were hard to come by, but the marines manufactured hundreds of meatball flags from old hospital sheets and either catsup or blood plasma. At 11:00 A.M., a Japanese air raid interrupted the trading and the 164th suffered their first casualty.

Vandegrift now had 23,000 troops on Guadalcanal and another 4,500 on Tulagi. Perhaps more important than the increase in numbers was the morale boost associated with the reinforcements. For the first time since the marines landed, someone besides the Japanese seemed interested in Guadalcanal.

U.S. Marines from the 2nd Marine Division evacuate a casualty from the front on Guadalcanal.

National Archives

Casualties were especially high throughout the battle for Guadalcanal.

National Archives

14

THE GROUND BATTLE FOR GUADALCANAL
OCTOBER 1942-JANUARY 1943

During the early morning of October 13, Admiral Kelly Turner, commander of the Amphibious Force South Pacific, successfully offloaded army reinforcements, equipment, and ammunition on Guadalcanal. General Vandegrift, commander of the ground forces on Guadalcanal now had 27,500 troops on Guadalcanal and Tulagi.

Admiral Isoroku Yamamoto, commander of the Japanese combined fleet, was not happy about the increase in Vandegrift's force. To show his displeasure, he sent the battleships *Kongo* and *Haruna,* a cruiser, and seven destroyers to bombard Henderson Field for more than an hour. Marines and soldiers suffered concussions, shattered bones and broken eardrums from the thousands of high-explosive shells that thundered over the area. Japanese floatplanes coordinated illumination for the ships for the entire period, allowing accurate fire to be placed upon the airfield, ration dump, ammunition stores, and other supply areas. When the Japanese navy finally withdrew, the runway was ruined, fuel and ammunition dumps were burning and exploding, and only 14 of 40 aircraft were operational. Army and marine casualties totaled 61, of which 41 were dead.

The following evening, cruisers *Chokai* and *Kinugasa* fired more naval gunfire into Henderson Field while Japanese transports unloaded 2,000 troops and equipment. Cruisers *Maya* and *Myoko* provided the naval gunfire on the evening of the 15th. By October 16, despite round-the-clock maintenance, Geiger had only 27 aircraft of all types that were capable of getting airborne.

Two transports arrived from New Caledonia on the 16th with

aviation fuel, parts, and maintenance crews for General Roy Geiger's "Cactus Air Force." Just before dusk, Marine Fighter Squadron 212 (VMF-212) arrived with 19 Wildcat fighters. The squadron commanding officer, Lieutenant Col. Harold Bauer, was airborne 60 minutes after arriving at Henderson and shot down four Japanese bombers. Despite the constant naval bombardment, Henderson Field was operational.

On October 15, orders were given for the next ground attack against Henderson Field. Much like his predecessors, Lieutenant Gen. Harukichi Hyakutake planned for simultaneous attacks by three separate units at widely separated points around the American defensive position. Hyakutake had 7,000 men for his main attack against what he believed to be a thin defensive line. His forces consisted of three battalions on the right commanded by Major Gen. Kiyotaki Kawaguchi, and three battalions on the left commanded by Major Gen. Yumio Nasu. Both groups were to be supported by anti-tank guns, mortars, artillery, and engineers.

In addition, Hyakutake activated an infantry-tank-artillery group under Major Gen. Tadashi Sumuyoshi with 16 tanks. Hyakutake held one infantry regiment in reserve. The ground attack was to be coordinated with naval gunfire and air support. From Rabaul would come bombers to pin down the enemy and rule the sky. Admiral Yamamoto would personally command a fleet of battleships and cruisers to destroy Henderson Field and all supporting facilities.

On October 16, well before Hyakutake's forces were in position for the attack, Japanese aircraft pounded Henderson and sank the seaplane tender *McFarland*, which was towing barges with 20,000 gallons of much needed aviation fuel. The fuel went up in flames. The next morning, large numbers of Betty bombers escorted by Zero fighters attacked Henderson. The Japanese lost eight fighters and eight bombers to Henderson Field fighters.

American defenders of Guadalcanal received some wonderful

news on October 18. In Washington, President Franklin Roosevelt and Secretary of the Navy, Frank Knox made a decision to hold Guadalcanal. More to the delight of the soldiers and sailors on Guadalcanal was the information that Vice Adm. William "Bull" Halsey was the new commander of South Pacific Forces. Halsey was well known and respected for being a fighter. When the information was received at Henderson Field, marines who were too sick from malaria to climb out of their holes were suddenly running around shouting the news like school children. Finally, the navy had a fighter in charge.

Halsey's reaction to his new assignment was no less colorful. "Jesus Christ and General Jackson," Halsey is reported to have said. "This is the hottest potato they ever handed me."[1] Halsey called a meeting of Turner, Vandegrift, Patch, and the marine corps commandant, General Thomas Holcomb, at his headquarters in Noumea. During the meeting Halsey asked Vandegrift if he could hold Guadalcanal. "I can hold," Vandegrift responded, "but I've got to have more active support than I've been getting." Halsey told Vandegrift to "go on back, I'll promise you everything I've got."[2]

While Vandegrift was in Noumea, Generals Kawaguchi and Nasu continued their march to their assault positions. The packs of the men were heavy, and the constant rain and chilly nights began to take a toll. Artillery and anti-tank weapons were especially difficult to lug through the jungle. Such equipment began to lag behind, and then became stuck and abandoned in the muck and mud of the various valleys and creeks that had to be crossed. Much to the commander's disgust, the attack had to be delayed for 48 hours, but the men moved on, sustained only by a few handsful of rice and rain water.

General Nasu's assault battalions were in place in the early morning of October 23, but Kawaguchi's were not. The attack had to be postponed until 5:00 A.M., the next day. In a fit of anger, the commander relieved Kawaguchi of his command and replaced him with Colonel Toshinaro Shoji. A report was sent to Admiral Yamamoto and General Sumyuyoshi advising them of the postponement. Sumyuyoshi never received the message. Consequently, the 16 tanks of Sumyuyoshi began their attack on October 23 as scheduled. With no other enemy to worry about, the marines took on the tanks in high spirits. In less than three minutes, the nine tanks that ventured out of the jungle were destroyed.[3] Three additional tanks and 600 Japanese infantry were killed by marine artillery that pinpointed Sumyuyoshi's assembly area.

At 3:00 P.M. on the 24th, as General Nasu and Colonel Shoji's groups began their movement to the attack positions, a heavy rain began that turned the jungle into a swamp. All communications between units failed, and it was midnight before the first flare was fired to signal the attack. Nasu's forces emerged from the jungle in the heavy rain and charged the American positions. Artillery and mortar fire tore into the Japanese and into their assembly area. Most of the initial attackers were killed by this fire. The remainder of the attack group were killed by Lewis Puller's battalion and soldiers of the 164th Regiment who were fed into the lines beside the marines. Side by side, soldiers and marines threw back the Japanese attack.

Early in the attack, about nine Japanese officers and men penetrated the marine lines and worked their way toward Henderson Field. One of the officers radioed Hyakutake that the airfield was in Japanese hands. Hyukutake, without confirming the report, immediately relayed the news to Rabaul. The news was a prearranged signal for Rabaul to land the Koli detachment at Lunga point. Meanwhile, 1,000 Japanese casualties lay in and around the defensive wire and foxholes of the Americans. More soldiers were moved into the front line positions to help the marines meet the next attack. Vandegrift reported 86 Americans killed and 119 wounded. He estimated Japanese casualties as 2,000.

Sumyuyoshi's 6-inch howitzers resumed their attack on Henderson early Sunday morning. All of Henderson Field's aircraft were grounded until the sun could dry the soggy runway. Japanese aircraft from Rabaul and Buin were quick to take advantage of the situation and took off in large numbers in hopes of destroying American aircraft on the ground.

While the marines and soldiers were drying out, digging in, and stringing more defensive wire, three fast destroyers rushed past Savo Island enroute to Sealark channel. The ships were carrying Hyakutake's Koli detachment to Lunga point in accordance with the prearranged signal that Henderson Field had been captured.

The landing of the Koli detachment was contested by two smaller U.S. destroyers, two tugs, and a few aircraft from Henderson that managed to slither down the runway and get airborne. The Japanese ships were bloodied and forced to retire, along with their cruiser escort, *Yura,* who departed on fire with a large section of her bow missing. Destroyer escort *Akizuke* was sunk.

Shortly after the unsuccessful attempt to land the Koli detachment, 16 Betty bombers and 27 Zeros arrived to bomb and strafe the airfield. Henderson Field dried out sufficiently to permit takeoffs, and 17 Zeros and five Bettys were shot down. Marine Lieutenant Joe Foss shot down four of the Zeros. The air raids and naval actions permitted the Japanese army to reorganize for another night attack. The attack began shortly after dark and ended in another defeat for the Japanese. General Nasu was killed as were most of his unit commanders. Half the officers of the Sendai Division died or were seriously wounded in the futile charge.

The Japanese, with no reserve force remaining, were forced to withdraw. Once again, the jungle ruined the complex tactical plans of coordinated fire and maneuver that are taught and practiced in the military schools. Once again, Japanese soldiers ate bark and roots, drank from dirty puddles of water, and gnawed their leather rifle slings for sustenance as they slogged back to Taivu. Unknown to everyone, this was to be the last Japanese attempt to seize Henderson Field.

The October 24 battle with the Sendai Division linked the marines and army forces as never before. Prior to the battle, marines customarily referred to members of the army as "doggies or dogfaces." After the battle, marines respectfully addressed the army troops as soldiers. Respect among the marines was so great that the commander of the First Marine Regiment penned the following letter to his army counterpart.

> The officers and men of the First Marines salute
> you for a most wonderful piece of work. Will
> you please extend our congratulations to all
> concerned.we are honored to serve with a unit
> such as yours."[4]

On Thanksgiving Day 1942, as soldiers and marines ate roast turkey and cranberry sauce, compliments of Admiral Halsey, the First Marine Division had a special reason to give thanks. Vandegrift's weary warriors received orders that they would be relieved in early December by the army's 25th Division. On the same day, Admiral Halsey received his fourth star and promotion to full admiral.

The First Marine Division departed Guadalcanal on December 7. Major Gen. Alexander Patch took command of all forces on Guadalcanal. Patch had a corps of three divisions and 40,000 men. By now, Henderson Field was an all-weather airfield, capable of supporting B-17 operations.

In mid-December, GHQ in Tokyo concluded that they could not adequately reinforce their forces on Guadalcanal. Japan had a severe shortage of combat ships, and American submarines were taking a heavy toll of their merchant shipping. The emperor reluctantly approved the recommended withdrawal, but admonished the military to, "Give enough thought to your plans so that Lae and Salamua (Papua) don't become another Guadalcanal."[4]

During the end of January 1943, another major Japanese air effort was launched from Rabaul. Coastwatchers reported Japanese ships massing in the Shortlands, and departure of the Combined Fleet from Truk. Halsey and Patch suspected another reinforcement effort by the Japanese. Patch broke contact with the Japanese forces and pulled his 25th Division back to defend the airfield area. His decision saved 11,000 Japanese lives.

At 9:30 P.M., on February 1, 1943, the first of 2,316 starving Japanese waded through the surf to the ramps of barges waiting to evacuate them. Three days later, the remnants of the Sendai Division embarked. On February 7, the rear guard of 3,000 men was similarly evacuated. During the six-day period, the Japanese navy safely evacuated 11,000 officers and men. Left behind were the remains of 21,000 of their comrades. Less than half that number died in combat. The remainder died of wounds, disease, or starvation.

The evacuation of the 17th Army from Guadalcanal is one of the greatest feats of the war. The plans were kept secret from all but the most senior commanders. To further ensure secrecy, Japanese reinforcements continued to arrive on Guadalcanal and were deployed to the front lines as late as January 15. The evacuation of forces by sea is a difficult proposition under the best of situations. Had Patch kept up his offensive pressure, the evacuation could well have been the ultimate catastrophe for the Japanese.

The ground battle for Guadalcanal lasted six months. Japan lost 800 aircraft, and, more importantly, 2,362 irreplaceable trained pilots and aircrewmen.[11] The battle forced Japan to change her strategy in the Pacific, and provided a much needed morale boost to the American people and our Allies. Like honorary Sergeant Major Vouza, the native scout that sent the following message to the First Marine Division in 1962, none of us should ever forget what brave men did on Guadalcanal.

> "Tell them I love them all. Me old man now, and me no look good no more. But me never forget."[5]

The Japanese lost more than 20 ships at Guadalcanal, and the battle was the Allies' first major victory in the Pacific.

US Navy

15

THE NAVAJO CODE TALKERS

One of the most interesting, important, and yet relatively unknown aspects of World War II was the role of the Navajo Indian code talkers. These native Americans volunteered to secure internal lines of communications for the marine corps in the Pacific theater. Without such communications security, the Japanese would have broken the codes used by the marines in the battles for the Pacific, resulting in far greater casualties and lengthening the war.

The United States and Canada experimented with the use of the Choctaw Indian language during World War I. The idea was great but the experiment was unsuccessful. The Choctaw language had few military terms in its vocabulary and the Choctaw Indians knew little English. The experiment did cause the German government to send "students" to learn every American native Indian language except one, Navajo.[1]

Credit for the use of the Navajo language for communications security belongs to Mr. Philip Johnston. Johnston was the son of a missionary to the Navajo nation. He was raised on the Navajo reservation and learned to speak fluent Navajo. He fought in WW I, and was aware of the Choctaw language experiment. He knew that the Navajo language was an unwritten language with no alphabet or other symbols and believed that it could provide the degree of desired security.[2]

When Johnston was nine years of age, he traveled with his father to Washington, D.C., to translate the discussion between the Navajo Tribal Council and President Theodore Roosevelt, concerning the fair treatment of the Navajo and Hopi Indians by the United States government.

PFC Preston Toledo (left) and PFC Frank Toledo (cousins) relay operational orders somewhere in the South Pacific during July, 1943.

US Marine Corps

The Navajo language was unique. It was confined to the southwest United States, was unwritten, had no alphabet, and had many dialects within the different Navajo clans. In 1942, it was estimated that not more than 30 non-Navajos (missionaries and anthropologists) could speak the language.[3] Since the language was unwritten, non-Navajos could not study its structure.[4]

During February 1942, Johnston contacted the U.S. Marines at Camp Elliot, California concerning his idea for using Navajo code talkers.[5] He met with several high ranking marine officers from the

Pacific theater and Headquarters Marine Corps (HQMC). Following the meeting, Colonel Wethered Woodward from HQMC was tasked to devise a test to measure the Navajo for a new top-secret cryptographic code program.

Johnson conducted the tests that had a Navajo male translating three-line English-language messages into Navajo and sending the translated message to a Navajo at the other end of the communication link. The second Navajo would translate the message into English and send it to the proper headquarters. Using such a procedure, the Navajo were able to complete messages in less than 20 seconds, a job that required cryptographic machines 30 minutes.[6] Subsequent tests proved the feasibility of Johnston's proposal and led to his enlistment in the marine corps.

By 1942, Japan had broken most of the American field codes that used a complex mathematical machine to send messages. This loss of tactical communications security was causing the marines to resort to human messengers, a slow and costly alternative to secure message traffic.

The initial induction of Navajo volunteers began in February 1942, at Window Rock, Arizona, with 29 recruits, some as young as 15, who lied about their age.[7] Upon completion of "boot camp" at San Diego, California, the Navajo men learned military skills and qualified with their individual weapons, usually the 30-caliber carbine, They then attended a four-week, field-signal-training school at Camp Pendleton, California. Training included vocabulary expansion, voice procedure, printing, message writing, wire laying, pole climbing, and learning the organizations of marine corps units. More than 200 military terms were memorized and translated into a Navajo equivalent. Then the men had to devise Navajo words for military terms that were not in their language. Completion of the course qualified them for assignment to operational units in the Pacific.

During this initial basic code development, a marine captain named Stilwell found that the process was too time consuming and the frequency of letter use was too high. He added 200 more words to the vocabulary (a total of 400), and alternative words for the 12 most frequently used words of the alphabet.[8] As a result of Stilwel's work, speed of translation increased and the frequency of letter usage decreased.

PFC Samuel Sandoval, a radio operator, relaxes under a torii gate during a break in the fighting on Okinawa.

US Marine Corps

Many of the translation words used common sense. Airplanes were named after birds (chicken hawk); a commanding general was (war chief), a major general was (two-star). Alternate words were created for each letter of the English alphabet that was used frequently. The letter A had three forms: ant, ax, and apple. Badger, bear, and barrel became substitutes for the letter B. If you were to listen to a code talker say the English word navy, you would hear, "tsah (needle), wol-la-chee (ant), ah-keh-di-glini (victor), and tsah-ah-dzoh (yucca)." Subtle differences in tone can change the meanings. Navajos used four different tones: low, high, rising and falling. As an example of tone difference, the words medicine and mouth have the same pronunciation but are said with different tones.

Navajo language also reflected the view of life incorporated in the world around them. Instead of saying, "I am hungry," they would say, "Hunger is hurting me." The Navajo had to memorize both the primary and alternate code terms because the vocabulary lists could not be carried in a combat area for fear of compromise.

The Navajo code talkers participated in every marine corps combat assault in the Pacific. They served in all six marine divisions and such major battles as Guadalcanal, Saipan, Bougainville, Tinian, The Marshall Islands, Okinawa, Tarawa, Iwo Jima and on mainland China.[9] Their primary job was to send vital information about troop strength and tactics over telephones and radios. The Navajo tribe had one of the highest percentages of its total population in the armed services of any American ethnic group. More than 3,600 Navajo men and women served in the armed forces with 400 of them being code talkers.

The success of the code talkers has never been in doubt, only the degree of their effectiveness. A marine signal officer may have exaggerated a bit when he said, "Had it not been for the code talkers, the marines would never have taken Iwo Jima and the other islands."[10] Following the war, Japan's chief of intelligence, Lieutenant Gen. Seizo Arisue, freely admitted that the Japanese were able to decipher the code of the United States Army Air Corps but could not decipher the Navajo code. The code sounded like gibberish to the Japanese. They could not write down the sounds, much less decipher them.

General Archer Vandegrift, commanding general of the First Marine Division on Guadalcanal, was so pleased with the performance of his code talkers that he requested 83 more "talkers" be assigned to the division. As more "talkers" became available, they were assigned in greater numbers to all the marine divisions.

Frank C. Willetto was one of the first to join the marines as a code talker. He tried to join at age 16 but his mother said he was too young. Six months later he was drafted, and following training, landed on Saipan. Willetto remembers that "every night someone got killed."[11] Preston Toledo weighed 119 pounds when he tried to enlist as a code talker. The minimum weight for his height was 122. Told to drink a lot of water, Toledo did and made the weight at 123 pounds. He served on Cape Gloucester, New Britain, Okinawa, and in Peking, China. Toledo earned the Bronze Star for his distinguished service.[12]

Francis Thompson remembers that seeing his buddies die all around him on Saipan was bad, but the worst was having his father die back home while he was overseas.[13] Samuel Sandoval remembers that several code talkers captured, butchered, and feasted upon some goats behind the front lines on Okinawa. The Navajo's main diet is mutton and goat, but it was never served in marine corps messhalls.[14]

The landing craft taking Merril Sandoval to the beaches of Iwo Jima was hit and sunk. He lost all of his equipment but was able to swim to shore. He recalls the tremendous noise of the main guns of the USS *Tennessee* and the shells passing over the heads of the marines as they landed on the beach. He also saw many planes diving at Japanese positions on Mount Surabachi. Some of the planes crashed into the mountains.[15] Wilson Price saw the flag raising on Mount Surabachi. He served with three of the marine corps divisions in the Pacific and participated in the battles for Guadalcanal, Iwo Jima, Okinawa, and Saipan.[16]

Keith M. Little recalls this story from his service at Roi-Namur: "During a lull in the battle for the Roi-Namur atolls in the Marshall Islands, our outfit was pulled off the front lines for some rest." The men were in a shell crater next to a steel-reinforced concrete building. One of the marines noticed that the heavy steel door of the building was slowly opening. "Out came a Japanese, naked except for what looked like a g-string, with his hands in the air. The platoon leader immediately ordered everyone to hold their fire, but apparently some trigger-happy marine . . . took a pot shot at the guy. Then 20 or more carbines blazed away. The Japanese took off and saved himself by diving into a shell hole." After an unmerciful scolding by the platoon leader for the horrible display of marksmanship, the Japanese was coaxed out of his shell hole, fed, clothed, and escorted to the rear. His only injury was a few scratches from his desperate dive into the shell hole.[17]

The use of the code talkers was one of the best-kept secrets of the war. So secret was the work that other American and Allied forces, and even some marine units, were unaware of the Navajos' presence among them. This secrecy caused the Navajo to have problems with our own forces. Navajo, because of their skin color and size, were often thought to be Japanese soldiers in marine uniforms. Cases of such mistakes often occurred when U.S. Army forces fought alongside marines. On Guadalcanal, an army unit apprehended a Navajo and notified the marines that they had captured a Japanese soldier dressed in a marine utility uniform and wearing identification tags. A marine officer was sent to "retrieve" the marine code talker from the army.

The code talkers were not recognized nationally until 1969, when the 4th Marine Division presented special medallions to their code-talking veterans. Subsequently, in 1971, Mr. Benis Frank, head of the Marine Corps Oral History Program, interviewed many of the survivors at a gathering in Window Rock. Later that year, the president of the United States awarded a Certificate of Appreciation to the code talkers.

On September 17, 1992, the "secret" label was officially removed from the code talkers when they were honored for their contributions to the defense of our nation at the Pentagon, Washington, D.C. During the ceremony, a permanent Navajo Code Talkers exhibit in the Pentagon was dedicated. Attendance at the dedication included 35 of the surviving code talkers and their families. The United States and the free world are in debt to the Navajo code talkers who did so much during WW II and asked for so little.[18]

PFC Carl M. Gorman observes the city of Garapan on Saipan, June 27, 1944.

US Marine Corps

16

SABURO SAKAI

Saburo Sakai passed away on September 22, 2000. He was 84, and a living legend in Japan during World War II. He was Japan's leading ace who survived the war. He shot down 64 enemy planes, but his legacy was for more than that. In more than 200 combat missions, Saburo is the only pilot who never lost a wingman in aerial combat.[1] Other pilots begged to fly his wing. In addition, Saburo never overshot a landing, never overturned his aircraft, or crash-landed his plane despite combat damage to the plane, personal wounds, and night or adverse weather conditions.

Saburo suffered a heart attack while enjoying dinner with U.S. Navy pilots at Atsugi Naval Air Station near Tokyo. He delighted in the friendships he made with American pilots and the many invitations to visit American aircraft carriers, warships, and aircraft. He was rushed to a nearby hospital but died a few hours later. Saburo was one of a growing number of Japanese pilots who have been able to reconcile with former enemies. For the past ten years, he questioned publicly why Japan went to war, and suggested several times the exoneration of Emperor Hirohito as a war criminal was a "whitewash."[2]

Saburo was born on a small farm near Saga City in Kyushu, Japan on August 16, 1916. Saga, with a population of 50,000, was one of the poorest of the self-sustaining provinces of Japan. His mother was widowed when Saburo was 11 years old, and was forced to care for the farm and seven children. His most poignant memory of his mother's hardship was seeing her bent over, nearly all day in the fields, with her youngest child strapped to her back.[3] Saburo had good grades in school but would not have gone to high school had his uncle, Mr. Hirokawa, not volunteered to finance his education.

After two years of high school, Saburo was at the bottom of his class academically and the top of the list for delinquency and disgraceful conduct. His uncle terminated his financial support and Saburo returned to Saga City in disgrace. On May 31, 1933, he enlisted, as a sixteen-year-old recruit, in the Japanese Navy. He suffered greatly at the hands of his petty officers during recruit training. Beatings with large wooden sticks were common, and Saburo drew far more beatings than his fellow recruits. Sometimes he received as many as 40 hard smashes with the stick, the pain causing him to lose consciousness. Unconsciousness was a short respite since the petty officer would dump cold water on him until he regained consciousness and then resume the beating.

The combination of scholastic failure, family disgrace, and recruit beatings taught Saburo humility and never to question authority. Following training he was assigned to IMS battleship *Kirishima,* and in 1935, he was promoted to seaman. He was then assigned to the battleship *Haruna* where he earned promotion to petty officer, third class. In 1937, he was one of 70 accepted for flight training out of 1,500 applicants.[4] Once again, physical ability became all important. Only those trainees that exhibited strong physical skills were permitted to continue training. After successfully completing a month of physical competition and ground training, flying lessons began. During the next ten months, 45 of the original 70 students were dismissed from training. Saburo was selected as the outstanding student pilot of his group. After additional training on aircraft carriers, he was sent to Kaohsiung Air Base on Formosa, and then to Kiukiang in southeastern China.

Saburo claimed his first aerial "kill" on May 21, 1938, despite forgetting most of the rules about aerial combat that he had been taught. He took off with 15 other Mitsubishi Type 96 fighters (Allied codename Claude). These were slow aircraft with fixed landing gear and open cockpits. When Saburo's' flight was attacked by Chinese fighters, he failed to jettison his highly explosive external fuel tank, he failed to turn into the enemy fighters when he was attacked, and was saved by another experienced pilot that observed his indecision. After doing everything wrong, Saburo was assisted by his fellow pilots into a position behind a Russian made E-16 fighter. The E-16 was faster, had retractable landing gear, and was more maneuverable than the "Claude."

Fortunately, the Chinese pilot was not very experienced. After a full minute of pulling the trigger of his guns to no avail, Saburo remembered to charge his guns. By this time the E-16 was only 200 yards in front of him. As Saburo fired, oily black smoke poured from the E-16, fell to its left and crashed to the ground. Upon landing back at Kiukiang, Saburo's flight leader was so angry at him for his "rookie" mistakes, that he could not talk. After trying to curse Saburo for his stupidity and realizing he was too angry for violence, the Captain turned his back and walked away.

Saburo did not fly another fighter mission until October 3, and that flight was unauthorized. On that day with no warning, 12 Russian SB twin-engine bombers attacked the Japanese airfield. The SB was the primary bomber of the Chinese Air Force. Following the attack, most of the 200 Japanese fighters and bombers were aflame and exploding. Saburo frantically searched among the exploding aircraft, found a Claude that was flyable and took off after the SBs. It took him 20 minutes at full power to catch the bombers and make a firing pass at them. As he fired, one bomber fell out of position and trailed smoke. As Saburo turned to finish the bomber off, he realized that he was 150 miles from his base at Hankow and nearly out of fuel. Showing far more intellect than his first fighter mission, he returned and landed safely at Hankow.

As Saburo climbed from his aircraft, the pain from his wounds caused him to collapse onto the runway. He was taken to the hospital where his shrapnel wounds healed slowly. Saburo was ordered to Omura, the nearest base to his home of Sago. Rather than being in trouble for his solo unauthorized attack against the 12 bombers, Saburo was told to rest and recover. He was considered a minor hero for his one downed aircraft and solo attack against

12 enemy bombers.[5] In November 1939, Saburo was granted overnight leave to visit his mother and family. When he arrived at the village, an hour's train ride from Omura, he was astonished to find the Village Master and a large crowd to welcome him home. "Welcome home, Saburo, the hero of our modest village," the Village Master proclaimed.[5]

Then began a party with food and many bottles of sake. Saburo was overwhelmed by the attention and had to be reminded by his mother to look pleasant and appreciative. The party lasted well into the night and after ensuring the welfare of his mother and family, Saburo returned to his base at Omura. He was put back on flying status and in January 1940, was selected as one of the pilots to fly an exhibition flight over Osaka. Following the flight, Saburo was visited at his hotel by the Niori family and their daughter Fujiko.

Fujiko and Saburo had never met and only knew of each other's existence because of Hatsuyo Hirokawa, the 16-year-old daughter of Saburo's uncle. Hatsuyo wrote to Saburo from Tokushima Girl's High School where she was studying and introduced her friend, Mikiko Niori. Hatsuyo described Mikiko as the most beautiful and brightest girl in her class. Based upon the picture and letter from Mikiko, Saburo had to agree. This initial introduction began a correspondence between Mikiko and Saburo that lasted until Mikiko's death in a traffic accident in October.

Hatsuyo, always the match maker, arranged for Fujiko Niori, Mikiko's sister to write to Saburo while he was at Omori recovering from his wounds. The two corresponded frequently with little hope of meeting one another until Saburo notified Fujiko that he would be flying to Osaka in the near future. Fujiko quickly responded that her family would travel there to meet Saburo.

Saburo was as nervous as he had ever been. He was taken to a famous restaurant in Tokyo for dinner with the family. The Niori family was one of the most distinguished families in Japan. They were from a famous Samurai group, and Mr. Niori had attained an acclaimed reputation as a college professor. The night went well and when it was over, Saburo thought he had passed the test to be a suitor of Fujiko.

Back at Omura, Saburo became depressed at the news that all of his fellow pilots were becoming aces in action against the Chinese and international pilots that flew for China. At last, he received orders to Kaohsiung, Formosa. When he arrived, he discovered that the Claudes had been replaced with the beautiful Mitsubishi Zero fighter. The Zero was sleek and modern. It had a powerful engine, enclosed cockpit, retractable landing gear, and four guns. It could fly at twice the speed and range of the Claude.

During an escort mission on August 11, 1941, Saburo was assigned to a Zero mission that flew 800 miles nonstop escorting seven Mitsubishi G4M (Allied code name: Betty) bombers for a strike on a Chinese airfield at Wekiang, China. Saburo and the escort Zeros strafed the field first, and Saburo destroyed two E-16 fighters as they tried to take off. The aircraft on the ground did not count towards ace status, but he shot down a brightly colored biplane on the way back to base for his second kill and the first while flying the Zero.[6]

On December 2, Saburo and his fellow fighter pilots began to fly fuel-conservation flights to determine if it would be possible to extend the range of the Zero to 1,200 miles nonstop. If they could do so, they would be able to attack the Philippines from Formosa without the use of carriers. Saburo set a fuel-consumption record of less than 17 gallons of fuel per hour during one of the tests. Normal fuel consumption was 35 gallons per hour. The fuel tests were successful, meaning that Japan was free to use its carriers elsewhere.

Saburo flew in the attack on December 8 (Philippine time) that caught Clark field in the Philippines with all their aircraft neatly lined up on the airfield. After the Japanese bombers destroyed the airfield, five P-40 aircraft were discovered to be airborne looking for a fight. Four of the P-40s scattered, but Saburo shot down the fifth, his third kill of an enemy aircraft in the air. On December 10, Saburo shot down a B-17 Flying Fortress over Clark Field and another on January 24 over Balikpapan, Borneo. Once these bomber kills were confirmed, Saburo was an ace.

By the end of February 1942, Sakai increased his kill number to 13. Most of the aircraft were P-36 Mohawks, P-40 Tomahawks, and Brewster F2A Buffaloes. They were flown by Dutch pilots from Surabaya and were no match for the Zero and the experienced Japanese pilots.

During March, Saburo was transferred to Rabaul in New Britain. The morning after he arrived, and before his squadron aircraft arrived, Rabaul was attacked by a dozen Australian B-26 Marauder aircraft. The raids continued for three consecutive mornings and greatly damaged the base and airfield. Saburo thought the base to be the most primitive and desolate he had ever seen. Conditions were about to change. For the next several weeks, there was a constant flow of fighters and bombers into the airfield as Japan prepared for the capture of Port Moresby, New Guinea.

On April 8, 30 pilots from Saburo's squadron were transferred to Lae, on the eastern side of New Guinea. Lae was only 180 miles from Port Moresby and provided an excellent base to attack the seaport, airfield, and city. Saburo found Lae to be far worse than Rabaul, worse even than the most primitive airfield in China.

There were no hangars, maintenance shops, or control tower at Lae. Rugged mountains towered above the 3,000-foot-long runway on three sides. The runway was dirt and became muddy when wet. Candles and a single kerosene lamp provided light. There were only three vehicles at the entire base: an ancient, rusty, noisy Ford sedan; one decrepit truck; and a single fueling vehicle. The briefing "hut" was made from mats and had no walls. Three crashed Australian transport planes lay at the end of the runway and a

WAR IN THE PACIFIC

War in the Pacific

Name: _____

Military service (Branch) _____ War, Crisis, or Period: _____

Message: _____

P.O. Box or Street Address: _____ Apt. _____

City: _____ State: _____ ZIP: _____

- -

Domestic orders (50 U.S. states) (USPS Priority Mail shipping included in price).

Total Volume I books _____ @ $25 ea. (soft cover) or @ $30 ea. (hard cover) = $ _____

Total Volume II books _____ @ $25 ea. (soft cover) or @ $30 ea. (hard cover) = $ _____

Total Volume III books _____ @ $25 ea. (soft cover) or @ $30 ea. (hard cover) = $ _____

Total Volume IV books _____ @ $25 ea. (soft cover) or @ $30 ea. (hard cover) = $ _____

Overseas (Foreign) orders (outside the 50 states) (Global Priority Mail included in price).

Total volume I books _____ @ U.S. $35 ea. (soft cover) or $40 ea. (hard cover) = $ _____

Total volume II books _____ @ U.S. $35 ea. (soft cover) or $40 ea. (hard cover) = $ _____

Total volume III books _____ @ U.S. $35 ea. (soft cover) or $40 ea. (hard cover) = $ _____

Total volume IV books _____ @ U.S. $35 ea. (soft cover) or $40 ea. (hard cover) = $ _____

Total 4-volume sets _____ @ U.S. $135 (soft cover) or $155 (hard cover) = $ _____

Total amount enclosed by check $ _____ (For foreign book orders, the payment may be sent by International Postal Money order, bank drafts against a U.S. bank, or cash dollars, sent by registered mail. Price includes shipping).

Send your order with payment to:

J. Hagen

47-446 Lulani Street

Kaneohe, HI 96744

E-Mail: Hagenj001@hawaii.rr.com

Fax: 808-239-1053

You may also order books online at www.warinthepacific.org

Volume III of *War in the Pacific* contains many topics that most Americans are not familiar with because not much has been written about them. Chapters include:

The Merchant Marines in WW II; Internment of Japanese-Americans, Japanese-Canadians, and the Aleut People during WW II; How the Navy salvaged seven of the battleships sunk at Pearl Harbor, six of which saw action in WW II.

There are chapters on such personalities as Hideki Tojo, Subhas Chandra Bose, Masanobu Tsuji, Joe Foss, "Bull" Halsey, "Weary" Dunlap, "Pete" Mitscher, Douglas MacArthur, and Chuichi Nagumo.

Battles and campaigns include Stilwell's Retreat from Burma, The Battle for Imphal, The Seige of Kohima, Victory in Burma, Bougainville, Tarawa, Peleliu, and Return to Guam, Saipan and Tinian.

If you enjoyed volumes I and II, you will find Volume III every bit as informative and enjoyable.

I will personalize and autograph each book if you will complete the personalizing information on the order form. Be sure to include any military service if appropriate. (For example: Thanks Gordon, for your service in the U.S. Navy during WW II; or Thanks, Don, for your service in the U.S. Army during the Korean War, etc.

Thank you for your order.

Semper Fidelis

Jerome T. Hagen

Brigadier General, USMC (Ret).

portion of a destroyed Australian merchant ship rose from the water near the primitive pier.

Saburo and 30 enlisted pilots lived in a six-by-ten-yard shack 500 yards east of the airstrip. A water tank for fresh water and a "pitifully inadequate" mess hall were behind the shack. Ten officer pilots lived 500 yards northeast of the runway and another 200 base security personnel and 100 aircraft maintenance personnel comprised the entire base complement.

For the next four months, Saburo rotated scheduled flights and alert status with the other pilots. On April 11, he accounted for two of the four P-39 Aircobras shot down near Port Moresby within five seconds of each other. On April 29, three B-17s attacked Lae while the Japanese pilots were finishing a breakfast honoring Emperor Hirohito's birthday. The attack destroyed five Zeros and damaged four more. Saburo was not able to get airborne in time to chase the B-17s. For the next few days opposing forces raided each other's airfields, destroying several aircraft on the ground. On May 1, he recorded his first triple kill, a P-40 and two P-39s near Port Moresby, using only 610 rounds of ammunition.

On May 2, Saburo recorded two more kills over Port Moresby, giving him a total of 22 planes shot down. He was back in the air on May 7, shooting down two more P-40s and again on May 8 and 9, when he shot down a P-39 and a P-40. He followed this up by shooting down a P-40 on May 10 with only four rounds of ammunition.

Saburo shot down an Aircobra on May 12, but lost his 20 year-old wingman, Naval Aviation Pilot Third Class (NAP 3/C) Honda, a day later while Honda was flying with another flight leader. The flight was attacked by P-39s near Port Moresby and the flight leader did not see them until Honda's plane was in flames. The loss was the first for the squadron since April 17 and had a profound effect upon the other pilots since Honda was the most popular pilot in the squadron. They all pledged revenge for Honda's loss.

Saburo's squadron was grounded on May 15 and 16 due to torrential downpours, but the rain did not stop 16 B-25s from cratering the Lae runway and damaging the maintenance shop. Repairs to the runway were quickly made and Saburo was at it again on May 17. Strafing of the Port Moresby airfield was ineffective, but the Zeros were attacked by a flight of P-39s as they turned to depart. Saburo received credit for two of the six P-39s that went down. As the 16 Zero fighters left the Moresby area, Sakai, Toshio Ota and Hiroyoshi Nishizawa left the formation and returned to the airfield at Port Moresby to put on an air show for the Australians on the ground. Three times the three Zeros performed triple loops as if tied together with short ropes. Not a single gun fired from the ground and no enemy aircraft appeared.[7]

Japan's leading ace, Saburo Sakai.

National Archives

Nishizawa, age 23, with 20 kills; Ota, 20, with 18 kills; and Sakai, age 26, with 27 kills knew they had nothing to fear from the Australians but were afraid of the repercussions if their squadron commander learned of their air show over the enemy airfield. They pledged silence to one another. Later that evening, the three pilots were called to the office of Lieutenant Sasai, the squadron commander. "Look here you silly bastards," Sasai began.[8] Sasai was red in the face and scarcely able to control himself as he waved a letter in the face of the pilots. The letter was in English and was signed by a group of pilots from the Port Moresby airfield. The letter had been air-dropped later that afternoon by a pilot from the Port Moresby airfield. The letter stated that the pilots were impressed by the airshow and were sorry they had not given the three Japanese pilots better attention. The letter asked for ". . . the same pilots to return again each wearing a green muffler around his neck. . . . we will see to it that the next time they will receive an all out welcome from us."[9] Lieutenant Sasai kept the unruly pilots at attention while he lectured them on their idiotic behavior, forbade them to ever do such a thing again, and dismissed them. It seems likely that Sasai had a twinkle in his eye.

The months of May, June, and July involved daily air-to-air combat for the squadron. The Zero remained the best fighter aircraft in the Pacific and Sakai's squadron boasted the most experienced and successful fighter pilots in the Japanese Navy. Although the Zero was a great fighter, it had no armor protection for the pilot, lacked self- sealing fuel tanks, and the pilots at Lac refused to wear parachutes because of their bulkiness. As the Allied pilots learned, a few 50-caliber bullets into the fuel tanks of a Zero would cause the plane to explode. Rounds fired into the cockpit area would penetrate the seat and fuselage and hit the pilot. This knowledge led to more precise aiming on the part of Allied pilots, with positive results.

Saburo shot down his 37th aircraft on May 21 without firing a shot. The P-39 he was chasing crashed into a mountain trying to escape. Nishizawa and Ota also received a kill for similar actions when aircraft they were pursuing crashed into mountains trying to escape. Saburo was credited with downing three B-25s on May 23 and 24 and a B-26 on May 28. He downed two more B-26s in early June.

On June 1, eighteen bombers from Rabaul, escorted by 24 Zero fighters, bombed and strafed the airfield at Port Moresby. They were met by 20 fighters that scattered the bombers. No aircraft were shot down by either side. On June 9, Saburo was credited with shooting down four of the 19 P-39s destroyed by his squadron. He now had a total of 43 victories. After five days of rest at Rabaul, Sakai was back at Lae on June 24, and shot down an enemy fighter over Port Moresby. A torrential downpour started on June 26th and grounded all aircraft in New Guinea for the remainder of the month.

July brought clear weather, clear nights, and enemy bombers to attack the Lae airfield every night. Mitchell and Marauder bombers flying as low as 600 feet knocked out the runway, destroyed maintenance shops, and kept everyone awake and confined to their shelters. Sakai and a dozen others were buried alive in one of the shelters when a bomb collapsed the roof and filled the crater with rocks and soil. Only the prompt action of Commander Nakajima and several men with shovels uncovered the men before they suffocated.

On July 4 (July 5 Port Moresby time), 21 Zero fighters from Lae added to the American independence celebration by attacking the airfield at Port Moresby. They met 20 enemy fighters and destroyed 12. In their absence, enemy bombers struck at Lae, destroying the fuel supplies at the base. As the Zeros glided towards the runway, seven Marauders flew across the runway dropping bombs to make it unusable. The first Zero to catch the enemy bombers crashed into the lead aircraft, sending both planes to their demise. Another B-26 was shot down before the Zeros had to return to land for fuel. The maintenance personnel on the ground quickly filled the bomb craters and the aircraft landed safely.

Lae was bombed daily from July 7 through July 10, but the runway was always quickly repaired and there were always Zeros available for bomber escort and fighter missions. On July 11, twelve fighters escorted 21 Rabaul-based bombers for yet another attack against Moresby, but six of the fighters, including Sakai, turned away to attack six B-17s that were on the way to bomb Lae. One Zero was lost to the B-17 gunners, the attack on Moresby was ineffective, and the Lae-based squadron was admonished for not staying with their bomber-escort mission.

On July 21, the Japanese army landed troops at Buna, 110 miles north of Lae, with the intention of crossing the Owen Stanley Mountain Range to attack Port Moresby. The effort ended with the eventual retreat and death of General Tomitaro Horii, the Japanese commanding general.[10] The Lae squadron kept at least six aircraft airborne over Buna to support the beachhead but support proved difficult. On July 22, Saburo claimed a Hudson bomber and a P-39 Aircobra near Buna, raising his total to 49. On July 26, he downed two B-26s near Port Moresby. This would be the last time he attacked aircraft on the Port Moresby side of New Guinea, as the Allies were landing troops on Guadalcanal and Tulagi.

On the last day of the month, Saburo shot down a B-17 near Buna, and on August 2, participated in the destruction of five B-17s and three Aircobras over Buin. Saburo was given credit for a B-17 and an Aircobra. The Lae squadron was returned to Rabaul on August 3 to begin flying missions against the Allied landing at Guadalcanal. The round trip distance would be 1,100 miles, without allowance for combat. The first attack on Guadalcanal occurred on August 7.

Twenty-seven Betty bombers escorted by 18 Zeros began launching at 8:00 A.M. for the long trip. As they neared Guadalcanal, the pilots were awestruck at the huge armada of ships on the horizon. As the bombers descended to 13,000 feet to commence their bombing runs, six Grumman F4F fighters attacked the bombers. This was the first time Saburo's group had seen the stubby U.S. Navy fighter. The bombing attack against American transports unloading at Guadalcanal was ineffective and the bombers turned for Rabaul. Saburo shot down the first F4F he saw and a SBD, his 60th kill. As he maneuvered to attack a flight of eight Avenger torpedo planes, he was hit by fire from at least two of the Avengers at the same time he began firing at them. The two Avengers were credited as his 61st and 62nd kills, but it hardly mattered.

Saburo was hit and hit hard. He lost consciousness as his aircraft descended. Only the cold air streaming through the shattered cockpit jarred him back to consciousness. Saburo was in a dream. He could not see and was tired. All he wanted to do was sleep. Suddenly, his mother's face appeared to him. "Shame! Shame! Wake up Saburo, wake up. You are acting like a sissy. You are no coward. Wake up."[11] Saburo opened his eyes but everything was scarlet. He thought the plane was on fire but there was no smoke. Unable to see, he found the stick and pulled back gently, enough to feel the plane stop its rapid descent. As he leveled off, the wind pressure abated.

His left hand would not move and he could not move his left leg. There was no pain, just numbness. Tears began to flow from his eyes and washed some of the blood from his face. He could not hear but he could see, a little. He could not read his instruments but as he looked out the side of the cockpit, he saw dark shapes moving past the plane at a high speed. The shapes had to be enemy ships. That meant he was at an altitude of 300 feet or less. He had to climb for more altitude but seemed powerless to do so.

Abruptly, his hearing returned. First he heard the roar of his engine and then the sharp cracks of enemy gunfire. The Zero shook from the shrapnel of near misses aimed at him, but he was unable to take evasive action. Gradually the sounds of shooting fell behind him. His thoughts came and went in short spurts. At one moment he would consider diving into the sea. A few moments later he would vow to return to Rabaul. Slowly Saburo regained an appreciation of his situation. Unable to raise or move his left hand, he used his right hand to feel his helmet. It was wet and sticky with what he knew was blood. There was a deep cut in the top of his helmet.

He probed the depth of the cut and found that it extended into his skull. He believed that the bullets that caused the cut in his helmet caused damage to his brain, which caused the paralysis to his left side. He felt his face and discovered it was puffy and swollen with tears in the skin and probable pieces of metal embedded in his skin.

As his mind continued to clear and the engine of the Zero began to run normally, Saburo felt better about his situation. Abruptly, his right eye began to pain. The throb was becoming unbearable. He covered his eye with his right hand. There was no loss of vision so he realized that he was blind in that eye. He used a piece of cloth from his flight suit to clean his left eye and discovered that he had good vision in that eye. For the first time he could see both his wingtips.

Tremendous head pain engulfed Saburo. Each time he would try to put a wad of cloth into his head wound, the wind would whip the rag away. Each time he let the stick go with his right hand to tear a piece of cloth, the plane would fall off on a wing and the cloth would be whipped out of the cockpit. Four times he tried to bandage his head wound and four times the wind took the cloth. He tried to cut his muffler into pieces to push inside his helmet. Twice the wind tore the pieces of muffler away. He only had one piece of the muffler left.

The throbbing continued and each time the pain would nearly cause Saburo to lose consciousness. He finally devised a plan to hold the stick in a slight climb with his good right leg. He added power to keep his speed up and then by leaning forward, removed his seat cushion. With the seat cushion removed, he was low enough in the cockpit to reduce the effect of the wind. Slipping to his knees, Saburo successfully inserted the muffler into the side of his helmet and worked it upward to the wound. Once the cloth was wedged into the wound, the bleeding subsided and the throbbing ceased.

Once again, an overpowering weariness overtook him. He would fall asleep and then wake when his chin contacted his chest. This occurred every 30 or 40 seconds for a long time. Each time he dozed off, the Zero would lose level attitude and either fall off on a wing or, on some occasions, become inverted. Saburo would right the aircraft and then fall victim to the warm comforting embrace of sleep. He tried hitting himself on the face to keep awake, but hit himself so hard that his face began to bleed and blood spilled from his mouth.

He tried to eat part of his lunch and immediately became violently ill. He threw up the food and suffered unbearable pain from his head wound. During these times, the Zero would lurch wildly, and without his left leg for rudder control, he was unable to keep the plane in balanced flight. He was often inverted or in a skid to one side or the other. As he alternated between asleep and consciousness, the plane continued to head northeasterly towards Rabaul. Or at least Saburo assumed he was headed northeasterly. When he was able to check the compass he found he had been flying a heading of 330-degrees. Instead of flying toward Rabaul, he was headed well east of the island.

Saburo turned the aircraft 90 degrees to the left to what he hoped might be the southern tip of New Ireland, and continued to fight the drowsiness that threatened to overwhelm him. Suddenly, the engine quit. He knew instinctively that his main fuel tank had run dry but could not reach across the cockpit with his right hand to turn on the auxiliary tank. In the meantime, the Zero slipped closer and closer to the ocean. Finally, with a superhuman effort, he jerked his arm across the cockpit and turned the lever that opened the fuselage fuel tank. The engine did not start. The fuel lines had been empty too long and it became necessary to use the emergency hand pump to fill the line with fuel. Saburo worked the pump fiercely as the Zero neared the top of the ocean swells. With a roar, the engine started and Saburo applied power to start a climb back to 1,500 feet.

After the fuel emergency, Saburo was thinking clearer than he had been since his ordeal started. He adjusted his rpm to 1,700 to give him the maximum cruising distance. One hour later, with 45 minutes of fuel remaining, he recognized Green Island, which was only 60 miles from Rabaul. Next came New Ireland with its highest peak at 2,400 feet. He knew if he could make it past New Ireland, he could make it to Rabaul. Weather over New Ireland forced him to detour around the island and use precious fuel. Just past New Ireland, he spotted two Japanese cruisers and considered a water landing beside them, but they were going the wrong way and may not have stopped to rescue him. So, he kept on his heading and altitude for Rabaul.

Finally the volcano at Rabaul came in sight. How was he to land? With his left side paralyzed and no rudder control, he decided to land in the water near the beach. He descended to 50 feet and then changed his mind. He believed that the water landing might knock him unconscious and, in his current state, he would probably drown anyway. As he added power to pull up and climb back to 1,500 feet for an approach to the runway, he was spotted by his fellow pilots that had landed two hours earlier. They rushed to the runway to watch his approach to the landing strip.

Using one hand, one leg, and one eye, Saburo lowered his flaps and landing gear and started his descent. Four times he tried to line the Zero up for a landing and each time he was unable to control the torque of the engine without use of the rudders. On his fifth attempt, he switched the ignition off with the top of his boot and glided to the runway. As he hit the runway, he pulled the stick back into his lap and the Zero rolled to a halt near the command post. Then, he passed out.

Friends carried the unconscious Saburo to a car and hurried him to the base hospital. The base surgeon cleaned his wounds, and removed some 50-caliber shrapnel from his skull, but there was little more he could do at Rabaul. Saburo would have to be evacuated to Japan where a specialist could tend to his paralysis and right eye. Four days later Saburo started to have feeling in his left hand and leg. He was put on a flying boat and, after a refueling stop at Truk, arrived at Yokohama.

Although it was Sunday, the chief surgeon and the best eye surgeon in Japan awaited Saburo's arrival. Saburo was strapped tightly down to a high bed and warned that the doctors could not use anesthetics. His head wound was cleaned and 14 stitches applied. Sakai was told to gaze at a red lamp hanging from the ceiling and never to take his gaze from it. If he did so, he could lose his total sight forever.

Saburo described the procedure as horrible. "It was the most frightful pain I had ever known. I screamed. More than once I shrieked like a madman from the terrible agony."[12] "Shut up!" the doctor roared. "You must endure this! Otherwise you will go blind." The operation lasted 30 minutes. When it was over Saburo was too weak to move a finger. For a full month he was confined to a hospital bed. Finally the doctor told him, "I did everything I could, but your right eye will never recover. Your left eye will be perfectly all right."[13]

Saburo soon had full use of his left arm and leg, and each week he submitted an application to be transferred back to Rabaul. Finally, the chief surgeon, tiring of his applications, told him that he was to have a six-month convalescence leave before he was assigned to duty anywhere. Saburo was sent to Sasebo Naval Base for convalescence and to be closer to his home in Sago. He was grateful for the opportunity to spend the time with his mother, family, and friends.

Before Saburo left for Sasebo, he was visited in the Yokosuka hospital by Fujiko and her father, professor Niori. After some small talk, Mr. Niori spoke solemnly, "Saburo-san, will you accept my daughter as your bride?" Saburo gasped at the surprise request. After composing himself, he answered, "I am greatly honored. But I cannot accept your offer." Saburo used the excuse of his being blind in one eye as not being an appropriate husband for Fujiko. Professor Niori and Fujiko were having none of Saburo's excuses. The lack of an eye meant nothing to them.

Saburo told them that he lacked a college education, and the loss of his eye would hamper his future and make him an unacceptable husband for Fujiko. In summary, Saburo said he did not deserve the love of Fujiko. It was almost an hour and many emotional outbursts and tears later before the professor and Fujiko left the hospital. Saburo would not see Fujiko again.

While at Sasebo, Saburo learned that Lieutenants Sasai, Ota, Yonekawa, and Hatori from his unit in Rabaul had all been shot down and killed during the battle for Guadalcanal. During January 1943, he was transferred from Sasebo to a training base in central Japan. Saburo loved flying the Zero again but soon became bored teaching the new recruits to fly. The war news was all bad for Japan, and Saburo began badgering his superiors for assignment to a combat theater. Instead, he was assigned as a flight instructor at Omura, a training base at Sasebo. He remained there until April 1944, when he was transferred to an air wing at Yokosuka.

On June 15, Japan was shocked when 20 B-17 bombers from China bombed northern Kyushu. Then they learned that Saipan had been invaded. The war was coming closer to Japan. The next day, Saburo's Yokosuka Wing was transferred to Iwo Jima, and Saburo was allowed to go with them. For the first few days, Saburo did not fly missions in support of the forces on Saipan, but on June 24 he and 80 other Zero pilots launched to meet an enemy attack enroute to Iwo Jima.

Saburo quickly shot down two Grumman Hellcats, the first

ones he had ever seen, and then fell into a trap involving 15 of the Hellcats. For nearly an hour the Hellcats kept Saburo inside their circle while they made continuous firing passes at him. Saburo was able to roll sharply to the left each time an enemy pilot started to fire his guns. He evaded the shells, but he could not break out of the circle. Finally, the circle of aircraft passed over Iwo Jima and the antiaircraft guns opened up. The sky was filled with flame as flashes appeared from all over the island. The Hellcats turned steeply and fled out of range. After landing, Saburo climbed down from the cockpit to be greeted by his fellow pilots that landed more than an hour earlier. After examining Saburo's plane, his crew chief reported that there was not a single bullet hole in his plane. His Yokosuka Wing was not so fortunate however; they lost 40 pilots to the navy Hellcats.

Saburo spent a week in the hospital with a bad case of diarrhea, likely caused by the rainwater that comprised the total fresh water at Iwo. As he reflected upon the recent air battle, Saburo felt that the war had come full circle. In the beginning, the experienced Japanese pilots and the Zero aircraft ruled the skies. Now, the Zero had become obsolete and the Japanese were the inexperienced pilots.

Enemy carrier-based aircraft attacked Iwo Jima on July 2. Fifty Hellcats escorted a group of Avenger torpedo-bombers and were met by the remaining 40 Zeros. As the fighter aircraft engaged, three separate groups of Avengers bombed and strafed the airfield complex on Iwo Jima. Saburo was not in the initial group of 40 Zero fighters that rose to meet the Hellcats. Now, on the ground, he wished he had been. The bombs were coming much to close. He sprinted to the only remaining Zero on the field. The engine had been reported as being underpowered, but Saburo didn't mind. The crew chief reported that he thought they had fixed the engine. Saburo started the plane and got airborne just as the fourth enemy bombing group arrived. As he headed for the group of fighters in the distance, a fifth group of Avengers dived on Iwo. When this bombing group departed, so did the enemy fighters.

The Yokosuka Wing lost 20 Zeros. It did not matter how many Hellcats were shot down. The U.S. Navy could replace their planes and pilots, Japan could not. The two landing fields on Iwo were in shambles. Ground crews cleared enough of one runway for their planes to land, but work on the runways continued all night. Next morning the Hellcats and Avengers attacked again and only nine Zero fighters returned from the dogfight. Again Iwo was razed. The installation was wrecked, buildings were on fire, the runway cratered, and many facilities destroyed.

A decision was made to attack the enemy carriers early on July 4 to repay them for their punishing bombing attacks. Before the Yokosuka Wing could take off, the enemy carrier aircraft hit them again. The runway was so badly damaged that no aircraft could takeoff. As soon as the runway was repaired, nine names were drawn; a pilot for each remaining fighter aircraft. Saburo was the ninth name to be called. Each Zero would be armed with a torpedo. (Saburo calls the weapon a torpedo, but it had to be a bomb, since the Zero could not carry a torpedo). Seven single-engine bomber aircraft would also accompany the fighters. The pilots were then assembled and told that they were to plunge their aircraft and weapon into an enemy carrier and sink it.[14] Saburo was stunned. This was the first time a Japanese pilot was ordered to make a suicide attack.

Eight Zeros and all seven bombers got airborne. After an hour flight, 50 or more Hellcats protecting the U.S. fleet met them. Saburo and his trio of aircraft tried to ignore the fighters and press on towards the enemy fleet, but it was impossible. Planes were being shot down all around them. Saburo shot down one enemy fighter and then took cover in a thunderstorm and tried to outrun the enemy fighters. His flight entered heavy rain and then it got dark. Saburo thought his only option was to try to return to Iwo Jima and live to fight again another day.

Two hours later he located Iwo Jima and, with the use of four lanterns that were turned on, he was able to land his flight of three aircraft. He found that one other Zero and a single bomber had also returned. Twelve aircraft were lost without reaching the enemy fleet.

The following day, 16 American warships pounded Iwo Jima. The bombardment continued for 48 hours. Every structure on Iwo Jima was destroyed-not even a tent remained. The five remaining aircraft were destroyed and the projectiles killed several hundred army and navy support troops. Iwo Jima was only defended by a battalion of army troops. It was available to the enemy with hardly a fight, but the U.S. Navy had other plans. Iwo Jima was bypassed and the navy turned to the Philippines. Iwo Jima would not be attacked again for eight months.

A few days after the naval bombardment, seven Betty bombers that had been converted into courier planes arrived to take the staff officers and pilots back to Japan. The aircraft loaded all but 11 of the more junior enlisted pilots and departed. Saburo was left behind with ten other enlisted pilots. The next day, a decrepit "flying wreck" arrived to return the last 11 pilots. The plane's engine had to be repaired for several hours before the plane could get airborne. Saburo was in a seat near the right engine and could see the engine vibrating so bad that it was in danger of breaking its mountings. "Turn back," he told the crew. "With that engine we will never make Japan."[15] The crew obeyed. The plane, after more repair and spark plug replacement, took off several hours later for another attempt to reach Japan.

An hour-and-a-half later, the plane encountered a violent thunderstorm. The plane was buffeted badly and leaked water from many openings in the fuselage. The pilot asked Saburo if he should try to go above the storm or below it. "Take it below," Saburo ordered.[16] The pilot took the plane down to just above the wave tops in an effort to reduce the pressure on the plane. "Where are we now?" the pilot asked Saburo.[17] "Get out of that seat! I'm taking over," Saburo ordered and scrambled into the pilot's seat. For another 90 minutes Saburo flew the plane in the pouring rain before Tokyo Bay came into view.

A month after returning to Tokyo, Saburo was promoted to the grade of ensign. He was assigned to the Yokusuka Air Wing as a trainer and a test pilot. He married his cousin, Hatsuyo, on February 11, 1945, following the second air raid attack of the day. Saburo had never forgotten Hatsuyo, largely through her efforts to keep in touch with him and her insistence upon marriage. She prevailed where Fujiko failed.

The following month, the Japanese Navy broke with precedent in announcing a special citation to NAP 1/C Shoichi Sugita and to Saburo. Normally such citations were awarded posthumously. Sugita was recognized for shooting down 120 enemy aircraft and shot down four more after the citation. Within a month he was dead, killed in his aircraft while taxiing for takeoff.

As the war wound down, B-29 bombing raids and then firebombing raids made Tokyo and its environs a terrible place to live. On March 10, 130,000 people died when Tokyo was firebombed and 19 square miles of the city were destroyed. On August 13, Saburo and the other pilots were notified that the emperor had decided to accept the terms of the Allied Potsdam Declaration (unconditional surrender). Later in the day, Sakai and his friend Ensign Jiro Kawachi made plans to move two Zero fighters to the runway and intercept a B-29 bomber if they were attacked that night.

Shortly before midnight, the air raid siren sounded and the two pilots ran to the aircraft they had moved to the edge of the runway. They discovered eight other Zero pilots had the same plan. All ten aircraft took off and climbed to 10,000 feet above Tokyo Bay. Kawachi and Sakai each made a firing pass on the superfortress and discovered that the other eight fighters were firing at the same B-29. Again and again the fighters attacked the huge bomber as it turned and headed south. Kawachi and Saburo followed, and were able to make one long firing pass each before the bomber dove away.

The bomber displayed no fire or smoke but it slowed and went into a long dive. By following it down, Sakai was able to see the huge bomber splash into the ocean several miles from shore. It disappeared under the water in less than a minute. The following day, the air commander grounded all pilots and aircraft. The war was over less than 12 hours later. At noon, the emperor read his surrender announcement. Men cried unashamedly and many killed themselves in front of the Imperial Palace. Saburo went home to Hatsuyo. The war was over, and he was Japan's surviving leading ace.

Saburo Sakai, Japan's leading WW II ace who survived the war.

John Connor

17

THERE'S MORE THAN SNOW AT NAGANO

The Rooftop of Japan

Nagano Prefecture in Japan hosted the XVIII Winter Olympics in 1998. The games, weather, and Nagano itself were the subject of extensive television, radio, and print media coverage as the games unfolded. Not mentioned in such coverage is the secret story of Matsushiro, a story even more chilling than the weather and solid rock surrounding Nagano.

In 1944, Matsushiro was a small village on a railway line, on the southern edge of Nagano. Today, it is part of the much larger city, but is still referred to as the "Little Kyoto of the Shinto region" of Nagano.

Nagano, often described as "the rooftop of Japan," is the most mountainous prefecture in a mountainous country. The three steep mountain ranges in the prefecture — the Hida, Kiso, and Akaishi ranges — with peaks extending to 3,190 meters, are snow covered all year long. The mountains were first described as "Alps" by English mining engineer William Gowland in 1881.

The secret of Matsushiro lies inside the mountains of the Japanese Alps, the mountains that provided the setting for the downhill, alpine, and other Olympic events. Within these mountains exist the tunnels prepared for Japan's Imperial Headquarters, and the memory of thousands of atrocities committed in the name of Japan's emperor.

The underground tunnels that form the Imperial Headquarters of Matsushiro were constructed to house Emperor Hirohito and the empress near the end of World War II. The fact that the tunneling was done through solid rock by the bare hands of thousands of Korean laborers is impressive. Even more impressive is the fact that the tunneling was done in complete secrecy. Such secrecy was essential because if the Japanese people had learned that the emperor planned to escape to Matsushiro, it would be obvious that Japan was losing the war. What is far from impressive is that the underground labyrinth was constructed at the cost of thousands of Korean lives.

Construction of the Imperial Headquarters began on November 11, 1944, and ended on August 15, 1945, with the emperor's announcement of unconditional surrender. Inside the headquarters are more than ten kilometers of underground tunnels with a floor space of 23,404 square meters that testify to the scope of this project.

Work on the underground headquarters was done by the Nishimatsu-gume construction company under army supervision. The conscripted Korean laborers toiled under relentless pressure to complete the project within the scheduled time. Ironically, one of the engineer supervisors, Mr. Kim Sok Ji, was Korean, but was not recognized as being Korean at the time because he graduated from Osaka University and used the name Mihara.

No one knows the exact number of Koreans who were worked to death and then cremated at Matsushiro. Japanese government officials burnt all the documentation concerning the tunnel before

American occupation forces could arrive. Yamane Masako, a Korean child whose father died working at Matsushiro, recalls that the Korean laborers were forced to work 12 hours a day, in skimpy clothing, bleeding feet wrapped in rags, and were fed a single bowl of sorghum each day. Masako also remembers that the smoke from the crematorium at Matsushiro never stopped. Every day Korean conscripts were brought directly to the crematorium ovens. Masako compares the ovens of Matsushiro to Germany's Auschwitz.

The entrance to the underground tunnel at Matsushiro.

J.T. Hagen

Masako also remembers that the Koreans who labored on the tunnels disappeared on August 15, 1945, the day that the emperor announced Japan's surrender. The men vanished without a trace. The assumption has to be that they were murdered and cremated in order to preserve the secret of Matsushiro, and for the Japanese to avoid prosecution for war crimes. Mr. Kim Sok Ji estimates the number of Korean laborers at about 7,000. He states that the workers were housed in 152 barracks and were worked unmercifully in unsafe conditions until they died.

Also at Matsushiro was a "comfort station" for the army officers who supervised construction of the complex. A Korean male, known as Haruyama, brought in the first group of young women from Korea. Later, more Korean women from northern Japan were brought to Matsushiro to act as sex slaves for the military.

The underground facility still exists, too large to ignore, but apparently best left alone and forgotten. Forgotten, and also left alone, are the pleas from family members of those who labored and died at Matsushiro. These few remaining relatives have waited for more than 50 years for some acknowledgment from the government of Japan as to what did happen at Matsushiro on August 15, 1945. Such an acknowledgment no longer appears likely.

The tunnel complex inside Matsushiro. Entrance to the tunnel is along the heavy line.

J.T. Hagen

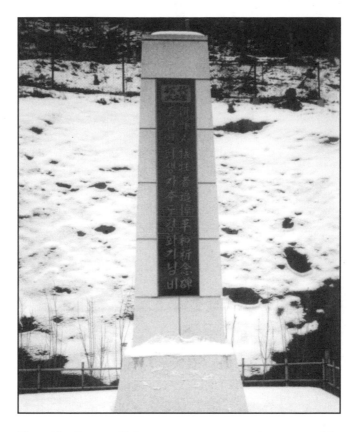

Matsushiro Oomoto Shrine — a peace monument in memory of the Koreans who died at Matsushiro.

J.T. Hagen

If you decide to visit "Nagano's secret," you will be able to get directions to Matsushiro. Once there, signs will direct you to the Zozan shrine and the Sanada clan temple, but you will have to find your own way to the underground Imperial Headquarters. Nagano prefecture officials do not mention Matsushiro.

Entrance to the tunnel is permitted on weekends, and although you will not find signs directing you there, you can get directions to the Meteorological Agency Earthquake Observation Station, which is located in the tunnels. Ask for directions to the seismographic facility in Matsushiro.

197

General MacArthur and his chief of staff, Lieutenant Gen. Sutherland, arrive in Leyte Gulf.

National Archives

18

THE BATTLE OF LEYTE GULF:
THE FIRST STRIKING FORCE

The Battle of Leyte Gulf is often referred to as the greatest naval engagement ever fought, and the largest naval battle in history. All aspects of naval warfare (air, surface, submarine, and amphibious) were involved in the struggle. Without question, it involved more ships (282), more men (200,000), and a greater area, (100,000 square miles), than any other naval engagement.[1] Leyte Gulf was the last gasp of the Japanese navy. If the Japanese Navy, with inferior forces, could not stop the Allied invasion of the Philippines, Japan was doomed.

The battle took place because of General Douglas MacArthur's dogged determination that the Allies should return to the Philippines rather than Formosa or China in their next leap across the Pacific. The first landing on Philippine soil was planned to be Mindanao on November 15, 1944. Once airfields and support facilities were established on Mindanao, Allied forces would invade Leyte Gulf, about December 20. These plans changed as the result of Admiral Bull Halsey's urgent message to Admiral Nimitz in September 1944.

Task Force 38, a fast carrier force, commanded by Vice Adm. Marc Mitscher, flew 2,400 sorties against Japanese targets in the central Philippines on September 12 and 13. As a result, Halsey found the Philippines to be "a hollow shell with weak defenses and skimpy facilities."[2] After a long period of consultation with his staff, Halsey sent an urgent message recommending that the planned operations against the Taluds, Mindanao, the Palaus, and Yap be canceled, and that Leyte be invaded as soon as possible.

Halsey's message stated that:

> the Japanese had few serviceable planes, most of their oil storage had been destroyed, and there was no shipping left to sink. On Leyte itself, there were no Japanese and the area was wide open.[3]

Nimitz forwarded Halsey's recommendation to the joint chiefs of staff, and made available his Third Amphibious Force and Twenty-fourth Army Corps, which were already loading at Pearl Harbor for the invasion of Yap. In less than two hours, Admiral Nimitz and General MacArthur were notified of the approval of Halsey's recommendation, and a target date of October 20 was established for the invasion of Leyte.

The Battle of Leyte Gulf involved many forces, fleets, and personalities engaged in events simultaneously. There were four separate engagements (Sibuyan Sea, Surigao Strait, Samar, and Cape Engano). In addition to the aspects of naval warfare listed earlier, the Japanese introduced kamikaze attacks on a large scale.

The actual assault on Leyte began on October 20, and relative to most amphibious operations in the Pacific, it was easy. The weather was perfect. There was no surf, no mines, or underwater obstacles, and more importantly, little enemy resistance. The main airfields were seized on October 21. By midnight, 132,400 men and nearly 200,000 tons of supplies were ashore.[4]

The naval battle began on the morning of October 23, when submarine *Darter* reported Japanese ships transiting Palawan Passage. *Darter* reported 11 vessels, estimated to be battleships, cruisers, and destroyers on a northeast course. These were part of the force later called Central Force. On the 23rd, *Darter,* joined by *Dace,* attacked the Japanese fleet in Palawan passage, sinking two heavy cruisers (flagship *Atago* and *Mayo*), and severely damaging *Takao.* These were the first ship casualties of the Battle of Leyte Gulf.

Halsey ordered search planes to locate the Japanese force attacked by *Darter* and *Dace,* and was rewarded on October 24, with a report that the force consisted of 27 ships, battleships, cruisers, and destroyers. The Japanese Center Force was passing the southern tip of Mindoro Island as if intending to enter the Sibuyan Sea. Also discovered by search planes on the same day was a smaller Japanese force, termed Southern Force, heading east in the Sulu Sea. Southern Force, was attacked by carrier aircraft that reported slightly damaging a battleship and a destroyer.

Southern Force consisted of two separate forces. The first was commanded by Vice Adm. K. Shima with three cruisers and four destroyers. The second was commanded by Vice Adm. S. Nishimura, and consisted of battleships *Fuso* and *Yamashiro,* heavy cruiser *Mogami,* and four destroyers. Halsey estimated that Southern Force would enter Surigao Strait to the south of Leyte Gulf and attack the landing force.

During the battle of Surigao Strait on October 24 and 25, Nishimura dashed ahead of Shima's force and came under torpedo attack from Destroyer Squadron 54. The destroyers sank Japanese battleship *Fuso,* three of the Japanese destroyers, and damaged the other destroyer. Later, as Nakashima's force exchanged fire with American cruisers and battleships, *Yamashiro,* Nishimura's flagship was sunk, taking with her the admiral and all but a few members of her crew.[5]

Admiral Kinkaid, commander of the landing force, at Leyte, estimated the Southern Force to consist of two battleships, eight cruisers, and ten destroyers. He announced his intention to prepare for a night surface engagement with Southern Force.

Center Force was commanded by Vice Adm. Takeo Kurita and was berthed at Lingga Roads, across the strait from Singapore. The movement of this force from Japan to Malaya was necessitated by Japan's inability to transport the necessary fuel for training by its navy. Kurita was 55 years old and had been an admiral since

1938. His mission was to proceed to Brunei, and from there to San Bernardino Strait, where he was to force passage, engage the enemy in a night action off Samar, and then destroy the enemy landing attempt at Leyte.

Kurita's only hope of success depended upon the ability of Vice Adm. Jisaburo Ozawa, commander of the Japanese carrier force, to decoy Admiral Halsey away from Leyte Gulf. The tasking for both men bordered on a suicide mission but neither objected.

Kurita left Lingga Roads on October 18, with the two super battleships, *Musashi* and *Yamato,* the mightiest warships in the world, and with the older battleship *Nagato,* the only three ships with 18-inch guns. Older battleships*, Kongo* and *Haruna* mounted 14-inch guns. Kurita also had 12 heavy cruisers and 15 modern destroyers.

When Kurita's force arrived at Brunei on October 20, they learned that they were expected to make a daylight attack upon the Allied forces. This change nearly generated a rebellion among division commanders and staff. They had planned and trained for a night action, and felt competent to conduct one. Kurita explained that by attacking during daylight they could be supported by suicide aircraft attacking the Allied fleet from land bases on Samar and Leyte. This would be the only air support they could expect.[6] The rebellion quickly subsided.

Halsey estimated that Center Force would pass through San Bernardino Strait and engage the landing force in Leyte Gulf. Halsey had three carrier groups maintaining position off Leyte Gulf consisting of 11 attack carriers, six battleships, nine cruisers, and 44 destroyers. To his commanders, he gave the position of the Japanese fleet and a one-word operation order, "Strike."[7] For three-and-a-half hours, the three carrier groups launched massive attacks against the Center Force ships. By early afternoon, pilots estimated that all five of the battleships they attacked had been hit and seriously damaged as was a cruiser.

Both *Musashi* and *Yamato* were thought to be listing and sinking. *Musashi* did sink, and cruiser *Miyoko* was disabled. At 2:00 P.M., Center Force reversed course and was reported heading west.

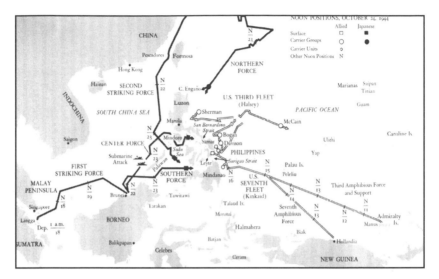

The approach to Leyte Gulf by the Japanese First and Second Stiking Forces, and the Northern and Southern Forces.

US Navy

Later that afternoon, Halsey sent a "Battle Plan" to his commanders in the event Center Force turned back east and entered San Bernardino Strait. The plan called for the formation of a new Task Force 34, with four battleships, five cruisers, and two divisions of destroyers to meet such a threat. Halsey intended the message only as an alert, and that Task Force 34 would only be formed when he so directed.

On the evening of October 24, scout planes reported three Japanese carriers, four or more cruisers, and six destroyers to the north of Leyte Gulf. This force was called the Northern Force. Halsey, impetuous as always, saw an opportunity to destroy the enemy carriers and other ships. After extensive consultations with his staff, Halsey made the decision to run north at top speed with all three of his carrier groups, "to put those (Japanese) carriers out for keeps."[8] He notified his fleet commanders that he was heading north at 25 knots and went to bed.

When Admiral Ozawa, commander of the Northern Force, returned from the disastrous defeat at the Marianas, Japan's carrier fleet had only 120 planes remaining. Ozawa had six carriers and two battleships converted to a flight deck that could accomodate 24 planes, but could only obtain fuel, crews, and supplies for four carriers for the Leyte Gulf battle (*Zuikako, Zuiho, Chitose,* and *Chiyoda*). What he did not have were planes and experienced pilots. Nevertheless, Ozawa's orders were to lure, engage, and destroy the enemy. One can only guess at Ozawa's true feelings. With a few airplanes, three cruisers, and some destroyers, he was to dispose of Admiral Halsey and the Third Fleet, and then attack and destroy the landing forces. Clearly, Ozawa needed a miracle.

As Halsey took the bait offered by Ozawa, he neglected to form Task Force 34 to defend San Bernardino Strait. Captain Arleigh Burke, Admiral Mitscher's chief of staff was the first to accurately pronounce the Japanese carriers as shells and therefore decoys. Burke reasoned that if the Japanese carriers had an offensive capability, they would have joined with the land based *kamikaze* aircraft during the day to exert greater punishment upon the Allied fleet. Burke was well aware of the slaughter of Japanese pilots and planes that took place in the Marianas (Marianas Turkey Shoot), and area around Formosa. The carriers are helpless he reasoned, and therefore only serve as bait to lure Halsey's Third Fleet away form Leyte Gulf to assist the Central Force.

Burke asked Admiral Mitscher to notify Halsey of his theory, but Mitscher refused to criticize Halsey's plan. Admiral Willis Lee, commander of Halsey's battle line for defense of Leyte Gulf, was not so reticent. He conveyed a similar message to Halsey, aboard USS *New Jersey,* by flashing light. His message was acknowledged but not acted upon. Halsey's staff considered the idea of using priceless carriers as decoys ludicrous.

Search planes from USS *Independence* reported that Center Force had reversed course and was headed toward San Bernardino Strait. Now more senior officers became alarmed. Admiral Bogan, commander of one of the carrier task forces with Halsey, asked Halsey's staff if they should not consider forming Task Force 34 and send it back to Leyte to meet the Center Force. Halsey's staff brushed off the advice, causing Mitscher to remark, If he (Halsey) wants my advice, he'll ask for it."[9]

At 2:00 A.M., on the 25th, a radar-equipped hellcat fighter made contact with Northern Force. The force was in two sections, and less than a hundred miles to the north. Halsey did not want his carriers involved in a night surface engagement and ordered Task Force 34 to be formed and sent ahead to engage the Northern Force. Halsey's message to Admirals King, Nimitz, and Kinkaid, plus General MacArthur, stated that his force was in three concentrated groups. If there had been any doubt, the message should have conveyed the obvious fact that Halsey in battleship *New Jersey* was with Task Force 34, hundreds of miles north of San Bernardino Strait. The message did not convey such meaning to any of the addressees of the message.

At 4:12 A.M., Admiral Kinkaid informed Halsey that the Southern Force was being engaged in Surigao Strait and asked if Task Force 34 was guarding San Bernardino Strait. There was no response from Halsey until 7:00, when he responded, "Negative. Task Force 34 is with carrier groups now engaging enemy carrier force."[10] Kinkaid was amazed and appropriately concerned.

Daylight came with no contact between Task Force 34 and the Northern Force. Admiral Mitscher launched a 180-plane strike from the three carrier groups hoping to attack the Japanese carriers before they could launch their aircraft. There were no Japanese carriers. At 7:10 A. M., a scout plane found the Northern Force much farther north than the initial report. The latest report indicated Northern Force as having 17 ships, including four carriers, two battleships with flight decks (the *Isye* and *Hyuga*), several cruisers, and eight destroyers. Halsey was pursuing with ten carriers, and a total of 64 warships.[11]

Kinkaid's next message was sent to Halsey at 6:23 A.M. and received at 8:02 A.M. Kinkaid reported that the Southern Force had been repulsed in Surigao Straight and was retiring. Halsey was delighted and looked forward to an even greater victory over the Northern Force. Halsey was surprised 30 minutes later when he received a plain-language dispatch that said the northernmost escort group (Taffy 3) off Leyte Gulf was receiving fire from enemy battleships and cruisers, some 15 miles distant. The enemy ships San Bernadino Straight during the night.

A few minutes later, Halsey received another message from Admiral Kinkaid announcing that, "fast battleships are needed immediately at Leyte Gulf."[7] With great reluctance, Halsey ordered one of his carrier groups to proceed to Leyte Gulf. After dispatching the force to Leyte, Halsey was handed a report of the first strikes against the Northern Force. His pilots reported one carrier sunk, two others damaged, and one cruiser badly damaged. The pilots reported no enemy aircraft opposition. A second strike was already on its way.

Northern Force was making 17 knots while Halsey's force was moving at 25. Halsey estimated that by noon his force would be close enough to engage the enemy in an old fashioned surface action, something that he had not participated in during his career. As Halsey anticipated such action, another plea for help arrived from Admiral Kinkaid. The message, received at 9:00 A.M., reported that an enemy force of four battleships, eight cruisers, and other ships was attacking the lightly-armed escort carriers in Leyte Gulf. The message requested surface ship and fast carrier support.

Halsey was fast running out of patience. His dream of

destroying the enemy by a surface action was only hours away, but he was being pressured to detach his forces and give up the opportunity.

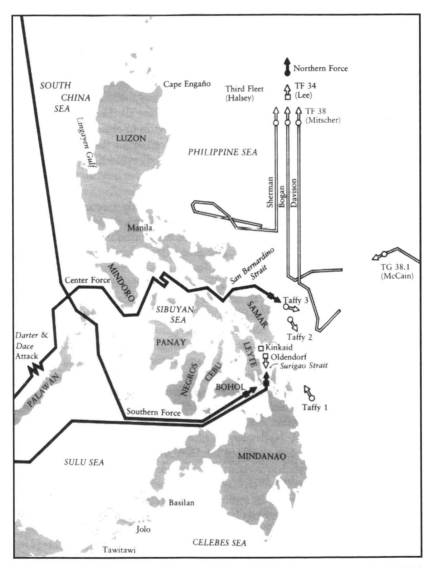

The Battle for Leyte Gulf on October 23-25, 1941. The lighter lines depict Halsey's Third Fleet chase of the Japanese Northern Force.

US Navy

Admiral William Halsey followed the Northern Force decoy while Admiral Kinkaid met with Japan's Central Force.

US Navy

Vice Adm. Ozawa was commander of the Northern Force and led Admiral Halsey away from Leyte Gulf.

National Archives

19

THE BATTLE OF LEYTE GULF:
THE JEEP CARRIERS

While Admiral Halsey pursued the Northern Force, Admiral Kurita's powerful Center Force passed through unguarded San Bernardino Strait, and engaged the six escort carriers of "Taffy 3," off Samar Island.

Taffy 3 was the designation of one of the three carrier task units that provided antisubmarine, antiaircraft, and ground aviation support for the amphibious force. The entire force consisted of 16 escort carriers, screened by destroyers and destroyer escorts. The three Taffy groups were located about ten miles apart. Perhaps the escorts carriers' finest hour came at Leyte Gulf.

The official name for the escort carriers was aircraft carrier escort (CVE), but everyone called them "jeep carriers" due to their diminutive size. The jeeps had few, if any, armor piercing bombs or torpedoes for use against battleships and cruisers, and were no match for Kurita's Center Force.

Henry Kaiser built 109 jeep carriers from June 1941 through June 1944. Of this number, 33 were delivered to Great Britain. The jeeps were built on construction lines on the west coast, and most of the workers were women. Because they were built so quickly, many of the ships had peculiar characteristics and makeshift arrangements that failed when least expected or desired.

Many of the ships were equipped with the Skinner Uniflow turbine engine. The engines were unique to a small class of ore carrying ships on the Great Lakes. Skinner had a surplus of the uniflow engines and the navy was quick to purchase them.

Because the engines were unique, their maintenance was not taught in the navy's technical schools. There were no manuals and few spare parts. None of the navy machinists or enginemen had any knowledge of how to maintain the uniflow. Of course they gained a great deal of knowledge over the four years the engines were used. A knowledgeable uniflow engine mechanic became a valuable commodity aboard a CVE.

The metal used for the skin of the jeeps was of a very thin gauge, that crinkled and crackled like a tin can in heavy seas. Sailors found the experience of going through a storm in a jeep to be an unnerving experience. How thin was the hull metal? It was so thin, that it failed to detonate the primers of Japanese eight-inch cruiser shells. Shells fired into *Mount Hood* passed through both sides of the ship and only exploded when they hit the water, because the water was harder than the steel of the ship.[1]

Jeeps began supporting amphibious assaults on November 24, 1943, at Makin Gulf. They also ferried aircraft from the U.S. to overseas locations.

The USS *Bismarck Sea* (CVE-95) loading planes from a barge.

US Navy

The first CVE casualty, *Liscome Bay*, was torpedoed by the Japanese submarine *I-175*, at Makin. The torpedo exploded in the bomb-storage area, resulting in subsequent explosions that essentially disintegrated the aft of the ship. *Liscome Bay* sank stern first, 23 minutes after being torpedoed. Only 272 of the crew of 913 officers and men survived.

On October 25, 1944, Admiral Takeo Kurita exited San Bernadino Strait with the world's largest battleship, IMS *Yamato*, several cruisers and destroyers. The ships were termed Center Force by the Allies. Kurita's mission was to destroy the Allied transports in Leyte Gulf. Because Admiral Halsey had taken the attack carriers north to engage the Japanese carrier force (Northern Force), the only force that stood between Kurita and the transports was Taffy 3.

Yamato was armed with 18-inch guns, the largest in the world. The cruisers had eight-inch guns and the "Long Lance" torpedo. The jeeps had the F4F fighter aircraft and a thin skin. All Japanese ships had a speed in excess of 30 knots. The jeeps' uniflow engine, when operating perfectly, could move the CVE at 18 knots. It promised to be a most uneven battle.[2]

As soon as Taffy 3 became aware of Kurita's presence, the goal was to put as much distance between themselves and the attacking force as possible, and to attack Kurita's forces with their aircraft. The CVEs were not able to steam into the wind because Kurita was in that direction. They had to turn southwesterly, and hope they had sufficient wind over the deck to launch aircraft continuously.

There was mass confusion when the aircraft returned from their short-distance bombing and torpedo attacks. Many of the aircraft were shot down and the escort carriers were receiving heavy shelling from *Yamato* and the cruisers. Aircraft landed on any deck they could find, rearmed, refueled, and took off again. This procedure continued for several hours since Kurita had no need to close the distance between the forces. His ships could remain "over the horizon" and lob shells fifteen miles into the jeep carriers.

Vice Admiral Fitzhugh Lee, commander of the jeep carrier, Manila Bay, recalled after the battle that one of the most unpleasant chores he had to perform that day was to load a TBM torpedo bomber from another ship with his last torpedo. The pilot had already made two attacks against *Yamato*, and had seen most of his squadron mates shot down. Lee's concern was that he had sent the young pilot to his death. He was delighted to learn that the pilot made the third torpedo attack, survived the ordeal, and landed on yet another carrier.[3]

The new *Essex* Class USS *Randolph* in the Pacific in January, 1944.

Two jeep carriers and three escort destroyers were sunk early in the battle. The American destroyers, although not credited with sinking any Japanese ships, gained praise for their continued daring torpedo attacks against the far larger Japanese ships. It seems likely that they created part of the confusion that influenced Kurita's subsequent decision.

At this time, no Japanese ships had been sunk, and it seemed only a matter of time before Taffy 3 would be completely destroyed.

Then a miracle occurred. Admiral Kurita, with a clear path to the transports, reversed course, and withdrew his force to the north. After the war, Kurita stated that he was confused by the aggressiveness of the CVE aircraft, thinking they may have come from the larger attack carriers, and that Halsey had returned from the north with such forces. Kurita knew he could not survive attacks by the attack carrier aircraft. Perhaps the real reason for Kurita's decision went to the grave with him. Certainly, it was the jeep carriers' finest hour, but the same could not be said for the mighty *Yamato* force.

Halsey continued to receive messages of alarm from Admiral Kinkaid, and one from Rear Admiral Ziggy Sprauge, commander of Taffy 3. The messages stated that Taffy 3 was under attack by battleships and cruisers located fifteen miles to the north. Kinkaid's messages asked for fast carrier support. The only available fast carriers were with Halsey, several hundred miles to the north.

The final blow to Halsey's plan to destroy the Japanese Northern Force in a ship battle came at 10:00 A.M., on June 25. Following two more messages from Admiral Kinkaid that pleaded for battleship and carrier aircraft support, Halsey received a message from Admiral Nimitz that asked, "WHERE IS RPT WHERE IS TASK FORCE-THIRTY FOUR RR THE WRLD WONDERS."[4]

Task Force-34 was the force Halsey planned to form and leave for protection of the landing force at Leyte Gulf while he pursued the Japanese Northern Force. He did not do so. The sentence, "THE WORLD WONDERS" was merely padding for the message added by a radioman, but Halsey did not know that and assumed Nimitz was censuring him for his decision to chase the Northern Force.

Thus ended Halsey's dream of destroying Northern Force and started what some describe as "Bull Run, or the Battle of Bull's Run,"[5] as Halsey turned his carrier forces and steamed at full speed to protect the amphibious force in Leyte Gulf. Long before Halsey's forces could arrive, Admiral Kurita departed Leyte Gulf. Halsey's fast battleships steamed 300 miles north and then 300 miles south without making contact with the enemy.

When Halsey's force reached San Bernadino Strait a little after midnight, the only Japanese ship remaining in the area was a destroyer picking up Japanese survivors from the Taffy 3 battle. Halsey, on his distant flagship, New Jersey, had to be content with watching his destroyers and cruisers destroy the Japanese destroyer. "The first and only surface action I saw during my entire career," Halsey lamented.[6]

Halsey's attack on Northern Force, termed the Battle off Cape Engano, resulted in the sinking of attack carrier *Zuikako*, three light carriers, and two destroyers. One cruiser was also damaged and subsequently sunk by an American submarine. Of the 13 ships in Northern Force, ten returned to Japan. It is conceivable that Halsey could have destroyed them all if he had been able to continue his pursuit. Perhaps two miracles occurred on June 25, one for each side.

Total losses for the Japanese navy were 306,000 tons of combatant ships, including three battleships, four carriers, ten cruisers, and nine destroyers. The U.S. Navy lost 37,000 tons of warships, including one light carrier, two CVEs, two destroyers, and one destroyer escort.

Later, when Halsey was criticized for taking the carrier force north, his decision was fully supported by Admirals Nimitz, and King, and General MacArthur. MacArthur sent a message to Halsey stating his complete confidence and inspiration when Halsey goes into battle, and King told Halsey that he had a green light on everything he did.

20

USS *FRANKLIN*

USS *Franklin* was a carrier of the new Essex class. She was damaged in the battle of the Philippine Sea, and returned to Bremerton, Washington, for repairs. In December 1944, she returned to the Pacific under command of Captain Les Gehres. The officer responsible for the control and training of 100 fighters, dive-bombers, and torpedo planes was Commander E. B. Parker.

Franklin arrived at Ulithi during January 1945. Besides Franklin, there were 30 carriers and dozens of battleships, cruisers, destroyers, ammunition ships and tankers. As *Franklin* passed the rows of ships at anchor, the ships' crews turned out on deck, honors were rendered, and the message, "Welcome back to the fighting forces,"[1] was flashed to *Franklin*.

Franklin departed the next day with a 4,800-man crew including the staff of Rear Adm. R. E. Davison, the task group commander. The task group consisted of four carriers (USS *Enterprise, Franklin, Independence,* and *Randolph*), and their escorts, and operated 45 miles off the coast of Japan. Their mission was to destroy aircraft and airfields on the Japanese islands of Kyushu, Shikoku, and western Honshu.

Early on March 19, 1945, as *Franklin* was launching her second strike of the morning, Rear Adm. Masafumi Arima, commander of Japan's 26th Air Flotilla, dove his Zero fighter at the flight deck of *Franklin*. He flew at low level for much of the distance of the flight deck, and then dropped two bombs just forward of the elevator. Both bombs exploded on the hangar deck right under the number one elevator. The first bomb wrecked the forward elevator, killed everyone on that part of the hangar deck, and started huge fires among the planes and ordnance on the hangar deck.

The second bomb exploded just below the flight deck, and started fires among the aircraft that were ready to launch. The aft elevator was ripped away and hung precariously out from the carrier. Planes were armed with combinations of rockets, torpedoes, and 500-and 100-pound bombs. Aircraft, fuel, bombs, and rockets began to explode, and sheets of flame and heavy smoke covered the entire ship.

The ship was quickly put into a 15-degree list to starboard, and manual steering allowed the crew to maintain control. Captain Gehres was out of action for 15 minutes due to smoke inhalation, but Commander Jurika started a right turn to put the heavy smoke away from the bridge. Speed was reduced while aircraft and ordnance continued to explode on both the flight and hangar decks. Some crewmembers had no choice but to jump overboard and destroyers trailed *Franklin*, picking up survivors.

The center of the ship was entirely in flames, making it impossible for the crew from one end of the ship to move to the other. Normal communications lines were not functioning and bullhorns could not be heard above the noise of the explosions. As a result, many of the crew, not knowing the extent of the damage but fearing the worst, continued to jump from the burning ship.

Captain Gehres recovered and decided that the ship could be saved. He told those officers and crew with whom he could communicate, to stay on the ship and put out the fires. Highlining of the admiral and his staff to the cruiser *Santa Fe* was started, and followed by the transfer of the air crews and wounded personnel. When the transfer was complete, *Franklin* was left with 772 men of the 4,800-man crew that was aboard before the attack.

Hundreds of dead and dying were laying on the flight deck, making Commander Joe Taylor's firefighting job difficult. Taylor was the executive officer and led the fire-hose and damage-control parties on the forward part of the ship. As Taylor's men worked, catholic chaplain, Father O'Callaghan, gave last rites to the dying.

When the fire and smoke were reduced somewhat, it could be seen that the flight deck from the forward elevator to the fantail was shredded. There were huge holes in the deck and the massive beams and girders were a tangled mass of metal.[2] Before the fires were extinguished, all the ammunition in lockers and gun mounts on the aft end had exploded.[3]

Franklin was taken in tow by cruiser *Pittsburgh*. Fires were extinguished and the 48,000-ton carrier began its slow journey back to the repair facilities. *Franklin* remained on general quarters all night, and on the 21st, was able to operate on two of its eight boilers. Cold "C" rations provided nourishment and there was always hot coffee.

Gradually, the 15-degree list was corrected, one degree at a time. During the night, water was pumped from the ship, the ship's radio was repaired, and all aircraft, parts and pieces of aircraft, scrap metal, and other wreckage were pushed over the side. Bombs that had not detonated were defused, and the dead were recovered from beneath the wreckage, identified, placed into canvas bags, and buried at sea. Near midnight, the ship's bakery was restored and men feasted on fresh bread with their coffee, beans and sardines.

The task group was attacked by *kamikazes* the next day, but the combat air patrol shot most of them down before they reached the fleet. The one Japanese plane that did attack *Franklin* was shot down by a marine manning a 40-mm gun above one of the destroyed five-inch guns.

On the 20th, *Franklin* was 125 miles off the coast of Japan and making five knots under its own power. *Pittsburgh* was relieved of its towing duties, and by March 21, *Franklin* was making 12 knots with three of its boilers operating.

At Ulithi, repair shops cut and pulled some of the twisted steel and shored up the bulkheads. Once it was determined that there was no damage to the propeller shafts or propellers, and with six boilers working, *Franklin* departed for Pearl Harbor.

Admiral Chester Nimitz, commander Pacific Fleet, and most of the navy personnel based at Pearl Harbor met *Franklin* when she arrived. Within 24 hours, she was enroute to New York via the Panama Canal. The crew had barely enough time to make a telephone call home, enjoy a hamburger, and beer, before departing on the 2,400-mile trip. *Franklin* steamed at 24 knots enroute to the canal, and reached the Brooklyn Navy Yard just as the last body was pulled from beneath the metal that covered it.

Actual casualties were 724 killed or missing and 265 wounded.[4] Casualties would have been much higher had not Chaplain O'Callaghan led two sailors below decks to help him wet down a five-inch magazine that threatened to explode and kill 300 sailors in the vicinity. Both courage and training permitted the saving of this proud ship. The firefighting parties of all ships were trained in proper techniques before going to sea. The training paid great dividends for *Franklin*.

Franklin did not return to the war, but most of her crew received two weeks leave and were ordered back to the Pacific to serve on different ships. USS *Franklin* has the distinction of being the most heavily damaged carrier in the war to be saved.

21

IMS *SHINANO*

No warships of any other nation, before or during WW II, could match the armament, full-load displacement, or speed of Japan's three *Yamato*-class ships, *Yamato, Musashi,* and *Shinano.* The battleship *Missouri* displaced 52,000 tons and mounted 16-inch guns. Germany's famed battleships, *Tirpitz* and *Bismarck,* each displaced 51,000 tons. In comparison, the Yamato-class ships displaced 70,000 tons, had a speed of 27 knots, and mounted 18.1-inch guns, largest in the world, each capable of sending a 3,200-pound shell 22-and-one-half miles.

At the end of the war, *Shinano* was rated at 72,000 tons, larger than either of her two sister ships, and the largest warship in history stalked and sunk by a submarine.

The keel for *Shinano* was laid at drydock number six at the Yokosuka Naval Shipyard on May 4, 1940. Like *Yamato* and *Musashi,* which were both named for provinces on Japan's main island of Honshu, *Shinano* was named for a prefecture in the center and broadest part of Honshu. Shinano is also the name of Japan's principal river, 243 miles long.

Following Japan's destruction of much of the U.S. Pacific Fleet at Pearl Harbor, work on *Shinano* was put on hold. *Yamato* was scheduled for completion on December 16, 1941, and *Musashi* on August 5, 1942. Japan already had a commanding lead in the number of battleships, and the war would likely be over before *Shinano* could be completed. These plans changed abruptly with the loss of carrier *Shoho* in the Battle of the Coral Sea, and the loss of four of Japan's finest carriers, *Akagi, Kaga, Soryu,* and *Hiryu* at the Battle of Midway. Construction of *Shinano* was accelerated, but significant changes were made. The hull of *Shinano* remained, but the ship itself was converted from a battleship to an attack aircraft carrier.[1] Completion was scheduled for February 1945.

Artist's painting of IMS *Shinano* during her maiden voyage. Note the unusual, canted funnel (smokestack.)

US Naval Institute

IMS *Shinano* as she appeared during her sea trials on November 4, 1944. The picture was taken by a civilian on a tug and never shown until after the war.

US Naval Institute

The Japanese Navy took exceptional measures to ensure secrecy of the ship conversion. A tall fence of galvanized steel was erected on three sides of the drydock, and a tall, steep limestone cliff provided a barrier for the fourth side. The thousands of dockyard workers who labored on *Shinano* were threatened with death if they uttered a word of the ship's existence.[2] The Japanese *kempeitai* (military secret police) enforced a strict ban against the possession of a camera within the shipyard. As the result of such secrecy, *Shinano* became the only ship built in the entire century that was not photographed during construction.[3]

However, at least two pictures of *Shinano* were taken, but none reached Pearl Harbor during the war. A picture taken by a B-29 bomber flying at 32,000 feet on November 1, 1944, appeared in April 1986, in a book on battleships. A second picture was taken on November 11, 1944, when *Shinano* was conducting builder's trials in Tokyo Bay. The photographer did not release this photograph until 1985. Consequently, no one in the U.S. Navy was aware of the existence of *Shinano*.

Shinano's flight deck was nearly 840 feet long. The flight deck was covered with 3.75 inches of steel, with nearly another inch of steel just below the flight deck. The hull of the ship was protected by large "blisters" of armor intended to cause torpedoes to detonate on contact with the blister rather than penetrate the main hull. The main (hangar) deck was protected by up to seven-and-a-half inches of steel. The weight of steel installed as armor plate weighed 17,700 tons, almost one fourth of *Shinano's* displacement, and similar to the total tonnage displacement of many light cruisers.[4] Shinano retained the distinction of being the largest warship ever built until the USS *Enterprise* was commissioned in 1961.

The ship's armament included 16 five-inch guns, 145 25-mm guns, and 12 multiple-rocket launchers, each capable of firing salvos of 4.7-inch rockets. Shinano's four steam turbines developed 150,000 shaft horsepower and moved the ship through the sea at a speed of 27 knots, well in excess of the speed of any submarine, surfaced or submerged.

In mid-June 1944, Japanese Naval Headquarters ordered the shipyard to deliver *Shinano* four months earlier than the scheduled February 1945 date. Captain Tatsuo Maeda, the engineering officer in charge, put his crews on a 14-hour day, seven-days-per-week schedule, but the work done under the longer hours was unacceptable.[5] Additional workers were added to finish construction, and *Shinano* was declared ready for launching on October 5, 1944.

Shinano left the shipyards on November 11 to conduct builder's trials in Tokyo Bay. Aircraft were recovered while the ship generated 24 knots. She was declared completed and the shipyard delivered *Shinano* to the Imperial Navy on November 19. Captain Toshio Abe was given command of *Shinano,* with orders to sail the ship to Kure in Japan's inland sea, where the ship would receive its complement of aircraft and be readied for the next great naval battle. Abe's request for a delay in departure due to the inoperability of four of the ship's 12 boilers, and the fact that the ship's 1,147 watertight compartments had not yet been tested for leakage was disapproved. Abe departed Yokosuka on Tuesday, November 28, at 6:00 P.M., just as the sun set. He had 2,176 officers and seamen, 300 shipyard workers, and 40 civilians on board. He also carried 50 *Ohka (baka)* suicide planes, and six *"Shinyos"* (suicide speedboats). *Shinano* was escorted by three battle-experienced destroyers, *Isokaze, Yukikaze,* and *Hamakaze.*

At 10:48 P.M., radar aboard the American submarine *Archerfish* detected *Shinano* at a distance of 12 miles to the northeast. *Shinano* was plotted on a southwesterly course at a speed of 20 knots. Commander Joseph Enright, commanding officer of *Archerfish* estimated the target to be an oil tanker with a single escort. *Archerfish's* radar pulse was detected by *Shinano,* whose radar detector operator correctly identified the pulse rate as coming from an American submarine. Both ships, *Shinano,* the hunted, and *Archerfish,* the hunter, were now very much aware of each other and thus began a six-and-one-half-hour battle that is well established in submarine history.

Shinano also intercepted the sighting report sent by *Archerfish* to submarine headquarters at Pearl Harbor. Although Abe could not decipher the message, he was certain that the transmission was a call to a submarine "wolfpack" that had been gathered to attack *Shinano*. Abe confided to his navigator, Captain Nakamura, that he suspected as many as seven submarines deployed against him.[8]

Commander Enright made the decision to run on the surface in an effort to maintain his position abeam the suspected Japanese tanker. He could maintain a speed of 19 knots on the surface, which appeared to be slightly less than the speed being maintained by the tanker. As the crew of *Archerfish* studied the ship they were tracking, it became obvious that it was not a tanker, but rather an aircraft carrier, and a carrier unlike any that were contained in their recognition manuals.

At 10:45 P.M., *Archerfish* was sighted by both *Shinano* and *Isokaze*. The destroyer ran at full speed towards the surfaced *Archerfish*. At her speed of 35 knots, *Isokaze* would be able to ram the submarine in less than seven minutes. Enright had a choice of diving to avoid the charging destroyer or maintaining his position on the surface in order to keep up with his intended target. He made the decision to stay on course at full speed. If the destroyer continued in an attempt to ram, he would turn into the attacking ship and launch a trio of torpedoes.

At a distance of three miles, *Isokaze* turned away and returned to a position just forward of the carrier. At the same time, *Shinano* turned 30 degrees to port, to a heading of 180 degrees. The turn was away from *Archerfish and* increased the distance between the two ships. The return of *Isokaze* and the port turn of the carrier were ordered by Captain Abe, who remained convinced that he was being pursued by a pack of submarines. He believed that any movement away from *Shinano* by his escort destroyers to attack a single submarine would only invite attack by other submarines.

Enright made the decision to maintain his course of 210 degrees in the hope that *Shinano's* port turn was only a zig in the carrier's zig-zag pattern, and that the huge carrier would return to its original course. At 11:30 P.M., Enright sent a message to Pearl Harbor notifying Sub Base of its tracking of the carrier. Enright's message was intercepted by Radioman Chisato Yamagishi on *Shinano.* As soon as Abe was informed of the message he ordered a turn to the right to 270 degrees. The turn was designed to foil the enemy wolfpack that Abe believed lay in position to attack on his course of 180 degrees.

As the crew of *Archerfish* cheered *Shinano's* turn to 270 degrees, the carrier turned further right to 275 degrees. The distance between the ships was now nine miles, too far for a torpedo attack. *Archerfish* could only remain on the surface, running at full speed in hopes of retaining its relative position to the carrier. *Archerfish* gained a small advantage in that *Shinano* was forced to reduce her speed from 20 knots to 18 due to a drive shaft overheating at the higher speed. Now both ships were moving forward at the same speed.

At 2:40 A.M., *Archerfish* sent an update message to Pearl Harbor. The message was immediately intercepted by *Shinano.* Abe was told that the message was sent from a position very close to the carrier, between 10 and 20 miles. Again, Abe believed that the message was sent to give his position, course, and speed to a pack of submarines attacking him. He ordered a 60-degree left turn to 210 degrees. In doing so, Abe turned directly into *Archerfish.*

Shinano's turn was so unexpected that Enright scarcely had time to turn to an attack heading of 090 degrees, ready the six, forward torpedoes, and dive. *Archerfish* leveled at 60 feet below the surface and raised periscope to sight the carrier. Range was 7,000 yards, at a bearing of 030 degrees. The depth of the Mark 14 torpedoes was set at 14 feet, and the torpedo doors opened. The range decreased to 3,500 yards as *Shinano* moved toward her attacker. At the moment Enright started to order the firing sequence of torpedoes, *Shinano* changed course and one of the escort destroyers headed straight for the submarine's position.

Enright retracted his periscope, maintained position, and the destroyer thundered directly overhead with ten feet of clearance. Once the destroyer was past, Enright ordered up-periscope, and marked the new firing position to the carrier. *Archerfish* intentionally fired four torpedoes, and unintentionally fired two more. Through the periscope, Enright saw the first fireball erupt near the stern of the carrier. The noise and shock of the first hit was followed by at least three more explosions. Then, *Archerfish* was forced to dive to 400 feet to prepare for depth charging from the attacking destroyers.

The first torpedo smashed into *Shinano's* hull, ten feet below the surface at 3:17 A.M. Within 30 seconds, three more torpedoes crushed the carrier's hull. The "blisters" had failed to explode the torpedoes short of the hull. The sea rushed into the hull from all four entry points and *Shinano* quickly developed a list to starboard of 13 degrees. At such a list, movement throughout the ship becomes difficult. Attempts were made to pump sea water into the port bilges to correct the list, but the hoses would not reach the water on the port side. Although 3,000 tons of water were shifted from starboard bilges to port, the list increased.

Shinano was still making 18 knots, so Abe headed the ship for Shiono Misaki, the nearest land in hopes of beaching the carrier. Shiono Misaki was 72 miles distant, and the sea water poured into *Shinano's* passageways and compartments. The watertight compartments that were never checked, leaked. The list increased to 15 degrees, her speed dropped to 10 knots. When the list reached 18 degrees, the freshwater evaporator shut down and the turbines stopped due to lack of steam. By 9:00 A.M., Shinano was dead in the water with a list of 20 degrees. Captain Abe never ordered "abandon ship," but started releasing members of the crew at 10:18 A.M. At 10:55 A.M., with Abe and Ensign Tadashi Yasuda clinging to the ship's railing, *Shinano's* stern dipped below the sea, and the ship began its three-quarter-of-a-mile plunge to the floor of the Pacific Ocean.[7] Approximately 1,080 of the 2,515 personnel aboard *Shinano* were rescued. The world's largest aircraft carrier sank 17 hours after embarking on her first voyage.

Archerfish remained on patrol to the east of Honshu, where the crew enjoyed turkey dinner and all the trimmings on Thanksgiving Day. On December 15, *Archerfish* completed her tour and returned to Guam. While on Guam, Commander Enright learned that navy intelligence would not support his claim of sinking a Japanese carrier. Since there was no record of such a carrier in Tokyo Bay, Naval Intelligence reasoned that *Archerfish* could not have sunk it. Eventually, *Archerfish* was given credit for sinking a ship of 28,000 tons, a compromise between Naval Intelligence and Enright. At 28,000 tons, the ship was in a class with U.S. carriers *Essex* and *Yorktown*.

Archerfish sailed from Guam on January 10, 1945, on her sixth war patrol. She was accompanied by two other submarines, *Batfish* and *Blackfish*. During a three-day period, *Batfish* sank three Japanese submarines. *Archerfish* returned in March for major overhaul and was back on station off Honshu by July 10.[8]

Following Japan's surrender, Commander Enright and the crew of *Archerfish* were able to visit the drydock at Yokosuka Naval Shipyard. They confirmed their knowledge that the huge carrier they sank was indeed produced at the site. Nearly a year later, the Joint Army-Navy Assessment Committee reviewed Japanese records and confirmed *Archerfish's* claim of sinking *Shinano*. The committee rated the carrier at 62,000 tons. Later in 1946, *Shinano's* gross tonnage was raised to 72,000 tons, and *Archerfish* was awarded a Presidential Unit Citation. Commander Enright was awarded a much-deserved Navy Cross medal.

Two of *Shinano's* escorts, *Isokaze* and *Hamakaze*, were sunk with *Yamato* on April 6, 1945, during *Yamato's* suicide mission to Okinawa. *Yukikaze*, one of the few Japanese ships to survive the war, was awarded to Chiang Kai-shek's Nationalist Navy, and remained on duty with that navy until 1971.[9]

22

SERGEANT RICHARD FISKE
Pearl Harbor and Iwo Jima

Richard "Dick" Fiske has the distinction of not only being on duty at Pearl Harbor on December 7, 1941, but of having two other family members there as well. His father, Francis, was stationed aboard USS *Tangiers* on the other side of Sand Island on the morning of the attack. Richard was a 19-year-old marine corps bugler aboard the USS *West Virginia*, and his brother Frank was a corporal in the army medical corps stationed at Schofield Barracks. All three of the Fiskes survived the attack, although they did not know it for some time afterward. Francis and Richard drove to Schofield Barracks on December 27, and found Frank. Francis' letters to his wife did not arrive in California until March 28, 1942. That was when she first learned her family survived the attack. Francis was medically retired in 1944 after 27 years of service in the navy. Frank mustered out in 1945, and Richard's side of the story is about to be told.

Richard was born in Boston, Massachusetts, in 1922, a navy port where his father was assigned. When his father received orders to San Diego, Richard went along and graduated from high school there. Following graduation, Richard enlisted in the marine corps in February 1941. He completed boot camp, and was assigned to Field Music School. He reported to the USS *West Virginia* (BB-48) during July 1941 as the ship's bugler, and, along with the crew complement of 1,587 men, was transferred to the Pacific Fleet at Pearl Harbor. The Fleet had been based at Pearl Harbor since May 1940, as a deterrent to Japanese aggression in the Pacific.

Private First Class Fiske had completed playing breakfast call on his bugle and was still on the navigation deck of *West Virginia* when the Japanese attacked. Two armor-piercing bombs struck USS *Tennessee,* moored alongside *West Virginia,* and jagged chunks of metal from *Tennessee* crashed through the bridge of *West Virginia,* critically wounding Captain Mervyn Bennoin, the ship's commanding officer. Nine torpedoes and two bombs sent *West Virginia* to the bottom of Pearl Harbor in less than 12 minutes. Fiske was thrown back ten feet by the first bomb explosion, and witnessed the death of the ship's captain before the order to abandon ship was given. Fiske, like most survivors, swam to Ford Island where he was helped from the water, fed, and provided a place to sleep for the night.

Following the attack of December 7, Fiske and many other survivors helped compile casualty reports, stood security watches, and assisted in various ways in the raising of six of the eight battleships and 15 of the total of 18 ships that sank. While he walked security post at night, he heard sounds of men trapped inside the hull of a sunken ship. When salvage crews raised the USS *West Virginia* six months later, they found the bodies of three of Fiske's friends huddled in an airtight storeroom. They also discovered a calendar on the bulkhead of the ship with 16 days crossed off. The sailors had lived that long, unaware of the situation outside their compartment.

Fiske remained assigned to USS *West Virginia* until January 1944, when he was promoted to field music sergeant and transferred to the Fifth Marine Division. On February 19, 1945, Sergeant Fiske landed on the hot sulfur sands of Iwo Jima, an island of eight square miles, 600 miles south of Tokyo. Fiske was assigned to the 13th Marine Regiment (artillery). The marine corps committed three divisions and 75,000 men to the battle before the island was finally secured on March 16. Marines suffered 25,851 casualties, including 6,318 dead. Japan started the battle with 22,000 troops. Only 1,083 were captured, the rest died during the battle. The battle for Iwo Jima is often termed the bloodiest battle in marine corps history.

Following the battle for Iwo Jima, where he was wounded,

Fiske was sent to the Big Island of Hawaii for training as part of the Fifth Marine Division artillery gun crew in preparation for the invasion of Japan. He and his fellow marines were scheduled to land on Southern Kyushu on November 1, 1945. They did not expect to survive the invasion of the Japanese home islands, and are grateful that the atomic bombs put an end to the war, and the hundreds of thousands, if not millions, of Japanese and American lives that would have been lost during an invasion of Japan.

Following the end of WW II, Richard enlisted in the newly established U.S. Air Force. He married Carmen, a lady he met while on leave in California. Following completion of aircraft and engine school, and completion of his private pilot's rating, he went on to serve during the Korean and Vietnam wars as a crew chief on KC-97 and KC-135 aircraft. He retired from the USAF in 1969 with the grade of master sergeant and moved to Hawaii in 1970.

Richard and I first met in Honolulu in September 1995 during the ceremonies marking the 50th anniversary of the end of the war. He was involved in bringing Japanese veterans that participated in the Pearl Harbor attack back to Honolulu for the 50th anniversary. At my request, he visited my WW II history class, War in the Pacific, and has continued to visit and speak to every class since.

Richard described to the class how his love for his shipmates killed by the Japanese on December 7, resulted in his total hatred for the Japanese people. "I would see a Japanese and my stomach would go into knots." Fiske explained that his hatred so filled his heart that he had no room for compassion or love. His marriage began to disintegrate and he lost many of his friends. As the direct result of his hatred, he developed a bleeding ulcer that medicine had a difficult time curing.

In 1965, during one of his frequent trips to Tripler Army Medical Center for treatment, a surgeon told him, "We can probably cure your ulcer, but we cannot cure your head." Fiske and the

229

surgeon talked for an hour or more and Fiske cried for an hour longer. The bitterness and hate disappeared as Fiske accepted the diagnosis and began to fill his heart with compassion and forgiveness. His work to bring the Japanese pilots back to Pearl Harbor for reconciliation was part of the effort to change his life.

Fiske began volunteer work as a Pearl Harbor survivor at the USS *Arizona* Memorial in 1982. He continues to serve as a tour guide and answers questions relating to the attack, the ships that were lost and the situation following the attack. He is also a self-taught counselor, talking with veterans that have not been able to put the bitterness of the war behind them.

Fiske first met with one of his Japanese counterparts, Mr. Takeshi Maeda, in Honolulu in 1991. Maeda was a torpedo pilot in the Japanese force that attacked USS *West Virginia*. Maeda was also president of Yokaren Unabarakai (Junior ROTC) and was committed to the philosophy of, "Never Again Pearl Harbor." The scars of war had taken a toll of both men. Their handshake and subsequent embrace released torrents of emotion and nightmares of the past. This simple gesture replaced hate with human kindness and compelled both men to devote their lives to assisting other Pacific war veterans to meet in friendship and reconciliation. The meeting led to the later reconciliation program in September 1995.

On September 4, 1995, Mr. Maeda, then president of the Japanese Naval Veterans Association (Unabara-Kai), placed a friendship plaque and spoke at the National Memorial Cemetery of the Pacific. Once again he committed himself to friendship between the two counties and "Pearl Harbor Never Again."

Richard Fiske has become Hawaii's symbol of forgiveness and reconciliation. He has been invited to memorial ceremonies in Japan and, in May 1996, received the Order of the Rising Sun with Silver Rays from Emperor Akihito of Japan. The award was presented by the Japanese Consulate to Hawaii, Mr. Kishichiro Amae.

Fiske, now 79, continues to play taps at the USS *Arizona* Memorial. At the request of Zenji Abe, a Japanese fighter pilot who bombed USS *West Virginia* on December 7, 1941, Fiske places two roses at the memorial every month and plays taps for all those who lost their lives. Abe, now 85, flew a type 99 dive bomber in the second wave of attacks on Pearl Harbor. He now pays for the roses and Fiske places them on the USS *Arizona* Memorial and plays taps. Fiske has not missed a month since he started playing at the memorial in May 1992. His bugle is new, but the mouthpiece is the same one that he used on that infamous day.

Master Sgt. Richard Fiske, U.S. Air Force (Ret.), and Mr. Zenji Abe, Japanese fighter pilot, embrace for perhaps the last time December 7, 2001, at the 60th anniversary of the attack on Pearl Harbor.

Honolulu Advertiser

The first wave of the landing force heads for the beach on D-Day at Iwo Jima. It would be the costliest endeavor in marine corps history.

US Navy

Marines and sailors unload supplies under fire after the initial assault came ashore.

US Coast Guard

23

IWO JIMA: FEBRUARY 1945
D-DAY

In the spring of 1998, James Bradley visited Iwo Jima. Bradley is the son of John Henry Bradley, a navy corpsman during the Battle for Iwo Jima, and one of the six men who raised the flag on Mount Suribachi. James Bradley, in his book, *Flags of our Fathers,* tells us those six men, all deceased, were calling to him to come to Iwo Jima and so he came.[1]

Bradley describes Iwo Jima as a trivial scab; barely cresting in the Pacific.[2] It was still seven-and-a-half square miles in size in 1998, with the beaches composed of soft volcanic sand, which swallowed the feet, ankles, and half the leg of anyone trying to cross it. Imagine if you will, the morning of February 19, 1945, when marines tried to run across this sand from the landing beach, with an additional 100 pounds of weapons, entrenching tools, canteens, full packs and ammunition, all the while receiving the full fury of Japanese preregistered weapons from 556-foot Mount Suribachi on their left, and hundreds of other camouflaged defensive positions to their immediate front. One of every three marines that landed on Iwo Jima on D-day became a casualty.

The Medal of Honor, our nation's highest award for valor, was earned by 22 marines and five sailors in the Iwo Jima campaign. Four of the sailors were navy corpsmen with the marines. The 22 medals are one-fourth of all the Medals of Honor earned by marines during World War II.

The conquest of Iwo Jima need not have been so costly. Following U. S. carrier aircraft attacks on July 4, 1944, and a 16-ship naval bombardment on July 6 and 7, Iwo Jima was defenseless.

Virtually every structure on Iwo was shattered. Nothing was left standing, not a single plane was operational. Several hundred troops were killed, many more were injured, and there remained less than a battalion of shell-shocked troops to defend the island.[3] But, the anticipated American landing did not occur. Unknown to the Japanese, Americans were shelling and bypassing Iwo as they headed for the Philippines. It would be eight months before the Americans returned, and in the meantime, Lieutenant Gen. Tadamachi Kuribayashi arrived with 17,500 soldiers and 6,000 navy personnel with orders to make Iwo Jima a mighty fortress.

Defense of the Bonin Islands (Haha Jima, Chichi Jima and Iwo Jima) became Tokyo's highest priority. Iwo's defense force increased until there was no room for more men. Fifty-two fighter planes, 14 large naval defense guns, and 30 antiaircraft weapons were installed.

Defending Iwo Jima were some of Japan's finest officers and men. Lieutenant Gen. Tadamichi Kuribayashi arrived in mid-June to command the island's defenses. Kuribayashi had been commander of the Imperial Guards Division that guards the Imperial Palace. The emperor, Prime Minister Hideki Tojo, and other leaders of Japan respected Kuribayashi and considered him well qualified for such an important and difficult position. His family was *samurai*, members of the warrior class loyal to the emperor. He completed tours of attaché duty in the United States and Canada, and fought in China and Hong Kong.

While on attaché duty in the United States Kuribayashi wrote his family twice a week and once told them that the United States is the last country in the world Japan should fight. He explained that the American industrial capacity far outstripped Japan's and the people were energetic and versatile. "One must never underestimate the American's fighting ability,"[4] he said.

Like Admiral Yamamoto and others before him, Tojo and the warlords ignored his counsel. Prior to his posting to Iwo Jima, he was honored with an audience with the emperor and received personal instructions from Tojo including, "The eyes of the entire nation will be focused on the defense of this island. Among all our generals, you are best qualified for the task."[5] Kuribayashi was honored to be chosen, but knew he would not leave the island alive.

On June 29, 1944, Major Yoshitaka Horie arrived in the Bonins. As a lieutenant in China in 1938, Horie had been badly wounded by machinegun fire. One of the bullets that entered his head clipped the motor nerves that controlled his legs. Horie recovered but remained crippled due to the wound. He overcame that adversity and was considered a first rate officer. Because of his previous staff position in Tokyo, with access to both army and navy message traffic, Horie, more than any other officer on Iwo, realized how badly the war was going. He knew there would be no Japanese navy coming to the rescue of the defenders of Iwo Jima.

Horie was sent to take charge of the logistic arrangements on the island of Chichi Jima, 150 miles to the north. Chichi had become Iwo's staging area. Troops, weapons, and supplies that came from mainland Japan were off-loaded at Chichi. Horie's job, with 3,000 men and 50 small vessels, was to store the weapons and materials, garrison the troops, and then deliver them at night to Haha Jima, 150 miles to the north. The material would remain during the day at Haha and travel the next night to Iwo. All off-loading, unloading, and movement from Chichi to Haha and eventually to Iwo had to be done at night to try to avoid Allied submarines and aircraft.

The Chichi garrison commander was Lieutenant Gen. Yosio Tachibana. Regardless of Tachibana's abilities, he will be forever remembered in disgrace as a war criminal that was hanged following the war. Under Tachibana's command, a dozen American airmen shot down in the Chichi Jima area were tortured, beaten, beheaded and mutilated. Believing that the flesh of an enemy boosted morale and improved ones' own health, body parts of some of the slain Americans were eaten at *sake* parties. From one aviator came the liver and a six-pound piece of thigh. The body of another flyer that had been buried for a full day, was exhumed and the liver removed for part of the menu.[6]

Lieutenant Col. Takeichi Nishi arrived at Chichi in mid-July to command the 26th Tank Regiment at Iwo. Nishi came from an old and wealthy family. He received the title baron from the emperor and gained a worldwide reputation by earning the gold medal in the Olympics in Los Angeles in 1912, in the individual horse-jumping event. He competed often throughout Europe, was widely entertained in the United States, and was well known to the troops on Iwo. He usually went about wearing cavalry boots and carried a riding whip. Wherever he went, he drew attention.

Nishi flew into Chichi Jima shortly after the transport *Nishu Maru* was sunk by the submarine USS *Cobia* near Chichi. Lost with the Maru were 28 of Nishi's tanks. Following a discussion with Kuribayashi concerning defense of the island, Nishi flew back to Tokyo in July to plead for more tanks. His trip was successful, but when the tanks arrived Kuribayashi had them buried, with only their turrets and guns in evidence. Greatly displeased, Nishi went back to Tokyo for more tanks that could be used appropriately, in his opinion, for defense of the island. Nishi was successful in obtaining 22 more tanks, but they also became part of the static "killing fields" developed by General Kuribayashi.

Lieutenant Col. Kaneji Nakane, "a God of infantry tactics," arrived in November 1944 to help raise morale and to train the defenders in sniper tactics from caves, bunkers, and pillboxes. He trained the men in night infiltration tactics and how to use wet straw matting to reduce the dust raised when the artillery pieces were fired.

Another Japanese Army draftee who arrived on Chichi Jima, was Nobuaki "Warren" Iwataki. In late 1940, Nobuaki was a U.S. citizen and a high school senior on Maui, Hawaii. His fisherman father drowned, and his mother took the five children to Japan to live with an uncle. Nobuaki was drafted into the Japanese Army, and was sent to Iwo Jima. A U.S. submarine sank Nobuaki's ship off Chichi Jima, where Nobuaki was rescued, but his unit lost all their artillery and other equipment, and remained at Chichi Jima.

Early on the morning of September 2, 1944, Nobuaki was digging a cave when he heard a shout, "An American plane is shot down."[7] Nobuaki ran to an observation spot, where he observed a pilot in a rubber boat in the ocean. U.S. carrier planes circled overhead, and a submarine surfaced to rescue the plot. Nobuaki thought, "Surely America will win the war if they care so much for one pilot."[8] The rescued pilot later became American President George Bush Sr.

Nobuaki also observed the death of another pilot, George Vaughn, who parachuted from his plane and was captured on Chichi Jima. Vaughn became one of those captured flyers brutally executed by Lieutenant Gen. Tachibana and members of his command.[9]

In early August, Rear Adm. Toshinosuke Ichimaru and 2,300 navy replacements arrived on Iwo Jima. Ichimaru was the senior naval officer on the island but his was not to be a typical navy command. Instead, he and his sailors would fight as ground troops from holes, caves, and fortifications that they would first have to construct. Ichimaru took the news well. He was grateful for the opportunity to fight, and stated that he wished to "fall like the flower petals in his garden at home."[10]

General Kuribayashi knew that every Japanese on Iwo Jima would die. He knew the Americans would be able to land on the only suitable beach on the island, and he knew that in time, with their superior numbers, they would overrun the island. His plan was to delay the inevitable. Kuribayashi's plan had its detractors. The Japanese army preferred to attack, rather than defend. Before the American invasion came, he replaced 33 of his staff officers that were not supporting his plan of defense.

His troops dug thousands of feet of tunnels, caves, and fighting holes throughout the island. He prepared false gun emplacements to draw the fire from the navy ships and aircraft he knew would attack. Against the strong objections of some members of his staff, he buried his tanks to permit their use as long as possible. His plan was to retreat slowly, and to make the marines fight and die for every inch of Iwo Jima. If he was successful, perhaps the United States would not land on the home islands of Japan, believing the price in human lives to be too high.

Opposing General Kuribayashi's forces were the entire Pacific Fleet, or as much as could be spared, and three marine corps divisions. Admiral Chester Nimitz, commander Pacific Fleet, now based at Guam, was in overall charge of the operation with Admiral Spruance in operational charge of the Fifth Fleet. According to U.S. Navy reports, there were 116 warships, including 16 aircraft carriers, 1,170 aircraft and 75,144 troops.

The "troops" were three marine divisions. The Fourth Marine Division was commanded by Major Gen. Clifton B. Cates, a future commandant of the Marine Corps. His marines conquered Roi-Namur, Saipan, and Tinian. The Fifth Marine Division was commanded by Major Gen. Keller E. Rocky. Rocky's division was to see action for the first time, but was loaded with veterans of Guadalcanal, Tarawa, and other Pacific campaigns. The Third Marine Division was commanded by Major Gen. Graves B. Erskine. Erskine's 21,000 battle-tested marines defeated the Japanese on Bougainville and Guam.

The divisions were under the Fifth Amphibious Corps, commanded by Major Gen. Harry Schmidt. Also very much in evidence was Lieutenant Gen. Holland M. "Howlin Mad" Smith, commanding general of Fleet Marine Forces Pacific, with headquarters at Honolulu. Smith, at 62 years of age and inflicted with severe diabetes, was not in the chain of command for the operation, but he was quick to make his views known at the highest levels and was dedicated to taking care of "his marines."

President Roosevelt knew Smith as a fighter and intervened with the navy to ensure that Smith was present for the operation. Back in the United States, Smith was blamed by many for the severe casualties suffered by the marines in the Pacific campaign. Roosevelt knew better, and was aware that Smith went head-to-head with the top navy brass before and after every battle over the lack of naval gunfire and air support that caused the high casualties. Iwo Jima would be no different. During the planning phase for the operation, instead of the ten days of bombardment needed by the marines, Nimitz and Spruance offered three. "Damn it Ray," Smith thundered at Spruance, "three days won't do the job."[11] Then, looking directly at Nimitz, Smith said in a low voice, "This will be the bloodiest fight in marine corps history." There was dead silence in the room, but Nimitz and Spruance had made their decision and the marines would have to take what the navy gave them. Smith knew that once again he would suffer insults and be accused of wasting the lives of young marines. The invasion date was set for February 19, 1945.

The first major raid on Iwo occurred on December 8, 1944, when 28 P-38s from Saipan surprised the garrison with a "Pearl Harbor Day" attack by bombing and strafing Chidori airfield. They were followed immediately by 62 B-29s and 102 B-24s that dropped more than 800 tons of bombs on the airfield and naval gun emplacements. Cruiser Division Five moved close to Iwo in the afternoon and shelled the island for 70 minutes. Damage was minimal. The airfield was made operational in five hours, and only four antiaircraft guns and six fighters were destroyed. On Christmas Eve, four navy cruisers moved to within a mile of shore to fire 2,000 rounds of eight-inch shells at suspected targets. On December 27, the cruisers fired another 1,200 rounds at enemy targets. For the next 70 days, Iwo would be hit daily by bombers or naval gunfire.

The problem with the earlier bombing and naval gunfire of Iwo was that it had not reduced the number of defense guns, antiaircraft guns, blockhouses, pillboxes, and artillery pieces, now estimated as 696 separate targets. In fact, the 305 targets plotted earlier by naval intelligence in October 1944, had more than doubled.[12]

What the landing force could not know at this time was that the blockhouses and pillboxes they could see were only the tip of a vast complex of tunnels, rooms, stairways, and passageways. More than 1,500 rooms connected by 16 miles of tunnels provided safe haven for the 22,000 defenders of Iwo Jima. Many of the rooms were ventilated and electrified, and all contained food, water, ammunition, and other supplies capable of supporting the defenders for five months.[13] Several hospitals were located throughout the complex including one with operating tables and 400 beds.

The pre-landing bombardment planned for the first day, February 16, was partially canceled because of weather. The aerial observers could not see the impact of the naval gunfire, and bombers from the Marianas could not see their targets. Only 17 of the 696 identified targets were accounted for on D-day minus 3 before the naval gunfire ships moved out to sea to spend the night. A big day for USS *Pensacola* was noted when its spotting plane, a slow OS2U (Kingfisher), was attacked by a much faster and more maneuverable Zero, and shot the Zero down.

D-day minus 2 weather was perfect for bombardment by ships and aircraft. USS *Nevada, Idaho,* and *Tennessee* commenced firing with their 14-inch guns at 8:40 A.M. Pensacola closed to 750 yards from the beaches and began blasting targets on Mt. Suribachi. A dozen rocket-firing minesweepers were firing even closer to the beach. Between USS *Pensacola* and the beach, another 12 gunboats and three destroyers blasted targets. As *Pensacola* moved in even closer to support the minesweepers, she was hit six times in less than two minutes. The only thing that saved her was the base of the Japanese 15-centimeter gun slipping away and causing the barrel of the gun to point skyward. *Pensacola* controlled her fires and flooding, but 17 men including the executive officer were dead and 120 were wounded. Kuribayashi won the first skirmish.

The minesweepers reported no mines, reefs, shoals, or obstructions to the beaches. At 10:30 A.M., the underwater demolition teams (UDT) or frogmen moved in small boats to within 500 yards of the beach. Their job was to clear the area from the beach to the line swept by the minesweepers. They were covered by 13 landing craft infantry (LCI) modified as gunboats. Kuribayashi could not count heads in the LCIs, he only knew there could be 2,400 marines in the 13 craft and ordered "Commence fire."

The LCI gunboats carried 50-man crews. When they reached a distance of 250 yards from the beach, every type of weapon on the island smothered them. In the next 90 minutes, every LCI was hit, 43 crewmen were killed, and 153 more wounded. LCI 473 had 189 holes in her hull. Two artillery rounds hit both of LCI 450's 40-mm gun mounts, fires broke out, and one shell cut the bow anchor cable, sending the anchor to the bottom. LCI 449 was hit three times, There was not a single unwounded man aboard. The commander, Lieutenant (j.g.) Rufus H. Herring, had three blood-gushing wounds but refused to be evacuated until all his remaining 20 men were taken from his craft. Herring, barely conscious when he was removed, earned the Medal of Honor for his actions.

Despite the horror inflicted upon the LCIs, the frogmen, clad only in facemasks, trunks, and fins, did their job. At noon, as the frogmen and their LCI gunfire ships withdrew on schedule, the naval gunfire and carrier airstrikes resumed. At the end of the day, only three of the 20 blockhouses had been damaged or destroyed, and perhaps five of the 316 pillboxes had been destroyed. As before, the gunfire directed at Iwo revealed new defensive positions faster than the navy could destroy the previously known positions. Where four antitank guns had been plotted, there were now 13 in concrete casements. Only one day of bombardment remained and little had been accomplished. The marines asked for another day of naval gunfire; the navy said no.

Sunday morning, February 18 dawned with only fair visibility and intermittent rain squalls. *Nevada* and *New York* began firing from 2,500 yards at beach defenses. *Tennessee* blasted positions on cliff batteries for five hours, and *Idaho* pulverized Suribachi all day. In late afternoon, the battleships withdrew. Church services began for the marines. General H.M. Smith went to his cabin in the *Eldorado* and read passages from his bible. He knew tomorrow would bring terrible casualties to his marines, and he could not prevent it. He prayed, as was his custom, turned out the light, and closed his eyes.

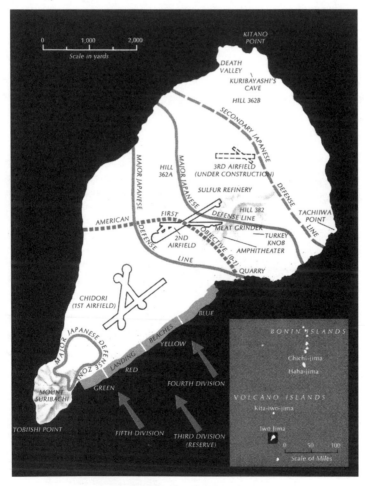

The U.S. invasion fleet approached Iwo Jima from the south east.

National Archives

At first light, one could see that Admiral Spruance aboard USS *Indianapolis* arrived during the night and brought Admiral Mitscher's Task Force 58 along. A total of 485 warships now circled the tiny island of Iwo Jima. Surely the Japanese defenders expressed awe, and perhaps some pride, at warranting such an armada.

D-day, Monday, February 19, began with slow deliberate fire from seven battleships and seven cruisers. At 8:00 A.M., 120 carrier planes attacked targets near the landing beaches using napalm, rockets, and 20-mm cannon fire. The final naval bombardment began at 8:25 A.M. More than 8,000 shells crashed into the island defenses in the next 30 minutes. Deep underground in their caves and tunnels the Japanese waited. Exactly at 8:30, the first wave of marines left the line of departure in 68 armored, tracked, landing vehicles (LVTs). In less than 45 minutes, 9,000 men should be ashore. Kuribayashi would not wait that long to send the marines back to the sea.

The first marine units landed at 8:59 A. M. The first loose sand terrace was only a few feet from the beach and rose almost vertically 10-to-15-feet high. Further to the right, some of the amtracs got up the first plateau, but nearer Suribachi, the terrace was impassable, even to tracked vehicles. The LVTs could not stay where they were because more "amtracs" were scheduled to follow at 15-minute intervals. Instead of moving inland to provide fire support and a defensive perimeter for the marines, they returned to the surf. Upon landing, a marine mortar man carried 122 pounds of equipment, corpsmen carried 51 pounds. Everyone else had packs weighing somewhere in between. The first 50 yards came easy. Then the soft, sucking sand started to swallow the feet of the heavily loaded marines. Most just flopped down where they were and waited for orders.

Since Japan no longer had a navy to contest the American invasion force on the sea, Kuribayashi's plan was to let the marines come ashore and destroy them on the beach. When the naval gunfire lifted, and the beaches were congested with men and equipment, he would first bleed them on the beaches and then drive them into the sea. As the numbers of enemy on the beach increased, it was almost time to do so. He would spring his trap at 10:00 A. M.

Major Louis Blissard was the executive officer of the First Battalion, 23rd Marines. A continuous torrent of fire from the defensive positions on Suribachi tore into the battalion's Charlie Company. Within 30 minutes, 17 marines were killed and 26 others wounded. Blissard was one of the eight survivors of the 39 battalion officers that landed that morning. He described the trip to the beach as exhilarating. Even a high-explosive shell that exploded off the bow of his LVT failed to dampen his enthusiasm. Blissard was in the sixth wave that landed on the beach at H+22 minutes. As soon as the LVT beached, Blissard was running inland as fast as he could. He ran about 150 yards before the sulfuric sand pulled him down. He rolled into a shellhole in order to pause and catch his breath, and found that he was already slightly ahead of the marine front lines. His runner arrived about the same time and they listened to the machine gun and mortar fire just in front of their position.

Blissard turned to his runner and said, "Preston, we're sure giving them hell with our machine guns aren't we?" Preston, with an astonished look replied, "Major, you don't think they're ours do you? Those are Jap machine guns."[14] Preston had seen combat before, Blissard had not. Blissard's position ahead of the beach was probably the best thing that could have happened to him. By now, nearly 30 minutes after the first landing, the Japanese were laying artillery, mortar, and machine gun fire directly upon the marines on the beach. Men were being blown to pieces, killed and wounded in terrible numbers.

The next morning, D-day + 1, Blissard's position was in a shell crater ten yards from the hole that sheltered his commanding officer. Two artillery rounds exploded in the hole next to Blissard, instantly killing the battalion commander, operations officer, communications officer, and severely wounding the adjutant. Blissard took command of the depleted battalion, which was put in corps reserve for two days to reorganize and assimilate replacements.

Japanese defenders on Iwo Jima used a complex tunnel system that allowed them wait for the marines to work their way inland, and then attack from behind.

US Marine Corps

Despite its casualties, Easy Company of the 28th Marines did move forward, thanks to the effort of PFC Douglas T. Jacobson. Jacobson, a veteran of the fight for Saipan, grabbed a fallen marine's bazooka and a satchel of explosives, and became a one-man demolition team. Crawling, running, and dragging his bag of demolitions, Jacobson first knocked out a pillbox-emplaced machine gun. With a blast of his bazooka he took out a second machine gun emplacement. Then he attacked and destroyed a concrete blockhouse, followed by numerous others. Finally, out of ammunition and demolitions, Jacobson returned for more, while Item Company continued the advance. Marines counted 75 dead Japanese and 16 reinforced positions destroyed as a result of Jacobson's heroics. Doug Jacobson became one of 27 Americans to earn the Medal of Honor on Iwo Jima, the largest group of such heroes in any battle in the history of the United States.

For the marines on the beach and those trying to advance from the beach, piles of sand became Japanese machine gun emplacements firing from openings barely visible above ground level. Mortar fire fell in cascades from concealed holes in the ground. Japanese heavy artillery and antiaircraft guns lowered their muzzles and fired directly into the troops on the beach and the amphibious vehicles bringing them ashore. Land mines exploded and tore off limbs as marines fell or stumbled upon them. Every square yard of the beach had been preregistered for defensive fire by Kuribayashi's forces.

By now, there were 6,000 marines on the beach. That means there were two marines for every yard of beach. Marines could not dig foxholes in the sand. As fast as one scooped out the loose volcanic sand, the hole filled up with more of the same. Landing craft were being destroyed at the beach and preventing following waves from coming ashore. Seven LVTs were destroyed within five minutes, sinking with their precious cargo of tanks, trucks, and ammunition.

Two miles offshore on USS *Eldorado*, Lieutenant Gen. Smith monitored the message traffic from unit commanders. Smith and Vice Adm. Kelly Turner were veterans of Tarawa, Peleliu, and other amphibious assaults in the Pacific, but never had the situation been so critical. Mortars and artillery pinned down all units. Machine gun and artillery fire was the heaviest ever experienced by the combat veterans. Kuribayashi was about to order his forces to counterattack and throw the invasion force back into the ocean from where they came. But, some 6,000 marines were ashore. They had a few tanks and bulldozers ashore and a few artillery pieces. They started to do what marines have always done; they attacked.

Marines ran to the pillboxes despite heavy casualties, and threw grenades inside. Then they entered the fortifications and came out with bayonets dripping blood. Marines died on each assault but others continued, blowing up some defensive positions and bypassing others. Lieutenant Frank J. Wright, a platoon commander, advanced across the entire island only to discover that from his 60-man platoon, only two marines were still with him. Lieutenant Wesley C. Bates did the same, and reached the far shore with five men remaining of his 60-man platoon. As he looked for other members of his platoon, a machine gun bullet broke his left forearm. Bates lost consciousness for awhile and then recovered to regroup his small unit for further combat.

Lieutenant Gen. H.M. Smith led the expeditionary force responsible for capturing Iwo Jima.

US Marine Corps

Gunnery Sergeant John "Manila John" Basilone, the first enlisted marine recipient of the Medal of Honor in WWII for his heroism on Guadalcanal, died with four other marines from a mortar round while trying to advance from the beach. Other marines rose to take his place. Tony Stein, a corporal from Dayton, Ohio, killed at least 20 Japanese in pillboxes as he advanced firing his machine gun from the hip. When he ran out of ammunition, he made eight trips to the beach for more ammunition before shrapnel killed him.

While the marines advanced singly, in pairs, and by small units, the situation on the beach became unimaginable. Disabled landing craft surged onto the beach with each wave, smashing into trucks, crates, and bodies at the water's edge. Just offshore other landing craft waited, looking for an opening in the carnage to land their cargo. The dead and wounded lay everywhere. The beaches became so congested that Vice Adm. Turner closed them to unloading until the wreckage could be cleared. General Kuribayashi was still very much in charge and remained so the first evening by consistently firing preregistered mortars and artillery on the beaches and at inland enemy positions.

More than a thousand American casualties were evacuated before dark on D-day and hundreds more lay on the beach awaiting evacuation. Many would die before morning. Shore parties worked all night to clear the beaches. Bulldozers cut roads leading from the beach; pulled pallets of water, food, and ammunition inland; winched equipment from landing vehicles destroyed in the surf; and opened the beaches to landing craft.

By nightfall on D-day, the marines' hold on the beaches of Iwo Jima was tenuous at best.

24

IWO JIMA: FEBRUARY 1945
D-DAY + 1

On the morning of D-day + 1, Robert Sherrod, a reporter with *Time* and *Life* magazines, surveyed the scene from his foxhole. Sherrod had been with the marines at Tarawa and Saipan. He told millions of readers that, "The first night on Iwo Jima can only be described as a nightmare in hell. About the beach in the morning lay the dead. They had died with the greatest possible violence. Nowhere in the Pacific have I seen such badly mangled bodies. Many were cut squarely in half. Legs and arms lay fifty feet from any body."[1] Eight dead marines lay less than ten yards from Sherrod and he counted 50 wounded marines still fighting within a hundred feet of his foxhole.

When morning finally came, General Holland Smith expressed amazement that the Japanese had not reverted to their usual *Banzai* attack, the one last charge to kill as many Americans as possible. "I don't know who he is, but the Jap general running the show is one smart bastard," Smith told reporters. In Washington, President Roosevelt was told of the 2,312 American casualties on the first day and shuddered at the news. It was the first time, "that anyone had seen the President gasp in horror."[2]

By 10:30 A.M., on D+1, elements of all eight assault battalions were ashore. The LSMs began bringing in tanks, bulldozers, and artillery. By the end of the first day 30,000 marines were ashore. Casualties were terribly high, just as Gen. Smith had warned Admiral Nimitz; but the marines were ashore, and they were there to stay. For the next four days, marines fought for control of Mount Suribachi. They had no choice. The 556-foot volcano dominated not only the beachhead, but the entire island. It was essential to capture and control this high ground.

Seizure of Suribachi was assigned to the 28th Marine Regiment of the 5th Division. The unit assigned to the left flank of the advance was pinned to the beach by the deadly fire from concealed positions at the base of Suribachi and seemed unable to move until the battalion commander, Lt. Colonel Chandler Johnson, moved among the men, shouting, "Okay, you bastards, let's get the hell off this beach!"[3] Marines responded and started for Suribachi.

By noon of the second day, Johnson's men had reached the foot of Suribachi, blasting 40 caves closed and killing hundreds of Japanese as they emerged from their holes and caves. By afternoon, tank support arrived and the marines moved forward another 200 yards. Early Wednesday morning, the 28th received naval gunfire support from cruisers and destroyers followed by close air support from carrier aircraft. Tough fighting continued all day. Marines were killed and wounded by mortars, artillery shells, mines, grenades, machine guns, and rifle fire. It was always the one or two heroic infantrymen that made advances possible. They rushed forward with grenades, demolition charges, and flame-throwers to blast the pillboxes and seal cave entrances. Often the Japanese defenders would move through tunnels from the destroyed concrete and rock positions to emerge from other prepared defensive positions.

February 23, D-day + four, was cold with a hard rain falling. The loose sand turned to gumbo making progress from the beach extremely difficult. But the battle for Suribachi continued. As platoon leaders were killed, corporals took command. Fighting became hand-to-hand as marines overran enemy positions and were met by grenades and bayonets. Navy corpsman John Bradley seemed to be everywhere administering aid and injecting morphine to ease the pain.

Marine tanks joined the battle along with 37-mm guns, 75-

mm half-tracks, and rocket trucks. By the time the 28ᵗʰ reached the base of the volcano, they destroyed more than 50 bunkers, pillboxes, and other defensive positions. Finally, the north and east sides of the mountain were cleared of Japanese; Suribachi was surrounded.

About 800 Japanese remained inside the mountain and around the base.[4] Perhaps half that number attempted to escape during the night, and many were killed as they made their way across the rubble of the mountain. On Friday morning, at 8:00 A.M., Sgt. Sherman Watson and three privates, started to climb the north face of Suribachi. When the unit reached the summit at 8:40, Colonel Johnson sent a patrol of 40 men to defend the summit and fly a 54-inch-by-28-inch flag. Four of the 40-man patrol survived to the end of the battle. The other 36 were either killed or wounded and evacuated from the island.

At 10:15 A.M, despite small numbers of Japanese who emerged from tunnels and charged the patrol, the American flag was raised atop Mount Suribachi. Secretary of the Navy, James Forrestal, from his position near the base of the mountain, turned to "Howlin' Mad" Smith and said, "This means a Marine Corps for the next 500 years."[5] Later, a larger flag was carried to the top of Suribachi, by PFC Rene Gagnon, and history was made by five marines, a navy corpsman, and Associated Press photographer Joe Rosenthal.

Hard fighting continued across the rest of the island. Four regiments from the 4ᵗʰ and 5ᵗʰ Marine Divisions made the initial assault to capture the two airfields and continue across the island to divide it. If possible, enemy fire was even more intense on the 5ᵗʰ Division landing beach than in front of Suribachi. The situation became confused on the beaches as boats landed wherever they could find a spot. Tanks were unloaded where no exits from the beach had been bulldozed. For the first time in the war, navy Seabees were landed with the assault troops rather than after them, and began using bulldozers to clear and clean the beaches. Artillery was ashore by late afternoon and began supporting the advance of the troops. The edge of the airfield, was reached 5:30 P.M., despite heavy casualties. Darkness fell at 6:45, however, Japanese preregistered artillery and naval guns continued to fire all night long.

Seldom were live Japanese seen. They would fire machine guns and mortars from their concealed positions and then quickly duck inside to avoid return fire. As marines bypassed enemy positions, the Japanese would emerge just far enough to throw grenades at passing marines and corpsmen. Eleven of the 23 corpsmen on the right flank were killed on the first day.

Marines of the 3rd Division landed on February 21, D-day + 2. They moved into position between the other two divisions and began to relieve some severely depleted units. The three divisions were generally on line, advancing northeast along the long axis of the island. Facing the marines was the Japanese 145th Regiment, commanded by Colonel Masuo Ikeda. The 145th was the best Japanese combat unit on Iwo, and although they respected the reputation of the U.S. marines, they would not back down for anyone. Forward movement of the marines was minimal, measured in yards with heavy casualties. Some companies were so badly depleted by nightfall that they had to be relieved. The situation remained static through February 23.

Marine artillery and naval gunfire began a massive barrage on Colonel Ikeda's front lines at 8:00 A.M. on February 24, D-day + 4. The barrage lifted an hour later, to allow carrier-based aircraft to attack targets in proximity to the front lines. Tanks moved through the front lines leading the marines towards the enemy positions directly ahead. Mines and buried torpedoes stopped the tanks and the advance 800 yards short of their objective, the intersection of the airfield's two runways. Mortar fire, artillery, machine guns and snipers took a heavy toll of the marines, and they were forced to stop their advance to call for more supporting arms. At 1:30 P.M., after a heavy barrage by naval gunfire, artillery, and close air support, marines neared the low ridge that was Ikeda's final defensive position.

Three times, the attacking platoons, now reduced to squad size, were thrown back from the objective. On the fourth attack, with less than 200 men remaining, the marines reached the front of their objective. As they did so, Ikeda's crack Japanese unit rose as one and charged the marines. Bayonets and swords flashed in the sun. Many of the marine's rifles were clogged with sand, so they fought with grenades, pistols, bayonets, knives, rifles as clubs, and shovels.

Men were choked to death, faces smashed, skulls and limbs were broken and blood poured from numerous tears, punctures and broken bones. Grunts, gasps, moans, and cries of pain accompanied the violence. What seemed hours to those that fought there was actually over in minutes. The marines, being larger and heavier, had a decided advantage in close combat. Fifty of Ikeda's finest lay dead on sand and rocks.

March 1, D-day + 10, started with the 3rd Division moving against the center axis, including airfield #3, and Motoyama Village. The 4th division, with a combat efficiency of 55 percent, continued its assault against the Meat Grinder, so named because of the large number of casualties being inflicted, while the 5th Division attacked along the left flank. Easy Company, the unit that raised the flag on Suribachi, had a particularly costly day, losing 38 men in the advance. Since D-day, the unit lost 90 men, 40 percent of its strength.

On March 2, the 5th Marines were moving from Hill 362A towards Nishi Ridge, 300 yards away. The ridges were mountains of stone, offering ideal hiding places for snipers and grenade throwers. Easy Company was the first unit of the 28th Marines to reach Nishi Ridge. Lieutenant Col. Chandler Johnson, the battalion commander, arrived at the ridge shortly after his troops seized it. As he stopped to examine a crater, a shell landed at his feet and blew him to pieces. The loss stunned his battalion, and especially E Company that had seen so much of the barrel-chested marine with the cocky looking fatigue cap and a .45-caliber pistol jammed into his hip pocket.

The 4th Division continued the assault on March 3, D-day + 12, with combat effectiveness down to fifty percent. The marines controlled about two-thirds of the island at a cost of 16,000 casualties, with 3,000 killed. Japanese losses were estimated at 18,000. Only 80 prisoners had been taken with more than half being Korean laborers. Seabees managed to put 1,000 yards of runway in operation to permit medical evacuation of casualties and emergency landings of B-29s from the Marianas.

The first B-29 to use the runway at Iwo was named Dinah Might. The plane was returning from bombing an aircraft plant south of Tokyo on March 4. The pilot, 1st Lt. Fred Malo, was unable to transfer fuel from his 1,000-gallon reserve tank and had only two options, ditch at sea or try a landing on Iwo Jima. Malo radioed his dilemma to a ship that passed the information to Iwo Jima. The marines were eager to clear the bulldozers and scrapers from the field just to see the Superfortress land. Malo made two low-level passes to familiarize himself with the coral runway and then set the huge plane down with a cloud of dust following it all the way to the near sanctuary of Suribachi. Less than an hour later, the fuel transfer valve was replaced and the crew was on their way to Saipan.

Lieutenant Malo and Dinah Might were back at Iwo on April 12, heavily damaged from antiaircraft fire over Tokyo. The crew had to leave the aircraft at Iwo and catch a ride back to Tinian. Within six weeks, the entire crew was dead, victims of antiaircraft fire over Honshu and a crash on take off on Tinian.[6] Landings of damaged Superforts on Iwo became a common occurrence, and from March 3 to the end of the war, 2,400 B-29s made emergency landings on Iwo saving 25,000 airmen that might have otherwise perished. From March 3 to March 26, an average of 124 casualties were evacuated daily by medically configured DC-3 aircraft.

March 5 was designated as a day of rest, reorganization, and resupply. Some marines were able to nap briefly in their foxholes, others near the beach chanced a quick dip in the ocean. Fresh water was available thanks to the Seabee drillers. More importantly, new men, some fresh from boot camp, joined depleted units to bring them up to strength. While the marines paused for breath, naval gunfire and carrier-based aircraft continued to bombard the enemy positions. Also on March 5, but known to only a few, a regiment of the 3rd Division, 3,000 marines that had not set foot on Iwo, were sent back to the Marianas to train for the invasion of Japan. With them went another 400 men of the three divisions that had been killed or wounded during the "Day of Rest."

Where the terrain allowed, the U.S. tanks scorched carefully prepared defensive positions.

US Marine Corps

There were now more than 50,000 Americans ashore.[7] All three division commanders were ashore as was the corps commander. On the right flank, the 4th Division moved against defense systems called "The Meat Grinder," "Turkey Knob," and

255

the fortified remains of the former village of Minami. The 3rd Division attacked airfield defenses, losing nine of 20 tanks during the day. Neither division made much progress during the costly and frustrating day. No one could know that the battle for the Meat Grinder would take many more days and many more casualties before it would end.

Lieutenant Gen. Holland Smith, third from left, leader of the Marine Expeditionary Force, briefs his senior-level commanders before wrapping up the campaign with a drive across northern Iwo Jima.

US Marine Corps

The 3rd Division was stopped in its advance to the sea by a strong point called "Cushman's Pocket," named after Lieutenant Col. Robert E. Cushman, commander of the 2nd Battalion, 9th Marines. On March 7, the 9th Marines conducted the marine's first night attack on the pocket, defended by Baron Nishi, and members of his tank regiment fighting as infantrymen. The marines were deep into Nishi's defensive area before they were discovered and moved quickly to the top of the hill. By 6:00 A.M., the marines reported that they had seized their objective, Hill 362C. As the sun came up, however, it became clear that it was the wrong hill. The objective was another 250 yards to the front.

Two battalions penetrated 200 yards into the pocket only to discover that Hill 362C had not been captured, and they were completely surrounded. Movement was impossible as heavy fire came from every direction. "Luckily," recounted Lieutenant Wilcie O'Bannon, "they (the Japanese) didn't charge. It would have been curtains for all of us."[8] Lt. Col. Harold Boehm's 3rd Battalion pressed on and seized Hill 362C despite 600 men killed or wounded, and then all attention was given to extricate the other two battalions. One company with 43 casualties and only 22 men fit to fight, was recovered during the night of March 7. The remaining marines were rescued the following day.

On the same day, the 5th Division suffered the loss of 43 men in a single explosion on a ridge near Kitano Point, Iwo's northernmost point. The Japanese blew the ridge with tons of explosives from a cave beneath it, resulting in an explosion that both buried and tore marines apart. The 4th division continued to be stopped by defenses on the Meat Grinder.

On the evening of March 8, General Sadasuc Senda and navy Captain Samaji Inouye disobeyed Kuribayashi's orders and led an infiltration of 1,500 Japanese through the marine lines. Before they left, they gave a grenade to each of the wounded men that could not travel with them. The grenade was to blow themselves up rather than be captured. Hopefully, they could each kill at least one of the enemy at the same time. Fortunately for the marines, the infiltration was discovered at dusk, and rockets, artillery, and mortars rained fire on the disorganized groups of infiltrators. Illumination disclosed additional groups of Japanese trying to infiltrate until morning. Japanese dead numbered nearly 800, and not all were killed by artillery fire. Many grenade battles ensued with some hand-to-hand fighting. Marines suffered about 300 casualties.

On March 9, two damaged B-29s landed on Iwo on their way back to the Marianas from firebombing Japan. The following day, the 4th Division captured and left behind two strong points that held up the division advance for two weeks. Movement of all three divisions increased dramatically, thanks to the ill-conceived night infiltration attempt on March 8th that claimed so many Japanese lives.

On March 10, units of the 5th Division approached the final strong point on the island, "The Gorge," or valley, was 500 yards south of Kitano Point, and extended 700 yards to the south. The Gorge contained 1,500 soldiers under direct command of General Kuribayashi, Admiral Ichimaru, and Colonel Ikeda. They fought from an elaborate complex of caves, tunnels, and boulders. Gains of the 5th Division were measured in feet, not yards.

Corporal Wilbur Young was one of those that were amazed at the Japanese ability to conceal themselves. "We would fight all day rarely see a Jap, and it seemed that as many marines were being shot from the rear as from the front."[9] On March 11, Young was ahead of his lines knocking out a machine gun nest with a grenade when one of those "seldom seen" Japanese stepped from behind a boulder and shot Young in the upper arm knocking him down and out of the battle. As the 5th Division slugged away at the enemy in the Gorge, the 3rd Division slowly reduced Cushman's Pocket, and the 4th Division closed around General Senda and his survivors. These two areas were declared secure on March 16, D-day + 25.

Combat efficiency of all three divisions was 40 percent or less at this time, with front lines manned by cooks, bakers, some artillery personnel, and other support troops. Replacements and junior officers with little combat experience manned most leadership positions. Companies were platoon size, and the men had become physically and mentally dazed by the long struggle.

Lieutenant Gen. Kuribayashi's defeat at Iwo Jima was announced in Japan on March 17 by Prime Minister Kuniaki Koiso, as well as Kuribayashi's promotion to full general. At the same time, Ichimaru was promoted to vice admiral, Inouye to rear admiral, and Nishi to full colonel. On the night of March 18, Baron Nishi, nearly blinded and led by his adjutant, took about 50 survivors on a suicide infiltration attempt. Once again, the infiltration was discovered and the Japanese were attacked by mortar, small arms fire, and grenades. Few survived, and those that did took their own lives rather than risk capture.

On March 19, remnants of the 4th Division embarked for Hawaii to train for the attack on the Japanese mainland. The 4th Division had completed four campaigns in 13-and-a-half months, and would require major reinforcement. The 3rd Division replaced the 4th, and the 147th Army Infantry Regiment took over garrison duties. The 5th Division continued to gain distances measured in feet and casualties in their assault on the Gorge. Kuribayashi sent a message to Tokyo on the 21st saying that, "We are still fighting. The strength of my command is now about 400 . . . .Food and water are gone, but our fighting spirit is still running strong."[10]

Marines also continued to fight, but their spirit was not so high. The average battalion that landed with 36 officers and 885 men now averaged 16 officers and 300 men. Companies that should have 250 men averaged 60 men. Platoons were commanded by noncommissioned officers. General Kuribayashi sent his final message to Major Horie on March 23. "The battle situation has come to the last moment. My officers and men are still fighting. All officers and men on ChiChi Jima goodbye."[11]

On March 25, day 34 of the battle, marines captured the

Gorge. This was thought to be the end of organized Japanese resistance on the island, but 3,000 Japanese remained scattered about the island, and they were not about to surrender. Several hundred of them infiltrated a rear tent area just before dawn, where they surprised and killed a number of soldiers and marines, 50 shore party personnel and Seabees, and wounded 100 more. Japanese losses were 250 killed and 18 captured.

One of the marines killed was 1st Lt. Hardy L. Martin, who earned the Medal of Honor earlier that morning. Martin was waiting for a ship to take him away from Iwo Jima when the gunfire grew louder and grenades and mortar fire began to fall very close to his tent. He quickly formed a firing line and stopped the Japanese attack. He was wounded twice as he moved from one position to another, killed four Japanese in a machine gun pit, and led the support personnel in a charge that scattered the Japanese. The remaining Japanese quickly regrouped, overran Martin's position and killed him. Finally, with the help of airmen, seabees, marines, and army medics, the Japanese were halted and thrown back. Martin was the last warrior to earn the Medal of Honor on Iwo Jima.

All records of the Japanese units on Iwo Jima and their battle flags were destroyed before the final days of the battle. Only 216 prisoners were taken, many of them Korean noncombatants from a supply unit. Consequently, little is known about the demise of the senior Japanese leaders. It is thought that Lieutenant Gen. Kuribayashi committed ritual suicide (seppuku) on Sunday March 18 after ordering the final banzai charge. Lieutenant Col. Kaneji Nakane is presumed to have severed Kuribayashi's head after Kuribayashi plunged the short knife into his abdomen. Nakane would then have killed himself.

Rear Adm. Toshinosuke Ichimaru led his sailors against the 5th Division on the western front of Iwo and died in battle. Captain Samaji Inouye, one of Ichimaru's naval commanders, led the thousand-man pre-dawn attack of March 18 and likely died in the attack. Colonel Masuo Ikeda commanded the 145th Infantry Regiment, Kuribayashi's best fighting force, and battled General Erskine's 3rd Division in a week-long slugging match that left both sides bloodied and decimated. Ikeda was likely buried alive in a cave that had the entrance blown closed.

Major Gen. Sadasue Senda, commander of the Second Mixed Brigade, committed suicide on March 14 by shooting himself in the head with his service pistol. Lieutenant Col. Takeichi Nishi, commander of the 26th tank regiment, promised his wife that he would do his best to survive but was unable to do so. The Olympic gold medal winner likely fought with the infantry when his tanks were destroyed and either killed himself or died in the battle of "Cushman's Pocket," on March 22. Colonel Shizuichi Hori also met his death.

Iwo Jima was declared "officially secured" on March 17, D-day + 26. Marine Corps casualties numbered 24,127 including 4,189 dead. It was the bloodiest and most costly battle in Marine Corps history. The final wrap-up phase of the battle took another ten days and cost another 1,724 casualties. Newsmen called Iwo Jima "the worst since Gettysburg" and Holland Smith prepared once again to face his critics in Washington.

Although three of the six "Rosenthal" Suribachi flagraisers, John Bradley, Rene Gagnon, and Ira Hayes, survived the battle and went on to help raise $26.3 billion in war bond drives, three of those marines did not survive.[12] PFC Frank Sousley, Sgt. Michael Strank, and Cpl. Harlon Block were subsequently killed on Iwo Jima. Two of the most renowned personalities of Iwo Jima were never there. They are Felix de Weldon, the sculptor of the Iwo Jima monument, and John Wayne, who played the lead in the movie, Sands of Iwo Jima. Perhaps the most renowned personality is Joe Rosenthal, the Associated Press photographer that took the famous picture. Rosenthal was on Iwo, but only briefly during the climactic moment when he snapped the picture.

Also renown is the quotation from Admiral Chester W. Nimitz as he summed up the collective heroism of the marines on Iwo Jima:

Uncommon Valor Was A Common Virtue

The marines of the Fifth Marine Division had no cover as they were welcomed aboard the fortified island by Japanese defenders.

US Marine Corps

25

THE POTSDAM PROCLAMATION: JULY 26, 1945

The Potsdam Proclamation demanded immediate, unconditional surrender of all Japanese armed forces, and offered Japan one alternative: prompt and utter destruction. The proclamation, released on July 26, 1945, was signed by President Harry Truman, British Prime Minister Winston Churchill, and agreed to by China's Generalissimo Chiang Kai-shek. The proclamation is often thought to be the major undertaking of the Potsdam Conference. It was not.

The Conference that convened on July 17, 1945, in Potsdam, Germany, just a few miles from Berlin in the Soviet sector, had the division of war-torn Europe as its purpose. In November 1943, President Franklin D. Roosevelt, Churchill, and Josef Stalin, president of the Soviet Union, met at Tehran, and again at Yalta in 1945. The purpose of these earlier meetings had been to prosecute the war against Germany. They were generally thought to have been successful. *Time* magazine cited the meetings as positive examples of how "The Big Three" were able to put aside partisan politics and achieve cooperation to defeat Germany.

Allied harmony ended at Potsdam. Roosevelt was succeeded by Harry S. Truman, and Churchill was replaced midway through the conference by the newly elected Clement Attlee. Maybe the issues were tougher at Potsdam. Maybe the difference was due to the change in participants, but, for whatever reason, stubbornness and aggressiveness replaced cooperation. The level of rhetoric was increased, diplomatic niceties disappeared, and previous conflicts were renewed.

Stalin came to Potsdam with agenda items that amounted to demands. Among his demands were the following:

❑ Division of the German merchant fleet and navy. While he was willing to share portions of the shipping, he wanted all he could get for Russia.

❑ Reparations in the amount of $20 billion from Germany and other Axis countries.

❑ Relocation of four-fifths of Germany's remaining heavy-industrial capacity to the Soviet Union.

❑ Russian trusteeships for occupied Europe.

❑ Safe satellite border states for the Soviet Union.

❑ Warm-water ports.

❑ Recognition of Poland's borders and admission of Poland to the United Nations.

❑ Diplomatic recognition of Finland, Romania, Bulgaria, and Hungary, all governments friendly to Russia.

❑ Elimination of the Franco regime in Spain.

❑ Acquisition of Port Arthur and Darien in China, the Kurile Islands, and the Manchurian railroads.

Churchill had much to say, but nothing of substance. Great Britain was prostrated by the war, physically and financially, and virtually capitulated to Stalin. Truman had his own agenda and disagreed with most of Stalin's demands. Germany's shipping would be needed for some time after the war to repatriate prisoners, and to transport food and supplies for refugees, Truman suggested it might be better to sink the German shipping than divide it. Regarding reparation, Truman doubted whether these war-torn countries could pay anything Russia, particularly since the United States expected was to provide massive amounts of aid just to keep them alive. Did Stalin expect the United States to send aid to Germany, and then have Germany forward such aid to Russia? If what remained of Germany's industry was moved to Russia, how would Germany ever recover from the war and be able to pay reparations? Likewise, the political issues involving recognition of Poland, Russia's desire to create friendly border states in Eastern

Europe, the Allied desire for recognition of the governments of Spain, Tangiers, Syria, and Lebanon revealed the "Big Three" to be far apart on such issues. President Truman knew that most of Stalin's demands were *fait accompli* anyway, and he did not intend to waste a lot of time debating them.

Winston Churchill, Harry Truman and Joseph Stalin at the beginning of the Potsdam conference.

British Information Service

Truman had not looked forward to Potsdam. He had never met Stalin, and only knew Churchill from Churchill's visits to Washington to confer with Franklin D. Roosevelt. Truman had spoken bluntly to the Russian Foreign Minister Vyacheslav Molotov, when Molotov stopped in Washington to pay his respects to Truman. Molotov told Truman that, "I have never been talked to like that in my life."[1] "Carry out your agreements," responded Truman, "and you won't get talked to like that."[2] Molotov would be at the conference, and Truman figured Molotov had a good memory.

President Truman embarked aboard the cruiser USS *Augusta,* on July 7, 1945, filled with concern, and a briefcase full of information and suggestions on things to say and do at the conference. At that time, he was a much different man than the confident Harry Truman that agreed to serve as chairman of the conference ten days later. The difference in Truman's confidence had everything to do with the results of the first successful nuclear bomb test on July 16, code-named "Trinity." A second cable on the evening of July 17, reported that a second bomb would be ready for use against Japan anytime after August 3. Truman now had a trump card that would match, or hopefully exceed, that held by Stalin; namely, that Russia already occupied much of Europe and was busy installing puppet governments sympathetic to the Soviets.

After July 17, Truman became a picture of confident energy and vitality. His strong positions on the issues and frank demeanor was in marked contrast to the ailing Franklin D. Roosevelt who represented the United States at the Tehran and Yalta conferences.

By the time Churchill was replaced by Clement Attlee, both Stalin and Truman realized a standoff had occurred. Truman created many confrontations with Stalin over the issues, but Stalin had not yielded on a single point. The power of the atomic bomb, if Stalin knew of the bomb at this time, had no effect on him. Russia had possession of most of Europe and America had the atomic bomb. Stalin and Truman could debate and threaten, but nothing would change the positions of the two countries. What Potsdam did accomplish was the design of the "Cold War" and the "Iron Curtain" that followed.

It would be 1946 before Winston Churchill used the term "Iron

Curtain," to describe the separation of Poland, East Berlin, Czechoslovakia, Hungary, Romania, Bulgaria, and Yugoslavia from the rest of Europe. Churchill, in a speech to an American audience, lamented that all the capital cities of the ancient states of Central and Eastern Europe were on the Soviet side of the Iron Curtain. The governments in Warsaw, Berlin, Prague, Vienna, Budapest, Belgrade, Bucharest, and Sofia were all controlled by Moscow. This was not the liberated Europe that America and Great Britain fought to create.[3]

If Truman was unable to force a change in Stalin's position in Europe, he was determined not to allow Stalin to intervene in the surrender of Japan. Truman was well aware of Japan's attempt to secure more favorable surrender terms by negotiating with Russia. U.S. intelligence intercepted Japan's Foreign Minister Shigenori Togo's radio message to their ambassador in Moscow, and promptly forwarded the decoded message to Truman. The message indicated Emperor Hirohito's desire to end the war as soon as possible, but stated that Japan would not accept unconditional surrender. Truman was also aware that Stalin was ordering his field commanders to move Russian troops as rapidly as possible to the Manchurian border in order to be in position to attack Japanese troops in China.

The Potsdam Proclamation was a Harry Truman initiative, sparked by the successful test of the first atomic bomb and the desire to keep Russia out of the war with Japan. Chiang Kai-shek, generalisimo of China, was not invited to the Potsdam Conference. Winston Churchill, representing Great Britain at the conference, was replaced by Prime Minister Clement Attlee, on July 28, following Churchill's defeat by the Labor party. Truman did not even show the draft proclamation to Stalin, since the Soviet Union was not at war with Japan. When Truman received Chiang's approval of the draft, he promptly released the document to the press. In reality, the only thing related to Potsdam in the Proclamation was that the document was released while Truman was in Potsdam.

That evening, Truman hosted Henry Stimson, his secretary of war; General George Marshall, chairman of the joint chiefs of staff; General H. H. "Hap" Arnold, chief of the army air force; and Ernest J. King, fleet admiral, to discuss the use of the bomb against Japan. Arnold said that "air power could end the war without the atomic bomb." Marshall wanted to warn the Japanese so that they would have a chance to surrender. King proposed a naval blockade to starve Japan into submission. Simply put, they all disagreed on Truman's plan to use the bomb against Japan. They also all failed to acknowledge the Russian equation. Truman promised them that he would not make a decision until he received a full report from Brigadier General Leslie Groves, the administrator for the atomic bomb project. [4]

Grove's report was read by Truman a few days later, and he was pleased by the bomb's potential. Truman knew that Stalin planned to have Russia join the war on Japan sometime after August 8, and there would be nothing that he could do about it. Truman wanted no part of the Russian "Bear" in Japan. The British were not needed to end the war in the Far East, and neither were the Russians. Truman wanted to end the war with Japan before too many Allies were involved, since they would only force another "Potsdam" to divide the spoils. Discussions with Japan would lead to protracted negotiations and Russian involvement. Truman did not know how to bring the war to closure before he arrived at the conference. Now he did, and he intended to do so.

The following morning, Truman showed both "bomb" cables to Churchill. The Prime Minister agreed that Stalin's aid was not necessary to defeat Japan, and, to keep the Russians out, they must not be told of the bomb. But then, Churchill began to pontificate about American public reaction to such an event, and what would be Stalin's claim to defeated Japan? Truman did not plan to wait for answers to these questions. Rather, he decided to play his trump card and end the war as soon as possible, thus reducing casualties and preventing Russia's involvement. At one point, Churchill referred to the need for Japan to surrender with honor. Truman replied that he, "didn't think Japan had any honor after Pearl Harbor."[5] For Harry Truman, the discussion was finished. He had made his decision.

British Prime Minister Atlee, President Truman, and Generalissimo Stalin at Potsdam during the second half of the conference.

US Army

We now know that Stalin was very much aware of the development and successful test of the atomic bomb. His frantic efforts to move forces to Manchuria were successful in the sense that Russia declared war on Japan and invaded Manchuria several hours before the second atomic bomb was dropped on Nagasaki, effectively ending the war.

The Soviets occupied Darien, Port Arthur, the Manchurian railroads, and Sakhalin. Truman ordered General Douglas MacArthur, supreme allied commander, not to discuss reparations or occupancy of mainland Japan with the Soviets. As a result, Russia was kept out of Japan, but she continued to occupy her Manchurian conquests until the communists drove Chiang Kai-shek from China. The Soviet Union continues to occupy Sakhalin and has never signed a peace treaty with Japan.

Australian troops storm ashore in the first assault wave to hit Balikpapan on the southeast coast of oil-rich Borneo in July of 1945.

US Coast Guard

26

THE HORROR OF SANDAKAN

Following Japan's seizure of Borneo in January 1942, Sandakan, located on the northeast coast of North Borneo, became a major port for exporting oil to fuel the Japanese military machinery throughout the Pacific. In addition to the port, construction of an airfield became necessary to provide a refueling point for Japanese aircraft flying from Singapore to the Philippines.

Local laborers were not available in sufficient numbers to build the airfield, consequently, the army made the decision to use POWs from the Changi POW camp in Singapore. At this time, Changi held more than 50,000 British, Australian, and Indian prisoners who were captured when Singapore surrendered. Many of the prisoners actually volunteered for the work detail because conditions were so bad at Changi, and the Japanese promised better conditions and more food if they volunteered.

Of the 2,500 POWs that were alive in the Sandakan POW camps in September 1943, only six survived to the end of the war, a survival rate of less than half-of-one-percent. Such a human tragedy demands that we not forget the horror of Sandakan.

The first group of 3,000 Australian POWs arrived at Sandakan in May 1942. These men did the initial work on the airfield and were later sent to work on the infamous "Death Railway" from Thailand to Burma. A second group of 1,494 POWs was shipped from Changi to Sandakan aboard the 3,000-ton cargo ship *Ubi Maru* in July 1942.[1] Upon arrival at the port, the POWs were forced to march the eight miles to the camp. Many of the men were sick or exhausted from the ten-day trip, having had very little food or water and enduring extremely cramped conditions. Some POWs were unable to walk and had to be moved to the camp by truck. The 1,494 POWs were crowded into a camp designed for 200 people.

Except for the overcrowding, the initial treatment of the POWs at Sandakan was an improvement over Changi. The men marched five miles from camp to the airfield each morning, worked from 7:30 A.M. to 5:00 P.M., and marched back. They had Sunday off, were paid a small amount for their labor, and could purchase food from a canteen. More importantly, the POWs were permitted to develop vegetable gardens. Captain Susumu Hoshijima, resident engineer for the airfield, was also POW camp commandant. Hoshijima left the supervision of the camp to subordinates, but took a personal interest in the airfield construction. He was well aware that the POWs were his prime source of labor, and, at least initially, he provided sufficient food for the POWs to survive.

During mid-1942, the Allies began their offensive in the Pacific. Coincident with Japanese losses at Guadalcanal and Papua New Guinea, conditions for the Sandakan POWs worsened. The POW food ration was reduced, consequently large numbers of men became ill from malaria, dysentery, beriberi, and tropical ulcers. Although medicine was available in large quantity it was not provided to the POWs. As more men became sick, work on the airfield began to fall behind schedule. During March 1943, 750 British POWs were moved to Sandakan from a POW camp in Kuching. In April, another 500 prisoners arrived from Changi.

The Japanese losses at Guadalcanal and Papua New Guinea, and the possibility that the Allies might try to retake Borneo lowered Japanese morale. Most of the Japanese Army guards were sent to operational units and replaced by Formosan guards. These guards, who had no status with the Japanese, began to take out their frustrations on the prisoners. The local *Kempeitai* (military police) were used to torture and obtain confessions from POWs suspected of obtaining illegal information and supplies. POWs and civilians were tried for these offenses and found guilty. Suspected ringleaders were executed and others were given long prison terms.

In November 1943, most POW officers were moved from Sandakan to the Kuching camp. Coincidentally with the removal of the officers, additional Formosan guards were added to each POW work detail. Sundays became workdays. Beatings increased and the Formosan guards proved to be much crueler than the Japanese. POWs thought to be shirking on the job were smashed with ax handles or clubs. Often the whole work detail of 40 or 50 men would be severely beaten due to the suspected infraction of an individual POW.

Prisoners would pass out from the beatings. While unconscious, their limbs would be broken or teeth smashed from their mouths. If a prisoner reported that his wounds prevented him from working, the guards would kick the wound or hit it with a club, causing tremendous pain to the helpless POW. Acts of suspected insubordination resulted in daily beatings and being locked inside a wooden cage five feet by three feet by two feet. Prisoners were confined in the cages for as long as 40 days. The first seven days in the cage, the POWs received no food. They had no water for three days. Each day they were taken out of the cage and beaten.

As the beatings and torture of POWs increased, their food ration decreased. In August 1942, POWs working on the airfield were given 750 grams of rice per day plus 600 grams of assorted vegetables. In 1943, rations were cut to 400 grams of rice per day and only a small amount of tapioca or sweet potato for vegetables. By September 1944, the food ration was cut to 100 grams of rice per day. A POW who arrived at Sandakan in August 1942, weighing 154 pounds, was down to 66 pounds in December 1944. His case is typical of all the Sandakan POWs.[2]

Sandakan was bombed by Allied aircraft for the first time on October 14, 1944. Bombing attacks continued on a near daily basis thereafter. Besides further lowering Japanese morale, resulting in more abuse to the prisoners, the bombings destroyed much of the local food crops that had been used to feed the POWs. All remaining food was seized by the Japanese and stored for their use. As could be expected, the mortality rate of the POWs increased dramatically. More than 400 POWs died in less than four months. At the end of 1944, only 1,850 POWs remained alive. Of this number, only 700 were capable of working.[3]

Continuous bombing of Sandakan rendered the airfield useless. Initially, the POWs were made to repair the bomb damage, but this was discontinued in early January 1945. By this time, the Allies had captured Palawan Island, to the northwest of Borneo, and the Japanese reorganized to meet the anticipated invasion of Borneo. Two of the three battalions at Sandakan, as well as other forces throughout Borneo, were moved to Brunei and Api on the west coast. The decision was made to use 500 POWs as bearers on the march from Sandakan to Api. The POWs were divided into nine groups of roughly 50 men per group. Each POW would be required to carry 65 pounds of battalion equipment and ammunition on his back. A rough path had been hacked through the jungle from Sandakan to Api, but the 204-mile trek was during the monsoon season, through rough mountainous terrain, through flooded valleys and swamps, and across rivers.

The first group of Japanese and POWs left Sandakan at 6:00 A.M., on January 29, 1945. The group was under the command of Capt. Shoichi Yamamoto. Yamamoto's battalion arrived in Borneo in October 1944, and had been engaged in construction of gun emplacements around Sandakan. A total of 470 POWs (370 Australian and 100 British) began the march. Prior to the march, Hoshijima gave the POWs the head, feet, and entrails of an old, skinny horse to eat,[4] and told them that they were being sent to a place where there would be good food and medicine, and where they would, at some time in the future, be repatriated. While Hoshijima was raising the morale of the POWs, Yamamoto gave orders to his guards that no prisoners were to be left behind once the march began. Any POW who fell out of line was to be disposed of.[5]

The Japanese plan for resupply and rest broke down immediately. There was barely sufficient food for the first group at the initial resupply point. The following groups received no food. Due to the monsoon, the marchers had to slog through heavy mud that was particularly difficult for the POWs who had no decent footwear. By February 12, about 120 miles into the march, 15 POWs and four Japanese soldiers from the first group had died. Group two lost a similar number of POWs and 11 Japanese soldiers.

POWs suffered greatly from their tropical ulcers, caused when a cut becomes infected, and, without medicine, an ulcer forms. Within a short time, the flesh begins to decay, forming large body cavities where the rotting flesh dissolves. The monsoon and difficulty of the march worsened the condition of the ulcers. There were also cobras, crocodiles, and huge leeches with which to contend. The loss of blood from leech bites further weakened the POWs.

The groups would stop in the evening to rest, but the POWs had nothing but leaves to cover themselves against the night rains. Each morning, those men who were still able to walk, got up and continued the march. Several guards would be left with the POWs who were too ill or exhausted to rise. Soon, shots would be heard and the POWs were never seen again. Prisoners that fell behind during the march were similarly murdered.

Group nine of the first march reached the 200-mile point on February 21. This group lost 18 POWs and seven Japanese soldiers. Groups six through nine were so weak, including the Japanese guards, that they were told to stay at the checkpoint and rest. Forty of the 200 POWs in these groups had died, and the rest were so weak that they continued to die at a rate of four or five per day. POWs in these groups were forced to exist on frogs, snails, and leaves.

Groups one through five reached Ranau, some 230 miles into

the march on February 19. Less than 200 POWs from the original 270 survived. The remaining POWs were unable to continue the march to Api. A decision was made for Yamamoto's unit to continue to Api, and the POWs were placed under the charge of Major Yoshio Watanabe. The POWs were put to work at Ranau repairing huts, carrying water, gathering wood, and doing other camp chores. Within a month, more than half of the 200 POWs died. The remaining POWs at Ranau were then forced to transport rice to the Japanese units (groups six to nine at Paginatan), the 200-mile checkpoint. POWs were loaded with 45-pound rice bags and made to carry them 30 miles to Paginatan. The round trip took five days. Any POWs who could still walk after their first trip were loaded up and sent again. One POW, Keith Botterill, made the trip five times. POWs who fell and could not get back up or continue were bayoneted or shot. Of 20 POWs who left Ranau on one such trip, only five survived. The POWs from Paginatan were moved to Api at the end of March. When all POWs from the first march finally assembled at Api, less than 150 prisoners remained from the 470 that left Sandakan.

When the first march left Sandakan in January, 1,300 POWs remained. By March, 10 to 12 POWs were dying each day due to illness and starvation. In April, all food and water to these POWs were discontinued. The prisoners were forced to scavenge for roots and insects, eat rats, and boil what foul water they could find. On May 20, Captain Hoshijima was transferred from Sandakan and replaced by Captain Takuo Tatakuwa. Tatakuwa had orders to move all POWs from the camp. On May 27, Sandakan was bombarded by Allied warships for the first time.

Tatakuwa made the decision to march 536 POWs (439 Australian and 97 British), using Formosan guards, to Ranau. He had the camp burned and destroyed excess ammunition. Some 288 POWs were still at the camp, too ill or starved to make the march. Organization of the second march was similar to the first, with about 50 POWs per group and a total of 11 groups. The second march began at 7:00 A.M. on May 29, with orders from

Tatakuwa to kill all stragglers. The POWs in the second march were much weaker than the POWs of the first march. Like the earlier marchers, they were forced to carry the rations of the Japanese soldiers and Formosan guards on their backs.

Many POWs were unable to continue after travelling a mile or two. Group seven lost six men in the first four miles. Escape for the POWs became impossible since they were in such poor physical shape that they could not survive in the jungle even if they could get away. Two POWs, however, proved to be exceptions. Dick Braithwaite and a POW named Campbell escaped into the jungle during the march, were discovered and cared for by local people, and were rescued by Allied forces in mid-August 1945.

Prisoners on the march existed on 85 grams of rice per day plus whatever they could dig, catch, or find to eat. Even the 85 grams of rice were discontinued before the march was completed. When the march reached Ranau on June 25, only 183 POWs from the original 536 survived.

Following the departure of the second march from Sandakan, 288 POWs remained at Sandakan. They were forced to improvise their shelter, since all camp buildings had been destroyed, and were not provided with any food or water. In addition to the POWs at the former camp, there remained one Japanese soldier, Staff Sergeant Hisao Mirozumi, 16 Formosan guards, and a few Javanese laborers. There was also a battalion of Japanese Army personnel in the Sandakan area. On June 9, Second Lieutenant Iwashita of the nearby Okuyama Battalion was assigned 75 of the remaining POWs plus 37 Japanese soldiers and told to march the group to Ranau. None of the POWs survived the march.

By July 12, the 185 POWs remaining at Sandakan had dwindled to 50. Staff Sergeant Hisao Mirozumi was told to take 23 relatively healthy POWs to an air raid shelter trench near the airfield and shoot them. Mirozumi used 12 Formosan guards to execute the

POWs. Their bodies were then dumped into the trench and covered with earth. The last of the remaining 35 POWs were killed on August 1.[6]

At the end of June, there remained 189 POWs at Ranau that survived the two marches. All of the survivors suffered from starvation and tropical diseases. The POWs were given 75 grams of rice per day, no vegetables, and were expected to put in a full day's work. They were dying at a rate of 10 to 15 per day. On July 7, Keith Botterill learned of Japanese plans to kill all the POWs. On July 7, Botterill, Dick Moxham, Nelson Short and a POW named Anderson escaped into the jungle. Anderson died during the escape, but the other three made contact with an Australian soldier, a member of a reconnaissance team. The three POWs were too weak to travel with the reconnaissance team, but were cared for by local people and were later rescued by the Allies.

On July 26, William Sticpewich was told by a Japanese guard that all POWs were to be killed. On the following day, the guards around the POW huts were doubled, but on July 28, Sticpewich and another POW named Raither managed to escape. Raither died in the jungle on August 1, but Sticpewich survived and was rescued in mid-August.

When Sticpewich and Raither escaped, the number of surviving POWs was down to 38. Of these, only 12 could walk. On the morning of August 1, the order was given to kill all the remaining POWs. Two large holes were dug at the end of the graveyard and POWs were forced to walk or crawl to the sites. Once there, they were shot and their bodies pushed into the holes.

During the Allied investigations of the POW situation at Sandakan, they found huge stockpiles of food and medicine. In a large storage room under the commandant's house, 90 metric tons of rice and 160,000 quinine tablets were found. Other stockpiles included huge amounts of quinine tablets plus vitamins A, B, C, and D tablets, and medical and surgical equipment. None of this material was ever given to the POWs.

Shortly after the emperor announced Japan's surrender to the Allies, the army ministry in Tokyo destroyed all files relating to prisoners and POW camps, and directed field commands to do the same. On September 17, the minister for the Japanese Army, Sadashi Shinomura, sent a message to all field commanders to place the blame for maltreatment of prisoners upon Korean and Formosan guards.

The Australian War Crimes Trials for the Sandakan massacre took place at Labuan, a small island in Brunei Bay, in January 1946. The first Japanese to be tried was Captain Susumu Hoshijima, commandant of the Sandakan prison compound. The prosecutor for the Sandakan trials was Athol Moffitt, a lawyer and officer in the Australian Ninth Division.[7]

Hoshijima was charged with cruelty, cruelty by confinement resulting in POW deaths, starvation and denial of medical attention causing deaths, and forcing sick men to do heavy labor.[8] Prosecution of the Sandakan war criminals was made difficult by the destruction of records, the murder of almost all of the POWs, and the opportunity for the suspected Japanese war criminals to develop and compare testimony prior to the trial.

Without the testimony of POW William Sticpewith, who was flown from Canberra to Lubuan to testify for the prosecution, there would have been no eyewitnesses to the starvation, torture, and murder of the POWs.

The systematic starvation and beatings of the POWs was determined to be a plot to weaken and kill all the prisoners. Evidence made clear that Hoshijima had far more rice and medicine than he could have ever used, but that he refused to provide such food or medicine to the POWs. Capt. Hoshijima was found guilty of all charges on January 26, 1946, and sentenced to death by hanging. His sentence was approved on review and Hoshijima was hanged at Rabaul on April 6, 1946. Hoshijima was defiant to the end, reportedly biting the hand of a guard that tied his arms prior to the hanging.[9]

The second Sandakan trial charged 11 Japanese; four captains, five lieutenants, a warrant officer, and a sergeant for murder and forcing POWs to make long, forced marches, under difficult conditions that resulted in many POW deaths. The lack of eyewitnesses and other evidence made prosecution of the defendants even more difficult than at the earlier trial of Hoshijima.

Only two POWs from the "First Death March," Keith Botterill and Dick Moxham, were still alive, but both were still in such poor health that they could not be returned to Borneo to testify. Both men wrote depositions that were used in court, but there could be no first- person identification of suspected murderers by means of a deposition.

The court, on January 28, sentenced ten of the defendants to death, and one officer to life imprisonment. The reviewing authority, concerned about the lack of eyewitnesses to the murders that took place on the march, ordered a new trial.[10] The second trial was conducted at Rabaul in May 1946. Keith Botterill and William Sticpewith both testified during the second trial. There was ample evidence that POWs that could not keep up with "The March" were killed by guards. Captain Shoiichi Yamamoto, officer-in-charge of the first march, and Lieutenant K. Abe were sentenced to death by hanging. The sentence was carried out at Rabaul on October 19, 1946. The other seven officers were sentenced to ten years imprisonment. Warrant Officer Gotunda and an unidentified sergeant were acquitted because neither could be positively identified as murderers of straggling POWs at the end of the line of march.

Captains Takuo Takakuwa and Genzo Watanabe, officers-in-charge of the "Second Death March," and massacres of POWs at

Ranau, were tried at Labuan in early January 1946. Both Takakuwa and Watanabe admitted the murder of POWs during the second march and at Ranau. The accused used the defense of military necessity for their actions. The court found each man guilty as charged. Takakuwa was sentenced to death by hanging and was executed at Rabaul on April 6, 1946. Watanabe was sentenced to death by firing squad and was executed on Morotai on March 16, 1946. In separate trials, Staff Sergeant Hisao Mirozumi was sentenced to life imprisonment for the murder of POWs at Sandakan. Only four Formosan guards received death sentences. The remainder received sentences of imprisonment for 12 to 15 years.

Lieutenant Gen. Masuo Baba, commander of the 37th Imperial Japanese Army, was tried in Rabaul in late May and early June 1947. Baba was the only Japanese general tried by an Australian court. Lieutenant Gen. Baba was charged with disregarding and failing to discharge his duties by allowing brutal atrocities and other high crimes against the POWs. Although not charged with any offense for his action, Baba refused to surrender his forces until September 10, three weeks after the emperor's announcement of surrender. His refusal to surrender in a timely manner resulted in additional casualties on both sides.

Baba's charges were similar to the ones lodged against General Homma for the "Bataan Death March," and General Yamashita for the "Rape of Manila." Baba was found guilty, his conviction was upheld upon review, and he was sentenced to death by hanging. He was hanged at Rabaul on August 7, 1947.[11] Colonel Tatsuji Suga, chief commandant of all Borneo POW camps, committed suicide on September 16, 1945, at Labuan.[12]

POW William Sticpewich was promoted to major. Sadly, this fine man that survived the horror of Sandakan, the Death March, and the jungles of Borneo, was no match for the automobiles of Melbourne. He was struck by a car and killed a few years after his testimony.[13]

281

The Sandakan Memorial Park, Labuan War Cemetery, Kundasan Memorial, and British Memorial at Kundasan, Sabah, all honor the memory of those that lost their lives in British North Borneo under the Japanese occupation from 1942 to 1945.

Sandakan was the worst tragedy suffered by Australians during the war. It seems appropriate to quote from some of the memorial plaques dedicated by the living.

THIS MEMORIAL GARDEN IS DEDICATEDTO THE MEMORY
OF THE 1,800 AUSTRALIAN AND 600 BRITISH
SERVICEMEN WHOM PERISHED IN THE P.O.W. CAMPS IN
SANDAKAN
AND IN THE 3 FORCED MARCHES FROM SANDAKAN TO
RANAU, AND OF THE MANY SABAHANS WHO SUFFERED
DEATH IN TRYING TO ASSIST THEM.

IN SANDAKAN
FROM SANDAKAN TO RANAU
1944-1945

"LET THEM NOT DEPART FROM THINE EYES, KEEP THEM
IN THE MIDST OF THINE HEART"
(PROV. IV.21)

THE MEMORY OF THEM SHALL LIVE FOREVERMORE.

Kundasan Memorial

Australian War Affairs

THEY ARE NOT DEAD, NOT EVEN BROKEN:
ONLY THEIR DUST HAS GONE BACK HOME TO THE EARTH:
FOR THEY, THE ESSENTIAL THEY, SHALL HAVE REBIRTH
WHENEVER A WORD OF THEM IS SPOKEN

Labuan War Cemetery

Dame Mary Gilmore

27

FLEET ADMIRAL CHESTER W. NIMITZ

History is replete with men who have been suddenly thrust into command positions with little or no time to prepare for the life and death decisions that must be made. During World War II, names like Winston Churchill, tasked with the survival of England; Douglas MacArthur, when he was ordered to leave Corregidor and proceed to Australia; Jonathan Wainwright, when he was suddenly left to defend Corregidor; and Harry Truman, with the agonizing question of whether to use the atomic bomb against Japan, come quickly to mind.

Perhaps none of these men, Churchill, MacArthur, Wainwright or Truman, felt the magnitude of the mission, heavy weight of responsibility, and loneliness of command more acutely than Chester W. Nimitz as he traveled from Washington, D.C., to Pearl Harbor to take command of the Pacific Fleet.

In early 1941, when President Roosevelt lost faith in Admiral James Richardson, commander of the Pacific Fleet, Chester Nimitz was strongly considered to be Richardson's relief. Nimitz, realizing that there were at least 50 deserving admirals senior to him, asked to be excused from consideration. He felt the ill will that would be generated by such advancement would be bad for the navy and his own career. Admiral Husband Kimmell accepted the appointment that Nimitz declined. In doing so, Kimmell jumped past 31 senior naval officers and probably earned the ill will that Nimitz avoided.

On December 16, Nimitz was notified by Secretary of the Navy Frank Knox, that he was to take command of the Pacific Fleet at Pearl Harbor. This time there was no opportunity for Nimitz to decline. America was at war. Now he would have the same seniority problem, plus the burden of relieving his good friend Admiral Kimmell. Knox told Nimitz that President Roosevelt said, "Tell Nimitz to get the hell out to Pearl and stay there till the war is won."[1] Nimitz made plans to leave for Pearl Harbor three days later.

Fleet Admiral Chester W. Nimitz, December 1944.

US Navy

Nimitz traveled from Washington, D.C. to California by train. Enroute he read the report of casualties from the December 7 attack, and carefully studied pictures of the sunken and damaged ships. USS *Arizona* had been Nimitz's flagship only three years earlier. Admiral Isaac Kidd had relieved Nimitz as the commander. Now, the Arizona was destroyed and sunk, and Admiral Kidd was missing and almost certainly dead, as were more than a thousand crewmembers. Nimitz's loss was both personal and professional. He was grateful for the train compartment that allowed him to express his emotions privately.

Nimitz also read secret documents that said Japanese forces had landed in Thailand and Malaya, and were advancing on Singapore. The British battleships, HMS *Prince of Wales* and *Repulse,* had been sunk by Japanese planes near Malaya. The small naval garrison on Guam surrendered, the Philippines and Gilbert Islands were being invaded by Japanese troops, and Japanese aircraft were bombing Singapore, Hong Kong, Midway Atoll, and Johnston Island. Only at Wake Island had the Japanese attack been repulsed.

Admiral Nimitz arrived at Pearl Harbor on December 25, 1941, in a steady rain. As he stepped from the plane, he was met by the repugnant stink of thousands of gallons of black oil, charred debris, burned and rotting bodies, and the news that Wake Island had surrendered.[2] As he was being taken from the seaplane to the pier in a filthy, oil-coated whaleboat, an escorting officer explained that the boats moving about in the harbor were still recovering the bodies as they floated to the surface.

A short distance away lay the new commander's navy. Only the hulls of USS *Oklahoma* and *Utah* were visible. USS *Nevada,* heavily damaged, was aground off Hospital Point. *California, West Virginia,* and *Arizona* were sunk in shallow water, and a minesweeper was lying on her side. "This is a terrible sight," said the shocked Nimitz.[3]

Nimitz was aware that morale of the navy at Pearl Harbor was extremely low. Like any commander, he would have liked the luxury of forming his own staff from people he respected and trusted. This was not to be. Those sailors and officers that formed the staffs of several Pearl Harbor commands, both ashore and afloat, had done nothing wrong and desperately needed leadership. Nimitz consoled Admiral Kimmel, promising him his personal support in the investigations that were certain to take place. He asked Admiral William S. Pye, who had relieved Kimmel for an interim period, to stay on and assist him. Then he called a conference of staff officers for the following morning.

It was a gloomy group of officers who assembled. They were prepared to be admonished and sent to unimportant desk jobs in naval districts all over the United States. Instead, Nimitz said he had complete confidence in them, did not blame them whatsoever for what happened, and asked them to stay and help him defeat the enemy. Most of the staff stayed; morale rose perceptibly.

This one action of Admiral Nimitz says volumes about the man. Here he was, in an unfamiliar environment of agony and defeat, most of his ships at the bottom of Pearl Harbor, no staff to assist him, and probably unpopular for being promoted ahead of so many senior naval officers. Instead of seeking compassion, leadership, and guidance, he provided it. From that moment, the Pacific Fleet was in good hands, and winning the war was only a matter of time.

Nimitz proved to be a sound advocate for the navy at the same time that he salved the wounds of the navy staff. The attack on Pearl Harbor was bad, he said, but not nearly as bad as it could have been. The Japanese missed the 4.5 million-gallon fuel farm. Had they set it afire, the Pacific Fleet would have been forced to retreat to the West Coast. Nor did the Japanese damage the carriers, because they were out to sea, and all but two of the eight battleships damaged at Pearl Harbor would be repaired and returned to the fleet.

Nimitz went on to explain, on at least three separate occasions, that had Admiral Kimmel been given notice of the enemy's approach, he would have sent his entire fleet to sea to engage the enemy. The Pacific Fleet would have had one carrier, USS *Enterprise,* against six modern Japanese carriers and aircraft. Japanese escort vessels were modern and capable of faster speeds than our slow battleships. Kimmel would have lost the entire Pacific Fleet in deep water along with 20,000 sailors and marines. More importantly, the attack galvanized a divided America and put us on a course to victory.

In describing Nimitz, one is tempted to compare him with his seniors, peers, and subordinates. His immediate senior, Admiral Ernest J. King, commander-in-chief U.S. Fleet, later chief of naval operations (CNO), assumed his duty the day before Nimitz became commander-in-chief, Pacific (CinCPac). King is generalized as being cold, aloof, and humorless. A navy officer once described him as, "Tall, gaunt and taut, with a high dome, piercing eyes, aquiline nose, and a firm jaw, somewhat resembling Don Quixote."[4] King had a well-deserved reputation as a stern taskmaster, hard on himself and on others. He rarely smiled and had no time for interest in others or for pleasantries. He inspired respect, but not love. He seemed to want it that way.

Perhaps Nimitz's only peer in the Pacific was Douglas MacArthur. The differences in leadership styles and qualities are striking. MacArthur, acknowledged as a brilliant strategist, was vain, with a high media profile; someone always obsessed with the press and the stories they printed. Nimitz had a low profile, with a dignified humility, that did not appeal to the press. When the press needed colorful stories concerning the navy in the Pacific, they turned not to Nimitz, but Admiral "Bull" Halsey.

Nimitz used his humility and fine sense of humor in staff meetings to gain the loyalty, and perhaps to some degree, the affection of his subordinates. MacArthur used his oratorical ability and arrogance, coupled from time to time with theatrical flamboyance, to gain the devotion of his subordinates. Loyalty, he believed, would come from victories in battle.

Admiral Nimitz found the time to demonstrate empathy for his people. He took a personal interest in those that worked for him and would ask them about their goals, their families, and their problems. By doing so, he gained their respect, loyalty and admiration.

Nimitz had the ability to motivate, and also to pacify. This ability served him well in his dealings with General MacArthur, senior officers from other services, and senior naval officers whose feathers became ruffled from time to time. The following story illustrates this ability.

> Once while walking in the environs of Washington D.C., with a friend, Nimitz passed under an overhanging branch of ripe cherries. Without hesitation, Nimitz used his walking stick to pull the branches lower so that he and his friend could pick and enjoy the cherries. While eating the cherries, the owner's wife came from the adjoining house, and accused them of being common thieves. When the lady stopped her tirade for a moment, Nimitz, with an expression of genuine regret, began complimenting her on the excellence of her cherries. He went on to praise the condition and appearance of her house and grounds. The lady began to smile, Nimitz smiled back, and the lady offered Nimitz and his friend all the cherries they wanted.[5]

Many of Nimitz's subordinates were men of stubborn convictions, some with a penchant for profane language. For this reason, they became favorites of the press. "Terrible" Ted Turner, H.M. "Howlin' Mad" Smith, and William "Bull" Halsey are not nicknames given by accident. They are well-deserved nicknames that also served the press well. It is a credit to Nimitz that he could absorb the directions of Admiral King, coordinate and cooperate with General MacArthur, and still mold his own strong-willed subordinates into the most effective fighting force in history.

Nimitz would have preferred more time to rebuild the Pacific Fleet, train the crews, and establish support facilities before he began offensive operations. Admiral King was having none of it. King pushed Nimitz to conduct carrier raids against the Gilbert, Marianas, Marshall, and Caroline island groups and to provide carrier escort for 5,000 marines that were being shipped from the west coast of the United States to Samoa to defend against further Japanese expansion.

Nimitz questioned his staff about offensive operations and received strong opposition to such a plan. His staff feared the loss of the carriers which were America's last mobile defense in the Pacific. The debate continued until January 7, 1942, when Vice Adm. William Halsey, back from chasing the Japanese fleet that attacked Pearl Harbor, barged into a staff meeting.[6] Halsey was appalled at the defeatism he found in Nimitz's staff and so informed Nimitz. Nimitz never forgot the support he received from Halsey and later in the war, when Halsey was being considered for censure, Nimitz refused to speak against his best supporter.

Halsey volunteered to lead the carrier raids against the Japanese-held Marshall and Gilbert Islands, and left Pearl Harbor with the USS *Enterprise* Task Force on January 11, 1942. On the same day, carrier *Saratoga* was torpedoed 450 miles southwest of Oahu, Hawaii. *Saratoga's* damage was extensive, requiring an estimated three months of repair. This left USS *Lexington* as the only carrier to guard the Hawaiian islands.

The risk taken by Nimitz and Halsey was huge. The Pacific Fleet now consisted of three carriers (*Enterprise, Lexington* and *Yorktown*), four old battleships, 11 heavy cruisers, four light cruisers, 36 destroyers, and 17 submarines. Not a bad fleet for a third-power nation, but insufficient to take the war to Japan.

Following the unopposed landing of the marines on Samoa, Halsey was joined by Admiral Fletcher with the *Yorktown* task force for the raid on the enemy islands. In actuality, the raids were ineffective, due to the inexperience of the navy pilots, extreme caution of Admiral Fletcher's task force, and the pilots overestimation of their achievements. Halsey was not about to add to the bad news being constantly received by the United States. His message to Nimitz read:

TOTAL DESTRUCTION OF TWO SUBMARINES

ONE LIGHT CRUISER

ONE SMALL CARRIER

FOUR AUXILIARY

WIDE SPREAD DESTRUCTION

THIRTEEN PLANES

CRUISER CHESTER

ENTERPRISE DAMAGED[7]

The press loved Halsey's report as did the American public. Banner headlines proclaimed, "Pearl Harbor Avenged,"[8] and morale received a much-needed boost. Actual damage to the enemy consisted of one transport and two smaller vessels sunk, damage to eight other ships, and minor damage to some shore installations. Halsey endeared himself to the press, and America was on the offensive.

Raids on Wake Island and Eniwetok, the battle of the Coral Sea, and Doolittle's Raid on Tokyo followed in quick succession. Nimitz retained Admiral Kimmell's intelligence officer, Commander Edwin T. Layton, and his assistant, Lieutenant Cmdr. Joseph J. Rochefort when he assumed command of the Pacific Fleet. Nimitz was displaying compassion at the time, but his leadership paid handsome dividends when the intelligence officers predicted the date and place of Japan's attack of Midway Island.

As the result of intelligence provided by his staff officers, Nimitz was able to preposition his forces to meet the Japanese fleet, resulting in a major victory and the sinking of four Japanese carriers during the battle that took place June 3-4, 1942. Following receipt of the battle reports, Nimitz extended his hand to Layton and Rochefort and stated, "Today, Gentlemen, Pearl Harbor has been revenged."[9]

Obviously a posed, and rather "tense" picture of admirals Nimitz, King, and Halsey.

US Navy

A dispatch was received by Nimitz during this time announcing that General Douglas MacArthur had been designated supreme commander, Allied Forces in the Southwest Pacific. The battle of

Midway stopped the Japanese advance in the Pacific, and the battle for Guadalcanal sent them retreating back towards Japan. Some may argue that Nimitz was tardy in providing the necessary support to the marines on Guadalcanal. One must remember; however, that the Pacific theater was only allocated 15 percent of America's assets. The remainder went to the European theater. Nimitz had little to provide.

Nimitz visited Guadalcanal on September 29. He was gratified to find that General Vandegrift and his men had high morale and intended to hold the island. What he needed, Vandegrift told Nimitz, was more men to man the defensive line, and more fighter planes to beat off the bombers that constantly attacked the airfield and marine defensive positions. Vandegrift also told Nimitz that far too many navy ship commanders seemed reluctant to risk their ships. Nimitz smiled but Vandegrift's message struck home. "I promise you support to the maximum of our resources," Nimitz told Vandegrift.

Once President Roosevelt announced his intention to hold Guadalcanal, and the army began to provide men and materials, Nimitz relieved Vice Adm. Robert J. Ghormley, South Pacific force and area commander, and replaced him with "Bull" Halsey. Halsey's reaction to the news was typical. "Jesus Christ and General Jackson!," he announced. "This is the hottest potato they ever handed me."[10]

In true Halsey style, he met with Vandegrift shortly after assuming command. He told Vandegrift, "Go on back (to Guadalcanal) I promise you everything I've got."[11] Unsaid was Halsey's intent to send his ships in harm's way to challenge Japan's nightly shelling of the marines on Guadalcanal. Halsey did exactly that, losing large numbers of ships, sailors, and ship commanders. Japan's navy lost even more, and the marines, with help from the army Americal Division, held Guadalcanal and sent the Japanese army and navy reeling back towards Japan. Never again would Japan mount a major offensive in the Pacific.

The date was January 1943. The battle for Guadalcanal took six months of coordinated land, sea, and air warfare by both sides. Following America's victory at Guadalcanal, the joint chiefs of staff decided to follow two separate paths to Japan. One route would be through the southwest Pacific to the Philippines. General MacArthur would command this drive. The second route would move across the central Pacific to Formosa (later changed to Okinawa), under command of Admiral Nimitz.

General MacArthur and Admiral Nimitz discuss Strategy in Honolulu in 1944.

National Archives

Although the Pacific Fleet was increasing in number of ships, Nimitz was sorely tested as he formed two fleets and two amphibious forces to support the two separate thrusts towards Japan. No less of a problem was dealing with General MacArthur, who argued that his drive should have priority. The United States Navy and Admirals King and Nimitz were not about to pass operational control of navy ships to MacArthur. To forestall such an event, Nimitz tasked Admiral Halsey to lead the attack on Rabaul under the command of MacArthur.

The actual plan, code named Cartwheel, called for Halsey to operate under general directives from MacArthur, but all ships, planes, and ground forces of the Pacific Command would remain under control of Nimitz.[12] The plan was unwieldy at best, but it worked. Halsey and MacArthur established a harmonious working relationship that made Nimitz's job of coordinating with MacArthur much easier.

The battles of the Pacific that took place between America's victory at Guadalcanal and the surrender ceremony on September 2, 1945, in Tokyo Bay, are well-documented in other chapters of this book and books by other authors. The remainder of this chapter concerns itself with Nimitz, the man and professional naval officer.

A typical Nimitz day began early by receiving intelligence reports and other priority matters in his office. His staff conference began at 9:00 A.M., and usually ended in an hour. Nimitz would often step out to his pistol range and practice shooting to relax. Promptly at 11:00 A.M., he received new commanding officers in his office. Nimitz would open the meeting with a few remarks about what the fleet was planning to do, and then ask each of the attendees what they were doing. "Some of the of the best help and advice I've had," Nimitz stated, "comes from junior officers and enlisted men."[13]

Nimitz often skipped the midday meal, but when he did have lunch, it was usually for further discussion. Sometimes he would take a walk or a short nap. Afternoons were spent in planning sessions with various staffs for future operations. His involvement was informal but thorough. Often he could critique war plans while they were in the draft stage, thus enabling revisions before they were sent to him for formal review.

When time permitted, Nimitz often strolled throughout the headquarters, talking to anyone or everyone he met. He would offer suggestions when appropriate and receive advice and information as well. On quieter days, he might visit navy or marine commands on Oahu.

The work day usually ended by 4:30 P.M. Nimitz would take a long walk, play tennis, and enjoy a horseshoe match. Dinner was always with guests and visitors, and the admiral's steward was an excellent cook. Occasionally, Admiral Spruance acted as bartender for the cocktail hour that preceded dinner. Nimitz had a rule that no more than two cocktails were to be served before dinner.

After dinner, Nimitz might show a movie or chat with his guests. The evening would end early, usually when Nimitz announced that he had to go back to his office to read the latest dispatches before sleep.

The CinCPac staff worked seven days per week. Nimitz would frequently organize picnics or beach outings for the staff, but they did not prove to be as popular as Nimitz would have liked. He wanted his staff to remain healthy and efficient, and encouraged them to participate in sports and exercise regularly.

When Admiral Spruance joined the CinCPac staff as chief of staff in 1942, the staff consisted of 45 officers. By 1944, the staff had grown to 250 officers. In addition to planning for the operations being conducted, many of the staff were involved with the supply and logistic functions, and garrisoning the islands captured from the Japanese.

On December 19, 1944, congress established a five star rank for four army generals and four navy admirals. The new rank was established to put American military leaders on the same level as some of the Allied military. The army promptly nominated and had confirmed General George C. Marshall, chairman of the joint staff; General Douglas MacArthur, commander of the southwest Pacific; General Dwight D. Eisenhower, supreme commander, allied expeditionary force; and General Arnold, chief of the army air corps.

The navy recommendations consisted of Admiral William Leahy, chief of staff to the president; Admiral Ernest King, chief of naval operations, Admiral Nimitz; and Admiral Halsey. Leahy, King, and Nimitz were quickly confirmed, but Admiral King was reluctant to have Halsey promoted if Admiral Ray Spruance was not. King sent a memorandum to Secretary of the Navy James Forrestal, naming Halsey, Spruance, and four other admirals as deserving of the fifth star. Forrestal was unwilling to make a recommendation, and deferred to President Truman. Truman lost no time in selecting Halsey and congress confirmed his promotion to fleet admiral.

Battleship *Missouri*, Halsey's flagship, was selected to be the site of the surrender ceremony in Tokyo Bay. The ceremony was conducted on September 2, 1945. Foreign Minister Mamoru Shigemitsu and General Yoshijiro Umezo, army chief of staff, signed the surrender document for Japan. Fleet Admiral Nimitz signed for the United States. When representatives from all Allied countries had signed, MacArthur announced, "Let us pray that peace be now restored to the world and that God will preserve it always. These proceedings are now closed."[14] With perfect timing, and a clear signal of Allied might, hundreds of navy and army air corps aircraft flew over the ships in Tokyo Bay.

Following the ceremony, Nimitz and his party went ashore for a final visit. They visited Admiral Togo's flagship *Mikasa,* with which Togo soundly defeated the Russian fleet in 1905. The ship was a national monument located at Yokosuka Naval Base. Nimitz arranged for a marine guard to be present aboard *Mikasa* to preclude damage or looting by sailors or marines in search of souvenirs.

The party then proceeded towards Kamakura to view the great Buddha. Each time the driver sounded the horn to alert pedestrians to the approaching car, the peasants would all fall on their knees and cover their eyes. "Why are they doing that?" Nimitz asked. The driver stopped and spoke to several Japanese. "In all of Japan, only the emperor has a horn like that," responded the driver. "When such a horn is heard, the people fall on their knees and cover their eyes."[15]

The following morning, September 3, Nimitz and his staff returned to Guam. A few days later, Nimitz flew to Pearl Harbor, and then, on October 3, to San Francisco to be greeted by thousands of people and Governor Earl Warren. Next, Nimitz and his wife flew to Washington, D.C., arriving there on October 5. Nimitz addressed the full Congress before beginning his parade along Pennsylvania and Constitution avenues to the Washington Monument. He was cheered by a half million people. Nimitz made his second speech of the day there, and then proceeded to the White House where President Truman presented him with the Distinguished Service Medal.

Nimitz traveled extensively and made numerous speeches on behalf of a strong defense and strong navy. On November 20, 1945, President Truman announced that General Eisenhower would succeed General Marshall as army chief of staff, and Admiral Nimitz was to succeed Admiral King as chief of naval operations. Admiral Spruance was named commander of the Pacific Fleet.

Nimitz relinquished his Pacific command on November 24, and was sworn in as chief of naval operations on December 15. Nimitz simply said that, "I have just taken on a great responsibility and I will do my best to meet it."[16]

The next two years were wonderful times for the Nimitzes. They both got along well with the president and Bess Truman, were greatly pleased to have an evening with former Prime Minister Winston Churchill, and enjoyed their home at the Naval Observatory. Nimitz stepped down as CNO on December 15, 1947, and retired to San Francisco.

Nimitz served in several posts with the United Nations until 1951, when he became a regent of the University of California. In

1960, Nimitz learned that the Russians wanted *Mikasa,* Togo's flagship, destroyed because they considered it to be a fortress. Nimitz donated funds and encouraged the Japanese people to contribute to restoration of *Mikasa,* and to be proud of the history associated with the admiral and the ship. The Japanese people were stirred into action, and *Mikasa* was rededicated on May 27, 1961. Nimitz then led an effort to restore the Togo shrine that had been damaged by the fire-bombing of Tokyo. His leadership resulted in sufficient contributions from Japanese citizens to restore the shrine.

In early 1961, the Nimitzes moved into quarters at the Yerba Buena Island Naval base. Nimitz fell and broke his right kneecap in 1963, and developed severe pain in his hip and lower back. He died on New Years Day, 1966. His wife was with him at the moment of his death, and his body was buried at the Golden Gate National Cemetery.

Fleet Admiral and Mrs. Nimitz at their
home in Berkeley, Calif. in the early 1960s.

National Archives

28

TRUK

One cannot hope to understand the *War in the Pacific*, without understanding the importance of the Japanese bases at Truk and Rabaul. Truk, Japan's mightiest Pacific naval base, nicknamed "The Gibraltar of the Pacific," ceased to be factor in the war after February 17, 1944. On that date, Vice Adm. Marc A. Mitscher's Fast Carrier Task Force 58 raided the stronghold. By the end of the second day of constant attack by naval aircraft, 34 naval vessels had been sunk, 204 aircraft and 40 buildings were destroyed, and most of the 450 coastal and antiaircraft weapons were destroyed or rendered unusable. Truk became the home of "The Ghost Fleet of Truk Lagoon," the Truk Lagoon State Monument, and a famous Mecca for diving enthusiasts from around the world.

Spain discovered and claimed Truk in 1565. Germany purchased the lagoon from Spain, following the Spanish-American War in 1899 for four million dollars. On October 12, 1914 near the end of WW I, Japan landed forces on Truk and received the surrender of the small defenseless German enclave. In effect, Japan annexed the islands, and in 1920, received a mandate from the League of Nations to govern the island. Japan immediately began to militarize the sheltered lagoon of more than 822 square-miles, and several islands large enough for land bases and airfields.

Japan withdrew from the League of Nations in 1935, and in 1938, closed the island to all visitors. At that time, Japan prohibited news of Truk being released to any outside agencies. Truk became the headquarters of the Japanese 4th Fleet in 1939, and in 1942, Admiral Isoroku Yamamoto arrived at Truk with the combined Fleet, including the two largest battleships in the world, the *Yamato* and *Musashi*. In 1942, an Australian Air Force plane succeeded in taking pictures of Truk Lagoon, revealing the huge fleet, runway, and large land installations.[1]

There are 15 islands inside Truk Lagoon with a total land area of 39 square miles. The Japanese Navy selected Dublon as the headquarters for its extensive submarine and seaplane base. Moen, the second largest island in the group was used for two airfields, and heavy coastal and antiaircraft defenses. More than 24,000 army and naval guard units defended Truk. All five entrances to the lagoon entrances were mined, and 365 aircraft were stationed there. The entire lagoon and its islands sat atop an extinct volcano.

Although Truk had sufficient forces and fixed defenses to defend against an amphibious assault, its real purpose was to act as a supply base for the Imperial Fleet. All of Japan's supply routes were channeled from Yokohama, 1,800 miles away, through Truk, and then to Japan's empire, including Rabaul, 695 miles to the south, Guam, 565 miles, and Saipan, 590 miles to the northwest.

Native Trukese were moved from Dublon, Moen, and Eten to the outer islands for work on farms, as were some 1,200 Naurans who were moved from Nauru to Truk to do forced labor. More than one-third of the Naurans would die from starvation, overwork, and beatings.[2]

As the result of communication intercepts and infrequent overflights, the Allies became well aware of the logistic base Truk had become. Not only did Truk provide men, bombs, food, ships and airplanes to other Japanese possessions in the South Pacific, aircraft from Truk could attack Allied naval forces as they moved toward the home islands of Japan. Faced with the possibility of invading this "Gibraltar," and with the horror of the Tarawa invasion still fresh, Admiral Chester Nimitz, Commander in Chief Pacific, was instructed by the joint chiefs to neutralize and bypass Truk.

As dawn broke on the morning of February 17, 1944 at Truk

Lagoon, a large concentration of ships lay at anchor. Included were cruisers *Naka* and *Katori;* auxiliary cruisers *Aikoku Maru,* and *Kiyosumi Maru;* submarine tenders *Rio de Janeiro Maru,* and *Heian Maru;* destroyers *Funitzuki, Tachikaze, Maikaze, Oite,* and *Nowake,* and many tankers and cargo vessels. The number of ships, under the command of Admiral Mineichi Koga, Commander of Japan's Combined Fleet, was not as impressive as it had been a few days earlier. On February 5, photographs taken by marine corps B-24 Liberators at an altitude of 22,000 feet, revealed the battleship *Musashi,* two carriers, 20 destroyers, 10 cruiscrs, 12 submarines, and more than 50 other surface vessels in the lagoon. Alerted by the photographic aircraft, Admiral Koga quickly departed Truk aboard *Musashi,* enroute to Japan. In similar fashion, Admiral Takeo Kurita's Second Fleet was on the way to Palau.

The photograph of Truk taken by Marine Corps PB4Y Liberators on February 5, 1944, twelve days before Admiral Mitsher's Task Force 58 raided the lagoon. Notice the cluster of ships surrounding Eten Island.

US Navy

Admiral Marc Mitscher's Task Force 58 reached a position off Truk shortly before daylight on February 14, and launched 72 F6F Hellcats from carriers *Enterprise, Essex, Belleau Wood, Intrepid, Bunker Hill,* and the new *Yorktown.* The Hellcat fighters would gain air superiority for the much slower Avenger torpedo bombers and Dauntless dive-bombers that followed. While the carrier aircraft proceeded toward Truk, Admiral Raymond Spruance maneuvered his screening force, including battleships *New Jersey,* and *Iowa,* cruisers *Minneapolis and New Orleans,* the carrier *Cowpens,* and four destroyers to intercept any ships that might escape from the lagoon. Spruance's fleet sank destroyer *Maikaze,* light cruiser *Katori,* a submarine, and the *Shonan Maru.*

Truk Lagoon with its protective coral reef.

Robert Carlson

302

Truk radar detected the incoming aircraft 30 minutes before they reached the reef, but the pilots at Eten received only 10 minute's notice since the air-raid sirens were not sounded until 7:14 a.m.. Pilots manned their planes, but many were unable to get airborne and were strafed on the runway and parking areas. There were a large number of unmanned aircraft on Dublon that were being readied for shipment to Rabaul. None of those aircraft got airborne. About 80 variants of the Zero (Zekes, Vals, Kates, and Jakes) did manage to take off to meet the attack. [3]

The carrier aircraft continued the attack during the evening of the 17th and morning of the 18th. It was the first time that torpedo bombers used radar to attack ships at night. Eight ships were destroyed and five damaged during these night attacks with the loss of one carrier-based aircraft. During the second day of the attack, the *Hikawa Maru*, a well-marked Japanese hospital ship, overloaded with injured Japanese military personnel was permitted to leave the lagoon. American losses for the two days were one ship damaged, 25 aircraft lost, and 40 killed.

Mitscher's pilots flew 30 separate attacks against the Japanese at Truk. Each attack consisted of more aircraft than either of the two Japanese attacks flown against Pearl Harbor. By the end of the second day, most of the Japanese ships were at the bottom of the lagoon, and the Japanese that were still alive suffered from shell shock, more commonly known to Americans as combat fatigue. Decomposing corpses lay everywhere under the hot sun. The air was filled with the sickening odor of human decay that quickly progressed from fly-covered, maggot-laced, rotting flesh, to decomposed skeletons with small bits of putrid flesh.

The Japanese took their revenge upon the POWs that they held. One of the young men of Truk, a boy named Afan, recalled that after the attack ended, a group of Japanese enlisted personnel led a blonde-haired American pilot to a clearing, forced the pilot to kneel down, and chopped off his head. [4] A similar fate was reported by Rambert Rayphand, a Trukese native that observed two American pilots viciously beaten, tied to stakes in the ground, dynamited so that the legs were blown off from both men, and then strangled by their Japanese captors. [5] Other American POWs were trussed between trees by ropes, and then used for repeated bayonet practice until they died. Following the war, evidence was produced to prove the murder of 10 Americans and 37 other POWs. Of the 137 Japanese tried for war crimes on Truk, 129 were convicted, including Vice Adm. Hara, who received a six-year prison sentence. [6]

Fighting on Truk ended on August 15, 1945. The formal surrender took place aboard USS *Portland* on September 2. On August 14, 1971 the "Gibraltar of the Pacific" became the Truk Lagoon State Monument.

Rombert Rayphand, a Trukese hospital aide for the Japanese obseved several atrocities committed on POWs by the Japanese. After the war, Rayphand became Municipal Judge of Udot.

R. Rayphand

29

RABAUL

Rabaul is located on the northeastern tip of New Britain Island in the Solomon Island chain. More than 1,400 years ago, the volcano on the Gazelle Peninsula underwent a major explosion that opened the eastern side of the caldera to the ocean, thus creating one of the finest natural harbors in the South Pacific. Simpson Harbor handled more than 300,000 tons of freight per year prior to the war. Rabaul was also the cultural and commercial center for northern New Britain. Rabaul has a climate of mild seasonal variations, with temperatures averaging 82 degrees and annual rainfall of 90 inches. Far more importantly, Rabaul had strategic implications to the Japanese, because the airfields and harbor facilities were only 440 miles from New Guinea, and 565 miles from Guadalcanal. Occupation of Rabaul would greatly assist Japan's effort to cut Allied supply lines to New Zealand, New Guinea, and Australia.

A panoramic view of Simpson Harbor under U.S. attack in September, 1943.

National Archives

Japanese conquest of Rabaul began in December 1941 with bombing attacks by 18 Truk-based, four-engine Mavis flying boats on the east airfield. The bombing attacks continued into January 1942, when the Australians removed their Lockheed-built Hudson bombers from the west airfield, leaving only a few Wirraway fighters (North American AT-6 trainers) at the east airfield.

Vice Adm. Chuichi Nagumo's carrier aircraft attacked Rabaul on January 22, and the Japanese landing force went ashore on New Ireland and New Britain. The 1,500-man Australian defense force was defeated the following day, with about 400 men escaping along the east and west coasts, and the remaining 1,100 being captured.

On June 22, the POWs and 200 Australian civilians were loaded onto the *Montevideo Maru,* bound for Japan. The ship was torpedoed by a U.S. submarine on July 1. There were no survivors. Shortly thereafter, 60 Australian officers and 19 Australian women were transported to Japan in the freighter *Naruto Maru.* These POWs did reach Japan.[1] Following the war, Japan reported that no POWs remained in Rabaul after July 1942. In actuality, a significant number of POWs, mostly Australian and American pilots were held at Rabaul. All Allied prisoners captured on New Britain or New Guinea were sent to Rabaul for interrogation and imprisonment. Sixty-nine such POWs were held by the 6th Field *Kempeitai,* and 20 by the Naval Garrison Unit of the 8th Fleet. Only eight of the 89 POWs survived the war. Some died of malnutrition and disease, to include diet experimentation. Some died of malaria to include malarial immunization experiments. Some were poisoned as the result of poison experiments, and 40 were massacred by the *Kempeitai,*

Japan occupied Rabaul and Kavieng, on the northern tip of New Ireland, and made Rabaul the operational center for southwestern Pacific operations. Simpson Harbor was constantly filled with warships and cargo vessels, airfields were built on surrounding plateaus, and more than 100,000 troops were deployed throughout New Britain. More than 360 miles of underground tunnels including living quarters, hospitals, supply storage, ammunition dumps, and reinforced concrete bunkers for senior members of the navy and army high command were constructed.

During March of 1942, Admiral Isoroku Yamamoto left Truk and arrived at Rabaul aboard the battleship *Yamato* to personally direct the campaign against Guadalcanal. At about the same time, Americans landed in the Russell Islands, about 60 miles north of Henderson Field on Guadalcanal, and the Seabees began carving a 2,000-foot runway out of the jungle and swamp that comprised the island. Alarmed, Tokyo ordered the Japanese commanders on Rabaul to send army reinforcements to Lae, Papua New Guinea, and to equip such forces to attack the new American airfields.

Early on March 2, eight troop transports with 7,000 troops, escorted by eight destroyers and Rabaul-based air cover left Rabaul's Simpson Harbor for Lae. The convoy was sighted on the same day it entered the Bismarck Sea, and for two days, was attacked by Australian Beaufighters, American B-17s, B-24s, and P-38 fighters. The bombers sank one transport and damaged two others while the P-38s kept the Zeros away.

On the third day, the Beaufighters strafed the convoy while army air corps B-25 Mitchell aircraft attacked the ships. The B-25 had an abysmal record of high-altitude bombing of ships at sea. As a result of this record of ineptness, Lieutenant Gen. George Kenney, USAAF, developed a new technique called skip-bombing. The B-25's approached the ships at mast-top height, dropped their 500-pound bombs with delayed fuses short of the target, and "skipped" the bomb off the water into the sides of the Japanese ships. The new technique was certainly more hazardous to planes and pilots than dropping their bombs from 25,000 feet, but the results were well worth it. All eight transports and four of the escort destroyers were sunk with a loss of most of the troops being transported. Lieutenant Gen. Hatazo Adachi and 2,400 Japanese soldiers were rescued from the sea and returned to Rabaul. Less than a thousand troops reached New Guinea. The Japanese lost 61 planes while the Allies lost four. Japan did not attempt to reinforce New Guinea by convoy again.

A Fifth Air Force B-25 skips two bombs off of the water near Wewak, New Guinea.

US Air Force

On April 7, Admiral Yamamoto, in his immaculate dress-white uniform, personally supervised the launch of more than 400 aircraft from Rabaul and Bougainville to attack Allied bases in the Solomons. When the pilots returned, they reported sinking 25 American transports, and shooting down 175 Allied planes. In actuality, the Americans lost only destroyer *Aaron Ward*, and four auxiliary vessels. Yamamoto, believing his forces had defeated the marines on Guadalcanal, cancelled further air attacks, ordered carriers back to Truk, and made plans to fly to Buin to congratulate his ground-based pilots.

Yamamoto's message to Buin with his itinerary was sent via a low-grade cipher, and was intercepted by Pearl Harbor intelligence. After obtaining approval from Washington, Admiral Nimitz authorized an interception of Yamamoto's flight. The aircraft was intercepted and shot down over Bouganville. Yamamoto died of bullet wounds received during the ambush of his aircraft.[2]

Following Japan's loss of Guadalcanal, the Japanese Navy enlarged the airfield at Munda Point on New Georgia, and built new airstrips on Vila, Kolombangara, Bouganville, and Buka. Two hundred planes were added to the 100-plus aircraft already attached to the 11th Air Fleet at Rabaul. The strategic location of Rabaul, its naval ship support facilities, and its four major airfields caused the American Joint Chiefs of Staff to institute Operation Cartwheel, the reduction of Rabaul.

The U.S. Navy responded by expanding Henderson Field into a full-scale bomber base, surrounded by three fighter strips. Carney Field, a new airfield five-miles west of Henderson, became operational in April 1943. More than 300 navy, marine corps, army, and New Zealand aircraft were based on Guadalcanal, all under command of Admiral Marc Mitscher, Commander Air Command Solomons (Airsols).[3]

Admiral Koga continued to launch attacks on Guadalcanal as late as June 7, when 27 of the 50 Zeros sent to attack Henderson Field were shot down, taking out only seven American planes. Airsols aircraft struck the Japanese airfields at Munda and Vila on Kolombangara to prepare for attacks on Bougainville and Rabaul.

Forces under General Douglas MacArthur moved up the New Guinea coast while Admiral William Halsey's forces advanced up the Solomon Island chain. This two-prong attack came together in the Bismark islands, and by late 1943, virtually surrounded Rabaul. Six naval battles were fought during the next six months in the waters of the central Solomons. Japanese commanders once again distinguished themselves by their night fighting ability and their destroyer captains through their use of the Long Lance torpedo. The last Japanese naval victory of the war occurred at night on October 1, when Japan was able to evacuate 500 men from Vella Lavella, and sink one American destroyer and damage another.[4]

The Allied effort to destroy Rabaul began on October 12, 1943, when more than 350 aircraft from the Army Fifth Air Force dropped 300 tons of bombs on northern New Britain. The raid was repeated six days later. Two months later, Rabaul was attacked daily by land-based F4U Corsairs, F6F Hellcats, and P-38 Lightnings from Henderson Field on Guadalcanal.

The Allied amphibious assault of Bouganville began on October 27. On November 4, 14,000 marines were ashore at Empress Augusta Bay. That night, Vice Adm. Sentaro Omori left Rabaul with two light cruisers and six destroyers intending to destroy the landing force. In the following engagement, Omori lost a cruiser, a destroyer, and suffered extensive damage to several other destroyers. The subsequent Japanese air attack at first light, by more than 100 aircraft, inflicted only minor damage to the American Fleet while the Japanese lost 17 aircraft.

On November 5, Task Force 39 launched 97 carrier based planes against Rabaul. Seventy-five Japanese fighters rose to meet them. Twenty-five Japanese planes were shot down while the U.S. Navy lost 10 aircraft. Again on November 11, Halsey sent carriers *Essex, Bunker Hill,* and *Independence* against Rabaul.[5] The aircraft damaged a cruiser and destroyer, and destroyed 121 of Rabaul's 173 land-based carrier aircraft. The following day, November 12, Japan withdrew all its carrier aircraft and cruisers from Rabaul rather than lose them to the daily poundings being inflicted by Allied aviation.

Halsey decided to bypass the Japanese stronghold of Kolombangara and seize Vella Lavella, to the northwest. Vella had ample flat areas of land suitable for airfields, and its occupation would permit the Allies to sever the Japanese supply lines from Rabaul to Kolombangara. On August 15, Americans landed on Vella. In September, a new airfield was in operation and the Japanese began to vacate Kolombangara.

Next, MacArthur's forces moved from Nassau Bay to capture Lae, New Guinea. The Japanese managed to evacuate some forces and equipment to Rabaul, and about 9,000 Japanese escaped into the mountains. By November, 1943 only Bougainville stood between the Allies and Rabaul.

Bougainville is 125 miles long, dominated by vast swamps and a tangled mountainous interior with two active volcanoes. At Buin, on the island's southern tip, the Japanese had four airfields and a seaplane base. At Buka and Bonis on the northern tip were two more airfields. At least 400,000 Japanese soldiers defended Bougainville. It would not be an easy conquest.

Halsey sought to confuse the Japanese on Bougainville and Rabaul as to his real intentions by bombing the Shortland Islands, a few miles north of Bougainville. He then landed Australian troops to seize the Treasury Islands during the evening of October 27. At midnight of the same day, 725 marines went ashore on the large island of Choiseul, southeast of Bougainville. The Japanese high command estimated that Choiseul was Halsey's target and deployed forces from Bougainville to defend against the Allied landing.

The Bougainville landing occurred on November 1, 1943. The airfields at Buka and Bonis were destroyed by naval gunfire while

311

Halsey landed his forces at Cape Torokina on Empress Augusta Bay. On November 2, Japan responded by sending three heavy cruisers, a light cruiser, and six destroyers to destroy Halsey's landing force. During the following battle, called the Battle of Empress Augusta Bay, the Japanese lost a light cruiser and one destroyer, while Rear Adm. Aaron Merrill had damage to four destroyers and drove back the Japanese.[6]

On November 5, ninety-seven planes from *Saratoga,* and *Princeton* raided Rabaul. They damaged seven warships and lost ten of their aircraft. Shortly thereafter, 27 B-24 bombers and 58 P-38 fighters unloaded 81 tons of bombs on Rabaul's wharf area. Six days later, planes from *Saratoga, Princeton, Essex, Bunker Hill,* and *Independence* sank a destroyer, damaged three destroyers and two light cruisers, and shot down more than a hundred Japanese aircraft. Following the raid, the Japanese moved their ships from Rabaul to Truk.

The battle for Bougainville raged for 17 days. American casualties were 1,000 dead. General Haruyoshi Hyakutake, commander 17th Army, lost 7,000 soldiers. On December 26, the First Marine Division landed near Cape Gloucester on the western tip of New Britain. Rabaul sent 70 to 80 aircraft per day to contest the landing, but they suffered the loss of dozens of aircraft each day. In three weeks, the marines cleared the Cape Gloucester area of all Japanese.

The Allies effectively reduced Rabaul to impotence following the seizure of Cape Gloucester. They left about 135,000 Japanese to exist as best they could on Rabaul without hope of reinforcement or supplies from Truk. General MacArthur objected strongly to the decision to bypass rather than occupy Rabaul, but the memories of American losses on Tarawa and Iwo Jima motivated Nimitz to bypass Fortress Rabaul.

30

THE UNITED STATES OF AMERICA VERSUS
TOMOYUKI YAMASHITA

There is a marble memorial in Nagoya, Japan honoring the Japanese war criminals that were ordered executed by the War Crimes Tribunals. The inscription on the memorial reads: "These trials were nothing but vengeance, the proud victors exercising arbitrary judgement over the vanquished."[1]

When I first learned of this memorial, I was filled with concern for a nation that would erect such a monument. The 28 men that were tried by the Tokyo War Crimes Tribunal were afforded every consideration possible under the American legal system. They were tried, adjudged, sentenced, and, where appropriate, executed after all appeals had been exhausted. What kind of people would ignore the testimony and evidence presented in a court of law and martyr those convicted? What kind of a society would refuse to study and debate the facts of this war, refuse to apologize to those people and countries that suffered so greatly under their occupation, and as a result, put the war behind them and get on with a new life? Perhaps they are the same people and the same society that build monuments to war criminals.

But, it may be that we judge those who erect such memorials too quickly. Perhaps the memorial honors other men than those convicted by the Tokyo War Crimes Tribunal. Perhaps the memorial honors General Tomoyuki Yamashita.

Tomoyuki Yamashita, "The Tiger of Malaya," was not always a tiger. He was born in 1885, in a small, isolated village in Shikoku, where he earned poor grades in elementary school. Only because of his grandmother's discipline, was he able to finish elementary school and attend high school. Away from home, his grades improved dramatically. He earned a scholarship and easily passed the examination for the military academy. He subsequently graduated from the academy with honors. Yamashita was remembered by his classmates as being simple, kind, and industrious. He never looked for leadership positions and was always calm and open-minded.

When he graduated in 1908, Yamashita quickly established himself as a hard worker and gifted leader of men. In 1914, he entered the prestigious Army Staff College, and served tours of duty with the general staff and war ministry. While with the war ministry in 1929, Yamashita drafted a plan to reduce men and weapons within the army. Kazushiga Ugaki, the war minister, approved the plan and sent it to the Diet where it was adopted, much to the displeasure of the army general staff and Lieutenant Gen. Hideki Tojo.

Tojo never forgot or forgave Ugaki or Yamashita. Later, when Ugaki was appointed prime minister of Japan, Tojo, a lieutenant general, and effectively in control of the military, refused to name a war minister to the cabinet, thereby forcing the cabinet to be dissolved and sending Ugaki into retirement. Yamashita, a major general at the time, was transferred out of the war ministry and assigned to command an infantry brigade in Korea. Tojo made certain that Yamashita remained in such out-of-sight posts until 1940, when Yamashita again went against Tojo's plans by predicting that if Japan went to war against America, Japan would lose.[2] Tojo banished Yamashita to Manchukuo, where his political views would not be likely to undermine the views of his fellow officers. Yamashita did not languish very long. Two months after his banishment he was recalled and ushered into the office of the chief of staff of the Imperial Japanese Army, General Hajime Sugiyama.

There, along with Lieutenant Generals Masaharu Homma and Hitoshi Imamura, he learned that he was to command the 25th

Imperial Army with the mission of invading and capturing as much of Malaya as possible. He was to hold his positions until reinforcements could arrive. Imamura would command the 16th Army with responsibility for capturing the Dutch East Indies, while Homma would direct the 14th Army against MacArthur in the Philippines.

Yamashita's mission with 30,000 men was not to capture Singapore, as British General Arthur Percival's 100,000-man army was thought to be far too strong. Rather, Yamashita was to fight his way down the Malay Peninsula, keeping as much pressure on Percival as possible, until additional forces could be moved from the Philippines and elsewhere. Yamahita's subsequent success was far greater than anyone could have imagined.

The amphibious assault was conducted at Singora, Patani, and Kota Bharu on December 8, 1941. Surprise was complete. On December 10, the day that British ships *Repulse* and *Prince of Wales* were sunk, Yamashita's forces reached the British Jitra defense line. The Jitra line had taken six months to construct. It was defended by a complete division, and was thought capable of stopping the Japanese advance for at least six months. In less than one day, Japanese troops sent the British reeling in full retreat. Yamashita pushed the British furiously. Whenever Percival's forces tried to make a stand, Japanese troops would quickly outflank the defenders and send them running. In 45 days, the Japanese moved 1,100 kilometers, relying primarily on "Churchill rations," the trucks, artillery, small arms, ammunition, food, and petroleum abandoned by the British during their retreat.

Yamashita and his staff drank a ceremonial toast and launched the invasion of Singapore on February 8, 1942. Six days later, General Percival discussed surrender terms with Yamashita. As Percival stalled, hoping for better terms, Yamashita, with one-third the forces of Percival, shook his finger at the interpreter and said, "There is no need for all this talk. It is a simple question, and

I want a simple answer: yes or no." General Percival nodded yes, and it was over. Churchill proclaimed the loss as the worst disaster in British history.[3]

Yamashita was proclaimed a national hero in Japan. The government celebrated Yamashita's feat by providing two bottles of beer and a packet of beans to every family, and a box of cakes and candy to each child. Yamashita refused the hero's mantle, insisting instead that the conquest of Singapore had not been brilliant, "It was a "bluff," he said, "a bluff that worked."[4]

To the Japanese people, Yamashita was a national hero, but to Prime Minister Tojo, he was still the enemy. Tojo had Yamashita sent to another unimportant post in Manchukuo and forbid him to stop in Tokyo to report to the emperor or to see his family. Yamashita, like his former academy classmate General Homma, was finding that there were more formidable opponents in war than the Allied powers. The Allied forces could be beaten; Tojo was quite another matter.

Yamashita remained essentially buried in Manchukuo until the fall of 1944. During July, when Saipan fell to the Allies, Tojo and his cabinet resigned. Pelielu fell to the Allies in September, and it became obvious that the Philippines would be next. The army desperately needed the genius of a Yamashita, and he was promptly recalled to relieve General Hisata Karuda, and to command the 14th Army in the Philippines. After only four days of briefings in Tokyo, Yamashita flew to Manila, where he found the defensive situation deplorable. Forces were scattered, supplies were scarce, the command structure was fragmented, and there were no reinforcements available. To compound the situation, MacArthur landed on Leyte on December 7, 1944.

MacArthur arrived in the Philippines with a vengeance. This was "his" country. These were "his" people. He had lived for this moment since he was forced to flee from Corregidor in disgrace. Now there was to be revenge and vindication for MacArthur and the people of the Philippines. The fact that his opponent was "The Tiger of Malaya," was all the better. Now the whole world would see how MacArthur could defeat the Japanese.

MacArthur's invasion was massive. Hundreds of thousands of soldiers, supported by thousands of aircraft and hundreds of warships rapidly pushed the weaker and poorly supplied Japanese forces back from the beachheads. The cries of "Remember Bataan," and "Avenge Corregidor," were on the lips of the American forces as they rapidly overran the Japanese defensive positions.

Yamashita was in an impossible situation. He commanded about 100,000 troops in northern Luzon, perhaps one-fourth of the number of troops opposing him. He had no air or sea support and no lines of supply. Even worse, he had not had time to familiarize himself with the geography of the country or capability of his forces. Despite his shortfalls in troops and supplies, General Yamashita stalled and embarrassed General MacArthur with his defense of Luzon. On the same ground, against similar odds, MacArthur's forces surrendered Corregidor less than 12 hours after the first Japanese set foot on the island. Yamashita's forces held the island for 11 days. In a similar comparison, MacArthur's forces, under Wainwright, surrendered after six months. Yamashita held out for eight months, and only surrendered then because the emperor surrendered Japan.[5]

Despite his success, Yamashita's only choice seemed to be fighting a delaying action in the mountains of Luzon. He ordered his troops out of Manila, and abandoned the city to MacArthur. Yamashita would later give three reasons for his decision not to defend Manila. First, he could not feed the million people of Manila. Second, the buildings were very flammable and not good for defensive positions. Finally, he had insufficient forces. On February 12, as Yamashita retreated from Manila, MacArthur proudly proclaimed that Manila had been captured like a "ripened plum."[6]

But MacArthur was wrong. Manila had not been captured by

the Allies and would not be captured until another month of hard fighting. What followed in Manila was a bloody scene of mass murder, rape, and atrocities on a scale similar to the Rape of Nanking.

When Yamashita retreated into the mountains, he left a small contingent of 1,600 men in Manila. These troops were to expedite the movement of gasoline and other supplies to Baguio, a city high in the mountains, north of Manila, where Yamashita planned to establish his headquarters. Unknown to Yamashita, there were another 20,000 sailors and marines, under the command of Admiral Sanji Iwabuchi, in and around the naval facilities of Manila Bay. Although Yamashita had ordered Manila to be abandoned, Iwabuchi had orders from his immediate superior, Vice Adm. Desuchi Okuchi, to destroy all naval facilities in Manila, and from Vice Adm. Gunichi Mikawa, to fight MacArthur "to the death."[7]

Iwabuchi made the decision to defend Manila. He commandeered Yamashita's 1,600 soldiers and prepared hasty fortifications to meet MacArthur's attack. Yamashita learned of Iwabuchi's insubordination on February 13, and ordered the sailors out of the city; but it was too late. MacArthur's forces had completely encircled Manila and trapped the naval contingent. As Yamashita's force retreated under heavy air and artillery bombardment, the Japanese naval forces in Manila engaged in an orgy of burning, shooting, rape, and torture.

Iwabuchi's troops knew they were to die for the emperor and were determined to kill as many Filipinos and Americans as possible. The sailors and marines were provided beer, wine, and saki in abundance, and, in a short time, the troops became a raging, drunken mob. In a final orgy of revenge, women of all ages were raped and beheaded. Men and boys were mutilated and murdered. Babies were bayoneted, their eyeballs ripped out and smeared across walls. Hospitals were burned with patients tied to their beds; doctors and nurses still inside.

American forces fought hand-to-hand, building-to-building throughout Manila. By the time the last American killed the last Japanese in the old walled city of Intramuros, 60,000 Filipinos lay dead.[8] Three-fourths of the homes and factories in Manila, and the entire business district was burned to the ground.

General Yamashita leads his staff down from the mountains of northern Luzon to surrender to General MacArthur's forces near Baguio.

US Army

When fighting stopped, and as soon as conditions permitted, MacArthur hurried to his former home, the penthouse atop the Manila hotel. He was told that the structure was still in good shape, but was in Japanese control. As he approached the hotel, the penthouse burst into flames. MacArthur watched the destruction of ". . . . my fine military library, my souvenirs, my personal belongings of a lifetime. I was tasting into the last acid dregs the bitterness of a devastated and beloved home."[9]

On August 14, 1945, communications personnel in Yamashita's army heard a radio broadcast from San Francisco announcing that the emperor had surrendered Japan to the Allied powers. A few days later, U.S. aircraft dropped leaflets on Yamashita's position instructing the Japanese to send an envoy to arrange a surrender. Yamashita decided to go in person to avoid any delays in the process. He was losing hundreds of men a day to starvation and disease.

The General Yamashita that surrendered his sword to a startled American officer on September 2, was not the same man that conquered Singapore. He had lost a lot of weight while starving with his troops in the mountains. His clothes were soiled and ragged, his face was worn, his eyes tired and defeated. He had done his best, but it was time to stop the killing. Too many of his men had been killed and were dying every day. Yamashita was hurried to a government house in Baguio, where he was required to sign a formal document of surrender. As Yamashita entered the room he was startled to see General Arthur Percival, his adversary from Singapore, seated across the table. Percival commanded no troops in the Philippines and had no reason to be there. General Percival was there at MacArthur's invitation. Much like Prime Minister Tojo, MacArthur had a long memory, and he was just starting to exact his revenge.

Following the brief surrender ceremony, Yamashita was taken to New Bilibid prison in Manila. For the first time, he learned of the atrocities that had been committed. Stunned initially by the news, Yamashita recovered and said, "If those crimes were committed, I positively and categorically affirm that they were against my wishes and in direct contradiction to all my expressed orders."[10] Questioning of Yamashita continued day after day, although Yamashita had not been provided with a lawyer or legal representation. After many days of interrogation, it became obvious to the prosecution that General Yamashita neither ordered nor knew of the atrocities committed in Manila.

Finally, after several weeks, Yamashita was escorted to the chapel to meet his lawyers. The Americans were not impressed. They saw a bull-headed man with no neck and narrow, inscrutable eyes. His stoic, inexpressive face obviously hid many tales of horror. However, as the lawyers questioned Yamashita they found a man of dignity and poise. When informed of the general charges against him, Yamashita was adamant that he had never heard of the rape, torture, murder, and destruction of Manila until after his surrender.

The senior defense attorney then asked the critical question. How could these atrocities have been committed without the commanding general being aware of them? Yamashita answered the question as he would answer the same question during his trial. Yamashita said that he had been given a very difficult mission under very difficult conditions. His communications with his forces were essentially lost as he began his retreat from Manila. Much of his force was fragmented and crushed by the superior American forces. When he reached his final defensive position, he was isolated from events outside his immediate mountain retreat. He had no way to know of the atrocities, and since he now understands that the naval forces that fought in Manila were all killed, there was no one to send such information even if they possessed such a communication capability.

General Yamashita was not charged with defeating General Percival at Singapore. He was not charged with responsibility for any atrocities in Malaya or Singapore. Nor was Yamashita charged with the brilliant defense of Luzon against MacArthur. In the pre-trial arraignment, Yamashita was charged with the responsibility for the rape of Manila, in that he failed to control the actions of members of his command. His trial was set for October 29, less than three weeks away. Two days before the trial was to begin, Yamashita's lawyers were handed an envelope outlining 59 new charges against Yamashita. The list of particulars had grown from 64 to 123.

The following day, defense lawyers requested a continuance so that they could prepare a defense against these new charges. MacArthur's hand-picked court disapproved the request. Later, a message from General MacArthur was found that said MacArthur was, "disturbed at reports of a possible continuance in the Yamashita case." MacArthur doubted the need of defense for more time and "urged" haste.[11]

The trial began on time. The prosecution reminded the commission of five general officers of the broad discretionary power given them by General MacArthur. The prosecution further reminded the commission that the rules of war did not apply to this case and that the commission was not a judicial body, but an executive tribunal established by General MacArthur. The prosecution went on to explain that it was MacArthur's desire to proceed as rapidly as possible, to permit no unnecessary delay, and to ignore the technicalities associated with criminal proceedings in civil law cases.

Yamashita's defense established that most, if not all, of the atrocities committed in Manila were done by the Japanese Naval Special Landing Force in direct disobedience to General Yamashita's orders. Not once during the eight days of the trial was Yamashita linked to the atrocities in any way. He had not ordered them and was not aware of them being committed. General Muto, Yamashita's chief of staff, testified as to the conditions that existed during the retreat from Manila to the mountains. Five prominent citizens of Japan testified about Yamashita's character, honesty, reputation, and political difficulties with Tojo.

Finally, General Yamashita took the stand to testify in his own behalf. Calm and courteous through 11 hours of cross examination, he told of the circumstances that existed during his retreat from Manila, and why he could not have known of the situation there. The prosecution ignored Yamashita's lack of personal involvement. It continued to bring forth witnesses that testified that atrocities were committed, that Yamashita was in charge, and maintained, therefore, that Yamashita was responsible for them.

The result of the proceedings was that the trial was never in doubt. *Newsweek* magazine reported that, "even third-hand evidence is admitted."[12] In the opinion of nearly every correspondent covering the trial, the military commission came into the courtroom the first day with the decision already in its collective pocket."[13] Robert Turnbull, correspondent for the New York Times, reported that, "All precedents in law have been thrown out the window. There are no regulations governing the American War Crimes Commission, except those it makes for itself, and it has made very few."[14]

The verdict was returned on Friday, December 7, 1945, the fourth anniversary of Japan's attack on Pearl Harbor. The commission found that atrocities by members of General Yamashita's command had been committed. It found, therefore, that Yamashita failed to provide effective control of his troops, and he was found guilty as charged. The Tiger of Malaya was sentenced to death by hanging. Yamashita was escorted back to his cell where he wrote the following *waka*.

> The world I knew is now a shameful place
>
> There will never come a better time
>
> For me to die

Yamashita's defense team knew that MacArthur would expedite the execution. It sent an urgent cable to the U.S. Supreme Court requesting a stay of execution until the court had the opportunity to receive and read the writ of Habeas Corpus that had been sent.[15] Two days before the scheduled execution, the secretary of war stayed the execution pending an appeal to the Philippine Supreme Court.

General Yamashita testifies in his own defense. Yamashita is wearing his uniform and military decorations. In a subsequent trial of General Masaharu Homma by the same commission, Homma was stripped of his uniform and had to appear in civilian clothes.

US Army

324

The Philippine Supreme Court heard Yamashita's appeal on November 23. The court ruled that it could not grant Yamashita's appeal, because to do so would interfere with the liberating U.S. Army. Once again Yamashita's lawyers cabled the U.S. Supreme Court asking for a stay of execution until the court could act on the writ of Habeas Corpus. This time the secretary of war radioed MacArthur and strongly advised him to stay the execution until the Supreme Court could make a decision. MacArthur refused. "The Supreme Court had no jurisdiction with this trial," he said. The execution would proceed.[16] The secretary of war then ordered MacArthur to postpone the execution, and MacArthur reluctantly complied.

On February 4, 1946, the United States Supreme Court ruled by a seven-to-two vote, that it lacked jurisdiction to hear the case. Justices Frank Murphy and Wiley Rutledge were not content to stop with the jurisdictional issue, and wrote a 32-page dissent in which they strongly criticized MacArthur for rushing the prisoner to trial under an improper charge, giving insufficient time to prepare a defense, eliminating all generally accepted rules of evidence, and sentencing a man to hang without even an attempt to prove that the prisoner committed a recognized violation of the laws of war.[17]

Murphy and Rutledge concluded their dissent by saying that, "Today the life of General Yamashita, a leader of enemy forces vanquished in the field of battle, is to be taken without regard to the due process of law. There will be few to protest. But tomorrow the precedent here established can be turned against others. A procession of judicial lynching without due process of the law may now follow."[18]

Yamashita was given a last meal of asparagus, bread, and beer on the evening of February 22, 1946.[19] The sentence was carried out at the Los Banos prison camp, 35 miles south of Manila, at 3:27 A. M., on the 23rd. Yamashita was kneeling in prayer when suddenly the door to his cell clanged open. "It is time," said one of the two soldiers. Yamashita rose and, as he did so, the soldiers saw for the first time this man convicted of such terrible atrocities. He was a burly man, thick and broad in the shoulders and chest, with the stomach of a sumo wrestler. He seemed to have no neck, a cannonball for a head, with no hair at all. He handed a paper to the army officer and asked him to please send his thanks to the lawyers who defended him.

One of the soldiers stepped behind Yamashita and handcuffed his wrists together. The officer, the prisoner, and the two soldiers left the cell and walked to a large courtyard. Slowly the prisoner began to distinguish the dim outline of a wooden gallows, the steps that led up to it, and the cross bar with a knotted rope hanging down from it. The officer read from a prepared statement, but the prisoner understood little of what was said.

A soldier stepped forward and put a black sash over the prisoner's head. With a soldier at each side, the prisoner walked the 13 steps to the top of the gallows. "Do you have any last words?" the officer asked. The prisoner was silent for a moment and then said, "I will pray for the Emperor's long life and his prosperity forever." A soldier stepped forward and fit the rope noose around the prisoner's short neck. The prisoner stood proud and tall, his shoulders squared, chin lifted high. Suddenly there was a shrill squeak, a dull thud, followed by a sharp crack.[20] It was done. General Douglas MacArthur and the people of the Philippines had their revenge.

Never before had a commander been convicted or executed by a victorious enemy on the grounds that he was negligent in the command of forces in the field. Never before had a military leader been prosecuted, convicted, and executed for a crime that he had not ordered, condoned, nor of which he was even aware.

While the trials at Nuremberg and Tokyo were models of legal decorum, the trial of General Tomoyuki Yamashita, and, immediately thereafter, that of General Masaharu Homma in

Manila, are travesties of the American justice system and deserve to be remembered as such.

General Yamashita and his academy classmate, Masaharu Homma, were men of character and honor. Nothing has been proven otherwise. They deserve to be remembered as such. Perhaps the monument at Nagoya does just that.

General Yamashita uses a GI helmet to wash his hands after his surrender and before signing the documents of surrender.

US Army

The wooden gallows prepared for General Yamashita. Note the 13 steps.

US Army

31

JONATHAN M. WAINWRIGHT

General Jonathan M. Wainwright was arguably the most famous American to survive World War II in the Pacific. Certainly he was the highest-ranking American officer held captive by the Japanese. Wainwright and his Philippine division were forced to retreat into the Bataan peninsula, and then to Corregidor during the Japanese invasion of the Philippines in December, 1941. Wainwright fought a defensive action from Bataan and Corregidor that lasted until May 12, 1942, when he surrendered all United States forces in the Philippines.

Colonel Wainwright as commanding officer, Fort Meyer, Virginia, 1937

US Army Signal Corps

After more than four years in Japanese prisoner-of-war (POW) camps, Wainwright returned to the United States as a hero, and on September 12, 1945 was presented with the Medal of Honor, our nation's highest military honor, by President Harry S. Truman. Wainwright's well-deserved recognition in 1945 was in sharp contrast to the future planned for Wainwright by the new army chief of staff, General George C. Marshall. In December, 1938, Marshall, anticipating war with Japan, decreed that any officer older than the age of 50 was too old to fight in the forthcoming war. Wainwright, at age 55, was well beyond the age limit and penciled in for retirement.

Most of Wainwright's contemporaries were forced to retire, but thanks to his friendship with the outgoing chief of staff, General Malin Craig, Wainwright was permitted a "retirement" tour of duty at Fort Clark, Texas, where he commanded the First Cavalry Brigade. Life at Fort Clark was easy-going and relaxed. Wainwright was doing what he loved most, being around the men and horses of the cavalry. Each afternoon, the Brigade would hold "beer call" at the officers' club where the men would gather to drink beer and share cavalry stories. Naturally, Wainwright led both the drinking and the story-telling.

Following his two- year "twilight" tour at Fort Clark, Wainwright fully expected to be retired. Instead, he received orders to the Philippines to command the American Division, an understrength division of about 7,500 men, most of whom were Filipino scouts. Wainwright's command included three infantry regiments, a cavalry regiment, two artillery battalions, plus the necessary engineer, ordnance, quartermaster, and military police units.

Life was good for an army officer in the Philippines in the late 1930s and 1940. Although military pay was low, it went a long way in the Philippines. Any officer could easily afford four Filipino servants. Even a private with monthly income of $21.00 could afford to hire a native to clean, wash, polish, and shine everything that did not move for $1.50 per month.

The good life continued until May 12, 1941, when the dependents were evacuated from the Philippines. By then it was far too late to recruit, equip, train, and organize a military force capable of defending the Philippines against a Japanese invasion.

During July 1941, General Douglas MacArthur, who had been field marshal of the Philippine Army, was recalled to active duty as the commander of the United States Army Forces in the Far East (USAFFE), a newly designated force of some 140,000 men. In September, MacArthur assigned Wainwright as senior field commander in the Philippines to command the North Luzon Force, considered to be the most important command in the Pacific theater, and the most likely site of a Japanese invasion. Brigadier Gen. George M. Parker commanded South Luzon Force, and Brigadier Gen. William F. Sharp commanded the Visayan-Mindanao Force. Wainwright now had three divisions under his command, but all was not well. The 31st Division had only a few weeks of training and no combat experience. The artillery had never fired a round of ammunition, and there were no antiaircraft weapons, transport vehicles, and very little small arms ammunition. Communications depended entirely upon commercial telephone lines.

The 11th Division, charged with defense of Lingayen Gulf, had to ask local merchants for barbed wire, tools, bamboo, and wood to prepare beach defenses. They also commandeered civilian automobiles, trucks, buses, and even drivers in the race to meet the anticipated Japanese invasion. The 21st Division, consisting of a cavalry regiment and Philippine scout battalion, with two batteries of 155-milimeter artillery and a battery of 2.95-inch mountain guns was better trained and would fight well.

Under Chief of Staff of the Army General Marshall, and due, in large measure, to the confidence of General MacArthur, U.S. policy became to defend the Philippines rather than a delaying action to slow the Japanese offensive. The War Department began to send men and supplies to the Philippines in August and September. By November, more than a million tons of equipment marked for the Philippines were in mainland ports awaiting transport.

New aircraft also began to arrive in great numbers. By December, 35 B-17s, more than half of all the B-17 bombers in the air corps were stationed in the Philippines, along with 197 Curtiss P-40 fighters. In November, as Wainwright trained his new forces, General Marshall, in Washington, announced to a number of newsmen that war with Japan was imminent. He stated that the Philippines had been fully armed and supplied, and that the 35 B-17s were capable of quickly destroying Japan's naval bases and major cities when war came.[1]

On November 24, Marshall approved a war warning that was sent to all American naval commanders in the Pacific, with orders to pass the message to all army commanders. The message warned that, "There are very doubtful chances of a favorable outcome of negotiations with Japan. This situation, coupled with movements of their naval and military forces indicate in our opinion that a surprise aggressive movement in any direction, including an attack on the Philippines or Guam, is a possibility."[2]

Two days later, MacArthur was warned by Washington that, "Negotiations with Japan appear to be terminated to all practicable purposes . . . Japanese future action unpredictable but hostile action possible at any moment."[3] Despite these clear warnings of war, MacArthur assured Wainwright that, "you'll probably have until April to train those troops."[4]

The following day, November 27, while Wainwright relocated to his new headquarters in north Luzon, MacArthur notified General Marshall that, "Everything is in readiness for the conduct of a successful defense."[5] It is well that Wainwright was not aware of MacArthur's message. Tasked to defend more than 600 miles of shoreline against a Japanese amphibious assault, with an untrained and still understrength force, Wainwright believed the situation to be hopeless. On the same day, he was directed to put his troops on a modified state of general alert.

Wainwright had a defense force of 50,000 men, and while that appears formidable on paper, most of them were untrained, poorly led, and poorly equipped. When the Japanese attacked a week later, many of the men did not even have a rifle to carry. Small wonder that desertions would reach epidemic proportions among local troops that had never seen combat and had no desire to do so.

Japanese aircraft started flying reconnaissance missions over Luzon on December 2. On December 4, MacArthur assured his American and British naval commanders that his forces would be ready to defend the Philippines by April 1942. MacArthur's commanders were not impressed. MacArthur's forces needed to be ready now, and they were not ready. On December 6, the U.S. cruiser *Pensacola* was enroute to Manila with a convoy carrying bombers, fighters, trucks, jeeps, ammunition, bombs, fuel, and 4,600 men. Also on December 6, a Japanese battle fleet was steaming toward Manila. The *Pensacola* convoy turned back, the Japanese fleet kept coming.

War came to the Philippines at 7:00 A.M., on December 8, (December 7, Hawaii time) by way of a phone call from Admiral Husband Kimmel, commander of the Pacific Fleet in Pearl Harbor. Wainwright was notified 15 minutes later, and, in turn, notified Clark Field to ensure that the B-17s and P-40s were not destroyed on the ground.

On Formosa, the Japanese strike force of 108 bombers and 84 zero fighters waited impatiently for the morning fog to burn off so they could strike Clark Field before MacArthur could launch a counter-strike against the Japanese airfields on Formosa.

At 8:00 A.M., the B-17s at Clark Field started to take off with empty bomb bays. MacArthur refused to let them bomb the Japanese bases on Formosa, and only approved their takeoffs so they would not be destroyed on the ground. By 9:00 A.M., American P-40s took off to intercept Japanese bombers that were bombing Baguio and other military installations in the north. At 9:25, MacArthur again refused a request to bomb the Japanese bases on Formosa. Shortly after 10:00, the B-17s and P-40s from Clark Field began landing to refuel. They lined up in neat rows, and the aircrews went to the mess halls for lunch. At 12:25 P.M, the Japanese bombed Clark Field. Ten hours after the disaster at Pearl Harbor, MacArthur's air force was destroyed on the ground. About 3:00 P.M., as Wainwright took a short break for lunch, he learned that Hong Kong was under attack, as were Wake Island, Guam, and Singapore.

Wainwright's first test came on the morning of December 10. A small Japanese force landed on the northern tip of Luzon. Wainwright's defense at this site consisted of one American lieutenant and 200 Filipinos with rifles and machine guns. The Lieutenant was ordered to drive the Japanese back into the sea. Instead, he and his men fled south without firing a shot. Next, Wainwright learned of Japanese paratroopers landing just north of his headquarters. Quickly he sent cavalry, tanks, self-propelled guns, and scout cars to stop the Japanese advance. The report proved to be erroneous, and, in the meantime, Wainwright's headquarters was bombed and severely damaged.

The Japanese force that landed on the northern tip of Luzon had advanced 50 miles south by December 12. The battalion of Filipino troops detailed to stop them in a narrow valley had retreated without offering any opposition. Also on the 12th, Japanese forces made a successful landing in southern Luzon. Enemy forces were now advancing on two fronts, with Manila, the capital city, as the goal. By December 20, Japanese forces moving south outflanked Wainwright's forces in the area of San Fernando, La Union, and sent the green Filipino troops reeling.

While Wainwright was coordinating a counterattack , he received information that the main Japanese attack would occur somewhere along the 120-mile coastline of Lingayen Gulf. A convoy of between 100 to 120 Japanese ships were expected to reach there the evening of December 21.

The entire Lingayen coastline was held by two divisions of the Philippine Army. They had four 155mm howitzers, and one .50-caliber and several .30-caliber machine guns. The Japanese landing was a minor disaster. The 85 transports unloaded some 41,000 troops eight miles out to sea. The choppy seas made it difficult to load the barges, the men became sick, radios were soaked and worthless, and many barges overturned. As a result, the second assault wave could not be launched and the transports had to move to the pre-scheduled debarkation sites. The only thing that prevented a total disaster to the landing force was that their landing was not opposed. By morning, the Japanese had established several beachheads that threatened the withdrawal of Wainwright's forces.

By December 23, Wainwright's forces had been badly mauled by Japanese forces moving south toward Manila. Late on the 23rd, Wainwright was informed by MacArthur that the defense of the Philippines was no longer possible, and that he was to withdraw his forces into the Bataan Peninsula and Corregidor to fight a delaying action.[6]

The problems facing Wainwright were tremendous. Had the order to withdraw been given several days earlier, an orderly withdrawal with adequate supplies for an extended defense could have been conducted. The Southern Luzon Force with more than 15,000 men would be crucial for the defense of Bataan, but they were now in danger of being cut off and captured by Japanese forces moving north to Manila. Somehow, Wainwright would have to hold critical positions with units that were manned with only a third of their authorized strength. Somehow, organizations that had collapsed during the earlier fighting would have to be reorganized and sent back into battle. Somehow, vital bridges would have to be held, and in some cases repaired until the South Luzon Force could cross, and then the bridges destroyed before the Japanese could use them. Somehow, the remnants of the North Luzon Force would have to protect its flanks long enough to disengage and move back to Bataan with whatever food, ammunition, and supplies they could salvage.

Wainwright was everywhere trying to put the withdrawal plans into effect. Everyone that was not directly engaged with the Japanese were put to work moving supplies from Manila to the mosquito-infested jungles of Bataan. Some 1,300 men worked around the clock to move as much as they could, and to destroy what they could not move. The civilian crewmen that manned the trains that could have moved supplies from Manila to Bataan deserted, leaving more than 50 million bushels of rice for the Japanese.

On Christmas eve, Wainwright received news that the Japanese had come ashore on Lamon Bay, 60 miles southeast of Manila. Here was another serious threat to the South Luzon Force. It would be a race to the Bataan Peninsula. On December 27, General Masaharu Homma, commander of the 14th Army, decided to halt his advance, consolidate his position, and bring up more men and supplies. At this time, Homma decided he would capture Manila first, and then mop up the American and Filipino forces on Bataan and Corregidor at a more leisurely pace. This decision would jeopardize Homma's career, lead to the Bataan Death March, and Homma's subsequent trial, conviction, and execution.

Somehow Wainwright's troops held, and the 51st Division of the South Luzon Force crossed the bridges early on New Years day. Later in the day, as Japanese forces approached the bridge, Wainwright ordered it and the nearby railroad bridge blown up. The four tons of dynamite on the road bridge and three tons on the railway bridge functioned perfectly, and both spans fell into the deep Pampanga River. For the first time since the Japanese landings on December 10, Wainwright had a few hours to plan for the defense of Bataan. On Corregidor, MacArthur watched through binoculars as the Japanese flag was raised atop the Manila Hotel, MacArthur's home until a few days before.

Bataan was perfectly suited for defense. At least it would have been if it had been properly prepared, supplied, and equipped. The peninsula was 29 miles wide, and 25 miles long. The land was mostly jungle, and mountains extended down the center of the peninsula, with Mount Natib (4,000 feet) in the north, and Mount Bataan (5,000 feet) in the south. The rugged terrain and thick vegetation provided cover from air surveillance, and the coastline was narrow and hilly.

To General Homma, Wainwright's forces were like a cat entering a sack. Now that the cat was in the sack, General Homma would pull the string tight and trap the cat. But it would not be that simple. Wainwright and Luzon Force would fight a defensive battle on Luzon for another four months before the lack of food, supplies, and medicine forced them to surrender. For most of the campaign, the men subsisted on 30 ounces (about 2,000 calories) of food per-man-per-day. The men on Bataan were already hungry, but they were going to get much hungrier before their ordeal was over.

Homma began his air and artillery bombardment of Bataan on January 9. The next day MacArthur and his staff from Corregidor made their first and only visit to Bataan. Homma had airplanes drop hundreds of leaflets warning that the Bataan troops were doomed and should surrender. At this time, there were about 90,000 men on Bataan and 11,000 more on Corregidor.

After four months of intensive naval gunfire, artillery, and aerial bombardment, Homma began his assault of Bataan on April 3, 1942. As the sick and starving men of Luzon force were pushed back , leadership in many of the Filipino units crumbled, and men faded into the jungle. Reestablishment of the defensive positions became impossible due to the lack of organized fighting units, the physical condition of the men, and Homma's constant artillery and air bombardment.

On February 23, President Roosevelt, knowing that Bataan could not hold much longer, directed General MacArthur to make plans to leave Corregidor. MacArthur was to go to Mindanao via torpedo boat, and then fly to Australia. Ordering MacArthur to leave the Philippines was an agonizing decision for the president. Wainwright's stand on Bataan was the only source of pride for the Allies in the Pacific. Ordering MacArthur out might appear to the world that the United States was abandoning the Philippines.

On March 2, MacArthur ordered the rations for the Bataan troops to be cut from one-half rations to three-eigthts. This dropped the calorie count per man to about 1,000 per day. The men resorted to eating caribou, cavalry horses, and lizards.

MacArthur, his family, and his entire military staff departed Corregidor on March 11. They used four torpedo boats to make the run to Mindanao, and were flown to Brisbane, Australia on three B-17s, sent to Mindanao from Australia for that purpose.[7] Wainwright was directed by MacArthur to move to Corregidor to exercise operational control, but MacArthur would exercise overall command from Australia.

General Marshall did not learn of MacArthur's plan to conduct the Philippines campaign from 4,000 miles distant until March 20. When he found out, he notified Corregidor and MacArthur that Wainwright was the Commanding General United States Army Forces Far East, and promoted him to lieutenant general the same day. MacArthur was not pleased, but could do little about it.

Wainwright designated Major Gen. Edward P. King as commander Luzon Force, and gave King the instructions he had received from MacArthur, and President Roosevelt. "There would be no surrender." King stated that he understood the instructions.[8]

The last two days of the defense of Bataan were days of disintegration and collapse. Communications were destroyed by Japanese aircraft, stragglers moved to the rear in a daze, and Filipino units disappeared into the jungle never to be seen again. Such organized forces that did remain in their positions were so weak from starvation that they could not move out, even if there were no enemy in front of them.

On the evening of April 8, General King assembled his staff and informed them he intended to discuss the surrender of the Luzon Force with the Japanese. "I have not communicated with General Wainwright," King said, "because I do not want him to be compelled to assume any part of the responsibility." Wainwright learned of King's intent to surrender at 6:00 A.M., the following morning. "They can't do it," Wainwright shouted, stunned by the news. "They can't do it."[9]

But, the deed was done. By noon on April 9, an awesome silence settled over Bataan. After weeks and months of continuous artillery fire, the sudden quiet was frightening. Shortly thereafter, Wainwright and his aides peering toward Bataan with binoculars saw long columns of bound captives walking north from Mariveles. The white flags of surrender dotted their columns. These were the defenders of Bataan. These were the men at the start of one of the greatest atrocities of the Pacific war. These were the men of the Bataan Death March. Of the 78,000 men that began the march, only 54,000 arrived at Camp O'Donnell POW camp, some 90 miles to the north.[10]

Lieutenant Gen. Wainwright announces surrender of all U.S. forces in the Philippines.

US Army

32

JONATHAN M. WAINWRIGHT
SURRENDER OF CORREGIDOR

General Wainwright seemed stunned to learn that Major Gen. King surrendered the Bataan Force on April 9, 1942. Yet, Wainwright had to have known that his own forces on Corregidor were not capable of holding out for much longer.

Homma began his bombardment of Corregidor on the afternoon of April 9, when 98 planes attacked the fixed naval gun emplacements. The guns were well fortified against attack from the sea, but were defenseless against bombing attacks. An even greater threat to Corregidor came from Bataan where the Japanese quickly relocated their artillery and began bombardment. Wainwright's engineers pinpointed the locations of all the new Japanese artillery positions when they fired and planned a massive retaliatory fire at 5:00 P.M., that day. Reluctantly Wainwright had to cancel the planned counter fire because the Japanese had positioned most of their artillery around some 4,000 sick and wounded Americans and Filipinos that surrendered on Bataan but had not yet moved. Wainwright postponed the counter fire for three days to allow the Japanese to evacuate the patients. Wainwright's decision was not popular with some of his men, many of whom doubted the Japanese would ever evacuate the patients.[1]

Wainwright was continuously among the men in the trenches and on the line. My presence is about all I can give them he reasoned. There were acute shortages of everything, and morale, especially among the Filipino troops was low. On April 29, Wainwright was able to evacuate 50 passengers, including 30 of the nurses on two PBYs from Australia that slipped through the Japanese blockade. On May 3, the submarine USS *Skatefish*, enroute to Australia after a patrol, penetrated the minefield at the harbor entrance and evacuated an additional 25 people, including 13 more nurses.

By May 1, it was clear the Japanese assault of Corregidor was near. There was no chance of defeating the assault, but Wainwright intended to buy as much time as possible. On May 4, all code books and secret files were destroyed. A day later Corregidor recorded its 300th air raid. At this time, all beach defense guns and fortifications had been destroyed and communications were virtually nonexistent.

During the evening of May 5, under cover of a massive artillery bombardment, Homma launched the first 2,000 troops of his amphibious assault. Colonel Sam Howard's Fourth Marines met the attackers at the beach and slaughtered 1,200 of them. Still, some 800 Japanese moved rapidly toward Malitna Tunnel, where the headquarters, hospital, and wounded were located. The starving men on Corregidor fought on, but on May 6, Homma put three tanks ashore. Wainwright had no weapons capable of stopping a tank, and the possibility of the massacre that would occur should the tanks fire their cannons point-blank into Malitna tunnel was simply unthinkable.[2]

General Wainwright made the decision to surrender at noon on May 6. He sent a final message to President Roosevelt: "With profound regret, and with continued pride in my gallant troops, I go to meet the Japanese commander. Goodbye, Mr. President." [3] All remaining weapons were destroyed, the American flag was lowered, and a white flag displayed in its place. A message announcing the surrender was sent three times to General Homma over the Voice of Freedom transmitter.

Wainwright tried to restrict his surrender to only those troops on Corregidor, but General Homma would have none of it. Wainwright must surrender all forces in the Philippines, including Mindanao and the Visayans, or the shelling, bombing, and advance on Malitna tunnel would continue. Wainwright could not know that at that very moment flame tanks were positioned to fire directly into the entrance to Malitna tunnel.

On May 8, with heavy heart, Wainwright was forced to announce to the people of the Philippines and to the remaining American and Filipino forces that he had surrendered all forces in the Philippines. The defense of the Philippines ended.

The captured Americans and Filipinos on Corregidor were put aboard three ships on May 23, docked at Manila, and forced to march through Manila to Bilibad Prison. The Japanese wanted the people of the Philippines to see how badly the enemies of Japan looked after their beating. Later, the men were trucked to Camp O'Donnell and joined the survivors from Bataan.

Wainwright and his 200 senior officers were sent to a POW camp at Tarlac, 85 miles north of Manila. The barracks consisted of a bare, two story, wooden building. The first floor was used as a primitive hospital and mess hall. There were no mattresses, blankets, mosquito nets, or pillows. Many of the men had no shoes, and were in terrible physical shape. Meals consisted of plain rice, twice a day.

Japanese rules were strict and simple, and never varied for the next three-and-one-half years. The Japanese demanded absolute obedience from Wainwright and the other captives. The lowest Japanese private or Korean conscript was superior to any prisoner. The POWs could expect no mercy or compassion. There was no restraint upon the guards in terms of brutality toward the POWs.

On August 13, 1942 Wainwright and the senior POWs were put aboard ship and moved to a POW camp named Karenko on the southern coast of Formosa. Wainwright would spend time in six different camps before he was liberated. Meals at Karenko consisted of rice and a cup of hot water. The men began to lose weight and develop malaria and beri-beri. They were also forced to work. Wainwright was assigned to tend a herd of 25 goats. Fortunately one of the enlisted aides, Sergeant Harry Greenleaf knew about goats, so Wainwright became his assistant.

On September 8, 1942 British Lieutenant Gen. Arthur Percival, and senior officers and civilian officials from Hong Kong, Borneo, Singapore, and the East Indies reached the camp. A few days later, Major Gen. William F. Sharp, commander of forces on Mindanao and 40 other senior POWs arrived. At this time, Karenko had to be the single most important POW camp in the world.

All the POWs took their share of slappings, beatings, and punching. During one such beating, Wainwright was slashed with a bayonet. On other occasions, he was slapped repeatedly about the face and knocked down. The thin and undernourished POWs barely survived the first winter at Karenko. Most had colds, fever, and chills. Several of the POWs died from their illnesses.

On April 2, 1943 Wainwright and 116 of the highest ranking POWs were moved 36 miles south to a new camp at Tamazato. The camp was for generals, governors, and chief justices only. The camp was quiet, restful, and had a moderate climate. No work was required of the POWs, and they were allowed to operate their own kitchen. The food, though never enough, was excellent by Karenko standards. Two weeks after arriving at Tamazato, the POWs were given their first Red Cross packages. Within a week, Wainwright gained seven pounds.

To date, the POWs had received no mail. While they worried about their families and loved ones, Wainwright also worried about America's perception of his surrender of the Philippines. He had periods of depression wherein he imagined himself as sharing the fate of Admiral Kimmel and General Short at Pearl Harbor. Both officers had been relieved of their commands. Worse yet, Wainwright thought it possible he could be disgraced by a general court-martial for his surrender. Such thoughts would haunt him for his entire captivity, yet he never failed to fulfill the role of leader to the rest of the senior POWs.

Wainwright and 89 of the senior POWs were moved to an undisclosed camp on June 1, 1943. They were only there for two-and-a-half weeks before they were moved back to Karenko. Instead of going into their former POW camp, they were stuffed into the small, filthy hold of a freighter that soon embarked. The men were packed into the hold so tightly there was only room to stand. When the hatches were closed and locked, the hold became stifling hot and there was no fresh air. The ship docked at Keelung, on the northern tip of Formosa, the following morning.

The POWs were moved 20 miles by railroad, put on trucks, and moved another five miles to the village of Muksag. Wainwright and the other senior members of his group would spend the next 16 months at Muksag. The treatment of the POWs at Muksag started very well. Too well for Wainwright. He immediately became suspicious of the Japanese motives. The men were given small rooms to live in with some furniture, the food was much improved, and there was no forced labor. A few days later Wainwright's suspicions came true. He was asked by Colonel Sazawa, the camp commander, to write letters and broadcast messages to President Roosevelt to end the war. Wainwright refused to even discuss the issue, as did all of the other senior officers.

A flood of Japanese now descended on Wainwright. Did he not appreciate the good treatment? Would he like to go back to the way it was at Karenko? The war was going badly for the Allies. Japan could not possibly lose the war. Far better to stop the war now and save lives. Roosevelt would surely listen to such an important person as Wainwright. Wainwright refused every attempt of the Japanese to even discuss the matter.

In May, 1944 Wainwright received the first letter from his wife since his capture. Naturally, it had been censored but it was enough for Wainwright to know that she was well and that their son was now in the military. About this same time, Wainwright's picture appeared on the cover of Time magazine, but Wainwright had no way of knowing that. The Time cover and accompanying article had this to say about Wainwright.

> He was ravaged by beri-beri, emaciated, he could hardly use his right leg; he dragged himself along with a cane. His faded breeches shrank up his legs. His shirt was ragged. His steely eyes were shrunken with fatigue. But his tours among the starved, tattered, forgotten men of Bataan were almost triumphal. They cheered him on the field. Behind his back they called him 'Old Skinny.' Some day in the not too distant future, the humiliation of the Philippines will be avenged. Wainwright and his soldiers wait. If they live they will learn that the nation has not forgotten the Philippines gaunt and ghostly men.[4]

On October 5, 1944 Wainwright and his group were moved to a new POW camp in the cold north of Manchuria, China. This would be about as far away from the advancing Allies as the Japanese could move their valuable prisoners. Enroute to China, the POWs spent several days at Beppu, Japan, where they were allowed to take hot baths, and more importantly, where some POWs read a bit of news in a Japanese newspaper, and learned that MacArthur had landed in the Philippines. Morale was never higher.

From Beppu, the men were moved to Pusan, Korea, and then to the cold and windy camp near Mukden in northern Manchuria. The camp was desolate and barren. The only thing that moved besides POWs and guards were hundreds of thousands of black crows. The sky was a dirty yellow color, and fierce winds blew sand and dust from the Gobi desert through the camp.

On November 28, Wainwright and the group that had been together at Muksag were informed they would be moved farther north to a more distant camp. This would be Wainwright's sixth POW camp. He was not certain he could survive any more moves. The camp at Sian was not pleasant. Wainwright's memories of this time are of mind numbing cold, hunger, and boredom. During the winter, temperatures dropped to 45 degrees below zero (Fahrenheit). In the summer, the sun baked the barracks and cracked the earth. Meals consisted of rice mush for breakfast and lunch, and a few vegetables for supper. Wainwright was down to less than 130 pounds. His weight before capture had been 160 pounds.

Wainwright's strength and spirits ebbed during his captivity at Sian. He was constantly humiliated by the guards and camp commander. He had trouble hearing and had to delegate certain of his responsibilities to other POWs, because his failure to hear and react quickly enough to Japanese guards could cause punishment for everyone.

On August 16, Corporal T. J. Willard, one of the American orderlies assigned to the camp congratulated a surprised Wainwright. Willard claimed he heard Japanese guards discussing that the war was over. The Emperor had surrendered. The war was over but it would be two whirlwind weeks before Wainwright would stand on the deck of USS *Missouri* to witness the surrender of Japan.[5]

From Mukden, Wainwright was flown to Chunking, the Capitol of China to meet with General Albert Wedemeyer, Chiang Kai-shek's chief of staff. On August 29, Wedemeyer entertained a group of officers and guests at his 30-room house on a cliff overlooking the Yangtze River, and presented Wainwright with the Distinguished Service Cross. Wainwright was unable to speak. With tears streaming down his cheeks he tried to explain that for the past three-and-a-half years he feared going home in disgrace. The medal made him realize that he and his men would be welcomed home. Indeed, the American people had not forgotten "Old Skinny Wainwright."

Wainwright was flown to Tokyo, where he was ushered in to see General MacArthur while MacArthur was having dinner. As

347

Wainwright entered the room, MacArthur rose from his chair and moved forward to greet him. MacArthur remembers being shocked at Wainwright's appearance. "He was haggard and aged. His uniform hung in folds on his fleshless form. He walked with difficulty and with the help of a cane .(Later MacArthur would recall that the cane was the one he gave Wainwright when he left Corregidor for Australia). His eyes were sunken, and there were pits in his cheeks. His hair was snow white and his skin looked like old shoe leather."[6]

The two men embraced, and MacArthur, not trusting his voice could only say, "Jim, Jim." Years later MacArthur would recall "The emotions that registered on that gaunt face still haunts me."[7]

Wainwright was up early on the morning of September 2. After a bountiful breakfast, he and Lieutenant Gen. Arthur E. Percival, Major Gen. Lewis C. Beebe, and other former POWs were taken to the dock at Yokohama, where they boarded destroyer USS *Nicholas* for the trip to USS *Missouri*.

The 45,000 ton-USS *Missouri* was the largest ship any of the men had ever seen. As they climbed the gangplank to the main deck a familiar figure reached down and grabbed Wainwright's hand. Big, gruff "Bull" Halsey would later recall that seeing Wainwright was so emotional he could not speak.

As Wainwright came on deck, he recognized more colleagues among the hundreds of officers facing the small table where the surrender ceremony would be conducted. Following the brief ceremony, during which MacArthur presented Wainwright and Percival with one of the pens used to sign the surrender documents, 400 B-29 bombers and 1,500 navy fighters and dive bombers flew over USS *Missouri*. World War II was over.

After the ceremony, Wainwright joined Admiral Halsey and other senior officers for coffee and pastries in Halsey's quarters. At 2:00 P.M., Wainwright and Percival were on a plane to Manila to witness the surrender signing ceremony at Baguio. Having General Percival, who surrendered Singapore to General Yamashita, and Wainwright at Baguio, was MacArthur's idea. Perhaps he believed that seeing their adversaries surrender would be good for both men, and would ensure that Yamashita received at least a small measure of the humiliation that Percival and Wainwright suffered.

The trip from Manila to Washington, D.C., took six days, with stops on Guam, Kwajalein, Honolulu, and San Francisco. While on Guam, Wainwright learned that President Truman had nominated him for the grade of General of the U.S. Army. For Wainwright it was the pinnacle of an impossible dream. From being a lonely POW, forgotten (or so he thought) by America and the world, with fear of being termed a loser, and possible court martial candidate, Wainwright had achieved the dream of every West Point graduate. The humble hero made no secret of his happiness and pride. San Francisco celebrated Wainwright's return with a large noisy parade up Market Street, and then it was on to Washington.

National Airport was bursting at the seams. Mrs. Adele Wainwright was there early, as were General George C. Marshall, many senior officers, the army's honor guard and band, American Legion units, amputees with front row seats, and more than 700,000 people that lined the route of march, all hoping for a glimpse of the nation's hero. Wainwright's plane landed at 12:26 P.M. and taxied up to the ramp. As the door opened, the band played ruffles and flourishes, and the crowd roared. Wainwright stepped out and the roar increased in volume as he descended the stairs, leaning on his cane.

To those that knew Wainwright well, he looked terrible. His legs wobbled, his clothes, though tailored for him were much too large, and his face was gaunt and drawn. "He looks like he may topple over at any minute," one radio announcer told his audience. After his reunion with Mrs. Wainwright, General Marshall escorted them to a car waiting to take them to the Pentagon. Waiting for them there were 47 veterans of Bataan and Corregidor. Wainwright plunged among them, greeting them all. Among those assembled were Colonel Sam Howard, commanding officer of the Fourth Marines who had done so much to stop the Japanese amphibious assault of the "The Rock" of Corregidor. Also present was Brigadier Gen. Carlos Romulo, probably alive only because Wainwright had ordered him to leave Corregidor before the final Japanese assault.

Next, the indefatigable Wainwright was driven to the Washington Monument, where some 400,000 people waited. Cannons, roared, bands played, and Carlos Romulo introduced Wainwright to the crowd. Romulo's words reflected his personal gratitude.

"We who last saw General Wainwright within the tunnel of Corregidor saw a leader bent under the tragedy of impending doom, a man left holding in his helpless hand the honor of America. . . . General Wainwright could not hold Corregidor, but he could hold fast to the standards of American decency, American honor, and American courage. Not once did he let the standards down; not even under torture did he let America down. . . . He was America on that bitter rock in Manila Bay. Now in this hour of flying flags and triumphant drums, he is the vindication of our democracy. He is your America and my America set free." [8]

Wainwright spoke briefly, recalling the brave men that defended Bataan and Corregidor, and especially those who died there or in prisoner camps in the Pacific. He thanked all Americans, in his name and those of his comrades, for devoting themselves to defending the freedom of America. He reminded all Americans to never again let our defenses crumble as we did before after WW I, and before WW II. Finally, he thanked God for his liberation, and the high respect that Americans had for the Philippine defenders during their years of imprisonment.

Next Wainwright was whisked to the rotunda of the Capitol

by the speaker, Sam Rayburn. Wainwright spoke in slow measured tones, expressing his gratitude for their recognition of his comrades in arms. He spoke briefly of his personal pleasure in the defeat of Japan, and of being present at the surrender ceremonies in Tokyo Bay and Baguio.

Cheering crowds welcomed Wainwright all the way from the Capitol, down Pennsylvania Avenue, to the White House. President Truman was waiting in his office. The two men shook hands and exchanged greetings, and then Truman suggested they step outside to the Rose Garden. Few people were aware of the president's secret intention. More than 100 people plus many reporters, photographers, and microphones awaited them.

Truman stepped to the microphones and read his prepared remarks. Suddenly Wainwright realized what was happening. He was being awarded the Medal of Honor by the President of the United States. After describing Wainwright's achievements and heroic conduct on Bataan and Corregidor, Truman grinned broadly and said, "and so it gives me more pleasure than most anything I've ever done to present General Wainwright with the Congressional Medal of Honor-the highest honor in the land."[9]

Wainwright was understandably overwhelmed with happiness and gratitude. "The moment was the realization ," he said, "of every dream of glory a soldier could have." He told Truman he expected to come home in disgrace. Truman assured him that he was a leader and a hero to the American people.[10]

Wainwright would go on to become commanding general of the Fourth Army at Fort Sam Houston in San Antonio, but most of his time was spent traveling across America to attend the numerous banquets, reunions and speaking engagements. Wainwright believed he owed America for the honors that the country bestowed on him. He retired on August 31, 1947, at age 64, after 45 years of service. He died of a stroke on September 2, 1953. His passing was mourned by all of the nation's leading newspapers, and his memorial service and burial at Fort Sam Houston was among the army's most elaborate and moving. The band played Wainwright's favorite songs, the ones he loved to sing with his cavalry troopers. Songs such as, The Girl I Left Behind Me, Garry Owen, and, She wore a Yellow Ribbon.

Wainwright never asked for much during his long army career. Many would say he never got much. But when war came, Wainwright was ready, even if the Army of the Philippines was not. He was ready, and he made the most of his opportunity. For that, a grateful nation remembers.

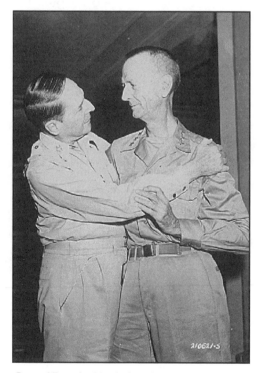

General Douglas MacArthur, Supreme Commander of the Allied Powers, welcomes Lieutenant Gen. Jonathan Wainwright in Yokohama, Japan, after Wainwright was flown from the Sian POW camp in northern Manchuria.

National Archives

33

MASAHARU HOMMA
LOS BANOS: APRIL 3, 1946

It is night at Los Banos, site of the U.S prisoner of war camp some 35 miles south of Manila. A soldier escorts a tall Japanese man to a large pole at the far end of the prison courtyard. The man is positioned with his back to the pole, and his arms are handcuffed, thus binding him to the pole. The soldier fixes a blindfold over the eyes of the man and steps away. Thirty feet in front of the man is a row of eight American soldiers, rifles at order arms. The soldiers are called to attention.

"Ready!" The rifles are brought to the firing position. "Aim!" Eight rifles are sighted on the chest of the man. "Fire!" The sound of the explosions is deafening in the small courtyard. The smell of gunpowder and the smoke from the rifles waft into the hot night air. The tall man that stood so erect and proud now sags to the side of the pole, his body kept erect only by the handcuffs that cut deeply into his flesh. Thus ended the life of Lieutenant General Masaharu Homma, conqueror of the Philippines.

Masaharu Homma was not your ordinary general officer of the Japanese Imperial Army. Even his friends acknowledged that he was quiet, withdrawn, and even aloof. His temperament was more of an artist than a samurai. He was emotional, sensitive, and easily hurt by the comments of others. Who exactly was this general that composed poetry in the midst of battle, wrote dramatic plays and talked of painters and sculptors?

Homma was born in 1887, the son of a wealthy landowner that died when he was a small boy. His mother never recovered from her husband's death, and paid scant attention to his development. At age 15, Homma made the decision to leave his mother and took the entrance exams for the military academy. Homma scored high on the tests, was admitted to the academy, and graduated at the top of his class. Even at this early stage, Homma was marked as a military genius, and a man to watch.

Following a tour with an infantry regiment, where he distinguished himself, Homma was assigned as attaché to Prince Chichibu, younger brother of the emperor. Homma went on to graduate with honors from the military staff college and was assigned duty as an observer with a British Expeditionary Force fighting in France and Germany. It was during his exchange tour with the British that his life changed dramatically.

Against the advice of all his friends and family, Homma married a beautiful woman named Toshiko Tamura while he was a military attaché. Toshiko was the daughter of a geisha from Akasaka, and Homma was very much in love. The couple soon had two children. While in Europe, Homma's mother sent him the news that Toshiko had left the children with Homma's parents and had become a prostitute.

The news devastated Homma. He went into a deep depression, started to drink heavily, and even attempted suicide. He was reassigned to the staff of Imperial Army headquarters in 1925, and seemed to have put the affair behind him. Once again, he became recognized as a military genius with a bright future in the army.

What many of Homma's seniors did not see, however, was his constant series of tragic love affairs. His romances became common gossip among junior officers, much to the chagrin of his family and friends. Homma's search for a passionate love that would last forever became the subject of ridicule among his fellow officers. Following Homma's affair with a 19-year-old geisha, he was introduced to a 21-year-old woman named Fujiko Takata. Fujiko had been married and divorced from a college professor and had traveled widely, including a long period in the United States. She seemed much like Homma, a gentle, cultured person with many western ideas.

Family and friends advised Homma not to continue with the relationship, but Homma listened to his heart and married Fujiko. He became a changed man. Their marriage was a happy one. With Fujiko as his wife, Homma stopped his heavy drinking and channeled his energy into his military career.

He was next sent to London as a colonel to attend the League of Nations disarmament conference. In 1933, he was assigned command of the 1st Infantry Regiment in Tokyo, promoted to major general in 1935, and put in charge of the Army Propaganda Department. Homma's moderate views toward war with Great Britain and the United States put him at odds with those radical army officers committed to throw the Western powers out of Asia, and marked him as an enemy of Prime Minister Hideki Tojo.[1]

Such was the situation on the morning of November 2, 1941, as Lieutenant Gens. Tomoyuki Yamashita, Hitoshi Imamura, and Masaharu Homma were ushered into the office of the Chief of Staff of the Imperial Japanese Army, General Hajime Sugiyama.

General Sugiyama greeted the three officers and offered them tea. Japan would be at war with Great Britain and the United States in less than three weeks, Sugiyama told them. "You will lead the imperial army to victory over the enemy. Lieutenant Gen. Yamashita will command the 25th Army and conquer Malaya and Singapore. Lieutenant Gen. Imamura will lead the 16th Army and conquer the Dutch East Indies. Homma will command the 14th Army and defeat the Philippines."[2]

Sugiyama went on to outline strategy, forces available, and estimated enemy strength. Homma keyed on Sugiyama's statement that he would have only two divisions to conquer the Philippines, and that he must complete his mission in 50 days. Yamashita and Imamura responded in humble and formal terms, thanking Sugiyama for his confidence in them and pledging their best efforts. Not so General Homma.

Homma began to question Sugiyama, quietly at first and them more vigorously. "How was the figure of 50 days to capture the entire Philippines decided?" Homma asked. "By the General Staff," Sugiyama responded. "But on what information?" continued Homma. "What kind of intelligence is available on enemy forces, dispositions, and equipment?" Before Sugiyama could respond, Homma continued, "Why is the 14th Army only being allocated two divisions? Who exactly decided that such a force was sufficient?"[3]

Stunned by Homma's challenge to his tasking, Sugiyama started to respond in a vague manner about the general staff review, but was interrupted by Homma. "The fact is, we really don't know the probable strength of the enemy, so it is not reasonable to ask me to take Manila in 50 days with only two divisions."

Imamura, Yamashita, and Sugiyama were shocked by Homma's outburst. It was well known that Prime Minister Tojo was looking for an excuse to remove Homma, considered to be too friendly to the Western nations. Tojo considered Homma to be too intellectual and too much of "a lover" to command armies in the field. Sugiyama and Homma had clashed before, and Sugiyama opposed giving Homma this important assignment. It was well understood, however, that Homma was one the most brilliant strategists in the Imperial Army, and, therefore, impossible at this time to bypass him for command. Homma had made no secret of his dislike for Tojo or his opposition to war against the West.

Sugiyama had quite enough of the brash Lieutenant Gen. Homma. "Whatever your opinions may be," Sugiyama responded angrily, "the 50-day period is firm and you will have to accept it." [4] Homma continued to question the validity of intelligence that would expect a force of 43,000 men to defeat MacArthur's 130,000-man army, and to conquer the entire Philippines in 50 days.

Sugiyama, his face reddened, and clearly at the end of his patience began a response, but both Imamura and Yamashita, good friends of Homma, interrupted and tried to explain to Homma that the 50 days was only a target date, not a guarantee. He was only expected to do his best to meet such a date. Homma knew better. His service on the general staff provided him with more information than was available to any of the other three officers present. He knew what intelligence was available on MacArthur's forces and he didn't agree with it. He believed that he was being put into a situation where failure was guaranteed. He also realized that further disagreement would solve nothing.

Slowly, the confrontation between Homma and Sugiyama subsided and the conversation moved to other matters. The meeting was over, but the hostilities between Sugiyama and Homma were only beginning. Homma continued to send sharply worded messages to Sugiyama, asking for clarification of his mission and detailed intelligence data. Sugiyama waited patiently for the right opportunity to punish his upstart commander.

As Homma and Major Gen. Masami Maeda, his chief of staff, studied the plans for the attack on the Philippines, it became obvious to them that the Imperial General Staff's assumptions were flawed. The staff assumed that MacArthur's forces would make a final stand trying to defend Manila. But what if MacArthur withdrew his forces to Bataan and Corregidor? The peninsula of Bataan was mountainous and surrounded on three sides by water. Defenders could concentrate all their forces to defend against a single front. With sufficient supplies, a force as large as the one commanded by MacArthur could hold out indefinitely.

Homma dispatched a cable to Sugiyama seeking further guidance on his mission: "What is my objective?" He asked. "Is it to occupy Manila or to destroy enemy forces in the field? If I am to destroy enemy forces in the field, this may not be possible if the main battle takes place on the Bataan peninsula. If the main battle takes place on the Bataan peninsula, the forces allocated to the 14th Army will be insufficient for the mission."[5]

Sugiyama answered that the main purpose of the attack is the occupation of Manila. "If the third-class, unworthy troops that face you retreat to Bataan, there is no reason why you should not blockade them there."[6] Finally, Homma had the guidance he needed.

Homma's forces landed on northern Luzon just after midnight on December 10 (Tokyo time) and advanced quickly with two divisions against MacArthur's ten. Sugiyama's estimate of the Filipino fighting forces proved to be accurate, as many of the Filipino soldiers ran from their positions at the first sign of the Japanese. The invasion advanced even faster than Homma expected. Within days, Manila was under attack from three directions. MacArthur abandoned his plan to defend the beaches and ordered his forces to fight a delaying action while falling back to the Bataan peninsula.

Within a few days, Homma's forces broke Major Gen. Jonathan Wainwright's defensive position. Wainwright was expected to hold his position long enough for MacArthur to move both troops and supplies to Bataan. More than 13,000 Filipino soldiers threw away their uniforms and melted into the jungle when Wainwright began his withdrawal from his defensive position.

By now it was clear to Homma that MacArthur was trying to evacuate his forces to Bataan. Homma was forced to make a decision to try and cutoff MacArthur's escape route to Bataan or capture Manila. He read once again Sugiyama's directive that stated the main purpose of the attack on the Philippines was to capture Manila. He could deal with MacArthur later. Homma pressed on to Manila. As a result of Homma's decision, MacArthur was able to withdraw the remainder of his army into the Bataan peninsula and onto Corregidor, but without the necessary supplies to maintain 80,000 soldiers and 25,000 civilians. There was only enough food to support such a force for a month. The entire force went on half-rations immediately.

Now both commanders made major mistakes. MacArthur overestimated Homma's forces as six divisions, precluding Wainwright from launching a counteroffensive that may well have succeeded, since his forces continued to outnumber Homma's by more than three-to-one. Homma, in turn, underestimated MacArthur's forces at 25,000. Both commanders provided their estimates back to their headquarters. As a result of MacArthur's estimate, a decision was made in Washington not to try and reinforce MacArthur against such a strong enemy force. The Philippines would have to be surrendered. In Tokyo, there appeared to be no need for concern since Homma's forces outnumbered the "unworthy" enemy. As a result, the blockade of Bataan would continue for months.

The general staff in Tokyo was thrilled that Manila was captured so quickly, but as the realization that Manila harbor could not be used until Bataan and Corregidor were captured, the euphoria began to wane. Sugiyama, when explaining the problem to the War Cabinet, stated that General Homma failed to display the proper qualities of leadership. Homma had run away, said Sugiyama, rather than cut off the enemy from retreat and force a final battle. To save his own face, Sugiyama argued that Homma should be recalled. "Homma was incompetent and afraid to fight."[7] The War cabinet decided to leave Homma in the Philippines, but to reduce the size of his command, since he faced such a small number of inferior forces and more soldiers were needed in Java.

On February 8, 1942, Homma called a conference of all his commanders to discuss future strategies for capturing Bataan and Corregidor. Before the officers could assemble, however, Homma received a message from Sugiyama stating that, "The Emperor is very concerned about your strategic situation. Why are you making no progress?" The sensitive Homma was in tears. He knew the message was from Sugiyama, not Hirohito, but he also learned for the first time that the man who gave him the mission to capture Manila as the first priority, the man who took away his forces when he needed them for an advance on Bataan, was now blaming him for the failure to capture the Philippines in 50 days.

General Homma during an inspection tour of troops in August 1942.

US Army

Homma dried his tears, listened to the recommendations of his staff, and then cabled Sugiyama that he could see no prospect of success against Bataan, based upon the enemy's strength and disposition. "We urge you to consider just how necessary it is to capture Bataan, and whether the expenditure in effort and casualties should prove worthwhile?"[8]

Sugiyama was furious and recommended immediate removal of Homma. Two concerns by the general staff prevented Homma's removal. First was the knowledge that every commander of an Imperial Army was considered to be appointed by the emperor. Removal of such a commander could be seen as a criticism of the emperor. Second, since the capture of Manila had been hailed as such a success, removal of the officer responsible could cause serious morale problems and embarrass the government. Sugiyama compromised. Homma would stay, but his chief of staff, Major Gen. Masami Maeda, would be recalled and replaced by a Sugiyama insider, Major Gen. Takaji Wachi. Another Sugiyama favorite, the infamous and widely detested Colonel Masanobu Tsuji, with a reputation for cruelty and barbarous conduct, was also sent by Sugiyama to be a member of Homma's personal staff. Tsuji was recognized as a staff headquarters spy wherever he was sent. He was known to have been responsible for the murders of more than 5,000 Chinese in China and Malaya.

Despite what he considered to be inadequate forces, Homma began an artillery shelling of the Bataan defenders on April 3, 1942. His advance, using armor, was a spectacular success, and Major Gen. Edward P. King, Jr., commander Luzon Force, surrendered Bataan on April 9. On May 5, Homma launched his attack against Wainwright's forces on Corregidor. The following day, Wainwright surrendered Corregidor.

While Homma was busy with the assault of Corregidor, Colonel Tsuji was busy issuing orders in Homma's name for disposition of the Bataan POWs. Homma had earlier approved a plan for the movement of 25,000 POWs from Bataan to Camp O'Donnell, a distance of 90 miles. The POWs were expected to walk the first 19 miles to a staging area at Balangas, and then be transported by truck some 33 miles to San Fernando. Two hundred trucks were allocated to transport the 25,000 POWs. From San Fernando, the POWs would be moved 30 miles by rail to Capas, and then walk the final eight miles to Camp O'Donnell. Field hospitals were to be established at Balanga and San Fernando, and there would be ample rest areas with water and other facilities. Homma approved the plan with the directions that POWs were to be treated "in a friendly spirit." He then turned his attention to Corregidor.

The POW plan, as approved by Homma, fell apart immediately. Instead of 25,000 POWs, there were 100,000. Instead of healthy young men, as assumed by the planners, the POWs were starved and suffering from malaria, dysentery, or both. Homma's plans estimated a 10-to-20 percent disease rate, but the actual rate was near 85 percent. Homma's plan was for the POWs to supply their own first day's rations, but there had been no rations for most of the POWs for many days. Few of the POWs were fit for any kind of a forced march, yet that is exactly what occurred.

It may have been impossible to correct the hopeless situation. There was not enough food, little medicine, not enough clothing, and 200 trucks could not move 100,000 men. There was only food for 25,000 men at Balangas, so the POWs could not be left there. Major Gen. Yoshi Kawane, overall commander of the POW movement to Camp O'Donnell, was overwhelmed by the numbers. He did not notify Homma of the problem, because there was nothing that General Homma could have done at the time to change the situation. The sea of human suffering began what the world would later call, The Bataan Death March."

POWs began dying all along the march to San Fernando. Men died from exhaustion, starvation, and disease. Thousands were brutally murdered. Japanese soldiers were in a vengeful mood. There were not enough supervisory personnel, most were fighting on Corregidor, and Colonel Tsuji had dispatched orders in the names of senior officers that all prisoners should be executed. About 78,000 POWs left Bataan, less than 58,000 arrived at Camp O'Donnell.[9]

During his trial, Homma argued that it was not until three years later that he learned of the Death March. The prosecution never argued that he had prior knowledge of the atrocities. Instead, as the commanding general, he was charged with overall responsibility for the Death March and for failing to prevent it.

After issuing orders in the names of senior staff officers to kill all prisoners, Colonel Tsuji undertook the destruction of General Homma as well. "Homma lacks ability," he secretly cabled Sugiyama. "His staff is dull and stupid."[10] Tsuji went on to say that Homma had been disobeying Sugiyama's direct orders to propagandize the Filipinos.

Sugiyama, armed with his cable from Tsuji, took the matter before the general staff. On June 9, 1942, Homma was relieved of his command and brought back to Japan disgrace. He was placed in a meaningless reserve unit and lived quietly with his beloved Fujiko until October 1945.

Following the end of the war, General Douglas MacArthur, as Supreme Allied Commander, established two separate war-crimes offices. The first was to bring to trial the major (class A) Japanese war criminals that would be prosecuted by the international military tribunal in Tokyo. Class A criminals were not charged with personally committing atrocities or murders, but for not preventing such atrocities from taking place and for leading Japan to war.

The second war-crimes office was to investigate and bring to trial all class B and C war criminals. Class B and C criminals may or may not have committed atrocities but were not considered important enough (such as Tojo) to be tried by the Tokyo tribunal. While Tojo and the other 27 class A criminals were afforded every legal safeguard possible, the trials of the 5,700 class B and C criminals were quite a different matter. Generals Yamashita and Homma were tried by the second type of war-crimes office.

General Masaharu Homma was arrested in October 1945. He was first questioned in a POW camp outside Tokyo by the prosecution. While held in close custody, he was informed that the Japanese War Ministry had decided to strip him of his rank and honors for a period of one year. The War ministry explained that they wished to distance themselves from Homma during his trial in the event they should be called upon to testify. Homma was stunned. First, he had been betrayed by the chief of staff of the army. Now, he was being cast-off by the very army he tried so hard to serve. Instead of a tall, erect, and proud officer in full military uniform, he would have to stand trial for his life in a dull, gray suit.

On December 8, 1945, Homma was transferred to Sugamo prison in Tokyo where his uniform and decorations were removed. A few days, later he was transported to the POW camp at Los Banos, south of Manila.

After the prosecution finished with their examination of Homma, he was allowed to meet his newly appointed defense attorneys. His trial date was only a month away and his lawyers knew their task was impossible. On December 18, Homma was brought before MacArthur's appointed five-general-officer commission for arraignment. Homma was charged with numerous atrocities committed during the Death March, violation of the open city status of Manila after MacArthur's departure, mistreatment of POWs in the camps, and isolated instances of brutality by Japanese soldiers against Filipinos in the field.

Homma's counsel asked for the prosecution to be more specific in its charges. Where and when did alleged atrocities take place? Who committed these atrocities? The presiding judge ignored the request and entered a plea of not guilty for Homma. Then the defense asked for more time to prepare its case. The presiding judge ruled that the trial would begin on January 3, 1946, as scheduled.[11]

Homma's trial took one month. The prosecution never attempted to prove that Homma was aware of the atrocities taking place. The prosecution asked for the death sentence because Homma should have known.

The prosecution brought in many Filipinos who displayed bayonet wounds received during the Death March, and women who testified of being raped by Japanese soldiers. American survivors of the Death March also testified as to conditions during the march and atrocities that were committed. In similar manner, hundreds of witnesses testified to the atrocities and murder of prisoners that occurred following The Death March. Since the prosecution did not present any evidence that indicated Homma ordered such atrocities or even knew about them, Homma's defense attorneys tried again to have the prosecution explain just exactly what Homma was accused of doing or not doing to enable them to defend against a negligence or disregard-of-duties charge. The commission refused to grant the defense request and the trial moved to a speedy conclusion.

Defense attorneys presented evidence to show that Homma had approved plans for the orderly movement and care of 25,000 POWs. There was testimony that showed Homma to be totally preoccupied with the Corregidor assault and that he left subordinates in charge of the Bataan POWs. For the one month following the capture of Corregidor, until he was recalled to Japan, Homma was shown to have been occupied by cleaning up insurgents around the islands, arranging for the surrender of guerrilla groups, and the establishment of an administration to govern the Philippines.

But, the defense had missed the point. MacArthur's prosecution proved that atrocities took place and that Homma was the commanding officer. Only once before had a commander been held to such a legal principle, that being the case of the U.S. versus Lieutenant Gen. Tomoyuki Yamashita. That case ended in Manila on December 7, 1945, with a guilty verdict against Yamashita. The principle that the senior officer "should have known" was established for the first time during Yamashita's trial, and became the guiding principle of the commission trying General Homma.

On January 13, for the first time since his arrest, Homma was permitted to visit his wife Fujiko in the guarded witness room. Homma gave his wife a small lacquered cigarette box that she accepted, knowing full well what was inside. Rumors were already prevalent that MacArthur intended to have Homma's body cremated and the ashes scattered so that the Japanese could never revere Homma's tomb.[12] The box contained a lock of Homma's hair and clippings from his fingernails. According to Buddhist religion, without a cremation of at least these body parts at an appropriate ceremony, Homma's soul could not go to heaven.

Many witnesses, including Filipino and British, testified on behalf of Homma's character. He was described as quiet and modest without any sign of arrogance. Finally, Homma and, later, his wife were called to testify. Homma answered every question asked of him and stated that he had done his job to the best of his ability. He explained the situation that existed when Bataan capitulated, and said that he was incapable of handling the situation differently. Fujiko testified about her husband being labeled pro-American due to his opposition to war with Great Britain and the United States. She said she was proud to be the wife of General Homma, and that she hoped their daughter might some day marry a man like Masaharu Homma. There were many moist eyes in the audience, including General Homma's when this dignified and poised lady finished her testimony. On February 11, 1946, the commission returned the verdict of guilty against Masaharu Homma. His punishment was set: death by a firing squad.

Homma wrote his last letter to Fujiko on the evening of April

2, 1946. He thanked her for her support and love, and promised to meet her in the other world. That done, he offered bottles of beer to the soldiers who came to his room to take him to his execution. The soldiers, unsure of the protocol involved, took a sip of beer in honor of this tall, gentle man, they had come to respect. Could he have possibly have done all the horrible things that he was said to have done?

"I am ready," Homma said. A soldier locked Homma's wrists behind his back with a pair of chrome handcuffs, and the small group moved slowly down the illuminated corridor to the prison courtyard.

General Homma testifies in his own defense before the commission appointed by General Douglas MacArthur, (February 6, 1946)

US Army

A despondent General Homma listens to testimony by victims of the Bataan Death March and the Rape of Manila.

US Army

34

CURTIS E. LEMAY

On January 6, 1940 Curtis E. LeMay was a 34-year-old lieutenant in the U.S. Army Air Corps. Five years later, he was a brigadier general, praised by military experts as the most innovative and successful aviation commander in World War II. LeMay would later earn the fourth star of a full general at age 45, the second youngest U.S. officer to hold the grade.[1]

LeMay's promotion to four stars came after three years as commander of the U.S. Strategic Air Command (SAC), and was long overdue. LeMay's unique accomplishments in both the European and Pacific theaters of war, and his subsequent development of SAC into the most efficient and powerful military organization in history, mark him as one of America's military giants.

Major Gen. Curtis E. LeMay, center, reads the report of the first low-altitude fire bombing of Tokyo in March 1945, with Brigadier Gen. Lauris Norstad, right, an army air corps representative from Washington, and Brigadier Gen. Thomas S. Power, who led the mission.

Wide World

In both Europe and the Pacific, LeMay's tactics were daring, ingenious, and effective. LeMay personally led his B-17 Flying Fortresses from England over fiercely defended German cities without fighter escort. Time after time, LeMay directed his forces from the lead aircraft in the attack force. Casualties to the bombers and the crews that flew them were mounting rapidly and were unacceptable to LeMay and the air force. If LeMay's bombers continued to suffer such losses, the bomber command would cease to exist. He developed the staggered-bomber formation that greatly increased the firepower of the bombers against German fighters, and pioneered the no-evasive-action, bomb-run procedure that improved the bombers accuracy. He also introduced the "hard-as-nails-training program" designed to save lives, airplanes, and improve morale.

B-29s that formerly flew under the command of General LeMay in China, move down a taxiway in Tinian for attacks against Japanese cities.

US Air Force

In the Pacific, LeMay introduced low-level, fire-bombing attacks that devastated Japan. The fire-bombing attack against Tokyo on March 30, 1945, destroyed 16.8 square miles of Tokyo, killed about 84,000 people, destroyed 267,171 buildings, and left a million people homeless. By June 1945, LeMay's B-29s flying from the Marianas had destroyed 105.6 square miles of the combined cities of Tokyo, Nagoya, Kobe, Osaka, Yokohama, and Kawasaki.[2]

Nagoya, Japan, under attack by B-29 bombers dropping incendiary bombs. More than 70 percent of the city was destroyed in this attack.

US Air Force

LeMay argued against the use of the B-29s to mine the inland sea of Japan, believing that the continued firebombing of Japanese cities would bring a quick end to the war. When the Joint Chiefs of Staff supported Admiral Chester W. Nimitz's request for the mine-laying operation, LeMay put his whole effort behind it. On March 27, the 313th bomb wing flying B-29s, dropped a thousand, one-ton magnetic and acoustic mines into the Shimonoseki strait of Japan's inland sea. During April, 18 Japanese ships were sunk, in May, 85 ships, and in June, 83 ships went down. Altogether, the B-29s seeded 12,000 of the anti-ship mines, sinking more than a half million tons of Japanese shipping, and reducing the volume of shipping in the inland sea to one-tenth the amount before the mines were laid.[3]

When President Harry S. Truman made the decision to use the atomic bomb against Japan, it was LeMay that made the crucial decision to send Colonel Paul Tibbets and the crew of the Enola Gay against Hiroshima, alone. A single, unescorted plane, he reasoned, would be considered a weather or reconnaissance plane and be ignored. A large fleet of bombers, all protecting a "queen bomber" in the middle of the formation would attract too much attention and resistance.

Following the emperor's surrender announcement on August 16 (Pacific time), LeMay sent out reconnaissance missions to pinpoint the location of Japanese POW camps. Then he launched airlifts of food, clothing, and medical supplies to the Allied POWs. Finally, he sent his aircraft to evacuate the POWs from Japan.

LeMay had come a long way from the humble workman's cottage on the east side of Columbus, Ohio where he was born in 1906. LeMay and his buddy, "Grizzy" Griswold from Ohio State University, enlisted as flying cadets in the fall of 1928, and left Columbus for March Air Field, California. When they arrived at Riverside, California, LeMay convinced Griswold to call March for transportation. The cadets were told to catch the next mail truck to the base. LeMay and Griswold received their wings and promotion to second lieutenant on October 1929. They forged a relationship that lasted throughout their military careers.

The Curtis LeMay who gained a reputation by low-level fire-bombing of Japanese cities, had a childhood not unlike most other boys growing up in America in the early 1900s.

LeMay's father Erving was nomadic, constantly moving in search of work. The LeMays lived at four different addresses in Columbus, Ohio, in other villages in Ohio, and in Pennsylvania, Montana, and California. Each move meant a change of schools and friends. LeMay was not much interested in school, but realized that he would have to get an education if he hoped to achieve his ambition of flying.

LeMay recalls that he had his first paper route when he was 11 years old, became a newspaper distributor when he was in high school, and used his earnings to buy a 22-calibre rifle. Before he had his own rifle, LeMay earned money by shooting sparrows with a friend's 22 rifle. An elderly lady gave LeMay a nickel for every sparrow he delivered. She fed the sparrows to her cat. LeMay's problem was that the cat's appetite could not keep up with his ability to supply English sparrows.

The greatest difference between LeMay and his friends may be that due to his various jobs, and interest in repairing automobiles, he had little time for socializing, especially socializing with girls. This dislike for making small talk stayed with LeMay for his entire life. Military personnel recall that you could be with LeMay in an automobile for an hour, and LeMay would not say a word.

LeMay probably earned the nickname, "the diplomat," as early as 1930 when he was stationed at Selfridge Air Base in Michigan. Several of the young pilots were bussed to Bradford, Ontario to witness a flying demonstration by a Canadian Air Force team. After the flying exhibition, LeMay was asked by the Canadian commander what he thought of the demonstration. LeMay responded, "Jesus Christ, aren't they lousy!" LeMay, for better or worse, would go through his entire air force career telling it like it was.

LeMay survived President Franklin D. Roosevelt's tasking of the army air corps to deliver the mail in 1934, but 65 aircraft and 12 pilots did not. The army fliers were not all-weather pilots in those days, and the mortality rate proved it. By May 1937, LeMay was the lead navigator for a B-17 force sent to intercept U.S. Navy forces at sea. The exercise received no publicity, but LeMay earned the unofficial title of "master navigator," and navigated several long-distance, good-will, and distance-record flights over the next few years.

For now, World War II was over and most of LeMay's most challenging work lay ahead. The first challenge to face Lieutenant Gen. LeMay after World War II was the Russian blockade of Berlin. LeMay was assigned as commander of the U.S. air forces in Europe in October 1947. On April 1, 1948, the Russians closed all road and train traffic through the Soviet zone that divided Berlin and the Western powers. Stalin meant to tighten the screws sufficiently that Great Britain and the U.S. would agree to Soviet control of Berlin.

LeMay began the Berlin airlift by flying sacks of coal in DC-3s (two-engine transports). After airlifting 300 tons of coal and other supplies over a three-week period, the Russians reopened the surface routes. LeMay's air force was bolstered by 28 B-29s on April 18. The Soviets, reacting to the B-29's role as a nuclear-weapon delivery vehicle, called the bluff, and on April 22, closed all passenger train traffic to the Western zones. They reinstituted a total blockade of road and rail in June. Once again, all sources of Allied supply to West Berlin were denied.

LeMay responded by asking for, and receiving the larger DC-4 aircraft (four-engine transports), and began an airlift that completed 426 round trips, carrying 2,047 tons of supplies by mid June. At the same time, he began construction of an additional runway at Templehof airport, in the Allied sector, that would increase the airfields traffic capacity by a third.

Soviet fighters began to make simulated firing passes on the transports and to harass them enroute to Berlin, but the airlift continued. By September 1949, when the Russians opened ground access to Berlin, the British and American airlift had delivered 2.3 million tons of food and supplies to the people of West Berlin. LeMay later recalled the airlift days with a touch of irony. A few years earlier he had, "battered it (Berlin), burned it, slain or mutilated many of the inhabitants. Now we are doing just the opposite, we are feeding and healing." [4]

While the Russians tried to blackmail the United States in Berlin, the chief of staff of the U.S. Air Force, General Hoyt Vandenberg, was concerned that his Strategic Air Command (SAC) could not perform its mission. Vandenberg sent for LeMay, who was about to take on his most challenging assignment.

When LeMay arrived in Washington, D.C., he was told not to unpack his suitcase. SAC was moving to Offutt AFB on the outskirts of Omaha, Nebraska. LeMay stayed in Washington just long enough to confirm his worst fears. SAC was in bad shape. With less than a positive frame of mind, LeMay boarded a plane and flew to Omaha. When he arrived, he was met by a host of newspaper reporters. LeMay's responses to the reporters questions were in keeping with his nickname of "the diplomat." "General, don't you think this will be a great thing for Omaha?"asked one reporter. "It doesn't mean a damn thing to Omaha, and it doesn't mean a damn thing to me," responded LeMay. "The diplomat" had wasted no time in introducing himself to the people of Omaha.

After thoroughly evaluating SAC's capability, LeMay pronounced his command as, "a very sad SAC."[5] Not only was SAC sad, so was Offutt. The field was an 1888 army cavalry station, originally named Fort Crook. The original officer's quarters and three barracks were abandoned, but still existed. The dominant feature of the base was the smell from the nearby Omaha stockyards. Also located nearby were several large factory buildings that were used by the Glenn Martin Company to build aircraft during Word War II. LeMay moved his people into the houses and barracks, and set up shop in the factory buildings.

Money was short and Congress was in a belt-tightening mood. Nevertheless, there was agreement on the part of the administration that SAC had to be improved. One of the quickest ways to build up SAC was to bring B-29s out of mothballs. It was only a short time before the B-29s delivered to SAC far exceeded the pilots and crews available to fly or maintain them. LeMay's lobbying for a mission-capable SAC was so effective that Secretary of Defense Johnson canceled a $188 million super carrier for the navy to fund more of the giant B-36 bombers for the air force.

By the end of 1948, SAC had 120 of the huge Consolidated B-36 "Peacemaker" bombers, with more scheduled to come. General Hap Arnold had started the B-36 program in 1941, and the planes were coming off the production line. The B-36 had been sold to Congress as the most efficient, and most cost-effective bomber in the world. The B-36 was to have longer range and greater payload than any other bomber. The initial problem was that many of the B-36s delivered to SAC were inferior in workmanship and materials. A tertiary problem was that the other services resented SAC receiving such a large share of the defense budget. By 1949, rumors about the deficiencies of the B-36 were so widespread that Congress investigated the B-36 purchase arrangement.

In April 1948, a B-36 flew 6,922 miles in 32-and-a-half hours. In May, the plane flew 8,062 miles in 36 hours and reached speeds well in excess of 300 miles per hour. In December, a B-36 dropped 42 tons of bombs from 36,000 feet. This was enough to convince the air force and LeMay that the plane was the logical successor to the B-29. LeMay's testimony to Congress was influential in saving the B-36, as was the discovery that many of the rumors concerning the B-36 inadequacies came from the navy.

Quite understandably, LeMay's ability to get money from

Congress for SAC did not endear him to the other services. Neither did his ability to convince the American public that SAC was the nation's most important defense capability. At this point in his life, most everyone agreed that LeMay did an outstanding job at SAC, but few would list him as a friend or a favorite person.

LeMay operated on the principle that he had to replace most of the people that he felt were incompetent, and to train the others from the ground up in his way of doing things. His lecture to his subordinate commanders included a warning that "we have a helluva job and they (his commanders) weren't worth a damn to start with, completely worthless".[6] LeMay replaced many of them with men that had worked for him in Europe and the Pacific. He then scheduled a simulated combat mission involving every crew and every aircraft flying at combat altitude against a radar target. Not a single aircraft was able to complete the short and relatively simple mission. LeMay was right. SAC was in sad shape.

A common theme wherever LeMay went was hard work and lots of it. When other commanders objected that SAC was getting more than its fair share of the air force budget, LeMay would respond that personnel in other commands worked an average of 20 to 30 hours per week. The people in SAC worked 90 hours per week and were still not receiving the funds they needed or deserved. In 1971, LeMay told an interviewer that, "I have always believed that you can work a man until he drops. All you have to do is convince the man that what he is doing is important, show some progress towards your goal, and show some appreciation for the effort."[7]

By March 1949, "Old Iron Ass" LeMay had whipped his command into shape such that he could state , "SAC could, in a matter of days, deliver a decisive attack against an enemy." His goal became to reduce the days to hours. By year's end, LeMay's SAC was meeting his high standards. SAC now consisted of 65,000 personnel, 1,000 aircraft, and 22 bases throughout the U.S. and Guam.

Now that SAC was able to perform its mission, LeMay turned his attention to housing, education, promotions, hobby shops, and other quality-of-life issues for the men and women of SAC. Within a short time, SAC bases became models for the other services. Next, LeMay instituted no-notice inspections to test the security of his aircraft, weapons, crews, and airfields. Officer and enlisted personnel were promoted, demoted, and reassigned as a result of these surprise operational readiness inspections.

During the Korean War, SAC deployed two bomb groups to Okinawa and Japan and flew tactical bombing missions in support of American forces on the ground. LeMay argued against the use of these strategic systems for tactical bombing, but supported the decision once it was made. "It wasn't our real mission. It was a disruption of our main purpose, but it had to be done," he rationalized.[8]

During June 1955, the first B-52 bombers were delivered to SAC as the replacements for the B-36. By April 1956, 47 B-52s had been accepted by SAC. Thirty-one others had been rejected for serious, but correctable problems in the electrical systems. The B-52s had engine-cooling and other problems, but soon began to phase out the B-36s. Following a series of nuclear weapons tests on Bikini atoll, code named "Operation Crossroads," a SAC B-52 dropped the first live hydrogen bomb from an American aircraft. This test was conducted on July 1, 1956, also on Bikini.

Concerned about the survival prospects of his aircrews if they should be forced down while on a practice mission somewhere in the world, LeMay founded the air force's first survival school near Reno, Nevada in 1952. By 1957, 23,000 crew members had graduated from the 17-day course.

Another problem that LeMay solved was the SAC aviation safety record. In 1948, SAC suffered 65 major aircraft accidents for every 100,000 hours flown. LeMay introduced an aviation-safety program and made Standard Operating Procedures (SOP)

378

mandatory. By 1956, LeMay's last year as commander of SAC, the accident rate had plummeted to nine accidents per 100,000 flying hours, and LeMay had a force of 3,000 nuclear-bomb-carrying jets located at 50 bases worldwide.

After nearly nine years in SAC, LeMay was promoted on April 4, 1957, to vice chief of staff of the air force. General Thomas D. White, the new chief of staff, selected LeMay for the job because "He was the best man to run the Air Force," while White devoted himself to his duties on the Joint Chiefs of Staff.[9] On June 30, 1960, President John F. Kennedy surprised not only LeMay, but the rest of the Air Force, by appointing LeMay as air force chief of staff. He became a two-term chief when Kennedy reappointed him in 1963. Why Kennedy reappointed LeMay, a man he seemed to oppose on so many issues, is not clear. Perhaps Kennedy respected LeMay's knowledge, but it seems more likely that Kennedy did not want to take on Congress, where LeMay was both respected and admired.

As service chief of staff, LeMay was increasingly frustrated by his inability to provide military information to the president or Kennedy's secretary of defense, Robert McNamara. A major reason for this frustration was because LeMay remained focused on conducting and winning a nuclear war, while McNamara and Kennedy sought to preclude such action. In reality, there was no communication because they were thinking and discussing different strategies. The dialogue between McNamara and LeMay reached the point where the secretary or president would often make their decision and issue their orders before asking LeMay or the chiefs for their views on the subject.

The basis for disagreements between McNamara and LeMay went far beyond nuclear strategy. The two clashed heatedly over such weapons systems as Minuteman missiles, and Polaris submarines to replace LeMay's B-52 bomber force. Simlarly, Congress was forced to intervene in the dispute over the B-70 bomber as a replacement for the B-52, the Boeing-General

Dynamics competition over the TFX fighter plane, and the Skybolt missile.

One of the negative legacies left by LeMay were the several State Department leaks during the Vietnam war that quoted LeMay as saying, "Maybe we ought to drop a nuclear bomb on Hanoi," and, "We ought to nuke the Chinks."[10] Even LeMay's own biographer, MacKinlay Kantor, quoted LeMay as saying that the way to handle the North Vietnamese was, ". . . to bomb them back to the stone age."[11] LeMay denies making the statements, but they are in keeping with his thoughts and blunt manner of speaking.

When asked, LeMay ranked two of his accomplishments above all others. First was the surrender of Japan without the need for an invasion. His B-29s destroyed the Japanese cities to such an extent that LeMay believes the emperor would have surrendered even without the atomic bomb. The second was development of the Strategic Air Command. LeMay believes that SAC preserved the peace for the many years following the end of World War II.

Most of those that knew LeMay well say that he was demanding, and exceptionally so. They also say that he was honest and always had the concern for his aircrews as his first priority. His superiors have gone on record to praise his work during the war and with SAC, but admit that he lacked the statesmanship for his job as air force chief of staff. LeMay could focus completely on his mission, be that the bombing of German or Japanese cities or developing the Strategic Air Command. What he lacked was the ability, or willingness, to understand the larger role of the air force and military in contributing to our national security through both the political and military process.

A most appropriate tribute to LeMay's effectiveness was made some years after World War II at a cocktail party where LeMay was not a participant. As the story goes, Judge Ralph Nutter mentioned at this party that he named his oldest child after Curtis LeMay. There was an awkward silence as the group around Nutter tried to reconcile Nutter's liberal views with the conservative views of LeMay. Nutter was a politically liberal California jurist that once was an American Civil Liberties Union attorney. The gap between Nutter and LeMay seemed nearly insurmountable. Finally, one asked, "How could you name your child after that right-wing son-of-a-bitch?" Nutter replied, "I served under him in England during World War II. I was a navigator in his 305th bomb group. He was so tough on us, he trained us so hard and prepared us so well, I honestly don't believe I'd have survived to have a child if not for Curtis LeMay."[12]

LeMay's distinguished military service earned him many awards and decorations from a grateful nation as well as from many foreign governments. Perhaps his most ironic award came in 1964, when he was presented the First Class Order of the Grand Cordon of the Rising Sun, the highest decoration that can be awarded to a foreigner by the Japanese government.[13] There must have been Japanese citizens who wondered why LeMay, credited with killing in excess of 200,000 Japanese by fire-bombing, received such an award.

Curtis LeMay retired on February 1, 1965. He had been a general officer for nearly 22 years and a four-star general for 13. Following his retirement from the Air Force, LeMay took a position as board chairman with Networks Electronics Corporation. While in this position he was a popular speaker with conservative groups and became a "hawk" on Vietnam. He suggested that the United States should "wipe out" Haiphong harbor and mass bomb large areas of North Vietnam, similar to what he did in Japan. He served as the running mate for George Wallace in the 1968 presidential campaign. The cry of "Bombs away with Curtis LeMay,"[14] became too much for Networks Electronics and he was fired from his position.

LeMay moved to Air Force Village, a retirement home for Air Force officers near March Air Force Base in Riverside, California. He grew even quieter in retirement, preferring to "just stay home and keep my mouth shut. That's always the best thing to do."[15] He died of a heart attack at March Air Force Base hospital on October 1, 1990, at age 83. His remains are interred at the Air Force Academy at Colorado Springs, Colorado.[16]

General LeMay on his last day of active duty, February 1, 1965. His retirement took place at the White House and then at Andrews Air Force Base near Washington, D.C. He is standing in front of a B-17 bomber with the markings of his old 305th Bomb Group.

US Air Force

35

THE SILENT SERVICE

The Bureau of Naval Personnel book, *United States Submarine Operations in World War II,* consists of 577 pages.[1] The book, *Silent Victory: The U.S. Submarine War Against Japan,* has 1,072 pages.[2] Dozens of other books about U.S. submarine operations in the Pacific total perhaps 10,000 pages.[3] My reason for mentioning these sources is to alert the reader to the fact that a short chapter in this book cannot do justice to the brave men of the Silent Service who took the undersea war to Japan.

U.S. submarines accounted for 1,178 merchant vessels, more than half (55%) of all Japanese merchant shipping sunk during the war, plus another 214 warships. During 1944, once their torpedo problems had been solved, U.S. submarines sank one-third of all Japanese warships that were sunk. Yet, at their peak strength, the submarine service accounted for only two percent of the U.S. Navy.

U.S. submarines sank in excess of 5.6 million tons of Japanese ships during the war. The price was 52 submarines, 374 officers, and 3,131 men. The Silent Service suffered 40 percent of all navy casualties in the Pacific.

The Japanese attack on Pearl Harbor took a heavy toll of the surface ships, but not the submarine force. The submarine base was not attacked. Within a week after the attack, three Pacific Fleet submarines (*Gudgeon, Pollack,* and *Plunger*) were on their way to Japan to execute unrestricted submarine warfare against Japan.[4] Three weeks later, *Pollack* sank two Japanese freighters, *Plunger* sank one, and shortly thereafter, *Gudgeon* sank the Japanese submarine *I-173,* thereby claiming the honor of sinking the first enemy warship, and the first enemy warship sunk by an American submarine.

Gudgeon's honor lasted until August 28, 2002, when the undersea research laboratory of the University of Hawaii discovered the Japanese midget submarine *I-22* in 1,200 feet of water three miles off the entrance to Pearl Harbor. The honor of sinking the first Japanese warship then went to the destroyer, USS *Ward,* who fired upon, depth-charged, and sank the midget submarine *I-22* at 6:30 A.M., on December 7, 1941.[5]

Sinking of the *I-173* by USS *Gudgeon* was such a joint effort that the story deserves telling. *I-173* was one of three Japanese submarines patrolling off the west coast of the United States in January 1942. Joseph Rochefort, head of the code-breaking team "hypo" in Pearl Harbor, knew they were there and when they were scheduled to depart. On their scheduled day of departure, *I-173* surfaced and fired a few cannon rounds into a refinery near Los Angeles. Rochefort learned of the shelling and decided to have his team track *I-173* and try to intercept it.

On the night of January 25, 1942, the three submarines passed Midway Island, surfaced, and fired a few shells at the island. Rochefort and his assistants plotted *I-173's* course and speed to Kwajalein and determined that *Gudgeon* was in its path. Lieutenant Cmdr. Joe Grenfell, commander of *Gudgeon,* was notified, and proceeded to the projected intercept point. *I-173* arrived exactly on schedule. *"I-173*, came along, fat, dumb, and happy. The boat was not even zigzagging, men were lounging on the upper deck, sunbathing and smoking."[6]

Grenfell fired three torpedoes and, after a run of 81 seconds, heard a dull explosion. When *Gudgeon* got back to periscope depth, there was nothing to see, and no propeller sounds on sonar. Grenfell reported the submarine damaged, due to lack of evidence of anything else, but Joe Rochefort in Pearl Harbor knew better. *I-173* never again transmitted, and disappeared forever. *I-173* was the first enemy combatant to be destroyed as the result of intelligence in WW II.

The early success of U.S. submarines against Japanese merchant and warships was impressive in light of the navy's torpedo problems. Few, if any, operational ordnance problems in WW II matched that of the Mk 14 torpedo. The weapon was slightly longer than 20 feet, with a 643-pound warhead, and was fitted with a regular exploder that detonated on contact with the side of the ship. Aditionally, a secret magnetic exploder was to detonate beneath the keel of a ship without contact. During the last weeks of December 1941, during 45 separate attacks, while firing 96 Mk-14 torpedoes, only three torpedoes exploded against Japanese ships. Small wonder that submarine commanders wanted to torpedo the Navy's Bureau of Ordnance. The Bureau rejected any and all complaints from the submariners, insisting that the problem was the submarine commanders, not the torpedoes.

Over time, submariners discovered that the Mk 14 did not run consistently at the depth set into its controls, and often went too deep for the magnetic exploder to function. Then they learned that the magnetic exploder itself was often defective, exploding before the torpedo reached the target. When submariners deactivated the magnetic exploder, they learned that the contact exploder was also faulty. Each of the defects hid the other, until all were discovered and fixed. It took 21 long months before the navy finally took the complaints seriously and solved problems with the firing mechanism, depth control, stabilizing fins, and magnetic triggers of the Mk 14. Much of the credit should go to Rear Admiral Charles Lockwood, Commander Submarines Pacific.

By early 1943, Lockwood had heard more than enough complaints from his submarine commanders about the faulty Mk 14. Lockwood and his assistants bought 500 feet of net from a local fisherman near Albany, Australia, modified a Mk 14 torpedo so that the explosive head was replaced by a dummy head, and did a series of test firings against the net. The first test firing was set to run at ten feet. The torpedo cut the net 25-feet below the surface. Additional torpedo tests all ran eight to ten feet deeper than set.

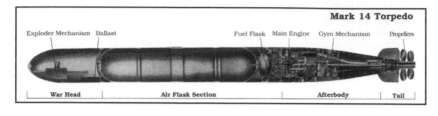

Thanks to Lockwood's tests, by August 1942, the depth mechanism had been isolated and corrected. Now the problem became the torpedo detonator. After months of firing duds at Japanese ships, Admiral Lockwood suggested at a conference in Washington that, "If the Bureau of Ordnance can't provide us with torpedoes that will hit and explode. . . then for God's sake, get the Bureau of Ships to design a boat hook with which we can rip the plates off a target's side."[7]

Lockwood's entreaties to the bureau proved fruitless, and on July 24, 1943, he ordered his submarines to deactivate the magnetic-influence detonators, and to rely on contact detonation only. This action only served to highlight the other problems inherent with the Mk 14.

Early in 1942, a German electric torpedo was captured and turned over to the Westinghouse Corporation to copy. Westinghouse produced the Mk 18 electric torpedo, and the submarine force was promised the weapon by summer 1942. It did not arrive. With the Mk 14 having so many problems, it was crucial that the Mk 18 become operational. Being electric, the torpedo had the advantage of having no wake, a feature that made observation difficult. The depth control of the Mk 18 was superior to that of the Mk 14, as was the exploder device. The Mk 18 could be manufactured for far less time and money than the Mk 14. The only negative with the Mk 18 was its slower speed, 28 to 30 knots, compared to 46 for the Mk 14 steam torpedo.[8]

Admiral Charles Lockwood, Commander Submarines Pacific.

US Navy

Operational development of the Mk 18 lagged so badly that submarine *Lapon* was sent to Newport, Rhode Island, to test-fire the Mk 18 and assist in operational questions. According to Commander Oliver Kirk and Lieutenant Cmdr. Eli T. Reich, commanding officer and executive officer, respectively, of *Lapon,* "what we found at Newport was simply sickening."[9] The Newport Torpedo Station had a "NIH" (not invented here) attitude that created apathy and a lack of interest in operational development of the promising torpedo. In fact, the personnel assigned to the Mk 18 had their own electric torpedo, the Mk II that they were developing in competition with the Mk 18. *Lapon* stayed at Newport for six weeks with Kirk and Reich agitating daily to overcome inertia and push the Mk 18 towards operational approval. Finally, both officers wrote memoranda that indicted the Navy's Bureau of Ordnance and the Newport Torpedo Station for the delay in operational development of the Mk 18.

The memos eventually reached the desk of Admiral Ernest J. King, chief of naval operations. King turned the matter over to his inspector general to investigate. Admiral Lockwood became very much involved in the controversy, and supported his submariners in every way possible. The Bureau of Ordnance was found to be at fault, and a higher priority was assigned to the Mk 18. The Mk 18 had a number of relatively minor problems that were quickly isolated and fixed. Some Mk 18s started to trickle to the fleet, but it was summer of 1944, before the Mk 18 development and production could meet fleet needs.

Until 1943, individual submarines conducted U.S. submarine warfare. On October 1, 1943, three U.S. submarines departed Midway for the East China Sea as the first American wolfpack of the war. The pack had average success, sinking a total of seven Japanese ships with a total of 22,607 tons. Three more subs left Midway on November 3, and sank an additional seven ships.

The wolfpack tactic continued into 1944, but never in the numbers or intensity of the German wolfpack attacks in the Atlantic. Japanese merchant shipping normally did not convoy, and their anti-submarine efforts were sporadic at best. There was no need to concentrate the submarine force to meet any threat.

As the Japanese began to move forces throughout the South China Sea in the summer of 1943, submarines began to sink larger vessels. USS *Bowfin* sank a 8,120-ton cargo ship on September 25. Two days later, *Bonefish* sank a 9,908-ton transport, and on October 10, sank a 10,086-ton transport. *Bonefish* left her patrol area credited with 24,206 tons of Japanese vessels.

USS *Bowfin* was positioned again off Mindanao in November 1943, and during a dark night with waves covering the periscope, found herself in the middle of a five-ship Japanese convoy. Under command of Lieutenant Cmdr. W. T. Griffith, *Bowfin* sank two tankers, a 5,000-ton freighter, a small coastal steamer, two large unidentified ships, and an escort vessel. Her attack on a 7,000-ton ship with her last two torpedoes resulted in a premature explosion of one torpedoe that sent the second off course. On her way to Freemantle, Australia, *Bowfin* made a surface attack upon a 75-ton oil-carrying yacht in Makassar Strait and destroyed the craft.

One of the more famous depth-charging stories belongs to the survivors of USS *Puffer*. On October 9, 1943, *Puffer* placed two torpedoes into a large Japanese merchant ship. The ship stopped, dead in the water, and began to list, but did not sink. Nine minutes later, Commander, M.J. Jensen, fired two more torpedoes at the ship. One detonated prematurely, the other missed or was a dud. By now, the merchant vessel began blazing away at *Puffer* with all her small-caliber guns. A few minutes later, a "pinging" sound was heard along with the sound of fast-moving screws. Jensen ordered "dive," but, because he planned to surface and finish off the merchant ship, he only dove to 400 feet.

Twenty minutes later, at 5:25 A.M., six depth charges exploded beside *Puffer*. The conning-tower door and hatch were blown open temporarily, admitting a shower of water. Several sea valves opened including a casting in the torpedo room which let in a constant stream of water. The rudder and stern plates were damaged. There were many additional "minor" damages throughout the ship, but *Puffer* was not seriously hurt. Jensen ordered a descent to 500 feet.

Ten more minutes, and another depth charge exploded near by. Fifteen minutes after that, four charges exploded at different depths above *Puffer*. It seemed obvious to Jensen that either escaping air bubbles or oil leaks were betraying his position to the Japanese escort vessel. The vessel would depart for as long as an hour, and then return to depth charge *Puffer*.

The crew was having trouble with the depth control of the sub. Much water had entered the bilges, and the main induction and supply lines were flooded. Gradually, *Puffin* drifted deeper until the control room was at an emergency-depth level. When the motors were used to move the sub, there was a 12 degree up angle on the bow. Few submarines had ever gone so deep. The air conditioning was stopped to conserve power and decrease noise. A bucket brigade was used to control the water level in the bilges, and to prevent drowning out the electrical motors.

After being submerged and under attack for 12 hours, a second anti-submarine vessel joined the first. Both vessels depth-charged *Puffer* until 1:15 A.M., on October 10, but neither vessel departed the scene. Finally, after keeping *Puffer* submerged for 31 hours, the escort vessels departed. Jensen wisely kept *Puffer* submerged until nightfall, another seven hours before bringing the listing and battered sub to the surface.

By early morning of the 11th, after hurried repair, *Puffer* was able to make a trim dive, and no serious leaks were found. *Puffer* stayed submerged all day to rest the crew and then headed for home. Once in port, the officers and crew were studied for their reaction to the long submergence. Several interesting conclusions were drawn. For example, the most serious impact upon crew morale occurred when the air conditioning was turned off. The heat became insufferable. Temperatures rose to 125 degrees in the maneuvering room, and the humidity was like a drug. Men gasped for breath and slipped on the greasy decks. Men thirsted for cool drinks, but all liquids were at room temperature. Swallowing the tepid liquid induced vomiting followed by thirst, more tepid liquids, and more vomiting until dehydration became a problem. No one wanted to eat anything.

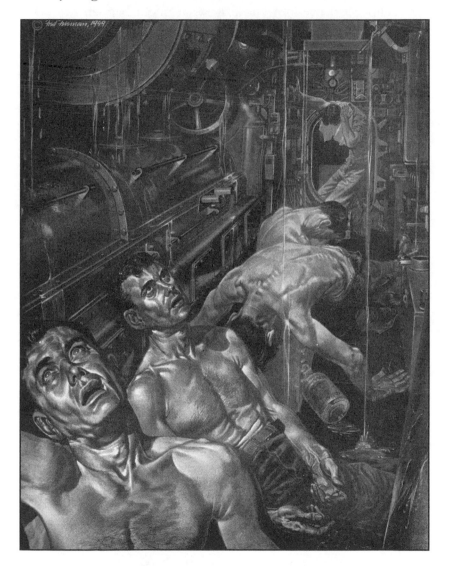

USS *Puffer* under attack. *Puffer* was submerged and depth charged for nerarly 31 hours.

US Navy

Those still working, such as the bucket brigade, struggled against extreme fatigue. Despite the use of CO2 absorbent and oxygen tanks, the air was foul, breathing was sluggish, and severe headaches were common. Some of the crew collapsed in a stupor, and were obviously well past caring what happened to them or their ship. Suspense, not knowing what might happen next, was also a negative morale factor. Although officers did pass through as many crew areas as possible and relayed up-to-date information, many crewmembers depended on their imagination to predict current and future events.

One seemingly innocent and reasonable event that backfired was the ordering of everyone to don life jackets. The psychological shock was profound. Experience had proven that one's chances of survival were much greater with a life jacket, but after so many hours submerged, the crew could only assume that the ship was doomed. Why else would they be suddenly be told to wear life jackets in the unbearable heat and humidity? As a result of the crew's interrogation, the navy determined that it would be best to leave the air conditioning on, keep everyone fully informed of decisions and the ship's status, and to keep everyone busy. Those crewmembers with few duties to perform tended to "imagine" the worst while those that were busy paid little attention to rumors.[10]

Many of the United States submarines sunk in the Pacific were lost as the result of minefields that guarded narrow channels or straits. The submarine may not have contacted a mine, but had to surface to penetrate the minefield. In doing so, the submarine became easy prey for antisubmarine vessels and aircraft. Such was the case with USS *Wahoo* that penetrated the La Perouse Strait and entered the Sea of Japan with USS *Plunger* in mid-August 1943. Targets were plentiful in the sea, but both subs had faulty torpedoes. Within the space of four days, *Wahoo* sighted 12 enemy vessels, and attacked nine of them with ten torpedoes, only to have all the torpedoes broach, make erratic runs, or fail to detonate upon contact with the target. *Plunger* had similar problems, and lost two of her motors due to burned out bearings.

When *Wahoo,* captained by Commander Dudley "Mush" Morton, returned to Pearl Harbor, he asked for the new Mk 18 electric torpedo and a chance to return to the inland sea. *Wahoo* was loaded with the newly arrived Mk 18s, and departed Pearl Harbor on September 9, 1943. She refueled at Midway on the 13th, and expected to enter La Peruse on the 20th. USS *Sawfish* trailed *Wahoo,* planning to enter the Japan Sea three days later.

With no way to detect enemy mines, U.S. submarines were forced to run near the surface, in the narrow straits and channels, making them easy targets. USS *Plunger* had been forced to dodge two Japanese destroyers while exiting the La Perouse Strait in August. Now, a few weeks later, the Japanese navy was alert and ready for *Wahoo's* return.[11]

Wahoo was never heard from again. *Swordfish* penetrated the strait but had no contact with *Wahoo*. *Swordfish* was attacked by a patrol plane while transiting the strait, on October 9, and the Japanese Navy reported depth-charging a surfaced submarine in the strait two days earlier. Records examined after the war gave credit to *Wahoo* for the sinking of four Japanese ships; the first on September 29, and others on October 5, 6, and 9.[12] Total tonnage sunk by *Wahoo* during this period was 13,429 tons, and included a steamer with 544 lives lost. Following loss of *Wahoo*, the Sea of Japan was abandoned as a submarine patrol area and was not invaded again until June 1945.

No chapter on U.S. submarines is complete without at least a brief mention of USS *Harder,* and her commanding officer, Commander Sam Dealey. Simply stated, Sam Dealey hated Japanese destroyers. American submarines were tasked to sink the merchant fleet of Japan and were doing a fine job of it, but the Japanese destroyers kept getting in the way. Submarine procedures called for submarines to run from Japanese destroyers whenever possible. After all, destroyers were there to destroy you, and they had the equipment to do it.

Dealey figured that if he took on the destroyers first, then he could dispose of the merchant fleet at his leisure. On June 6, 1944, Commander Dealey was tasked to pick up a team of British and Australian commandos that had been operating behind Japanese lines for two years. The fact that three other submarines had tried to rescue the commandos and failed, only added suspense to the mission.

As Dealey raised the periscope in Sibutu Passage, a narrow strait that separates Borneo from Tawi Tawi in the Philippines, he spotted a convoy about 12 miles ahead. It was night, dark clouds partially covered the moon, and Dealey could make out the silhouette of three tankers and three destroyers. At six miles distant, the moon broke through the clouds, and *Harder* was spotted immediately by the destroyer escorts. One destroyer broke away from the convoy and sped directly toward *Harder*.

As the destroyer closed, Dealey ordered, "Take her down," and then, "Left full rudder."[13] "Up scope," and there she was, just as Dealey planned. The destroyer was going directly over the spot where *Harder* had been. Dealey ordered "fire," and three torpedoes sped toward the destroyer. The first missed ahead, number two ripped the destroyer's bow with a tremendous explosion, and number three hit under the bridge. The destroyer *Minatsuki* rose stern first and slipped beneath the waves.

Dealey surfaced to pursue the convoy and another destroyer headed for *Harder*. Dealey dove and tried the same tactic but this time the destroyer captain would not follow a straight line. He zigged and zagged, making a torpedo shot most difficult. Finally, Dealey fired six torpedoes, but the destroyer turned hard starboard and all torpedoes missed by a few feet. Now the destroyer had the advantage and subjected *Harder* to a furious barrage of depth charges. Finally, the destroyer departed, once her convoy had cleared the area.

Still enroute to the rendezvous area on June 7, Dealey was

interrupted by another destroyer. This vessel followed the pattern of *Minatsuki*, and at the range of 300 yards, suffered two torpedo explosions, one of which was likely in her magazine. In less than a minute, *Hayanami* disappeared forever. Within 16 hours, *Harder* sank two enemy destroyers. In more than three years of war in the Pacific, American submarines had never sunk more than single destroyer on a given patrol.

Suddenly, *Harder* was rocked by blasts from 11 depth charges. A destroyer had arrived to avenge *Harder's* latest kill. For two hours *Harder* lay on the bottom of the sea, hoping for the best, and fearing for the worst. When Dealey did surface, he discovered six destroyers waiting for him. Six destroyers were a bit too much for even Sam Dealey. With a shake of his head, he went back down to wait a bit longer.

On June 8, some 48 hours late, *Harder* arrived in a shallow bay off the Borneo coast. The landing party was put ashore in canvas and rubber boats, and in two hours were back with the commandos. As the commandos ravished steak and ice cream in the wardroom, Dealey discovered that two destroyers had closed his exit through the strait. The destroyers steamed broadside across the channel entrance fully aware that *Harder* was inside. "Make ready four fish," ordered Dealey. Then, moving slowly and submerged so that only the tip of his periscope showed above the water, he closed the distance to the destroyers.

Sam Dealey did not want to waste a single torpedo. He wanted to fire his torpedoes as the two destroyers passed one another, so that four torpedoes could sink both ships. When ready, he ordered, "fire." Then, he raised the periscope to full height and watched. Number one torpedo missed ahead of the first destroyer. The second and third torpedoes crashed into the nearest destroyer, and a blinding sheet of fire destroyed the cover of darkness. The fourth torpedo tore into the second destroyer just as it emerged from behind destroyer number one. Just as Dealey had planned. In short order, both destroyers slid beneath the surface. Dealey surfaced and brought his crew on deck so they could witness the fruit of their efforts. Congratulations did not last long. The tolling of midnight was broken by the roar of an aircraft that dropped bombs that exploded nearby. *Harder* dived as deep as she could and exited the bay that enclosed her.

The next day Dealey sighted another large Japanese convoy. This one was a fighting force of three battleships, four cruisers, and eight destroyers. The crew of a submarine would never implore the commander to run, but that had to be in the mind of most of the crew. They had already sunk four Japanese destroyers, how long could their luck last? Sam Dealey had similar thoughts. Eight destroyers were suicide odds. Besides, he had the commandos to consider. He did not rescue them just to have them die at the bottom of the ocean. Dealey figured if he attacked, his chances of getting out of it alive were one in a million.

Dealey's musings were broken as *Harder* rocked from the explosion of bombs dropped from escorting aircraft. *Harder* had been seen, and now a destroyer was charging at her at full speed. Sam's decision was simple. He had to kill the destroyer or be killed by it. At 1500 yards, Dealey fired three bow torpedoes with no gyro angle. It was what the submariner's call a "down the throat or head on shot." *Harder* dove, went to full speed, and right full rudder. As *Harder* passed 80 feet, a deafening series of explosions rocked the sub. These were not depth charges, but the destroyers boilers or magazines, or both exploding.

The remaining enemy destroyers now began a serious depth-charging. *Harder* "sweated" it out although the senior commando approached Dealey and asked if it would be all right to just take them back to Borneo. Their life had been far simpler behind the Japanese lines. Three long hours of depth-charging took a toll of men and machine. Suddenly, it was over. *Harder* rose to periscope depth and found a clear horizon.

Harder and her crew won the admiration and respect of the entire navy for destroying five enemy destroyers in one mission. Commander Sam Dealey earned the Medal of Honor, but posthumously, since USS *Harder* and her entire crew disappeared on August 24, 1944.

Three U.S. submarines, *Darter, Shark II,* and *Tang* were lost on October 24, 1944. The first, *Darter,* ran aground in the Paladin passage after attacking and sinking the heavy cruiser *Atago* (Admiral Kurt's flagship), and closing in to finish off a second heavy cruiser, *Takao.* USS *Dace* rescued *Darter's* crew, and USS *Rock* tried to sink *Darter* with ten torpedoes. Unfortunately, *Darter* was high aground, and the torpedoes exploded on the reef. Next, USS *Nautilus* closed and fired 55 six-inch shells into *Darter.* Although *Darter* remained on the reef, Lieutenant Cmdr. G. A. Sharp, commander of *Nautilus,* pronounced *Darter* useless to the enemy.[14]

Shark II apparently attacked and sank an unmarked Japanese prison ship carrying 1800 Allied POWs near Hainan Island. *Shark II* was quite possibly rescuing survivors when she was attacked and depth-charged. According to Japanese post-war records, 17 depth charges were dropped on *Shark II,* and bubbles, heavy oil, clothing, and cork rose to the surface.

Tang's loss was particularly grievous, due to the crew's recent success and terrible misfortune. During *Tang's* October 1944 patrol northwest of Formosa, she torpedoed and sank two heavy freighters on October 10-11. Twelve days later, Commander O'Kane, the sub's skipper, discovered three cargo ships, one or more tankers, a troop transport, and several escorts in convoy. O'Kane drove *Tang* into the center of the convoy on a night surface attack. Firing from bow and stern tubes, *Tang* soon had ships burning, freighters blowing up, and escorts dashing about in a frenzy. *Tang* weaved and bobbed like a boxer to dodge the bullets and shells hurled in her direction.

Suddenly, through the smoke of battle, the troop transport bore down on *Tang* to ram her. "Emergency speed and hard right rudder," ordered O'Kane with *Tang* still on the surface. The maneuver saved *Tang* for the moment, but now she was boxed by three burning ships on one side, and a freighter, transport, and several destroyers closing in from the other. O'Kane turned *Tang* to meet her attackers and fired a salvo at the transport and freighter. Both were hit and damaged. Now O'Kane turned to meet the charging destroyer head on and rang up full speed. The bluff worked. *Tang* had empty torpedo tubes, but the destroyer wanted no part of a possible head-on torpedo attack and veered away. *Tang* roared away to quieter water, submerged, and reloaded her torpedo tubes. O'Kane reported seven ships sunk, but postwar Japanese records list three ships as sunk.

After USS *Darter* ran aground, it was wrecked to prevent capture.

US Navy

Commander R.H. O'Kane, commander of USS *Tang*.

Twenty-four hours later, *Tang* found a second convoy. O'Kane reported seeing tankers with aircraft on their decks, and troop transports loaded like camels with crates and large boxes on all after decks. Once again O'Kane conducted a night surface attack. The escorts took *Tang* under attack immediately, with five-inch and 40-mm fire. O'Kane ignored the destroyers and drove *Tang* to within 1,000 yards of the convoy, where he fired six torpedoes, two at a transport, two at a second transport, and two at a tanker. All torpedoes hit and exploded. A large transport and a tanker were now astern of *Tang,* and three destroyers were rushing at *Tang* from the two sides. O'Kane rang full speed ahead, and charged straight at the destroyers. Closing the range, he fired three torpedoes in front of him. One hit a tanker that promptly flamed, a second hit and stopped a transport, and the third exploded and stopped one of the charging destroyers.

Tang dashed away to load the last two torpedoes into her tubes. Zig zagging and darting, *Tang* returned to the attack with her last two torpedoes. The first torpedo ran true for the crippled transport. The second swerved sharply to the left, porpoised, and made a sharp turn. It was making a circular run. O'Kane shouted for emergency speed and threw full rudder into the turn. Twenty seconds after launching, the torpedo struck and exploded in the stern of *Tang*. The blast threw O'Kane and eight others from the bridge. Inside *Tang*, men were hurled against bulkheads, arms and legs were fractured, and *Tang* began her 180-foot plunge to the bottom.

After destroying codebooks, and following a Japanese depth-charge attack, crewmembers followed emergency procedures, and in the smoke, fire and flooding, 13 men escaped from the forward compartment. Eight of the men reached the surface alive, and five swam all night until picked up by a Japanese destroyer in the morning. Three of the nine men that were blown from the conning tower survived the long night, including O'Kane.

Blows, kicks, and clubbings greeted the submariners as they were taken aboard the destroyer escort. The beatings were bad, but seemed somehow acceptable considering that the burned mutilated Japanese doing the beatings were themselves victims of *Tang*. Following the war, *Tang* was credited with sinking seven ships during her last patrol with a tonnage of 22,072. Only one other submarine (*Tautag*) would go on to sink more ships than the 24 recorded by *Tang*. *Tang* was awarded a second Presidential Unit Citation, one of only three warships to receive such an honor twice. Commander R. H. O'Kane survived captivity, and was awarded the Congressional Medal of Honor by President Harry Truman in April 1946.[15]

During June 9-25, 1945, a classified operation termed Barney involved the intrusion of nine U.S. submarines into the well-defended Sea of Japan. The Japanese Navy considered the Sea of Japan impregnable; so much so, that merchant vessels followed peacetime rules when operating in the sea. The nine submarines spent 15 days in the sea, sinking 28 Japanese ships, including a large submarine, and a total tonnage of 70,000 tons. Japanese losses would have been much higher had the navy been able to conduct such an operation earlier. By June 1945, much of the Japanese merchant fleet had already been destroyed. USS *Bonefish* and her crew were lost during this operation.[16]

The success of Operation Barney is attributed to the leadership and energy of Admiral Lockwood, and his demand for a device that would permit his Pacific submarines to locate and evade underwater minefields. That device, frequency modulated sonar, (FMS),[17] enabled the crew of the submarine to follow a narrow, shallow, entrance channel to a harbor or inland sea, to see and hear nearby surface vessels, and to avoid minefields that protected a narrow channel. Even after FMS was developed and tested, Lockwood had to overcome the conservatism of his submarine skippers, who demanded to be shown that FMS worked before endangering their ship and crew to such a device.

General Billy Mitchell, speaking in the 1920s, was quoted as saying, "The best defense against submarines is another submarine."[18] USS *Batfish,* with Commander J. K. Fyfe, took Mitchell's advice to heart. During the evening of February 9, 1945, *Batfish's* radar operator detected a Japanese submarine at 11,000 yards. Fyfe closed the range to 1,850 yards and fired four torpedoes. All torpedoes missed. Shortly after midnight, the visual lookouts spotted the submarine at 1,020 yards. Fyfe fired three torpedoes, a violent explosion occurred and the radar indication disappeared. The submarine was later identified as Japan's *I-41*.

The next evening, *Batfish* again detected a submarine. The submarine was sighted visually, and as *Batfish* maneuvered to fire its torpedoes, the submarine submerged. A short time later, the submarine reappeared at a distance of 8,650 yards. Fyfe closed the distance to 6,000 yards and fired four torpedoes. As on the previous evening, an explosion, flash, and roar blew the submarine apart. The vessel was later identified as *RO-112.*

Two days later the *RO-112* scenario was repeated. Another enemy submarine was first located and closed to 7,150 yards when it submerged. Radar contact was then established at 6,800 yards. Fyfe's first torpedo destroyed *RO-113* in less than 30 seconds. *Batfish* still holds the record of three submarines sunk in three days.

But, among the many navy successes, were several mistakes. On the night of June 13, 1945, USS *Spadefish,* operating with eight other submarines in the Sea of Japan, torpedoed and sank the 11,000-ton Russian ship *Transbalt.* The commander's defense was that, "The ship had no lights burning and was not following a designated Russian route." Nothing happened to the sub commander. He increased the number of Russian ships sunk by American submarines to five.

On April Fool's Day 1945, USS *Queenfish,* operating in dense fog off the China coast, fired four torpedoes at, and sank, what the sub's commander believed to be a destroyer escort. The ship was actually the Japanese transport *Awu Maru* that had been given safe conduct from Japan to Saigon to carry 10,000 Red Cross food packages to POWs there. The ship was marked with white crosses, which were to be lighted at night, but could not be seen in the fog. *Awu Maru* was not sounding her fog whistle as required by international regulations.

Japanese diplomats around the world lamented the sinking of *Awu Maru* and demanded justice and vengeance. The secretary of the navy, following a general court martial, gave *Queenfish's* commander a letter of reprimand that did nothing to harm his career. [19]

Submarines laid mines, carried fuel, transported men and equipment, provided weather reports and forecasting, and evacuated personnel. During the Battle for Guadalcanal, USS

Amberjack delivered 9,000 gallons of aviation gasoline, 200 bombs, and 15 aviation personnel to Tulagi, enough for two days of operations. Delivery came at a critical time when the U.S. Navy was about to write Guadalcanal off as a failure.

On February 6, 1942, USS *Trout* left Corregidor with 20 tons of gold and silver, much of the national treasury of the Philippines. The cargo was safely delivered to Australia.

A lesser known, but most important, role of the Silent Service, was the rescue of downed airmen at sea. Submarines spent 3,272 days on lifeguard stations in the Pacific, and rescued 504 pilots and airmen. One of them, a navy pilot, named George Walker Bush, would go on to become President of the United States.

Historians and military personnel, both American and Japanese, agree that the war against Japan's shipping was the most decisive single factor in the collapse of the Japanese economy and their inability to logistically support their army and navy. Simply stated, Japan was exhausted, starving and burned, well before the atomic bombs fell on Hiroshima and Nagasaki. The Silent Service can justly claim credit for playing such a decisive role in the war against Japan.

Sunk by her own torpedo, and her last, USS *Tang* lies in the Formosa Strait. Only eight of the submariners who escaped, made it to the surface.

US Navy

36

THE COMFORT WOMEN

One of the most tragic and unresolved issues of World War II is that of the comfort women. Comfort women were usually young, uneducated women who were forced into a life of prostitution for the Japanese military. Many of these women were made to sexually service as many as 40 Japanese men per day, some for as long as four-and-a-half years.

We will never know the exact number of women who were kidnapped and beaten into sexual slavery. The highest estimate is about 200,000.[1] Between 80 and 90 percent of the women were Korean, and 90 percent of the women died during the war or just after.[2]

The Korean and Chinese comfort women were very young. Eighty percent were between 14 and 18 years of age, with some only 12 and 13 years old. Nearly all were virgins and free of sexually transmitted diseases. A common ruse was to offer the girls employment in Japan working in defense factories as part of the Women's Defense Corps. The civilian recruiters of the women promised good food, excellent living conditions, and good pay. Japanese citizens and members of the Korean police force worked closely together to procure the young women. The women were further duped by their teachers and village authorities who feared Japanese reprisals if they did not cooperate in meeting the local quota for young women. As the need for more women increased following Japan's Pacific conquests, procurers resorted to force and even murder of family members in order to meet their quotas. Once the women were collected and forced onto ships going to Japan or trains going to China, they were beaten, raped repeatedly, and forced into a life of sexual slavery.

The first military comfort station was established in Shanghai in 1932, according to Lt. General Yasuji Okamura, deputy chief of staff in Shanghai.[3] The women were Koreans from the north Kyushu mining area of Japan. Some of these early comfort women may have been professional prostitutes, and, when offered pay, may have volunteered for the work. There were also a small number of Japanese prostitutes in military brothels during the war, but they were reserved for senior officers and were treated much better than the non-Japanese sex slaves. Pay was not something the comfort woman received. Soldiers would either pay a fixed amount or provide a coupon to the manager for the women's services, but coupons were seldom collected by the women, and money was never received by them. All income for the women's services was kept by the civilian contract agents or by the army.

Korean women wade through the Hwang Ha River. They are happy and laughing with joy because they believe they are going to a good job in a manufacturing company. Instead, they became comfort women for the Japanese soldiers.

National Archives

Comfort stations multiplied rapidly and were soon found wherever Japanese troops were located: from Myitkyina in Burma to Sabah in Northern Borneo, and the home country of Japan. There were even comfort women at the notorious underground headquarters project at Matsushiro. (See the chapter titled

"Nagano" in this book.) The number and size of comfort stations were directly related to the military strength in the area. Initially, a program was developed to kidnap young women from Korea and China for service in the stations, but as Japan's conquest of the Pacific progressed, women were obtained from Burma, the Dutch East-Indies, Formosa, Hainan, Hong Kong, Malaya, Okinawa, the Philippines, Singapore, and Thailand.

The Japanese navy also exploited comfort women. Documents dated May 30, 1942, by Rear Admiral Nagaoka Takasumi, head of the Ministry for the Navy, reveal instructions for the movement of 165 comfort women to four navy facilities in Southeast Asia. This was the second shipment of women to these bases.[4]

The term "comfort" may have been appropriate for the soldiers who visited the stations, but there was no comfort for the women who provided sexual service. Living conditions for the women varied considerably, but even the best conditions were bad. Stations near the Soviet border and close to the front lines consisted of tents with partitions that allowed a five-foot-by-three-foot space per woman. Often, papers or a dirty, smelly blanket was the only item on the dirt floor. Stations farther from the front lines were temporary wooden shacks or large buildings divided into many small rooms, each just large enough for a person to lie down. Sometimes a filthy mattress would be on the floor, and often the women were provided with a wash basin to be used after each man satisfied his sexual needs. Sometimes comfort women near the front lines would be forced to take their blanket and travel between foxholes and bunkers to service the soldiers who could not leave their post.

Women generally were awakened between 6:00 A.M. and 7:00 A.M. They had to clean their rooms, clean themselves, perhaps clean and wash the kitchen, eat, and start their sexual service by 9:00 A.M. Each soldier was allocated 30 minutes, and the women would have only a minute or two to clean up after each man. The day would usually end about 10:00 P.M, after each woman had serviced between 30 to 40 men. Sometimes, officers would elect to spend the night with the women.

Comfort women were inspected at regular intervals for venereal disease. Soldiers were required to use condoms, but many refused. If the women protested they were beaten, burned with cigarettes, and stabbed. Many had limbs broken and others died trying to protect themselves.

Food varied depending on location and the quantity available. Early in the war, when food was relatively plentiful, the women received rice, soup, some vegetables, and barley. Comfort women in Korea received kimchee, pickled cabbage, and some bean sprouts. Later in the war, when the Japanese were starving on bypassed Pacific Islands, the women starved with the men. Most comfort women wore baggy trousers and a cotton jacket with an open front. They shared such luxuries as soap, gauze, and tooth powder when it could be obtained. It was not uncommon for overly amorous soldiers to bring gifts to the women, especially if they were about to go into battle and did not believe they would survive.

Keith Howard edited the English translation of the book, *True Stories of the Korean Comfort Women*, in 1995. The book includes the stories of 19 Korean women who were kidnapped and forced into prostitution for the Japanese military. These 19 women testified to the Korean Council for Military Sexual Slavery by Japan, or to the Research Association on the Women Drafted for Military Sexual Slavery by Japan. A summarization of a few of these testimonies follows.[5]

Kim Haksun was the first Korean comfort woman to publicly tell her story. In 1941, at age 17, Kim and another foster daughter were taken from Seoul, Korea, to Beijing, China, by the girls' foster father in hopes of finding suitable employment for them. They were too young to work in Korea and their family was unable to support them.

Shortly after arriving in Beijing, Kim's father was accused of being a spy and was led away by Japanese soldiers. The two girls were kidnapped by other soldiers. The following day the girls were repeatedly raped, despite their protests and struggles. The girls were put into a house with three other women, two age 19 and one age 22. Each woman was allocated a small space separated by a flimsy curtain. They were provided with beds, blankets, a wash basin, and forced to provide sex to soldiers.

The entrance to a comfort station in Shanghai. Signs on stations commonly offered encouragement to Japanese soldiers fighting the war for Japan.

National Archives

Kim, with the help of a Korean civilian who entered the comfort station undetected by the guards, managed to escape after four months of confinement. She posed as the man's wife, and they found refuge in the French district of Shanghai. At age 18, Kim became pregnant. She gave birth to a girl, and at age 21, had a boy. Following the liberation of Korea in 1945, Kim and her live-in husband were repatriated and returned to Seoul. Due to a cholera epidemic, they were forced to spend three months in quarantine near the dock area where Kim's daughter died of the disease. With no family or friends, the couple managed to exist until 1953, when Kim's male friend lost his life in an industrial accident. Kim lost her son in a swimming accident while he was in the fourth grade. Despondent, Kim tried to commit suicide several times but was unsuccessful. She worked at heavy labor and as a domestic until 1987, when she met an elderly woman who was a victim of the atomic bomb. The woman convinced Kim to speak out and to tell the story of the comfort women.

Now, at age 74, Kim resents the life of shame and degradation she has been forced to endure and no longer dreams of growing old with a family and children who could love and care for her.[6]

In 1944, Kang Tokkyang was a freshman attending high school in Korea. She was sent, along with 150 other girls, to work in an airplane factory in Hujiko, Japan. Instead of work at the factory, Kang was sent to Matsushiro, near Nagano, Japan, where she and a half-dozen other women were forced to provide sex to 10 or more soldiers a day with no time off. Kang was housed in a tent, partitioned into six cubicles. She was often required to leave her tent late in the evening to service countless soldiers on the mountainside. By morning she would be so weak and sick that she would have to be dragged back to her tent by the last man to have sex with her.

Kimmiko Kaneda was 17 years old in 1939 when she made the mistake of believing a Japanese man in Seoul who promised her a lot of money if she would go to work in a factory in Japan. Kimmiko was taken to China, beaten, raped, and forced to work for six years as a sex slave, servicing 40 to 50 Japanese soldiers per day. Because of her shame, Kimmiko could not return to Korea. She lives alone in a Tokyo suburb, surviving on painkillers and tranquilizers, to ease the pain and illness caused by her ordeal. Kimmiko has no future. Her only joy in life is feeding birds in the park. Perhaps the birds take the place of the family she will never have.[7]

A 15-year-old-girl in Malaya, we will call her Madame X, was at home with her family when Japanese soldiers entered her village and broke into their home. She was raped in front of her parents and brother. When her father tried to assist her, he was knocked down and kicked in the head. Madame X was taken to Jalan Ampang, where she was forced to provide sex to numerous soldiers in various comfort stations. She was closely supervised to prevent escape and was often beaten for no reason.[8]

Kim T'aeson was born in Korea in 1926. She was an orphan living with her uncle in 1944 when a Korean and a Japanese male entered her uncle's house and led Kim away for work in a factory, where she was promised a large salary. Kim and many young women like her were escorted by bus, train, and ship to Osaka, Japan. From Osaka, a large transport ship, the Aribiya Maru, took the women south to Okinawa, where about 60 of them were taken off the ship. The ship traveled only at night for fear of Allied bombing raids, and many soldiers guarded the women. The ship stopped at Saigon, but Kim and about 20 other women were taken to Rangoon, Burma, and then trucked north for three hours to the side of a mountain.[9]

Kim was quartered in one of two large buildings, with 10 small rooms in each building. Each room measured about three-feet-by-five-feet, the entrance was closed by a small curtain, and the women were given two blankets. The women were fed rice three times a day, pickled radish, and soya bean soup. Kim was forced to begin her sexual service the next morning at 9:00 A.M. This was the first time Kim had experienced sexual intercourse and she was in constant pain.

Well before 9:00 A.M., soldiers would start lining up outside the building in orderly rows. When they came to the women's rooms, they would leave their shoes on and just pull their trousers down. The women would pull their baggy pants and underwear down. By saving time in this manner, the women were forced to serve 30 or more soldiers per day. Condoms were provided, but there were never enough. To help guard against venereal disease, the women collected the used condoms and washed them in a nearby stream.

In early December 1944, the Allied bombing attacks became frequent and it was obvious to the women that the Japanese military was preparing to leave. The two comfort station buildings were demolished and the women were told to climb onto the back of one of the trucks. Before long, Kim and the other women realized that all the Japanese soldiers had gone and they were left alone in the back of the truck. After discussing their situation, the women decided to walk south at night to avoid the bombing attacks. After a few days, they came to a Burmese village where they obtained some food. On New Years day, the women tried to cross a large river on a small boat, but the boat capsized and all 20 women fell into the river.

Many rivers and much illness later, only Kim and another comfort woman, Haruko, were still alive. Haruko died from cholera, but in May 1945, Kim walked into Rangoon. She had wandered in the jungles of Burma and survived for nearly six months. Kim was repatriated to Korea, where she worked in a restaurant, lived with a man, bore two daughters who know nothing of her past, and receives medical treatment for illness associated with her experiences. Kim goes to church, prays daily, and would like to be able to forget her past. She claims to feel some sense of relief since telling her story.

Comfort women, wherever located, had little hope of escape and could offer no resistance to their tormentors. Many of the women contracted venereal disease and were killed and buried in unmarked graves. One comfort woman who tried to resist a soldier was taken to the courtyard, and, in front of the other women, her head was cut off and her body chopped into small pieces. Another woman was tied by her limbs to horses and her body was pulled apart. Still another woman refused to bathe in the hopes that soldiers would be discouraged from coming near her. She was suspended upside down from a tree, her nipples were cut off, and she was shot with a rifle through the vagina.[10] Make no mistake, the penalty for less then full compliance with the will of the soldiers was a painful death. Total submission was essential for survival.

Comfort women were often forced to commit mass suicide as the Allies moved toward their locations. If they did not kill themselves, they were murdered by the men they served in order to preclude evidence and testimony after the war. Following the war, only the Dutch military tribunal, of all the Allied nation tribunals, prosecuted Japanese military personnel for allegations of sexual slavery. The Dutch tribunal found nine Japanese army personnel guilty of sexual crimes against 35 Dutch women during the war. Punishment for these offenses included the death penalty.

Most of the comfort women who survived the war were so embarrassed by their ordeal that they refused to come forward and testify. As of early 1991, only three Korean women had publicly discussed their past as comfort women. Gradually, as international awareness grew, more women came forward to tell their stories. A novel and book were published about forced prostitution in Taiwan. In 1992, a Dutch woman, Jeanne Ruff-O'Hearne, spoke at a public forum in Tokyo about her experiences as a comfort woman. A woman from Java described in an article in May 1993, how she and her sister were abducted, taken to Borneo, and forced into prostitution.

Jeanne Ruff was one of the 35 Dutch women forced into prostitution after Java fell to the Japanese. She was taken to a comfort station in Semarang and forced to service Japanese soldiers. Ruff testified that she fought every rapist. She kicked, scratched, fought, cried, and protested to no avail. She was always thrown down by the stronger soldiers, her dress torn from her body, and forcibly raped. Each day the horror began anew. Ruff would try to hide, but was always found and dragged back to her cubicle and beaten. Still, she continued to resist with all her might. When she was released in the summer of 1944, she was near death. "The Japanese had abused me and humiliated me. They had ruined my young life. They stripped me of everything, my self-esteem, my dignity, my freedom, my possessions, my family."[11]

Maria Rose Hensen was a Filipino girl of 15 when she was

abducted and imprisoned in a "comfort station" in Angeles, Pampanaga. She was forced to have sex with numerous Japanese soldiers every day. "Every day, from two in the afternoon to 10 in the evening, the soldiers lined up outside my room and the rooms of the six other women there. I did not even have time to wash after each assault. At the end of the day, I just closed my eyes and cried."[12] Maria was 68 when she became the first Filipino to end the decades of silence borne by the comfort women. In the 173 cases of documented comfort women in the Philippines, 27 have already died.[13]

LILA Filipina, an organization of seven women's groups was formed in the Philippines in 1994 in an effort force Japan to take legal responsibility for its actions, apologize for the crimes, and pay reparation to the surviving comfort women. To date, Japan has refused to accept responsibility or offer an official apology to the comfort women. In 1995, Prime Minister Ryutaro Hashimoto offered a personal apology and reparation of $18,600 to the surviving Filipino comfort women from a private fund, but the offer was rejected since it did not come from the government of Japan.

In December 1991, three Korean comfort women sued the Japanese government for 20 million yen as reparation for their suffering and loss of livelihood. In April 1993, Filipino women did the same. Initially, Japan insisted that the comfort stations were operated by private parties, but in 1991, Japanese Defense Agency archives revealed that Japan's military organized and directed the establishment of comfort stations for its troops.[14] In August 1993, Japan formally acknowledged enslavement of the comfort women by the Japanese Imperial Forces. Prime Minister Kiichi Mizawa went so far as to acknowledge the Japanese government's responsibility and extended its "apologies and remorse to all those who suffered immeasurable pain and incurable physical and psychological wounds as comfort women."[15] Japan did not offer compensation, however, and claimed that the issue of reparations had already been settled in 1951. On August 31 1994,

Japanese Prime Minister Tomiichi Murayama refused to admit Japan's legal responsibility towards the victims and refused to pay monetary reparation. Murayama proposed instead that Japanese businesses would establish a foundation to pay "gifts of atonement" to families of the victims.[16] Murayama's proposal was never accepted by Japanese business or the comfort women.

Since the Muriyama proposal, the International Commission of Jurists issued a 240-page report concluding that the comfort women must be compensated by the Japanese government.[17] In October 1998, a Japanese court ruled that no individual has a legitimate position to stand under international law before the courts, and that the U.N. does not have the authority to deal with issues that occurred before its creation.[18] Nobukatsu Fujioka, a professor of education at Tokyo University, has become a leading "revisionist" historian for the government, claiming that the comfort women were ordinary prostitutes who were paid for their services. Fujioka demands that the government of Japan retract such weak apologies that have been made on the subject and remove all references about comfort women from Japanese textbooks.[19]

While the issues of apology and compensation languish in the courts, the surviving comfort women continue to die. The women are in their early to mid-70s and, due to their trauma and illness, do not have many years left. Perhaps Yun Yuri, a Korean girl abducted from Pusan Korea, at age 17, and forced into a life of sexual slavery speaks for many of the surviving women when she says, "I want to be born as a woman again. I want to be able to study more. I want to live with my parents in a good and just society. I want to marry and have children. But what am I now? I am unmarried. I sleep alone at night. Why am I living alone? Who made me feel this way? When I see families passing with children, I feel miserable. I ask why, if others can have children, is my life so hard?"

"Japan ruined my life. How can Japan now dare to evade the

issue? They ruined my life. They took away my chance to get married. Could a verbal apology from them ever be enough? I will never forget what I had to go through so long as I live. No, I will not be able to forget what happened even after I die."[20]

Japan's failure to compensate the surviving comfort women caused the government of South Korea to approve a plan to compensate South Korean women who were enslaved as prostitutes in Japanese army brothels. The South Korean government will pay each of the 152 surviving South Korean women $27,000 in recognition of their pain and suffering.[21]

37

SHIRO ISHII (UNIT 731)

One of the most evil but least known war criminal's of World War II was Shiro Ishii. Not much is known about Ishii because after the war he made a secret agreement with General Douglas MacArthur, supreme allied commander, that guaranteed him and his accomplices immunity from prosecution.

Ishii was born on June 25, 1892 in the village of Kamo near Tokyo. Shiro was the fourth, and brightest son of a wealthy landowning family. During his childhood he was described by his peers as an individual with determination and arrogance. Ishii graduated from the medical program of the elite Kyoto Imperial University in 1920, and immediately joined the Imperial Army as a surgeon. He returned to Kyoto University in 1924 to pursue his graduate studies, and married Kiyoko, the beautiful daughter of Torasaburo Akira, the university president. Ishii was awarded his Ph.D. in 1927.

Ishii, now a captain, was sent to Europe in 1928 as a military attaché and spent the next several years surveying biological research in western countries. When Major Ishii returned to Japan in 1932, he was convinced that biological warfare was the most effective way for Japan to fight a war. Subsequently, he studied information provided by the *Kempeitai* (Japanese secret police) concerning the use of germ warfare by the Russians, and the success of the Italian Army with aerial spraying of mustard gas in Abyssinia.

Outwardly, Ishii was not an impressive person. He was a small, thin man, but had a powerful personality. His belief in the potential effectiveness of biological warfare soon became an obsession. Biological weapons were most appropriate for Japan, he argued, because they are economical to produce, and because Japan had few raw materials for the production of expensive conventional weapons. If this logic failed to convince his audience, Ishii further argued that biological weapons had to be effective because the League of Nations was trying to prohibit their use.[1] His final and, perhaps, most powerful argument was that his travel and research convinced him that the western nations regarded biological experimentation on human beings as unacceptable. If Japan could conduct such experiments in secret, they could attain an unequaled lead in biological warfare.

During 1935, Ishii was authorized to establish a germ-warfare research study at the army hospital in Harbin, China. Ishii's argument that the formal prohibition of biological warfare gave Japan a tremendous advantage convinced the army leadership to permit his research. China was the perfect place for such experimentation because the unsanitary conditions there would hide evidence of the research. Human experimentation began at Harbin shortly after the research center was established. The bodies of the Chinese "patients" were burned in an electric furnace so as to leave no evidence.[2]

In 1937, Ishii was authorized to build the world's first major biological and bacteriological warfare center. In two short years, Ishii had climbed from a position of relative obscurity to the director of a top-secret, nationally funded program.

The site chosen by Ishii for the warfare center was a three-square-kilometer site near a small village called Pingfan, 40 miles south of Harbin, and adjacent to the South Manchuria Railroad. The center, called the Pingfan Institute (also known as Unit 731), was completed in 1939. It consisted of 3,000 scientists, technicians, and soldiers, 150 buildings, many of which accommodated the Japanese assigned there, a high wall for privacy, and high voltage wires to discourage intruders. The institute had its own electrical power units, an incinerator, a farm with animals and 50,000 chickens, and produced its own vegetables. There was a school for the children of the Japanese workers, a hospital, and a nearby airfield for transport and field trials of aerial-delivery methods.[3] The innocuous title of the institute was the, "Epidemic Prevention and Water Supply Unit for the Kwantung Army."

Three of Ishii's brothers, Takeo, Mitsuo, and Shiro worked at Pingfan. Takeo was the prison commander. Guards for the prison, called the Special Squad, came from Ishii's village of Kamo. Ishii and his senior assistants, Kitano Masaji and Wakamatsu Yujiro, began to grow bacteria in huge quantities. Included in the horrific menu were anthrax, botulism, cholera, gas gangrene, glanders, plague, salmonella, smallpox, tetanus, tick encephalitis, tuberculosis, tularemia, typhoid, and typhus. In 1949, Russian investigators estimated that the production capacity of the institute had been eight tons of bacterial and biological agents per month.[4]

Inside the institute at Pingfan was a large square-shaped building known as Ro block. Ro, in Japanese, means square-shaped. Although Ro block looked square from the outside, hidden from view were two other buildings called blocks seven and eight. Ro block was the center of bacteria production and disease research. Blocks seven and eight had a more sinister purpose.[5]

Administratively, the institute was divided into seven divisions. These were the bacteriological-research division (Ro block), warfare- research-and-field-experiments division (blocks seven and eight), the bacteria-mass-production-and-storage division, an educational division, a supply division, a general-affairs division, and a clinical-diagnosis division, also blocks seven and eight.

The prison in Ro block resembled many accounts of hell. Spyholes were cut into the steel doors so that the prisoners could be observed in their cells.[6] Prisoners were called *Marutas,* meaning "blocks of wood" in the Japanese language. Many prisoners were chained to the walls. Some had rotting limbs, with pieces of bone protruding through their skin. Others had high fevers, writhed in agony, and moaned in pain. Most were emaciated and had open wounds. Through the spyholes, Ishii's doctors would note the symptoms of human beings infected with the worst diseases known to man. The Ro block prison housed about 200 inmates, but could be expanded to 400 when necessary. Block seven housed only males, block eight held both men and women. Marutas were used up at a rate of two-to-three per day.

Unit 731 had its own squadron of seven aircraft to conduct experimental field tests, and manufactured its own bombs for aerial delivery of bacteriological agents. The bombs were made of clay so that they would shatter into fragments upon detonation. The stabilizer fins and fuses were combustible so that no trace of the delivery weapon could be found. Field tests of aerial delivery agents were conducted at Anta (also spelled Anda), a large plain about 146 kilometers from Pingfan. During one such test, 30,000 plague infested fleas were dropped using the clay bombs. Survival rate of the fleas was 80 percent. Since even one flea bite could be fatal to a human, Ishii knew he had a new and most effective weapon.[7]

Nine different types of bombs were developed including the *Ha* bomb for disbursement of the deadly anthrax disease spore. The *Ha* had a thin steel wall and contained 1,500 small, razor sharp pellets immersed in half-a-litre of anthrax emulsion. The bomb was set to explode above ground and scatter the pellets over a diameter of 40 meters. If untreated, a person infected with the anthrax virus would die within four days. The mortality rate during these tests was 100 percent.[8]

There were hundreds of bomb experiments including the dropping of disease laden feathers and chaff. Rats and fleas were also packaged in a cardboard container and dropped from aircraft. Upon touching the ground, the paper cylinder would split apart, and the rats and fleas would disperse. The cylinder would then be consumed by fire, destroying all evidence of the bomb.

Ishii had 11 workers under Dr. Yukimasa Yagisawa conducting research on crop destruction. The squad used smut and nematosis as agents. They found that as little as five kilograms of nematosis per acre would ensure complete destruction of wheat crops. In addition to unit 731, Ishii created unit 100, with the responsibility for sabotage using bacteriological and biolological agents developed at Pingfan. Ishii truly built a mighty empire. Hundreds of talented scientists and thousands of military personnel labored for him, and his "troops" were attached to every division of the Japanese Army.

By 1935, the human experimentation at Harbin had progressed to a point where Ishii was showing motion pictures of his human experiments to senior staff officers of the Kwangtung Army, including General Hideki Tojo, who at the time was Chief of the Police Affairs Section of the Kwangtung Army *Kempeitai*. By the time that the Pingfan Special Military Zone was established, human experimentation had become routine.

Ishii was promoted to Lieutenant Gen. on March 1, 1941 and Unit 731 was granted a citation for heroic conduct for contaminating the Khalkhin-Gol River as the Russians drove the Japanese back during the battle of Nomonhon. They used typhus, paratyphus, and cholera bacteria to contaminate the river. In October of that year, Prime Minister Hideki Tojo personally presented Ishii with Japan's highest award for technical achievement.

During the Chekiang Campaign, Ishii's unit used germs of cholera, dysentary, typhoid, plague, anthrax to cause "inestimable" casualties to the Chinese.[9] Ishii's good work was also a disaster for the Japanese as they suffered 10,000 casualties when their troops overran one of the contaminated areas.

Some of Ishii's research has been recently documented. In 1993, Masataki Mori provided documentation that revealed bubonic plague attacks on Chinese cities in the early 1940s that killed at least 400 Chinese.[10] The information was found by Mori during a visit to Zhejiang, China in 1991. These attacks were first revealed in 1985, by Kentaro Iwane of Chuo University. Iwane discovered documents in the U.S. national archives that gave details of germ raids against the port of Ningpo, south of Shanghai, on October 27, 1940, and the dropping of ears of corn and chaff infested with plague-carrying fleas on Yiliao in September 1942. Keiichi Tsuneishi, a leading researcher of Unit 731 activities, verified that the biological attacks occurred, but estimates the number of casualties at Ningpo and Yiliao as no more than 100.[11] Takai Matsumura, a Japanese historian and economist at Tokyo's Keio University, says that germ-warfare experiments were conducted in at least 10 cities in China, including Beijing, Nanking, and Canton, as well as Singapore.[12]

About 20 kilometers from Pingfan, the *Kempeitai* ran a detention camp called Hogoin. The camp was under the command of Major Gen. Akikusa, chief of the Harbin Secret Service. The camp housed about 150 inmates, most of whom were Russian dissidents. The purpose of the camp was to provide live prisoners for research at Pingfan. No one knows how many prisoners were killed in this manner, but most estimates put the number between 2,000 and 3,000. What is known is that those sent to Pingfan never came back.

About 75 percent of the prisoners at Pingfan were Chinese men, women, and children, including babies of only a few months, but smaller numbers of Korean, Russian, and Allied prisoners were also used for research projects. When Ishii wanted to know if biological agents worked differently on Caucasians, he sent researchers to a POW camp near Mukden that contained Allied prisoners. Under the guise of providing healthful inoculations, the POWs were divided into groups and injected with typhoid and smallpox bacteria. The results of the inoculations were then monitored until the prisoners died.[13]

Robert Peaty was a major in the Royal Army Ordnance Corps and the senior British officer at one of the POW camps near Mukden. Peaty kept a secret diary in which he recorded these injections of infectious diseases disguised as preventative vaccinations. His entry for January 30, 1943, records: "Everyone received a 5cc typhoid paratyphoid A inoculation." His entry for February 23 reads: "Funeral service for 142 dead. 186 have died in 5 days, all Americans. Further inoculations followed. By August 6, the death toll reached 208."[14]

In similar fashion, American POWs Greg Rodriguez, Frank James, and Herman Castillo were victims of grotesque biological warfare experiments. Castillo, after being stuck with hypodermic needles was thrown into a tiny wire cage, and told, "Now you are a carrier for life."[15]

A deathbed confession by an 83-year-old Japanese that was involved with the murder of many human guinea pigs in Pingfan confirmed the earlier reports. In 1993, three days before his death, Jintaro Ishida confessed to his granddaughter of his role in these 1942 experiments. The tape-recorded confession was nearly four hours in length. Ishida's duties included the recording of lab data and keeping a daily log of medical officers' reports. He also had access to all classified records at the Institute. On the day that the emperor announced Japan's surrender, Ishida burned all classified documents in an incinerator, and saw all remaining prisoners being injected with potassium cyanide. He then incinerated all the corpses.[16]

The *maruta* were kept in Ro block until they were killed under scientifically controlled conditions. Dr. Sueo Akimoto, a young serologist in Unit 731, describes the feelings of the Japanese staff: "Very few of the scientists had a sense of conscience. They treated the patients like animals. The prisoners were the enemy; they would eventually be sentenced to death. The prisoners would die an honorable death if they contributed to the progress of medical science."[17]

Prisoners were taken from their cells and infected with the selected bacteria, and then thrown back into their cells. Some would be allowed to live until the disease claimed them. Others would be given lethal doses of morphine at various stages of the disease, their bodies then opened, and the progress of the disease noted. Some prisoners had their blood siphoned from their bodies and replaced with horse blood to determine the effect. Prisoners were burned alive with flame-throwers to measure the results. Prisoners were also tied to stakes, their bodies exposed, and then subjected to explosions of bombs laced with anthrax. The pieces of shrapnel, due to their penetration of the body, would cause illness and death in 90 percent of the prisoners.

Experiments on live prisoners included bombardment with lethal doses of x-rays, being whirled to death in giant centrifugal machines, and being subjected to such high pressures in a sealed chamber that the POWs' eyes would pop out of their sockets. POWs were routinely tied to stakes in a testing ground called Anta. Planes would spray the zone with the plague virus or some other culture to infect the prisoners. The POWs would then be returned to their cells to be clinically studied until they died.

Other POWs were electrocuted, dehydrated, frozen, and boiled alive. To research the effects of frostbite, prisoners were taken outside during freezing weather, stripped naked, and doused with water. An arm would be repeatedly drenched with water until the frozen limb made a sound like a board when struck. As a result of such experimentation, the Kwantung Army modified its treatment of frostbite victims.

Prisoners were electrocuted to death, but never immediately. Instead, the amount of electrical charge was slowly increased to study how much of a charge the prisoner could take before lapsing into unconsciousness. The prisoner was then revived and the experiments continued until the person died. Other tests involved hanging prisoners by ropes to see how long it took them to strangle to death, injecting air into prisoners to obstruct blood vessels to study the effects, and injecting horse urine into the kidneys of prisoners. Prisoners would frequently be shot with pistols and rifles to provide opportunities for the surgeons to practice removing bullets from a live body.

Young Japanese surgeons were encouraged to practice their skills on live prisoners in blocks seven and eight. The prisoner would be strapped to the table, and, according to Dr. Ken Yuasa, a surgeon in China during the war, " We would do an appendectomy, amputation of an arm or leg, and finally, a tracheotomy. If the prisoner was still alive after the 90 minute surgery, they might be killed by an injection".[18] The prisoners were not anethesized; most died on the operating table. Dr. Yuasa, now deeply apologetic for his actions in Unit 731, also recalls cultivating typhoid germs that were used to infect the wells of villages in communist-controlled China.

Surgical experimentation was not limited to Pingfan. Teddy Ponzcka, an American airman from a B-29 bomber crew, bailed out after his aircraft was rammed by a Japanese *Zero* over Fukuoka, Japan. He suffered a knife wound when he was captured and was taken to the anatomy department of Kyushu University in Fukuoka, where he expected medical treatment for his wound. Instead, a surgeon there removed one of his lungs, and, according to another surgeon present, Dr. Tono Tarusu, his body was injected with salt water, and he was left to bleed to death.[19] The salt-water injection experiment was done to determine if seawater could be used as a substitute for sterile saline solution on Japanese patients.

Eight other Americans were captured with Poncka. They suffered a similar fate. The Japanese wanted to know if a patient could survive the partial loss of his liver. They wanted to know if removing part of the brain could control epilepsy. Experiments were also done on the prisoners spines, throats, and necks. All of the Americans died.

It remains unclear whether Emperor Hirohito was consulted about the experiments, but his younger brother, Prince Mikasa, toured the institute at Pingfan and saw pictures of field activities in which Chinese prisoners died from poison gas experiments.[20]

By June of 1945, the Pingfan flea factory had 4,500 breeding machines in operation, producing 100 million fleas every few days. Plans were made for the feeding of 3,000 rodents, mostly rats. Enough pague, typhoid, cholera, and anthrax had been produced to infect half our planet.

Early on the morning of August 9, 1945 the Soviet Army swept across the border into Manchuria and Korea with one-and-a-half million men, 5,500 tanks, and 5,000 planes. The following day, Ishii received orders to destroy Pingfan, and to burn and bury all evidence of its existence.[21]

Approximately 600 Chinese and Manchurian laborers were machine-gunned to death and buried in a huge hole that was bulldozed in the earth to receive the physical remains of the institute. All human captives waiting biological testing were gassed or poisoned, and their bodies cremated in a giant incinerator. All bodies, records, and remaining equipment, including enough biological organisms to wipe out the entire human race, were pushed into the hole, ignited with gasoline, and burned before the hole was filled and covered with earth. It took the engineers three days to demolish the reinforced concrete structures. Any remaining equipment was sent to the Japanese colony of Korea.

Ishii provided poison capsules for all the Japanese at Pingfan and urged them to commit suicide rather than face Allied justice. Less than a thousand did so. The rest, including Lieutenant Gen. Ishii, fled from the fast-advancing Russians aboard 15 freight trains that took them to Korea and the port at Pusan.[22]

In the process of destroying all evidence of the institute at Pingfan, Ishii loosed thousands of plague-infested rats on the countryside of Pingfan. As the direct result of Ishii's final act, 30,000 Chinese died from a massive plague outbreak.[20] Sheldon Harris, author of the book, *Factories of Death,* estimates that

200,000 Chinese were killed in germ-warfare field experiments.

On August 19, the first Ishii unit personnel arrived at the ancient Noma Shrine in Kanazawa, Japan. They collected money and supplies that had been placed there, changed into civilian clothes , and disappeared. Each day more men arrived and departed until September 22, when the shrine was vacated.[23] A systematic destruction of all records of units 731 and 100 was ordered by the war ministry.

The Tokyo War Crimes Tribunal indicted thirty Japanese medical personnel from mainland Japan in March 1948. These men were not members of units 731 or 100. Charges against them ranged from vivisection, wrongful removal of body parts, and cannibalism. Twenty-three were found guilty of one or more of the charges, although the cannibalism charge was dismissed. Five of the defendants were sentenced to death, four to life imprisonment, and the other 14 to shorter prison terms. In September 1950, General MacArthur reduced most of the sentences, and, by 1958, all of the convicted felons were free. None of the death sentences were carried out.[24]

General Shiro Ishii and his Pingfan associates were not tried as war criminals. Ishii lived peacefully until his death from throat cancer on October 9, 1959 at age 67. He had six children. His grave is in gekkei-ji temple, and one of his bones was buried beneath unit 731's memorial, the Seikon Tower, in Tokyo Toma cemetary. Several of his senior assistants went on to become such prominent figures as governor of Tokyo, president of the Japan Medical Association, and head of the Japan Olympic Committee.[25] Lieutenant Colonel Ryo'ichi Naito assisted Ishii in brokering for immunity and returned to academic research at his university. Lieutenant Gen. Kitano Masaji became a millionaire in the blood-plasma business.

Exactly why Ishii and his Unit 731 cohorts were allowed to escape justice remains a mystery. Information that was provided by Ishii in return for immunity was promptly secured in U.S. and British archives and remains unavailable. Gavin Daws, in his book, *Prisoners of the Japanese*, speculates that MacArthur was authorized to make the secret deal with Ishii to keep the biological-experimentation data from the Russians. If Ishii and his associates had been indicted, the long investigation would have to involve the Russians, since they occupied Harbin and all of Manchuria.

Other reasons advanced for the grant of immunity included the fact that the United States was rushing to end the war trials and sign a peace agreement with Japan. The cold war with the Soviet Union was well underway by 1958, and the United States wanted to restore relations with Japan in order to have a base of operations near the Soviet Union. This theory has credence, since, by December 1958, all Japanese sentenced to prison for war crimes were free men. Some researchers believe that the United States intelligence service had no information at the time concerning human biological experimentation. Since it took the better part of 50 years for information on Comfort Women and Nagano to be known, this theory seems quite possible. It is known that the information U.S. Intelligence obtained was kept from the War Crimes Tribunal, as well as from the public record. It has even been suggested that MacArthur was so disgusted by the information that was available, that he decided to spare the parents and families of missing POWs the agony associated with a public trial.

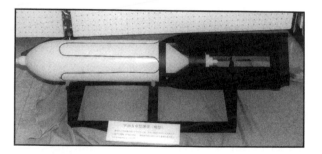

The Uji-50 bacterial bomb was developed by Shiro Ishii.

National Archives

NOTES

Chapter 1 The Tanaka Memorial: 1927

1. Tanaka 1924, p.5.
2. Tanaka 1924, p. 57.
3. Tanaka 1924, p.10.
4. Tanaka 1924, p. 11.
5. Tanaka 1924, p. 12.
6. Tanaka 1924, p. 16.
7. Tanaka 1924, p. 17.
6. Tanaka 1924, p. 46.
7. Hagen 1995, p. 4.

Chapter 2 Chinese Military Victories

1. The Japanese Army in China was called the Kwantung Army.
2. Dorn 1974, p. 65.
3. Dorn 1974, p. 129.
4. Dorn 1974, p. 129.
5.Tanaka 1934, p. 13 (Document first circulated in China in 1927).

Chapter 3 Chungking: 1937-1941

1. Sheen 1943, p.338.
2. Sheen 1943, p.339.
3. Moser 1978, p. 8.
4. White 1962, p. 52.
5. Adet 1975,p. 128.
6. Snow 1958, p. 267.
7. Snow 1958, p. 267.
8. Adet 1975, p.130.
9. Crozier 1976, p. 333.

Chapter 4 Chiang Kai-shek

1. Clark 1943, p.110.
2. Clark 1943, p.78.
3. Clark 1943, p.52.
4. Crozier 1976, p.145.
5. Crozier 1976, p. 151.
6. Crozier 1976, p.210
7. Crozier 1976, p.251.

Chapter 5 Captain Claire Chennault: The Flying Tigers

1. Moser 1978, p. 59.
2. Moser 1978, p. 60.
3. Moser 1978, p. 60.
4. Moser 1978, p. 64.
5. Schultz 1987, p. 162.
6. Schultz 1987, p. 230.
7. Schultz 1987, p. 229.
8. Schultz 1987, p. 230.
9. Schultz 1987, p. 236.
10. Moser 1978, p. 67.
11. Schultz 1987, p. 227.
12. Schultz 1987, p. 253.
13. Moser 1978, p. 179.
14. Moser 1978, p. 186.
15. Schultz 1987, p. 306.

Chapter 6. Roosevelt Knew

1. Toland 1982, p. 17.
2. Layton 1985, p. 529. The Roberts Commission, The Hart Inquiry, The Navy Court of Inquiry, The Army Board, The Clarke Investigation, The Clausen Investigation, The Hewitt Inquiry, and The Joint Congressional Committee Investigation. In addition, Frank Knox, did a personal inquiry on December 11 and 12, 1941. The 79th Congress's hearings before the Joint Committee on the Investigation of the Pearl Harbor Attack, included the Robert's Commission Report and the proceedings of several other courts, commissions, and inquiries.
3. Layton 1985, p. 21.
4. Layton 1985, p. 99.
5. Layton 1985, p. 21.
6. Persico 2001, p. 57. On February 13, 1941, President Roosevelt approved establishment of a small intelligence and fact-finding unit under columnist Carter that reported directly to the president.
7. Persico 2001, p. 187. Donovan traveled extensively to Europe on behalf of President Roosevelt from July 1940 until summer 1941 when he accepted Roosevelt's offer as director of Civilian Intelligence Agency (CIA). Donovan and the CIA were never accepted by others in the cabinet. As a result, Roosevelt created the Office of Strategic Services in July 1942, with Donovan in charge but with much less investigative authority.
8. Layton 1985, p. 117.
9. Layton 1985, p. 137.
10. Rusbridger 1991, p. 180.
11. Layton 1985, p. 179.
12. Layton 1985, p. 193.

13. Toland 1982, p. 280.
14. Layton 1985, p. 195.
15. Layton 1985, p. 209.
16. Holmes 1979, p. 26.
17. Toland 1982, p. 311.
18. Costello 1981, p. 4.

Chapter 7. Gregory "Pappy" Boyington

1. Boyington 1958, p.16.
2 Boyington 1958, p. 40.
3. Boyington 1958, p. 81.
4. Walton 1986, p. 100.
5. Sakaida 1996, p. 20.
6. Sakaida 1996, p. 20.
7. Sakaida 1996, p. 20.
8. Sakaida 1996, p. 21.
9. Tanaka 1998, p. 175.
10. Sakaida 1996, p. 20.
11. Sakaida 1996, p. 95.
12. Sakaida 1996, p. 20.
13. Brown 1995, p. 68.
14. Hagen 1995, p. 270.
15. Walton 1986, p. 184.
16. Walton 1986, p. 189.
17. Walton 1986, p. 190.
18. Sakaida 1996, p. 26.

Chapter 8 Hector C. Bywater: 1941

1. Honan 1991, p. 15.
2. Honan 1991, p. 90.
3.Honan 1991, p. 27.
4. Honan 1991, p. 178.
5. Hagen 1995, p. 27.
6. Honan 1991, p. 272.

Chapter 9 Ensign Jimmy Daniels, U. S. Navy

1. Captain James G. Daniels, US Navy (Retired) has been a guest speaker at my War in the Pacific course many times. All the quotes in this chapter except for the following two are from Captain Daniel's classroom presentations. Captain Daniel's has edited this chapter.
2. Cressman 1989, p. 46.
3. Cressman 1989, p. 57.

Chapter 10 Operation Watchtower: The Battle for Guadalcanal

1. Frank 1990, p.11.
2. Spector 1985, p. 191.
3. Frank 1990, p. 31.
4. Sakai 1978, p. 193.

Chapter 11 Martin Clemens: Coastwatcher

1. Rhodes 1982, backcover.
2. For information concerning Australian forces deployed to Rabaul, Timor, and Ambon, see chapter 40, volume 1.
3. Feldt 1959, p. 13 and 24.
4. Feldt 1959, p. 92.
5. Feldt 1959, p. 92.
6. Clemens 1988, p. 159.
7. Clemens 1988, p. 198.
8. Clemens 1988, p. 210.
9. Clemens, p. 27.

Chapter 12 The Ground Battle for Guadalcanal: August-September 1942

1. Newcomb 1961, p. 158.
2. Hoyt 1982, p.50.
3. Griffith 1963, p.83.
3. Costello 1981, p. 328.
5. Griffith 1963, p. 114.
6. Griffith, 1963, p.115.
7. Frank 1990, p. 53.

Chapter 13 The Ground Battle for Guadalcanal: Sep-Oct 1942

1. Griffith 1963, p. 117.
2. Griffith 1963, p. 122.
3. Griffith 1963, p. 100.
4. Hoyt 1983, p. 127. Author Samuel E. Morrison on page 133 of "The Struggle for Guadalcanal," states that Kiashi fired only four torpedoes.
5. Morrison 1949, p. 133. Morrison assumes that Japanese submarine *I-15* which was in the area torpedoed USS North Carolina. Such has not been verified.
6. Griffith 1963, p. 137.
7. Griffith 1963, p. 138.

Chapter 14 The Ground Battle for Guadalcanal; October 1942-January 1943

1. Griffith 1963, p. 163.

2. Griffith 1963, p. 164
3. Griffith 1963, p. 167.
4. Griffitj 1963, p. 233.
5. Griffith 1963, p. 246.

Chapter 15 The Navajo Code Talkers

1. Bixler 1992, p.38.
2. Bixlcr 1992, p.125.
3. Brechting 1998, p. 3.
4. Brechting 1998, p. 63.
5. Hitt 1999, p. 1.
6. Lapez 2001, p. 1.
7. Kawano 1990, p. 11.
8. Brechting 1998, p. 6.
9. Kawano 1990, p. 94.
10. Lapahie 1999, p. 1.
11. Kawano 1990, p. 94.
12. Kawano 1990, p. 91.
13. Kawano 1990, p. 87.
14. Kawano 1990, 9. 80.
15. Kawano 1990, p. 79.
16. Kawano 1990, p. 70.
17. Kawano 1990, p. 68.
18. Brechting 1998, p. 9.

Chapter 16 Saburo Sakai

1. Sakai 1978, p. ix.
2. Honolulu Star Bulletin August 31, 2001.
3. Sakai 1978, p. 3.
4. Sakai 1978, p. 10.
5. Sakai 1978, p. 33.
6. Sakai 1978, p. 40.
7. Sakai 1978, p. 123.
8. Sakai 1978, p. 123.
9. Sakai 1978, p. 124.
10. Hagen 1996, p. 241.
11. Sakai 1978, p. 177.
12. Sakai 1978, p. 200.
13. Sakai 1978, p. 200.
14. Sakai 1978, p. 255.
15. Sakai 1978, p. 276.
16. Sakai 1978, p. 276.
17. Sakai 1978, p. 277.

Chapter 17 There's More Than Snow at Nagano

1. Cook 1992, p. 433.
2. Hicks 1994, p. 108.
3. Hicks 1994, p. 108.
4. Cook 1992, p. 436.
5. Hicks 1994, p. 109. See Chapter 14, The Potsdam Proclamation: July 26, 1945.

Chapter 18 The Battle for Leyte Gulf: The First Striking Force

1. Cutler 1944, p. xiv.
2. Potter 1985, p.277.
3. Potter 1985, p.277.
4. Morison 1963, p. 436.
5.Morison 1963, p. 447.
6. Hoyt 1972, p. 11.
7. Potter 1985, p. 291.
8.Potter 1985, p. 296.
9.Potter 1985, p. 298.
10. Potter 1985, p. 301.
11.Potter 1985, p. 300.

Chapter 19 The Battle for Leyte Gulf: The Jeep Carriers

1. Wooldridge 1993, p. 204.
2. Wooldridge 1993, p. 206.
3. Wooldridge 1993, p. 303.
4. Potter 1985, p. 303.
5. Potter 1985, p. 304.
6. Potter 1985, p. 304.

Chapter 20 USS *Franklin*

1. Jurika 1990, p. 250.
2. Jurika 1990, p.258.
3. Morison 1960, p. 97.
4. Morison 1960, p. 98.

Chapter 21 IMS *Shinano*

1. Roscoe 1949, p. 491.
2. Naval History Division, Office of CNO 1963, p. 1.
3. Enright 1985, p. 11.
4. Tompkins 1981, p. 18.

5. Enright 1985, p. 13.
6. Enright 1985, p. 14.
7. Enright 1985, p. 16.
8. Enright 1985, p.30.
9. Toyoda 1980, p. 229.
10. Roscoe 1949, p. 529.
11. Enright 1985, p. 216.

Chapter 23 Iwo Jima: February 1945 D-day

1. Bradley 2000, p. 3.
2. Bradley 2000, p. 6.
3. Blissard 1945, p. 1.
4. Ross 1984, p. 18.
5. Ross 1984, p. 19.
6. Wheeler 1980, p. 39.
7. Kraus 2002, p. A25.
8. Kraus 2002, p. A25.
9. Kraus 2002, p. A25.
10. Wheeler 1980, p. 44.
11. Ross 1984, p. 32.
12. Newcomb 1965, p. 60.
13. Newcomb 1965, p. 68.
14. Blissard 1945, p. 2.

Chapter 24 Iwo Jima: February 1945 D-day +1

1. Ross 1984, p. 80.
2. Ross 1984, p. 81.
3. Newcomb 1965, p. 93.
4. Wheeler 1980, p. 214.
5. Newcomb 1965, p. 146.
6. Ross 1984, p. 277.
7. Wheeler 1980, p.250.
8. Wheeler 1980, p.298.
9. Wheeler 1980, p.312.
10. Wheeler 1980, p. 324.
11. Ross 1984, p. 321.
12. Bradley 2000, p. 294. The tour by the Suribachi survivors doubled the
fund raising goal. Americans pledged $26.3 billion. That was almost half of the
entire U.S. budget for 1946 ($56 billion).

Chapter 25 The Potsdam Proclamation: July 26, 1945

1. Mee 1975, p. 18.

2. Mee 1975, p. 18.
3. Churchill 1960, p. 87.
4. Mee 1975, p. 107.
5. Mee 1975, p. 208

Chapter 26 The Horror of Sandakan.

1. Wall 1997, p. 9.
2. Wall 1996, p. 27.
3. Wall 1996, p. 53.
4. Moffitt 1995, pp.89-90.
5. Wall 1996, p. 65.
6. Wall 1996, pp. 108-110 and Wall 1993, p.163.
7. Moffitt 1995, p. vii.
8. Moffitt 1995, p.71 .
9. Moffitt 1995, p.92.
10. Moffitt 1995, p. 107.
11. Moffitt 1995, p. 130.
12. Wall 1993, p.13.
13. Moffitt 1995, p.13.

Chapter 27 Fleet Admiral Chester W. Nimitz

1. Potter 1976, p. 4.
2. Casad 1983, p. 137.
3. Toland 1972, p. 33.
4. Potter 1976, p.31.
5. Potter 1976, p. 164.
6. Pfannes 1983, p. 104.
7. Casad 1983, p. 147.
8. Pfannes 1983, p. 105.
9. Casad 1983, p. 166.
10. Griffith 1963, p. 163.
11. Griffith 1963, p. 165.
12. Potter 1985, p. 210.
13. Potter 1976, p. 222.
14. Potter 1976, p. 396.
15. Potter 1976, p. 398.
16. Potter 1976, p. 411.

Chapter 28 Truk

1. Hinz 1995, p. 74.
2. Stewart 1985, p. 72.
3. Stewart 1985, p. 27.
4. Stewart 1985, p. 68.

5. Stewart 1985, p. 68.
6. Stewart 1985, p. 105.

Chapter 29 Rabaul

1. Tanaka 1996, p. 14.
2. Sakaida 1996, p. 7.
3. Miller 1995, p. 375.
4. Miller 1995, p. 282.
5. Miller 1995, p. 385.
6. Miller 1995, p. 184.

Chapter 30 The United States of America versus Tomoyuki Yamashita

1. Moffitt p. 30.
2. Taylor 1998, p 108.
3. Hagen 1998, p. 71.
4. Taylor 1981, p.111.
5. Bergamini 1972, pp. 1345-1346.
6. Taylor 1981, p.120.
7. Taylor 1981, p. 123.
8. Taylor 1981, p. 124.
9. Taylor 1981, p. 125.
10. Taylor 1981, p.142.
11. Taylor 1981, p. 156.
12. Bergamini 1972, p. 1347.
13. Taylor 1981, pp. 157-158.
14. Bergamini 1972, p. 1347.
15. Taylor 1981, p. 196.
16. Taylor 1981, p. 198.
17. Taylor 1981, pp. 206-207.
18. Bergamini 1972, p. 1351.
19. Bergamini 1972, p. 1352.
20. Taylor 1981, p. 7.

Chapter 31 Jonathan M. Wainwright

1. Schultz 1981, p. 62.
2 Schultz 1981, p. 63.
3. Schultz 1981, p. 63.
4. Schultz 1981, p. 63.
5. Schultz 1981, p. 64.
6. Morton 1952, p. 560.
7. MacArthur 1964, p. 145.
8. Schultz 1981, p. 236.

9. Schultz 1981, p. 241.
10. Hagen 1996, p. 42.

Chapter 32 Jonathan M. Wainwright: Surrender of Corregidor

1. Some of the patients died, some were murdered, and some survived.
2. Morton 1952, p. 560.
3 Morton 1952, p. 561.
4. Schultz 1981, p. 378.
5. Hagen 1996, p. 225.
6. MacArthur 1964, p. 272.
7. Schultz 1981, p.400.
8. Schultz 1981, p. 409.
9. Schultz 1981, p. 411.
10. Schultz 1981, p. 419.

Chapter 33 Masahuru Homma: Los Banos: April 3, 1946

1. Taylor 1981, p. 47.
2. Taylor 1981, p. 54.
3. Taylor 1981, p. 54.
4. Taylor 1981, p. 55.
5. Taylor 1981, p. 57.
6. Taylor 1981, p. 57.
7. Taylor 1981, p. 69.
8. Taylor 1981, pp. 82-83.
9. Refer to chapters, Death March: Bataan, April 1942, and Death March: Camp O'Donnell, in Volume 1 of War in the Pacific.
10. Taylor 1981, p. 99.
11. Taylor 1981, p. 172.
12. Taylor 1981, p. 188.

Chapter 34 Curtis E. Lemay

1. The youngest US officer to be promoted to the grade of full general was Ulysses S. Grant, at age 44.
2. Official Japanese figures: Coffey 1968, p. 164.
3 Coffey 1968, p. 168.
4. Coffey 1968, p. 267.
5. Coffey 1968, p. 271.
6. Coffey 1968, p. 274.
7. Coffey 1968, p. 291.
8. Coffey 1968, p. 306.
9. Coffey 1968, p. 344.
10. Coffey 1968, p. 427.
11. Coffey 1968, p. 3.

12. Coffey 1968, p. 439.

13. Edoin 1987, p. 238.

14. Los Angeles Times, 2 Oct. 1990, p. A-1.

15. The Washington Post. 2 Oct. 1990, p. B-6.

16. http:www.xs4all.nl/~ejnoomen/wwgrave.ntml.

Chapter 35 The Silent Service

1. Roscoe, Theodore 1949, pp.1-577.

2. Blair, Clay Jr. 1975, pp. 1-1072

3. For example, Schratz, Paul R. 1988, Submarine Commander, pp.1-322; Gray, Edwyn 1988, Submarine Warriors, pp. 1-324; Galantin, I.J. Take Her Deep, 1988, pp. 1-300; Gannon, Robert Hellions of the Deep, 1996, pp. 1-240; Lockwood, Charles A. Hellcats of the Sea, 1955, pp. 1-335; Ruhe, William J. 1994, War in the Boats, pp. 1-303; Gugliotta, Bobette, 1984 Pigboat 39, pp. 1-224; Kimmet, Larry, 1996. U.S. Submarines in World War II. Pp. 1-157.

4. Blair, Clay Jr. 1975, p. 106.

5. Cole, William. Minisub's owner yet to be decided. The Honolulu Advertiser, Sept 8, 2002, p. A28.

6. Blair, Clay Jr. 1975, P. 118.

7. Blair, Clay Jr. 1975, p. 403.

8. Roscoe 1949

9. Blair, Clay Jr. 1975, p. 402.

10. Roscoe 1949, p. 275-277.

11. Roscoe 1949, p. 240.

12. Lockwood1955, p. xi.

13. Warshofsky 1962, p. 130.

14. Roscoe 1949, p. 395.

15. Roscoe 1949, p. 422.

16. Lockwood 1955, p. 102. The abbreviation FMS was later changed to QLA, which were not initials for any words.

17. Lockwood 1955, p. 80.

18. Roscoe 1949, p. 449.

19. Roscoe 1949, p. 460.

Chapter 36 The Comfort Women

1. Howard 1993, p. v.

2. "Wounds of War", The Honolulu Advertiser, 3 February 1993, C1.

3. Tanaka 1998, p. 94.

4. Tanaka 1998, p. 98.

5. Howard 1993, p.p 43-192.

6. Howard 1993, p. 40.

7. Sakami 1996, p. 26.

8. Hicks 1994, p.12.

9. Howard 1993, pp.151-157.

10. Tanaka 1998, p.93.

11. Chang 1998, p.53 and Tanaka 1998, pp. 92-94.

12. Galang 2000, p. 55. (Filipina March 2000).

13. Galang 2000, p. 56. (Filipinsa March 2000).

14. "The Comfort Women"; The Honolulu Advertiser, 14 June 1996, p. 6.

15. "Japan Will Compensate WW II Comfort Women"; The Honolulu Advertiser, 15 June 1995 A4, and and MacGregor 1995, "Private comfort women fund threatens to backfire in Japan"; The Honolulu Advertiser, 27 December 1995.

16. "Panel Advises $40,000 for Comfort Women"; The Honolulu Advertiser, 22 November 1994, A6.

17. Howard 1993, p. 193.

18. Chang 1998, p.209.

19. Howard 1993, p. 192.

20. Howard 1993, p. 193.

21. "South Korea to aid former sex slaves"; The Honolulu Advertiser, 14 April 1998, A2.

Chapter 37 Shiro Ishii (Unit 731)

1. Harris 1982, p. 82.

2. Williams 1989, p. 32 and Gold 1996, p. 41 and Harris 1982, p. 83.

3. Harris 1982, p. 83.

4. Harris 1982, p. 84.

5. Gold 1996, p. 39.

6. Gold 1996, p. 40.

7. Harris 1982, p. 1.

8. Harris 1982, p. 84.

9. Guyatt (online) 1999, p.1.

10. The Nation, January 12, 1993, p. A-5.

11. Kristof 1997, p. 4.

12. Kristof 1997, p. 3.

13. Williams 1989, p. 59.

14. Guyatt(online) 1999, p.1.

15. McLaughan 1998, p.1.

16. The Honolulu Advertiser 1995, p. A-8.

17. Williams 1989, p. 38.

18. Kristof 1997, p. 6.

19. Easton 1999, p. 2.

20. Kristof 1997, p. 5.

21. Gold 1996, p. 231.

22. The Other Holocaust (online) 1999, p.8. and Gold 1996, p. 232 and 196.

23. Kristof 1999, p.4.

24. Easton 1999, p. 3.

25. Kristof 1999, p.7.

BIBLIOGRAPHY

Adet, Anor and Meimei Lin. *Dawn Over Chunking*. New York: Da Capo Press, 1975.

Agawa, Hiroyuki. *The Reluctant Admiral: Yamamoto and the Imperial Navy*. Tokyo: Kodansha, 1979.

Alexexander, Joseph H. *Edson's Raiders*. Annapolis: Naval Institute, 2001.

Arthur, Anthony. *Deliverance at Las Banos*. New York: St. Martins, 1985.

Asahi News Service. "Confession describes Japan's WW II atrocities." *Honolulu Advertiser*. 23 Nov. 1995. Sec. A, p. 8.

Bain, David H. *Sitting in Darkness: Americans in the Philippines*. Boston: Houghton Mifflin, 1984.

Ballard, J. G. *Empire of the Sun*. New York: J.G. Ballard, 1984.

Ballard, Robert D. *Lost Ships of Guadalcanal*. New York: Warner Books, 1993.

Barker, A.J. *Okinawa,* New York: Gallahad, 1981.

Beaumont, Joan. ed. *Australia's War*. St. Leonards NSW, Australia: Allen and Unwin, 1996.

Bix, Herbert P. *Hirohito and the Making of Modern Japan*. New York: Harper Collins, 2000.

Bixler, Margaret T. *Winds of Freedom: The Story of the Navajo Code Talkers of World War II*. Darien, CT: Two Bytes Publishing, 1992

Blair, Clay Jr. *Silent Victory*. New York: Bantom, 1975.

Blow, A. J. *The History of the Atomic Bomb*. New York: American Heritage, 1968.

Bo, Ma. *Blood Red Sunset,* New York: Penguin, 1995.

Boardman, Robert. *A Higher Honor*. Seattle: Boardman, 1968.

——, *Unforgettable Men in Unforgettable Times*. Mukilteo, WA: WinePress, 1998.

Boyington, Gregory. *Baa Baa Black Sheep*. New York: Bantam, 1958.

——, *The Black Sheep Squadron: Devil In The Slot*. New York: Bantam Books, 1978.

Boyne, Walter J. *The All-American Airman*. Air Force Magazine, March 2000, 52-60.

Brechting, Colleen and Flora Gonzalez. *Navajo Codetalkers*. Allendale, MI: Grand Valley State University, 1995.

Braddon, Russell. *The Naked Island*. London: Pan Books, 1955.

Bradley, James. Flags of our Fathers. New York: Bantam Books, 2000.

Breuer, William B. *MacArthur's Undercover War*. New York: John Wiley, 1995.

Bryan, J. III, and Phillip G. Reed. *Mission Beyond Darkness*. New York: Duell, Sloan and Pearce, 1945.

Bryant, Arthur. *The Turn of the Tide*. New York: Doubleday, 1957.

Burgess, John. *"Rewriting the Rape of Nanking,"* Washington Post National Weekly Edition, February 11, 1985, 18.

Caidin, Martin. *Fork Tailed Devil: The P-38*. Des Plains, IL: Bantam, 1994.

Caren, Eric C. *Pearl Harbor Extra: A Newspaper Account of the United States' Entry into World War II*. Edison, NJ: Castle Books, 2001.

Casad, Dede W. and Frank A. Driscoll. *Nimitz: Admiral of the Hills*. Austin: Eakin Press, 1983.

Chang, Iris. *The Rape of Nanking,* New York: Basic Books, 1997.

Churchill, Winston. *The Second World War*. New York: Time, 1960.

Clark, Blake. *Remember Pearl Harbor*. Honolulu: Mutual Publishing, 1987.

Clark, Elmer T. *The Chiang's of China*. New York: Abingdon-Cokesbury Press, 1943.

Coffey, Thomas M. *Iron Eagle: The Turbulent Life of General Curtis LeMay.* New York: Avon, 1986.

Clemens, Martin. *Alone on Guadalcanal.* Annapolis: Naval Institute Press, 1998.

———, *"Awaiting the Fleet Majestical."* Naval History, 56-61 (Dec 1998).

Crenshaw, Russel S. Jr. *South Pacific Destroyer.* Annapolis: Naval Institute Press, 1998.

Cressman, Robert J. and J. Michael Wenger. *Steady Nerves and Stout Hearts.* Missoula, MN: Pictorial Histories, 1992.

Crost, Lyn. *Honor by Fire: Japanese Americans at War in Europe and the Pacific.* Novato, CA: Presidio, 1994.

Cressman, Robert. *The Gallant Ship: USS Yorktown (CV-5).* Missoula: Pictorial Histories, 1985.

Crozier, Brian. *The Man Who Lost China.* New York: Charles Scribner's Sons, 1979.

Daniels, James G. "The Tragedy of VF-6 at Pearl Harbor." (Naval Aviation Museum) Foundation 7 (1986): 80-86.

Davidson, Edward and Dale Manning. *Timeline of World War II.* Londen: Cassell and Company, 1999.

Day, David. *The Great Betrayal.New York:* W.W. Norton, 1989.

De Latil, Pierre. *Enrico Fermi.* Paris: Savants du Monde Entier, 1966.

Dorn, Frank. *The Sino-Japanese War 1937-41: From Marco Polo Bridge to Pearl Harbor.* New York: Macmillan, 1974.

———, *Walkout: With Stilwell in Burma,* New york: Thomas Y. Cromwell, 1971.

Dupuy, Trevor. *Asiatic Land Battles: Expansion of Japan in Asia.* New York: Franklin Watts, 1944.

———, *Asian and Axis Resistance Movements.* New York: Franklin Watts, 1965.

Editorial Board. Nanjing Archives. *Historical Data of Nanjing Massacre.* Nanjing, China: 1985.

Edwards, Bernarde. *Blood and Bushido: Japanese Atrocities at Sea 1941-1945.* New York: Brick Tower Press, 1997.

Ellis, John. World War II: The Encyclopedia of Facts and Figures. United States: Military Book Club, 1995.

———, *The Sharp End: The Fighting Man in World War II.* New York: Charles Scribner's Sons.1980.

Elphick, Peter. *Singapore: The Pregnable Fortress.* London: Hodder and Stougton, 1995.

Enright, Joseph. *Shinano.* New York: St. Martins, 1985.

Ethell, Jeff. *Flying the Hump.* Osceola, WI: Motorbooks International, 1995.

Evans, Stephan R. *Sabah: Under the Rising Sun Government.* Singapore: Tropical Press, 1991.

Fallows, James. *Looking at the Sun.* New York: Pantheon, 1994.

Fane, Francis D. *The Naked Warriors: Navy Frogmen.* New York: Appleton-Century-Crofts, 1956.

Feldt, Eric. *The Coastwatchers.* New York: Bantam, 1979.

Fessler, Diane Burke. *No Time for Fear.* East Lansing: Michigan State University Press, 1996.

Flaherty, Thomas H. Jr. ed. *The Aftermath: Asia World War II,* Alexandria, VA: Time Life Books, 1983.

Flanagan, E. M. *Corregidor: The Rock Force Assault.* Novato, CA: Presidio, 1995.

Fletcher-Cook, John. *The Emperor's Guest 1942-1945.* London: Leo Cooper, 1994.

Forty, George. *Japanese Army Handbook: 1939-1945.* Gloucestershire: Sutton, 1999.

Frank, Richard B. *Guadalcanal: The Definitive Account of the Landmark Battle.* New York: Penguin, 1990.

Fraser, George MacDonald. *Quartered Safe Out Here: A Recollection of the War in Burma.* London: Harper-Collins, 1995.

Galang, M. Evelina. "Lola Lucia Alvarez." (Japanese Comfort Women) *Filipinas,* March 2000: 54-57.

Galantin, L.J. *Take Her Deep.* New York: Pocket Books, 1987.

Gannon, Robert. *Hellions of the Deep.* PA: Pennsylvania State University Press, 1996.

Garfield, Brian. *The Thousand Mile War.* New York: Bantam, 1982.

Gause, Damon. *The War Journal of Major "Rocky" Gause.* New York: Hyperion, 1999.

Gold, Hal. *Unit 731 Testimony.* Singapore: Yenbooks, 1996.

Goodwin, Michael J. *Shobun, A Forgotten War Crime in the Pacific.* Mechanicsburg, PA: Stackpole, 1995.

Grace, James W. *The Naval Battle of Guadalcanal.* Annapolis: Naval Institute Press, 1999.

Gray, Edwyn. *Submarine Warriers.* New York: Bantam, 1988.

Green, Michael. *MacArthur in the Pacific.* Osceola, WI: Motorbooks International, 1996.

Greenfield, Kent R. ed. *The War Against Japan: United States Army in World War II.* Washington: Office of the Chief of Military History, 1952.

Grey, Denver G. "I Remember Pearl Harbor," *Nebraska History* 62, no. 4 (1981): 437-480.

Gugliotta, Bobette. Pigboat 39: *An American Sub Goes to War.* Lexington: The University Press of Kentucky, 1984.

Gunther, John. *The Riddle of MacArthur.* New York: Harper and Brothers, 1950.

Hagen, Jerome T. *War in the Pacific, Vol. I.* Hawaii: Hawaii Pacific University, 1996.

Halter, John. *Top Secret Projects of WW II.* New York: J. Messner, 1978.

Hammel, Eric. *Guadalcanal: Decision at Sea: The Naval Battle of Guadalcanal.* Pacifica, CA: Pacifica Press, 1988.

_____, *Munda Trail: The New Georgia Campaign June-August 1943.* Pacifica, CA: Pacifica Military History, 1989.

Harris, Robert and Jeremy Paxman. *A Higher Form Of Killing.* New York: Hill and Wang, 1982.

Harris, Sheldon H. Factories of Death: *Japanese Biological Warfare 1932-1945 and the American Coverup,* New York: Rutledge, 1944.

Hart, B.H. Liddel. *History of the Second World War.* New York: G. P. Putnam's Sons, 1970.

Heatherington, John. *Blamey: The Fighting Field Marshal.* London: Horowitz, 1954.

Hess, Gary. *The United States at War, 1941-1945.* Wheeling IL: Harlan Davidson Inc., 1986.

Hicks, George. *The Comfort Women.* New York: W.W. Norton, 1994.

Hitt, Jack. *Navajo Code Talkers:America's Biggest World War II Crypto-Secret.* http://www.rense.com/politics5/code.htm.

Hixon, Carl K. *Guadalcanal: An American Story.* Annapolis: Naval Institute Press, 1999.

Holmes, W.J. *Double Edged Secrets.* Annapolis: Naval Institute Press, 1979.

Holsinger, Chuck. *Above the Cry of Battle.* Phoenix: ACW Press, 2001.

Honan, William H. *Visions of Infamy.* New York: St. Martin's Press, 1991.

Hoopes, Townsend and Douglas Binkley. *Driven Patriot: The Life and Times of James Forrestal.* Annapolis: Naval Institute Press, 1972.

Howard, Keith. ed. *True Stories of the Comfort Women.* New York: Cassell, 1995.

Howarth, Stephen. ed. *Great Naval Leaders of World War II.* New York: St. Martin's Press, 1992.

Hoyt, Edwin P. *The Men of the Gambier Bay.* New York: Avon, 1979.

_____, *Closing the Circle: War in the Pacific: 1945.* New York; Van Nostrand, 1982.

_____, *Deadly Craft.* Boston: Little, Brown and Co., 1968.

Hsi-sheng, Chi. *Nationalist China at War: Military Defeats and Political Collapse, 1937-45.* Ann Arbor: University of Michigan Press, 1982.

Ienaga, Saburo. *The Pacific War: 1931-1945.* New York: Pantheon, 1978.

Illustrated Story of World War II. Pleasantville, NY: The Readers Digest, 1969.

Inoguchi, Rikihei and Tadashi Nakajima. *The Divine Wind: Japan's Kamikaze Force in World War II.* Annapolis: Naval Institute Press, 1958.

Ireland, Bernard. *Battleships of the 20th Century.* New York: Harper-Collins, 1996.

Irons, Peter. *Justice at War.* New York: Oxford University Press, 1983.

Ito, Masanori. *The End of the Imperial Japanese Navy.* New York: W.W. Norton, 1956.

Jasper, W. J. *The USS Arizona.* New York: St. Martin's Press, 2001.

Jones, H.I. *Manchuria Since 1931,* London: Oxford University Press, 1949.

Kawano, Kenji. *Warriers Navajo Code Talkers.* Arizona: Northland, 1990.

Keith, Billy. *Days of Anguish, Days of Hope.* New York: Doubleday, 1972.

Kemp, Peter. *Decision at Sea.* New York: Elsevier-Dutton, 1978.

Kimball, Warren. *Forged in War.* London: Harper Collins, 1997.`

Kimmett, Larry and Margaret Regis. *U.S. Subamarines in World War II: An Illustrated History.* Seattle: Navigator Publishing, 1996.

Kinney, John F. *Wake Island Pilot.* Washington, DC: Brassey's, 1995.

Knebel, Fletcher and Charles W. Bailey II. *No High Ground.* New York: Harper and Brothers, 1960.

Knox, Donald. *The Death March.* New York: Harcourt Brace Jovanovich, 1981.

Kramer, Paul. Ed. *The Last Manchu: The Autobiography of Henry Pu Yi, Last Emperor of China.* New York: Pocket Books, 1987.

Kristof, Nicholas. "Unlocking a Deadly Secret. http://www.cs.umn.edu/~dyue/wiihist/ germwar/germwar.htm (8 Nov. 1997).

LaFeber, Walter. *The Clash.* New York: Norton, 1997.

Lawson, Don. *An Album of WW II Homefronts.* New York: Franklin Watts, 1980

Lawson, Fusao Inada. ed. *Only What we Could Carry,* Berkely, CA: Heyday Books, 2000.

Lawson, Robert L. *Carrier Air Group Commanders.* Atglen, PA: Schiffer Military History, 2000.

Leach, Douglas E. *Now Hear This.* Kent, OH: Kent State University Press, 1987.

Leach, E.R. *Political Systems of Highland Burma.* Boston: Beacon, 1954.

LeMay, Curtis E. with Mackinlay Cantor. *Mission with LeMay,* Garden City: Doubleday, 1965.

Leary, William M. ed. *We Shall Return: MacArthur's Commanders and the Defeat of Japan 1942-1945.* Lexington: University of Kentucky Press, 1988.

Li, Lincoln. *The Japanese Army in North China 1937-1944.* London: Oxford University Press, 1975.

Li Ting-yuan. *Record of the Mission to Liu-ch'iu Chi.* (Ryukyu) Peking: published privately.1802.

Liang, Chin-tung, *General Stilwell in China 1942-1944: The Full Story.* New York:

St. Johns University Press, 1972.

Linebarger, Paul M. *The China of Chiang Kai-shek*, Boston: World Peace Foundation, 1941.

Linn, Brian McAllister. *Guardians of Empire: The U.S. Army and the Pacific: 1902-1940*. Chapel Hill: University of North Carolina Press, 1997.

Lockwood, Charles A. and Hans C. Adamson. *Hellcats of the Sea*. New York: Greenberg, 1955.

Lomax, Eric. *The Railway Man*. New York: W.W. Norton, 1995.

"Lost Fatherland and People under Compulsion," Korea-Japan Problems Research Institute, Asia Press, 1945.

Lotz, Dave. *World War II Remnants: Guam, Northern Mariana Islands*. Honolulu: Arizona Memorial Museum Association, 1998.

Ma Bo. *Blood Red Sunset: A Memoir of the Chinese Cultural Revolution*. New York: Penguin, 1995.

MacCarthy, Adian. *A Doctor's War*. London: Robson Books, 1979.

Mackay, James. *Betrayal In High Places*, Auckland: Tasman Books, 1996.

Matsushima, Keizo. *Admiral Nagumo Tragedy: From Pearl Harbor to Saipan*. Tokyo: Tokuma, 1967.

Marshall, S.L.A. *The River and the Gauntlet*. Alexandria, Va: Time-Life Books, 1953.

Matsushima, Keizo. *The Tragedy of Admiral Nagumo*. Tokyo: Tokuma Books, 1967.

Matthews, Tony. *Shadows Dancing: Japanese Espionage Against the West, 1939-1945*. New York: St. Martin's, 1993.

McCombs, Don and Fred L. Worth. *World War II: 4139 Strange and Fascinating Facts*. New York: Wings, 1983.

McEwan, James. *The Remorseless Road: Singapore to Nagasaki*. Cornwall: Airlife, 1997.

McCully, Newton A. *The McCully Report: The Russo-Japanese War, 1904-05*. Indianapolis: Naval Institute Press, 1977.

Mee, Charles L. Jr., *Meeting at Potsdam,* New York: M. Evans and Co., 1975.

Mikesh, Robert C. *Zero*. Osceola, WI: Motorbooks, 1994.

Miller, Nathan. *War at Sea*. New York: Scribner, 1995.

Millot, Bernard. *Divine Thunder,* New York; McCall, 1970.

Moffitt, Athol. *Project Kingfisher*, Marickville, NSW, Australia: Southwood Press, 1995.

Molnar, Alexander. *Navajo Code Talkers: World War II Fact Sheet*. http://www.history.navy.mil/faq61-2.htm1.

Morison, Samuel Eliot.*The Rising Son in the Pacific; 1931-April 1942*. Chicago: University of Illinois Press, 2001.

_____, U. S. Naval Operations in World War II, Vol. 7, *Aleutions, Gilberts and Marshalls: June 1942-April 1944*. Boston: Little-Brown, 1968.

_____, History of U.S. Naval Operations in World War II. *Breaking the Bismarks Barrier:* 22 July 1942-1 May 1944. Edison, NJ: Castle, 2001.

_____, History of U.S. Naval Operations in World War II. *The Struggle for Guadalocanal: August 1942-February 1943*. Edison, NJ: Castle Books, 2001.

Moser, Don. *China-Burma-India,* Alexandria: Time-Life Books, 1978.

Morley, William. Ed. *Deterrent Diplomacy Policy; Japan, Germany, and the USSR*. New York: Columbia University, 1976.

Morris, Eric. *Guadalcanal: The End of the Line*. New York: Stein and Day, 1981.

Mueller, Joseph N. *Guadalcanal 1942,* Oxford, England: Osprey Publishing, 1992.

Naito, Hatsuho. Thunder Gods: *The Kamikaze Pilots Tell Their Stories*. Tokyo: Kodansha, 1982.

Naval History Division, Office of Chief of Naval Operations, *U. S. Submarine Losses, World War II*. Washington: U. S. Government Printing Office, 1963.

Nichols, Charles S. Jr. and Henry I. Shaw, Jr. *Okinawa: Victory in the Pacific*. Washington: Historical Branch, Headquarters U.S. Marine Corps, 1955.

Newcomb, Richard F. *Iwo Jjima*. New York: Bantam, 1982.

Norman, Elizabeth M. *We Band of Angels*. New York: Simon and Scuster, 1999.

O'Connor, Richard. *Pacific Destiny*. Boston: Little Brown, 1969.

Okinawa War Pictorial: *The Last Battle of Japan*. Naha: Okinawa Monthly, 1977.

Oleksy, Walter. *Military Leaders of World War II*. New York: Facts on File, 1994.

Orita, Zenji with Joseph Harrington. *I-Boat Captain*. Canoga Park, CA: Major Books, 1976.

Otani, Keijiro. *Singapore Atrocities*. Tokyo: Shinjinbutsu Oraisha, 1973.

Owens, William J. *Green Hell: The Battle for Okinawa*. Central Point, OR: Hellgate Press, 1999.

Parker, John. *The Gurkhas*. London: Headline Book, 1999.

Potter, E. B. *Nimitz*, Annapolis: Naval Institute Press, 1976.

_____, *Bull Halsey*, Annapolis: Naval Institute Press, 1985.

Powell, John J. "Japan's Germ Warfare," Bulletin of Concerned Asian Scholars 12.4 (October-December 1980) 2-17.

_____, "Japan's Biological Weapons, 1930-1945: A Hidden Chapter in History," Bulletin of the Atomic Scientists 37.8 (October 1981): 44-52.

Preston, Anthony. *Aircraft Carriers: An Illustrated History*. London: PRC, 1997.

Raymer, Edward C. *Descent into Darkness: A Navy Diver's Memoir*. Novato, CA: Presidio, 1996.

Regan, Stephen D. *In Bitter Tempest: The Biography of Admiral Frank Jack Fletcher*. Ames, Iowa: Iowa State University Press, 1994.

Reynolds, Quentin. *The Man Who Wouldn't Talk*. New York: Random House, 1953.

Rhodes, F. A. *Diary of a Coastwatcher in the Solomons*. Fredericksburg, TX: Admiral Nimitz Foundation, 1982.

Rhodes, Richard. *The Making of the Atomic Bomb*, New York: Simon and Schuster, 1968.

Romanus, Charles F. *Time Runs Out in CBI*. U.S. Army in World War II. Washington DC: 1958.

Rooney, David. *Burma Victory: Imphal and Kohima*. London: Cassell, 1992.

Roscoe, Theodore. *Submarine Operations in World War II*. Annapolis: Naval Institute Press, 1949.

Ross, Bill D. *Iwo Jima: Legacy of Valor*. New York: Vanguard Press, 1985.

_____, *Peleliu: Tragic Triumph*. New York: Random House, 1991.

Roush, John H. Jr. ed. *World War II Remembrances*. Kentfield, CA: John H. Roush Jr.,1995.

Ruhe, William J. *War in the Boats: My WW II Submarine Battles*. London: Brassey's, 1994.

Rusbridger, James, and Eric Nave. *Betrayal at Pearl Harbor: How Churchill Lured Roosevelt into WW II*. New York: Summit Books, 1991.

Sakada, Henry. *Japanese Army Air Force Aces 1937-1945*. London: Osprey, 1997.

Sakaida, Henry. *The Seige of Rabaul*. St. Paul, MN: Phalanx, 1996.

Sano, Iwao P. *!,000 Days in Siberia*. Lincoln, NE: University of Nebraska Press, 1997..

Schaffer, Ronald. *Wings of Judgement: American Bombing in World War II*. New

York: Oxford Press, 1985.

Schratz, Paul R. *Submarine Commander.* KY: University Press of Kentucky, 1988.

Schultz, Duane. The Maverick War: *Chennault and the Flying Tigers.* New York: St. Martins, 1987.

_____, *Hero of Bataan: The Story of General Jonathan M. Wainwright.* New York: St. Martins, 1981.

_____, *Wake Island.* New York: St. Martins Press, 1978.

Seagrave, Sterling and Peggy Seagrave. *The Yamato Dynasty.* New York: Broadway Books, 1999.

Sears, Stephen W. *Eyewitness to World War II.* Boston: Houghton Mifflin, 1991.

Seichi, Morimura. *Akuma no Hoshoko* (The Devil's Gluttony) Tokyo: Kodansha, 1981.

Senso, Hanzi. *War Crimes.* Tokyo: Shinjinbutsu Oraisha, 1975.

Setysuko, Chichibu. *The Silver Drum.* Folkstone, Kent: Global Books, 1996.

Sheen, Vincent. *Between the Thunder and the Sun.* New York: Random House, 1948.

Sides, Hampton. *Ghost Soldiers.* New York: Doubleday, 2001.

Simons, Gerald. ed. *Japan at War: World War II.* Alexandria, VA: Time Life Books, 1980.

Sledge, E.B. *With the Old Breed.* New York: Oxford, 1990.

Smith, Carl. *Pearl Harbor.* Oxford: Osprey Publishing, 1999.

Smith, S.E. ed. *The United States Navy in World War II.* New York: Ballantine, 1966.

Snow, C.P. *The Physicists: A Generation That Changed the World.* Boston: Little, Brown, 1981.

Snow, Edgar. *Journey to the Beginning.* New York: Random House, 1958.

_____, *The Battle For Asia.* New York: Random House, 1941.

Steinberg, Rafael. ed. *Return to the Philippines: World War II.* Alexandria, VA: Time Life Books, 1980.

Stewart, William H. *Ghost Fleet of the Truk Lagoon.* Missoula, MT: Pictorial Histories, 1985.

Sulzberger, C.L., *Pictorial History of World War II.* Volumes 1 and 2, New York: The American Heritage Foundation, 1966.

Tanaka, Giichi. *The Tanaka Memorial.* Seattle: Columbia Publishing Company, 1934.

Tanaka, Yuki. *Hidden Horrors: Japanese War Crimes in WW II.* Boulder: Westview Press, 1996.

Tapert, Annette. *Lines of Battle.* New York: Times Books, 1987.

Taylor, A.J.P. *The Second World War: An Illustrated History.* London: G.P. Putnam's Sons, 1975.

Taylor, George. *The Struggle for North China.* New York: AMS Press, 1940.

_____, *The Struggle for North China.* New York: Institute of Pacific Relations, 1978.

Taylor, Lawrence. *A Trial of Generals.* South Bend: Icarus, 1981.

Teller, Edward. *The Legacy of Hiroshima.* Garden City: Doubleday, 1962.

Tenny, Lester I. *My Hitch in Hell: The Bataan Death March.* London: Brassy's Inc., 1995.

The War Against Japan: A Pictoral Record. Washington: Chief of History, Department of the Army, 1952.

Thomas, Gordon and Max M. Watts. *Enola Gay.* New York: Stein and Day, 1977.

Thomas, Lowell and Edward Jablonski. *Dooolittle: A Biography.* New York:

Doubleday, 1976.

Tibbets, Paul W. *Mission Hisoshima.* New York: Stein and Day, 1981.

Tolley, Kemp. *Yangtze Patrol: The U. S. Navy in China.* Annapolis: Naval Institute Press, 1971.

Tollischus, Otto D. *Tokyo Record.* New York: Reynal and Hitchcock, 1943.

Tuten, Frederic. *The Adventures of Mao on the Long March,* New York: Citadel Press, 1971.

Ugaki, Matome. *Fading Victory: The Diary of Admiral Matome Ugaki 1941-1945.* Pittsburg: University of Pittsburg Press, 1991.

Valentine, Douglas. *The Hotel Tacloban.* Westport, CN: Lawrtence Hill, 1984.

Van der Vat, Dan. *The Pacific Campaign: W. W. II.* New York: Simon and Schuster, 1991.

Wall, Don. Abandoned Australians at Sandakan. Monte Valle, NSW, Australia: D. Wall. 1990.

_____, *Kill the Prisoners.* Monte Vale, NSW, Australia: D. Wall, 1990.

_____, *Sandakan: The Last March.* Monte Valle, NSW, Australia: D. Wall, 1995.

Waller, Jane and Michael Vaughan-Rees. *Women in Uniform 1939-45.* London: Macmillan, 1989.

Walton, Frank. *Once They Were Eagles: The Men of the Black Sheep Squadron.* Lexington: University Press of Kentucky, 1986.

Warshofsky, Fred. *War Under the Waves.* New York: Pyramid Publications, 1964.

Wetzler, Peter. *Hirohito and War.* Honolulu: University of Hawaii Press, 1998.

Wheal, Elizabeth-Anne, Stephen Pope, and James Taylor. *Encyclopedia of the Second World War.* Secaucas, NJ: Castle, 1989.

Wheeler, Keith. *Bombers Over Japan.* Chicago: Time-Life Books, 1982.

Wheeler, Richard. *Iwo.* New York: Kensington Publishing, 1980.

White, Theodore H. ed. *The Stilwell Papers.* New York: MacFadden, 1962.

Williams, Peter and David Wallace. *Unit 731.* New York: Macmillan, 1989.

Wilson, Dick. *When Tigers Fight.The Story of the Sino-Japanese War: 1937-1945.* New York: Viking, 1982.

Wooldridge, E. T. ed. *Carrier Warfare in the Pacific.* Washington: Smithsonian Institution Press, 1993.

Wright, Michel. ed. *The World at Arms: The Reader's Digest Illustrated History of World War II.* London: The Reader's Digest Association 1989.

Wu, Tien-wei. "A Preliminary Review of Studies of Japanese Biological Warfare Unit 731 in the United States." http://www.cs.umn.edu/~wiihist/germwar/731rev.htm#korera (8 Nov. 1997).

Y'Blood, William T. *The Little Giants.* Annapolis: Naval Institute Press, 1987.

_____, *Illustrated World War II Encyclopedia.* Vol. 20 (Russia's War Against Japan) Monaco: 1966.

Yoshida, Jim. *The Two Worlds of Jim Yoshida.* New York: William Morrow, 1972.

Yoshimura, Akira. *Battleship Musashi.* Tokyo: Kodansha, 1999.

Young, Peter. Ed. *Illustrated World War II Encyclopedia.* Vol. 18 (The War in China) Monaco: H. S. Stuttman, 1978.

Young, Stephen B. *Trapped at Pearl Harbor: Escape from Battleship Oklahoma.* Annapolis: Naval Institute Press, 1991.

Ziemke, Earl Frederick. ed. *The Soviet Juggernaut: World War II.* Alexandria, VA: Time Life Books, 1980.

INDEX